Sculpting the Human Figure

JOHN W. MILLS

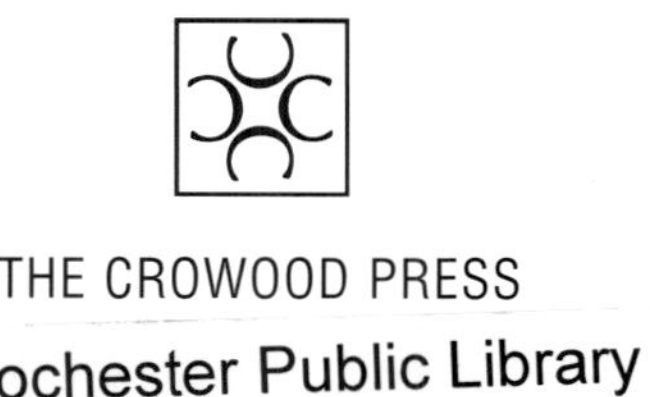

THE CROWOOD PRESS

First published in 2006 by
The Crowood Press Ltd
Ramsbury, Marlborough
Wiltshire SN8 2HR

www.crowood.com

British Library Cataloguing-in-Publication Data
A catalogue record for this book is available from the British Library.

ISBN 1 86126 866 1

EAN 978 1 86126 866 2

Unless stated otherwise, all photographs are by the author.

Designed and typeset by Focus Publishing, Sevenoaks, Kent

Printed and bound in Singapore by Craft Print International

Contents

Preface

The dissemination of knowledge pertaining to the skills and techniques of sculpture has been a constant concern for me over the past forty-five years; it is a common ground that all sculptors should be able to enjoy. Just after the end of the Second World War, I received training at art school in London. There, at the age of fourteen, I encountered skilled and committed artists of many disciplines, who were anxious not only to get back into the swing of things after the long war years, but also to teach us skills that encouraged the creative rather than the destructive processes of life that wartime had brought in the preceding years. They were concerned with ideas and concepts – as all artists are, and must be – but they did not consider them to be separate entities (as many do today). As artists, they were makers and communicators of images of all kinds and recognized the vital interdependence of ideas and skills. This is what defined their teaching and their art.

The values to which I was introduced in those days have sustained me over the intervening years, and I have sought to encourage similar thoughts and attitudes in young artists through my teaching, my writing and my sculpture. I do not like the notion of secret processes in the visual arts, believing rather in the free interchange of technical information. It is what you make that should concern you, and the viewer of your sculpture, not the complexity or indeed the purity of the technical methods involved. There is no greater joy for an artist of any kind than the knowledge that the fingers can do the dancing, giving the brain the freedom to design the steps and explore the joy of the dance. The reverse is also true of course: a lack of skill will imprison the brain and the body, restricting the freedom of expression to a narrow activity.

The term 'sculpture' in the art world today has come to have so many meanings that there exists a certain confusion in the mind of those coming to study the art form for the first time, either as practitioners or as enthusiastic observers. In the modern world, a video recording or a page of typescript may be described as sculpture, displayed in a prestigious art gallery setting, and assessed as sculpture by prominent art critics. This book, however, will deal only with the making of sculpture based on the human figure. Obviously this is open-ended, since the infinite variety of human beings and their interaction with worldly affairs provides the greatest continuous creative stimulus, more stimulating for instance than a self-conscious searching for originality and trying to invent new art forms to support such apparent originality.

Introduction

Traditions and Inspirations

The description 'traditional' has in some quarters become a criticism, usually referring pejoratively to figurative but not abstract sculpture, even though both can be of poor quality (and, indeed, often are). It is an attitude that reflects a poor understanding of art history, and reveals a preoccupation with contemporary idioms gleaned for the most part from the influential art media, including franchised glossy art magazines and televised arts forums. The printed media in particular exercises an invidious influence, illustrating a chosen few artists in all the capital cities around the world at the same time – I call this 'air mail' culture. This gives a false impression of what is actually happening in the arts today, and in sculpture in particular. It allows those few artists to have too great an influence on young minds, and seems to encourage an ignorance or neglect of true traditional standards, values and attitudes. Tradition means more than just a constant reference to the past, and a preoccupation for or against selected periods in the history of mankind, as it is reflected in the creative expression of those times.

Great traditions – those that have had a long-lasting influence – are represented globally by past grand civilizations, now easily identified by their scholarly titles – Mesopotamia, Assyria, Ancient Egypt, Greece and Rome, Ancient China, Africa, Japan, and so on. It is now clear that each evolved by allowing for and accepting the need for constant appraisal and reappraisal of expressed doctrines and social mores, with all their accompanying ideas and images. The consequent inheritance, in which we can all take pleasure, is a rich international collection of sculptured personalities of all kinds – innumerable images, predominantly three-dimensional, but usually explored in all the visual media. Some significant sculptured icons were repeated over and over by succeeding generations, gradually being honed and refined to better communicate the meaningful figures of each culture. Such refinements reflected social or religious adjustments to the perception of those leaders, chiefs or deities, effectively contributing to what was to become our 'tradition'. Those powerful images not only fulfilled the various functions of their time by communicating with the contemporary populous, but also command interest and even awe in viewers today.

Studying Sculpture

Much of this great inheritance is stored in museums, which are full of fine sculptures from all historic periods and cultures. Aspiring sculptors should visit these store houses as often as possible, to gain particular visual sculptural experiences and to 'file away' memories of history's wide variety of expression. In this way, you will become aware of the enormous potential that still exists, which is always available to you for your unique interpretation.

Too often, the study of art history is divorced from that of social history, and vice versa, but in fact the two are mutually influential. Social history is sometimes taught with the aid of art and artefacts, but the reverse is less often the case. In fact, the social mores of any society affect the creative impulses of their time, and are reflected in the activities and products of artists, poets and painters, musicians and sculptors, architects and engineers, scientist and philosophers, Popes and politicians; nothing happens or exists in isolation. Visits to museums of all kinds, and to designated art galleries, allow for a study of the interplay of artistic and social activities, and an insight into that fine meld of ancient and modern social expression. This will lead to a greater understanding of the usefulness of art and design in the world at large, and, possibly, direct your own ideas.

Whenever possible, sculpture should be examined on the site and in the environment for which it was designed and

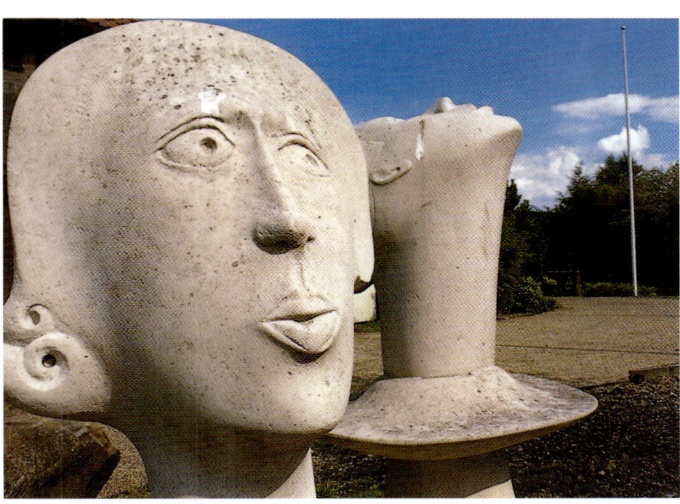

Harlequin and Columbine, *by Peter Nicholas, in Portland stone.*

made, where it is truly 'site specific'. Taking note of the suitability of the work in all its elements to its position is a rewarding study. On-site encounters with sculpture will often provide the opportunity to experience sensations peculiar to this three-dimensional art. Interacting with the physical presence of a sculpture, gaining experience of its true volume, poise and texture, is a learning experience of great value, whether the work is good, bad or just mediocre. Perhaps the absence of any guardians will allow 'hands-on' study – sculpture is after all a tactile art form and it is important to become familiar with the feel of different materials. The coldness of metal as distinct from the warmth of wood, or the rough feel of sandstone compared with the almost sensual feel of polished marble, are all part of the joy of materials, which is vital to the expression and appreciation of sculpture.

All sorts of examples should be observed – good, bad and indifferent. It is often possible to learn more from something that does not work, when the faculties are not dazzled by the success of a master work or the fame of great sculpture in its setting, and when the mind is allowed to indulge in a spate of creative criticism.

What is Sculpture?

Sculpture is the art of making an image in three dimensions, using any materials that can be modelled, carved, moulded, cast, or assembled. It can be made in the round, which means it is a free-standing and self-supporting object, once described as being different from painting, because 'it is something you could bump into in the dark and come away with a bruise'. Alternatively, the image can be made in relief, which is a projection from or a depression into a surface, thus 'relieving' that surface. Relief sculpture is probably the oldest form of sculptural expression, possibly started by someone scratching marks into mud or sand, and then building up from those marks to develop a more recognizable image. Such techniques are identifiable in ancient artworks, such as prehistoric cave paintings that sometimes lead on to rudimentary sculptural expression. Images have been found that evolved from artists scratching, colouring and embellishing rock forms that already resembled the shape of observed creatures. These renderings of animals are often extremely sophisticated and accurate, demonstrating man's powers of observation and his skilful depiction of the natural world, but in all cases they are interpretations of the observed world. The artists were obviously working from memory, deep in caves, far away from their subject and any direct reference. This aspect of interpretation is important and will be repeated throughout this book; making a simple replica is not making a sculpture.

History and Influences

All cultures across the world and throughout history have produced sculptures, both in relief and free-standing, and in all kinds of materials that can be modelled, carved, moulded, cast or assembled. Perversely, modern history has seemed to encourage appreciation only of those sculptures made from materials that have survived the tests of time and elements, particularly those made from stone, marble, wood, terracotta and bronze. Furthermore, the current appearance of such images now encountered in museums and galleries and collections all over the world, with their rich and varied patination, the result of weather, wear, tear, adulation and abuse, has intruded into our cultural thinking, affecting our perception of the appearance of sculpture. In the past, sculptors have attempted to replicate such ancient patinas and continue to do so today, spending hours working out complex formulas for the chemical patination of metals, for instance.

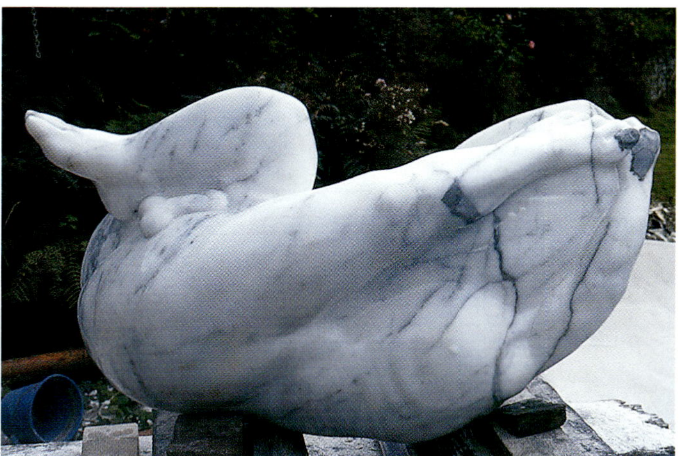

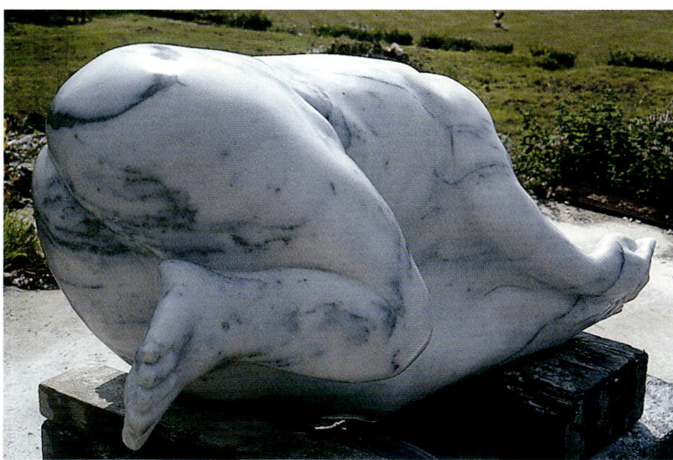

Hercule, *by Peter Nicholas, in marble.*

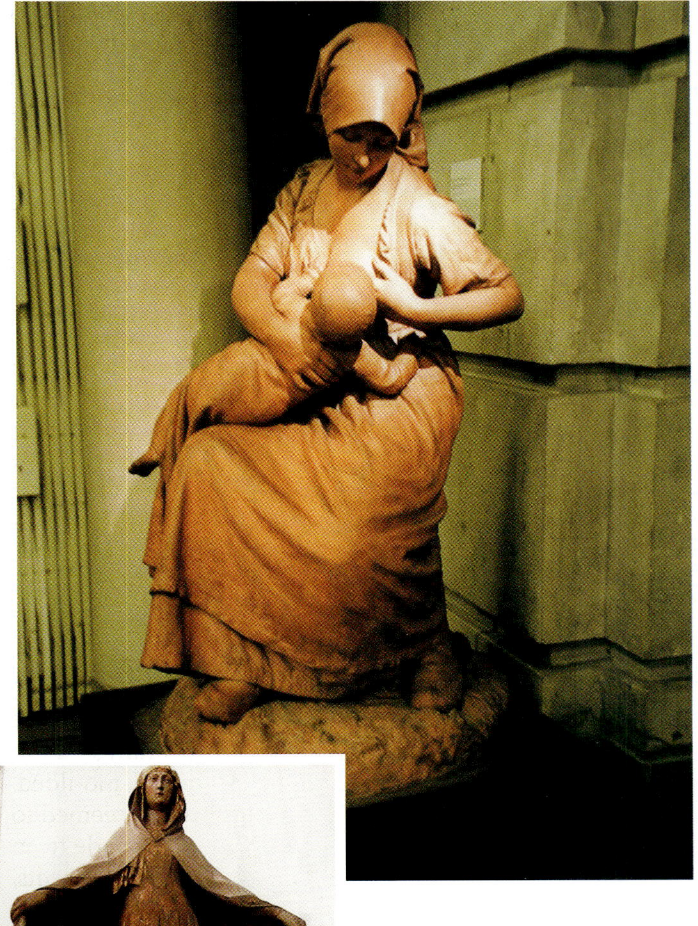

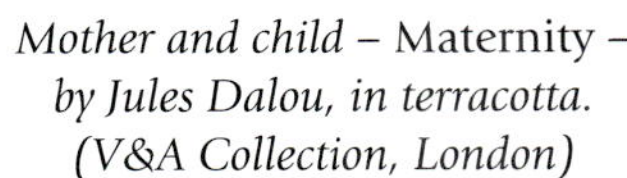

Mother and child – Maternity – *by Jules Dalou, in terracotta. (V&A Collection, London)*

Madonna Misericordia: *medieval woodcarving, coloured and gilded, by Tolentino.*

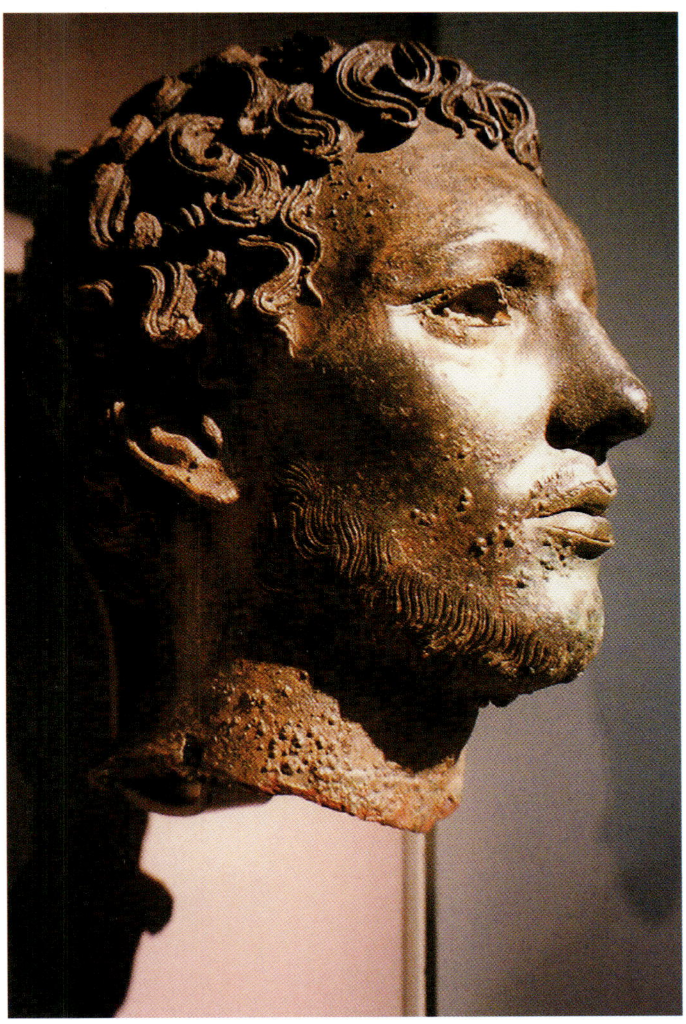

Head of a Young Man, *from Ancient Greece, in bronze. This is a fine impression of reality but still full of classical interpretation. (The British Museum, London)*

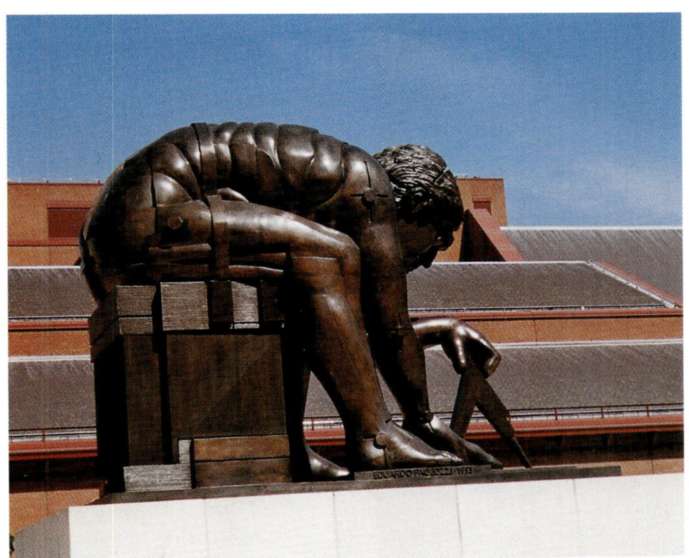

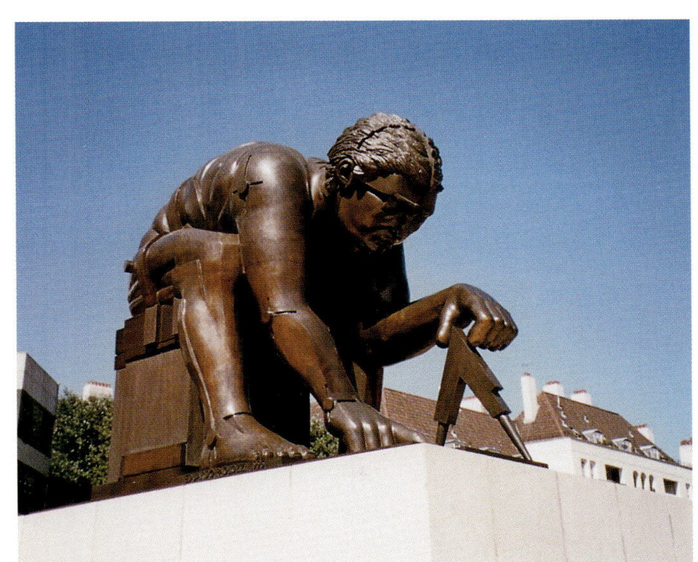

Newton, *by Edouardo Paolozzi, outside the British Library, London.*

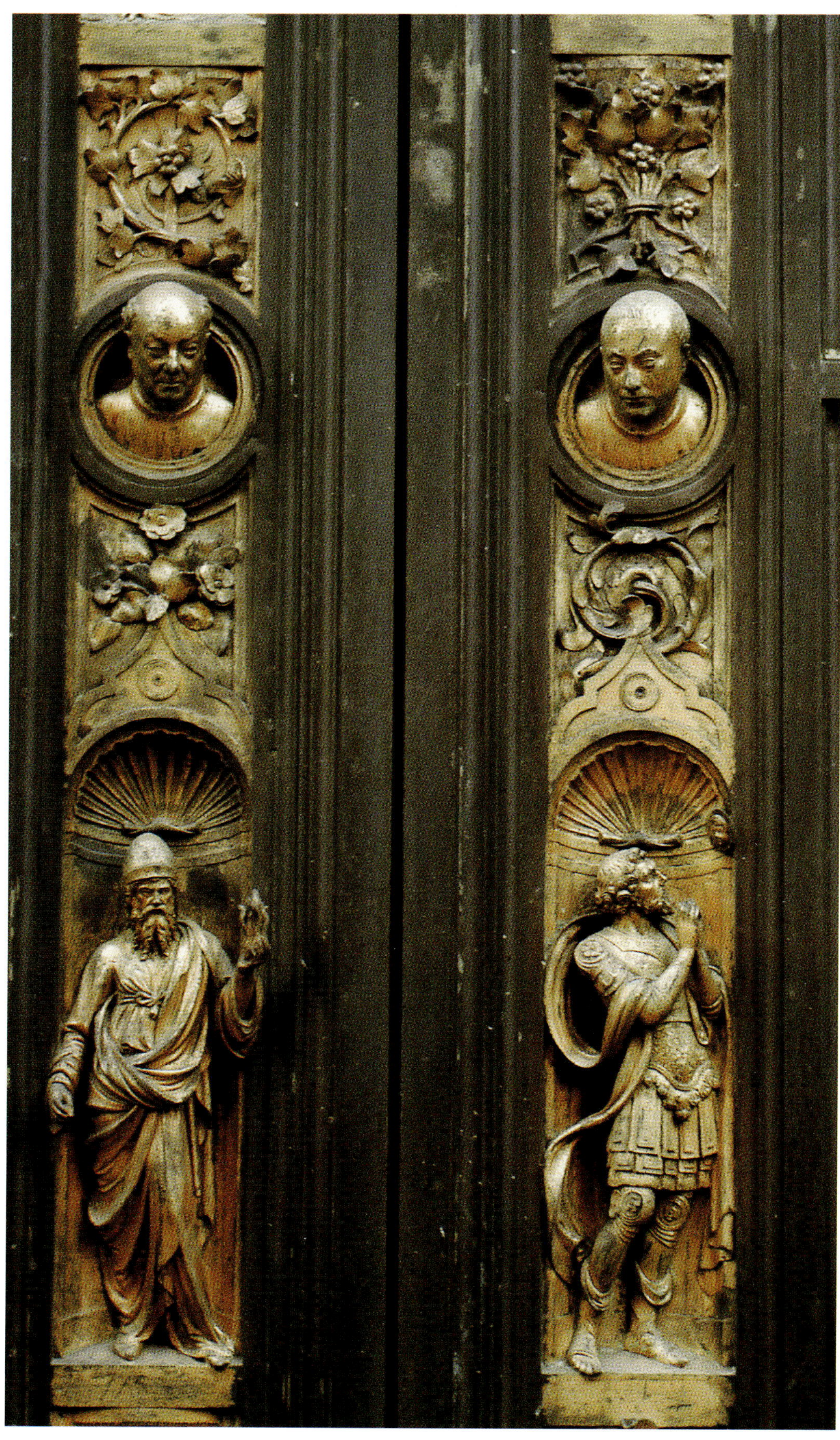

High relief, self-portrait in gilded bronze: Gates of Paradise, *by Lorenzo Ghiberti. (Baptistery, Florence)*

Until the time of the Italian Renaissance, most sculpture was embellished with colour and gilding, or both. With the influence of the archaeological discoveries and the scholarship of the Italian Renaissance, the fashion changed, and the preference for natural patinas continues today. Although polychrome sculpture is occasionally seen today, it is not common, despite the occurrence of super-realistic images that occasionally crop up. In an art-historical context, however, colour is an integral factor in terms of social/religious communication and is an element that should be studied, along with any other technique. Close examination of global art history shows that mankind will fashion images from whatever material is available, not just from those materials that can withstand the ravages of time or the elements (or, too often, the violent vandalizing reactions of mankind).

Study of the strange and powerful images that are now recognized as sculpture – images that intruded on the self-conscious European art world of the 1920s – will prove to be a liberating factor when making research into sculptural influences. The anthropological artefacts produced by so-called primitive or tribal cultures were brought back to Europe at that time and displayed as curiosities. They fascinated those who saw them, and had an influence on all the visual arts – and continue to do so to this day. Inevitably, they are seen in comparison with the sophisticated statuary of the 'civilized' nations, which formed the cultural background to most intellectuals of that period. This will provide rich lessons in respect of the growing antipathy to what was seen as merely academic, and the freedom to use anything available to create an image.

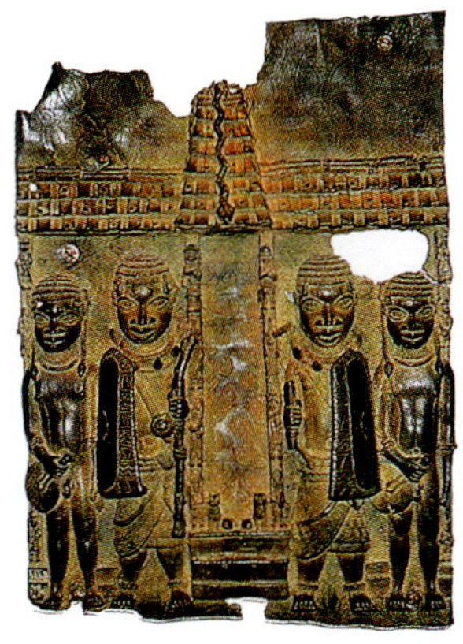

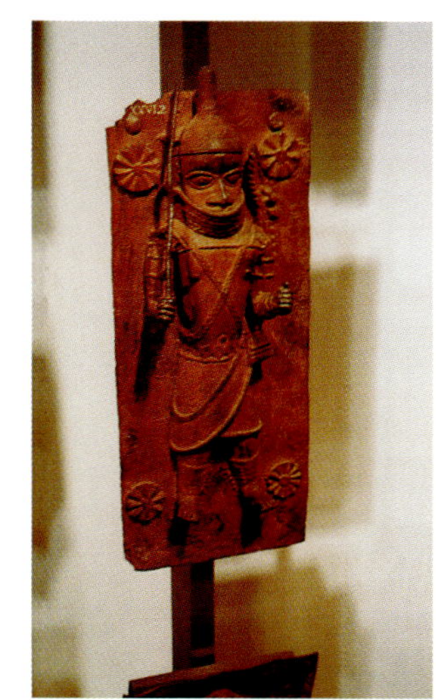

Fine bronze reliefs from the Benin tribe of Africa.

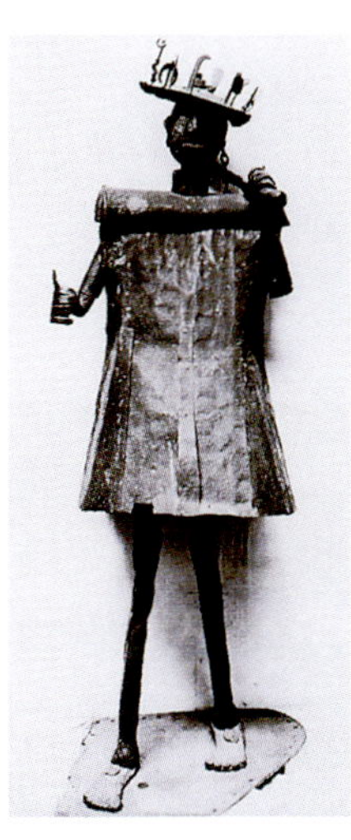

AFRICAN SCULPTURE.

RIGHT: The God of War, *Ebo tribe. Iron.*

BELOW LEFT: *Nigerian Yoruba woodcarving.*

BELOW MIDDLE: *Nigerian deity, Yoruba woodcarving.*

BELOW RIGHT: *Nigerian mask, Yoruba woodcarving.*

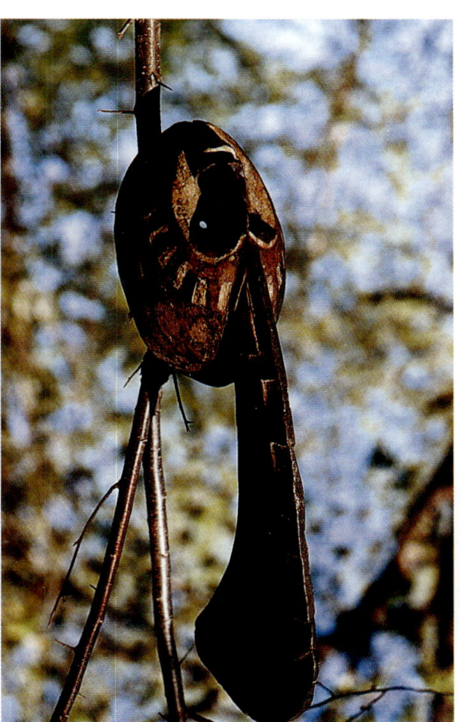

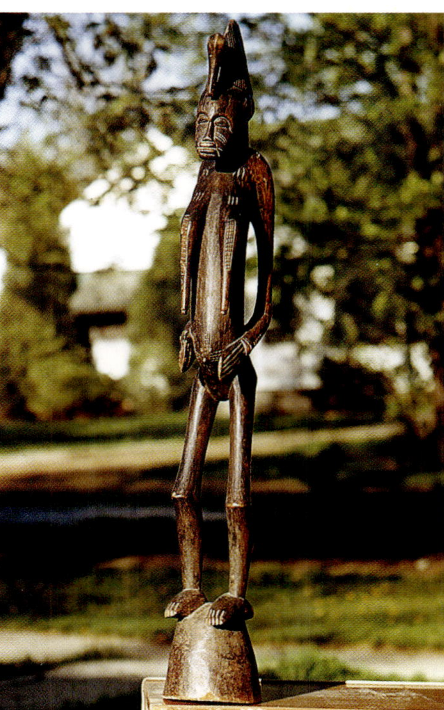

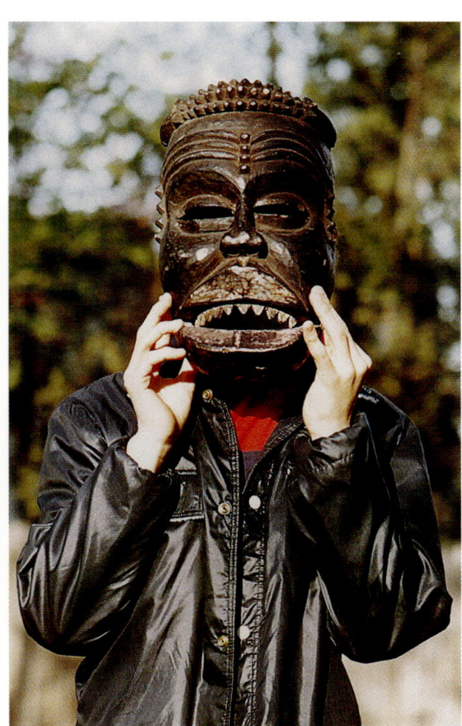

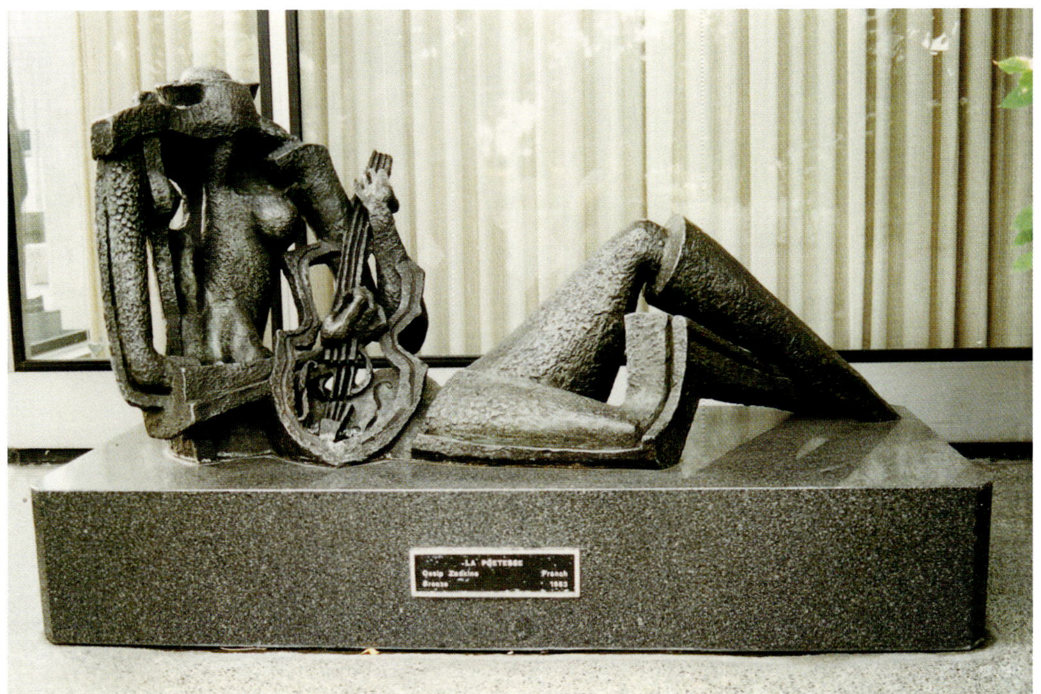

The Poetess, *a Cubist-influenced figure in bronze, by Osip Zadkine.*

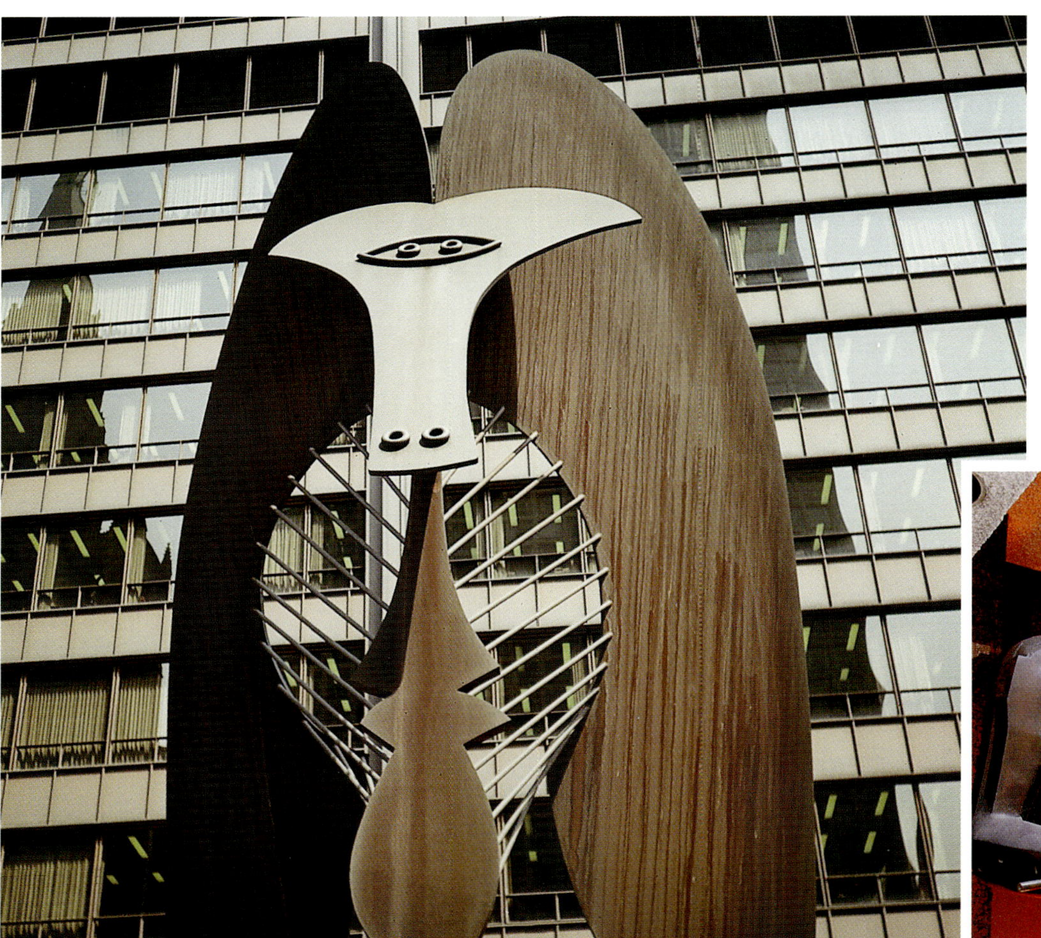

LEFT: *A welded steel image on a very large scale:* Head of a Woman, *by Picasso. (Chicago, USA)*

BELOW: Man, *by Edouardo Paolozzi. This very strong image in bronze is influenced by Cubism. (London)*

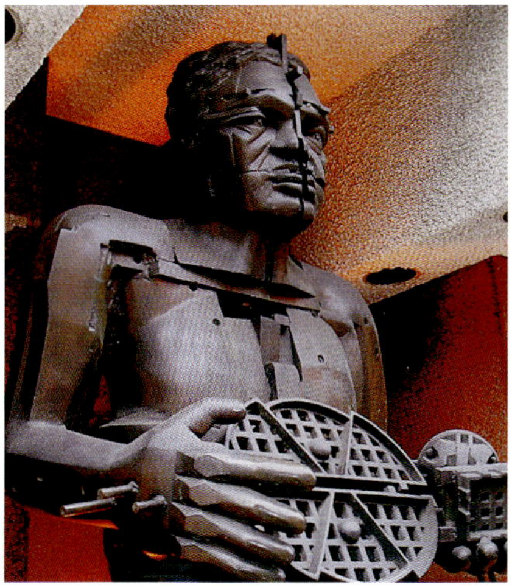

History has produced sculpture of all types, made for all social and religious purposes. There are works incorporating every sort of stuff, from bark and shells to feathers and fabrics, as well as clay, stone, wood or metal. Using such diverse materials can engender a huge sense of excitement, and this was the sensation that forced one of the great art revolutions of the twentieth century: Cubism. It was an art movement that led the race away from the academic – for good or for bad.

A kind of corollary to this free use of materials can be found in the great European courts where sculptors, even some of the big names such as Michelangelo, Da Vinci and Bernini, were often involved in making images from whatever ephemeral materials came to hand, fashioning things that were destined to last for only a day or so, to embellish parties, fetes, festivals or ceremonies. Such works by sculptors who were highly regarded in their time, although necessarily made to a high standard, were incidental to their more serious work, which was produced in marble and bronze. It precedes by centuries what has become a modern major preoccupation with so-called 'conceptual' work, sometimes referred to as 'happenings' (but that is another story).

A sculptor's reasons for making sculpture are many and varied, but all cultures have used both three- and two-dimensional imagery as a means of communicating succinctly to the greatest number of people; in order to identify and record the actual or spiritual presence in their community of deities, religious, royal and fearful; and to to inspire awe, fear or adulation. To a certain extent, this remains the reason for making sculpture: to create a reaction – preferably favourable but sometimes hostile – in those who encounter it. If a sculpture can be easily ignored it is deemed to have failed in its role.

The difference today is that the propagandizing role in society is forcefully taken by the modern communications media, particularly those associated with the electronics industry and all its needs. Its constant and all-consuming demand for material creates a pollution of information of every kind, and drains the supply of creativity from all the arts, not only the visual. Similarly, printing and literacy in the past usurped much of the need for visual depictions of deities, saints and sinners, in two and three dimensions. In a literate society, the need to make visual images became a very personal affair; there was no longer a strong social need to communicate definitive visual icons, common across society, and artists therefore gained a freedom of expression that they had never before experienced. They became dependant only upon themselves and their own ideas.

Such freedom brings certain problems with it, sometimes creating a sort of introversion and making the sculptor inward-looking, and the consequent imagery may be somewhat self-possessed. It is possible perhaps to connect this concern for the expression of the 'self' with that period in European history when publicly published words

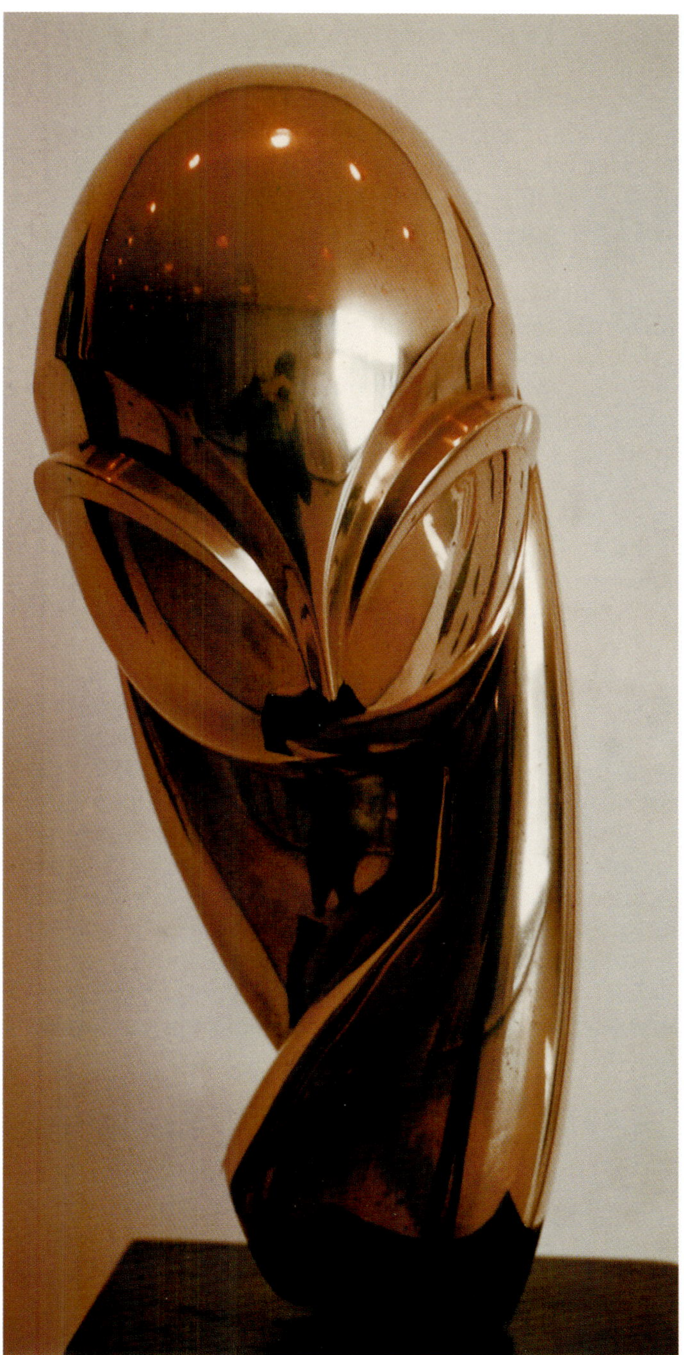

Mlle Polgany, *a very formalized interpretation in polished bronze, by Constantin Brancusi. (Albrigh-Knox Museum Collection, Buffalo, USA)*

became as widely available as pictures. As time passed, the printed word became increasingly important, creating a dilemma that affected all artistic expression, and the visual arts in particular. This complicates the vital task of finding meaningful imagery, which, when expressed externally, should eventually become identifiable as a personal statement and style. Of late, 'sensation' for its own sake has seemed to be a priority for a large number of sculptors and painters. It comes from the need to communicate that is felt by all artists, but too often the work lacks subjects and characters to interpret that are socially and spiritually significant in modern society. Perhaps there is a lack of the traditional skills, too, which has led to the violent and awful becoming so dominant in figurative sculpture now; after all, it is easier to make a monstrous or cadaverous violent-looking image of power than it is to make a powerful statement using a subject of beauty.

Society recognizes that in other disciplines such as dance, music, poetry, writing, medicine, and most of the sciences, reference to the past is embedded in the acquisition of skills needed for the invention, expression and resolution of new ideas. I was once able to ask a Nobel Laureate if he thought it was essential to have a profound knowledge of the history of his subject to be able to make the leap into the dark that leads to the discovery of something new. His reply was that accumulative knowledge usually supplies the springboard for such a leap, and without such knowledge the chances of discovery are diminished. He added that only knowledge, plus hard work, could lead to those other essential happy ingredients for discovery: 'luck' and 'inspiration'. For some reason today in the leading visual arts of 'painting and sculpture' accumulative knowledge will often seem to be ignored or frowned upon. The resulting desperate search for 'originality', or something new, often ends in banality. The artist should not abandon the search for knowledge, but must believe that concentrating on all that impacts upon his or her speciality, including anything that may be gleaned from the past, can only lead to his or her future, whatever that may be. It might even be of great originality.

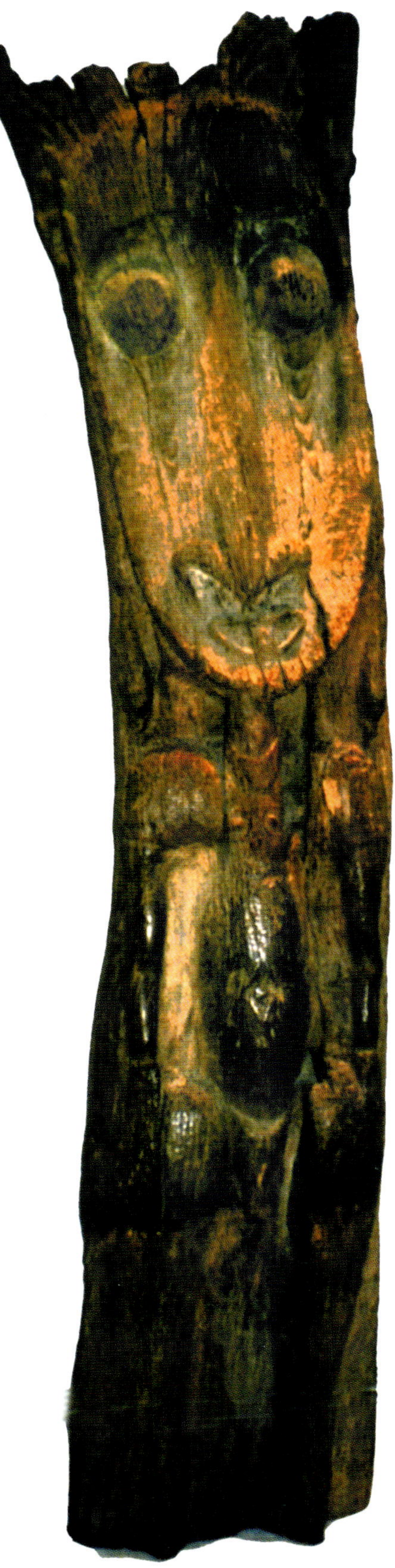

An African woodcarving of a wood spirit, exploiting the shape of the original tree trunk.

Picasso – The Master of Innovation

Pablo Picasso was probably the master of innovation in painting, sculpture and many other disciplines. He had a kind of instinct that enabled him quickly to use the good qualities of any new process he encountered. This intuition seemed to guide him, allowing him to flit from one discipline to another, seemingly without a learning interval. No matter how experimental and innovative the images and processes he explored, his underlying skills were so soundly

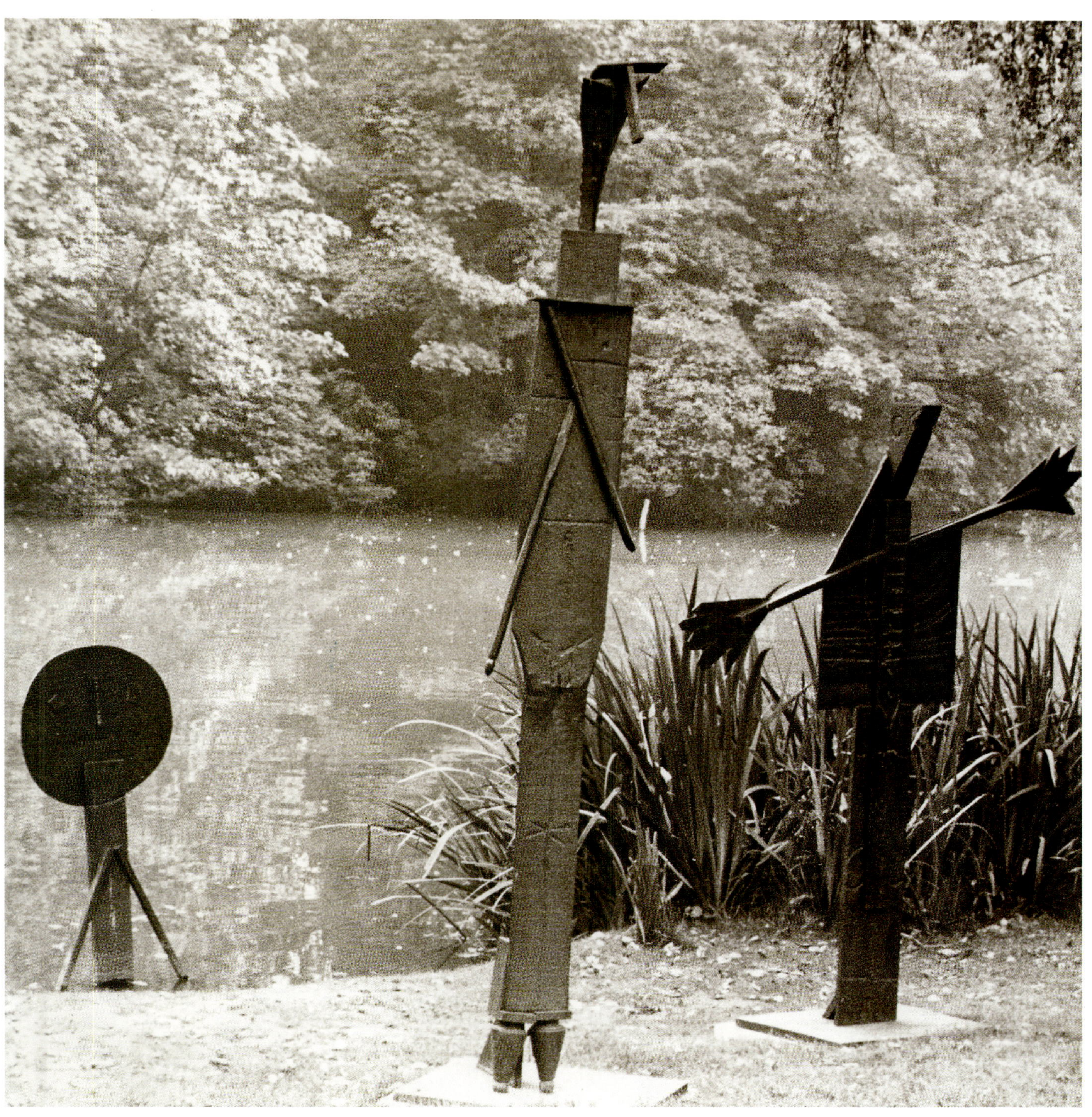

Bathers, *by Pablo Picasso, in bronze. The figures were assembled from timber finds and then cast in bronze. (Battersea Park exhibition, London, 1960)*

based in tradition that it allowed him choice and the necessary freedom to explore. When he first encountered 'primitive' tribal artefacts in Paris at the turn of the twentieth century, it was this factor that caused him to see with fresh eyes that it was possible to make significant works from any material that could be modelled, carved, cast, or assembled. (Paradoxically, after enjoying the freedom of assembling disparate items to form a strong sculptured personality, he would have the sculpture cast in bronze, making the ephemeral permanent. This probably had much to do with marketing and museum economics, a reflection of another important modern phenomenon that affects the art world.)

Picasso made powerful sculptures based on this newfound freedom, released from what had become in his view the very narrow academic thinking of the time. The academies against which he and other artists railed had come to represent a very narrow view of art. The 'academic norm' that became the basis for so much bad teaching in the western world and beyond was based on a formulaic interpretation of classical ideals, inherited third hand from Ancient Greece via Rome and the Italian Renaissance. This interpretation paid scant attention to everyday reality. It insisted on standard poses for art school models, who would take up the archetypal classical postures of a Venus or an Apollo regardless of their own physical shape. Formulae were devised for the perfect figure and head, resulting in the notion of ideal proportions for man and woman. This academic attitude caused many artists to rebel, and Picasso to declare at one point, 'I can draw like Raphael but I cannot draw like a child.' He raged against the formulaic; he longed to express the simple perception of reality of a child, but with the caveat that it should be used together with the accrued confidence and freedom of expression that can come only with practice and knowledge. Of course the innocence of early childhood lasts a short time, altering as the complexities of life loom large, but the retention of a degree of early innocence helps the artist to absorb influences and to take a sideways look at tradition, so that it becomes a tool and not a stick with which to be beaten. This naive quality can be seen in the tribal imagery that came to have such a profound influence on modern art, because of the direct interaction between the artists, the required icons and the material from which they were made, but there was greater sophistication there than at first appeared.

Personal Influences

Being influenced by others is predictable, but it is no bad thing. However, being influenced by a single source can be detrimental to the development of personal expression. It is better to investigate as wide a range of artistic activity as possible – not only sculpture and painting, and not only figurative art, but all that leads to the interpretation of human form. The visual and actual characteristics that shape men and women have preoccupied artists since the dawn of civilization and remain a mainstay of artistic endeavour today; even in the world of abstraction, which apparently has little or no reference to the human form or

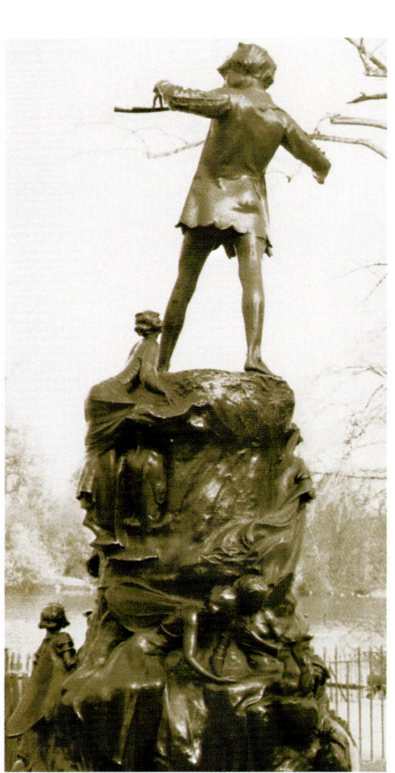

LEFT: Peter Pan, *by George Frampton, in bronze. (Kensington Gardens, London)*

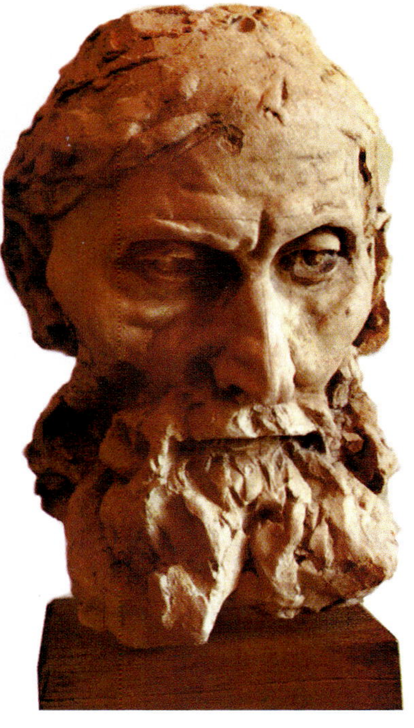

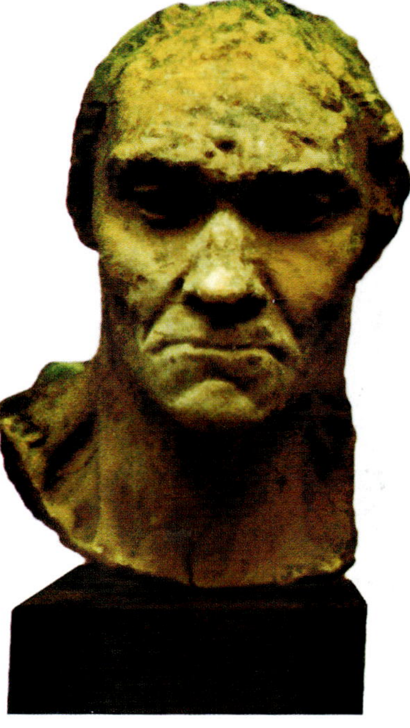

ABOVE: *Plaster heads, Auguste Rodin. (Rodin Museum, Philadelphia, USA)*

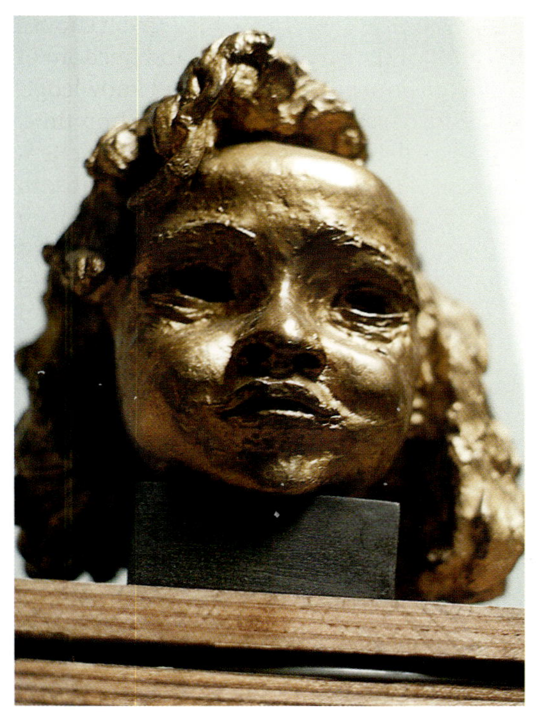

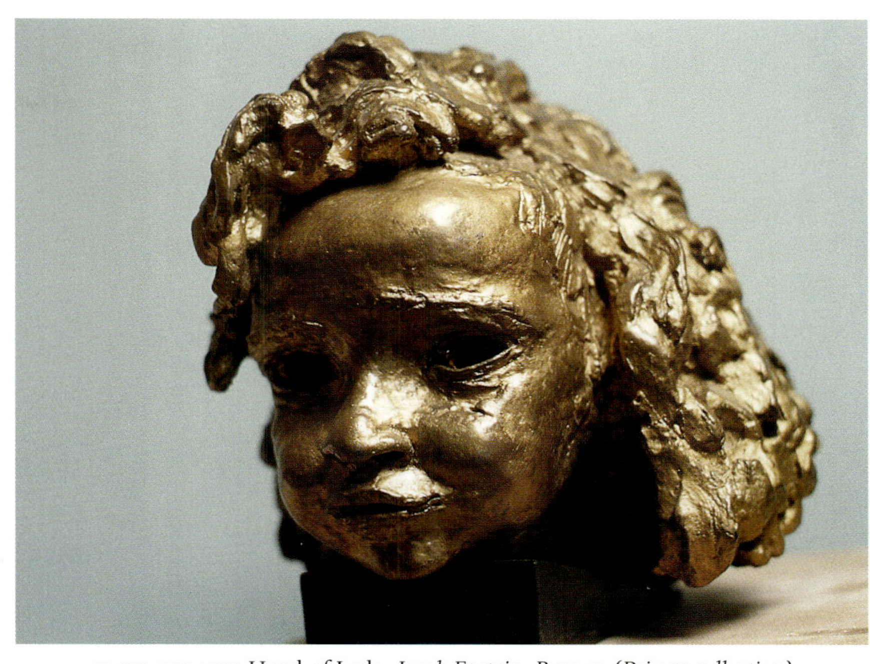

ABOVE AND LEFT: Head of Leda, *Jacob Epstein. Bronze. (Private collection)*

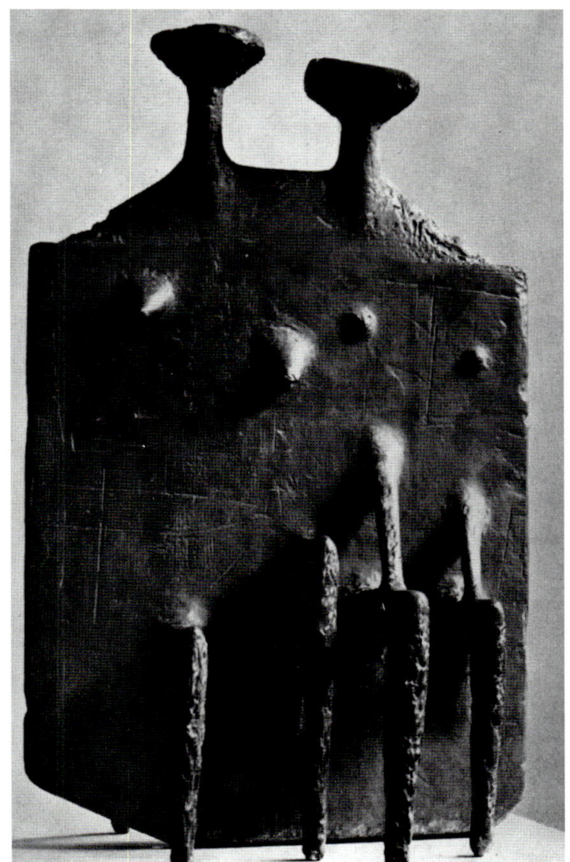

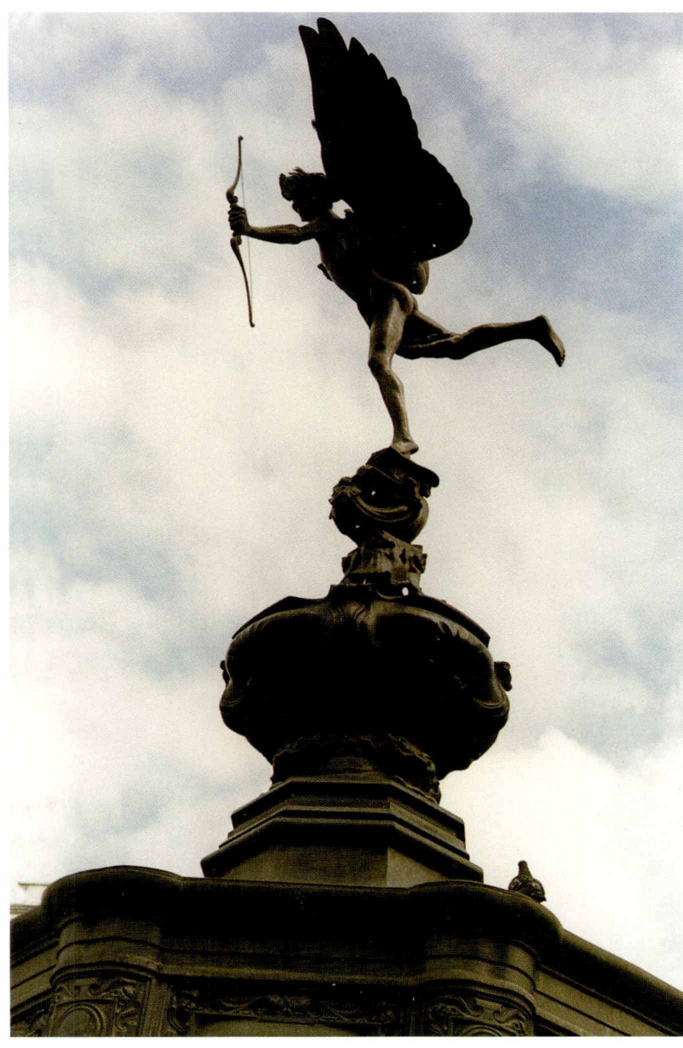

ABOVE: Diarchy, *by Kenneth Armitage, in bronze. (Battersea Park exhibition, London, 1960)*
RIGHT: Eros *at Piccadilly Circus, London, by Alfred Gilbert, in aluminium. This lively image explores action and silhouette to great effect.*

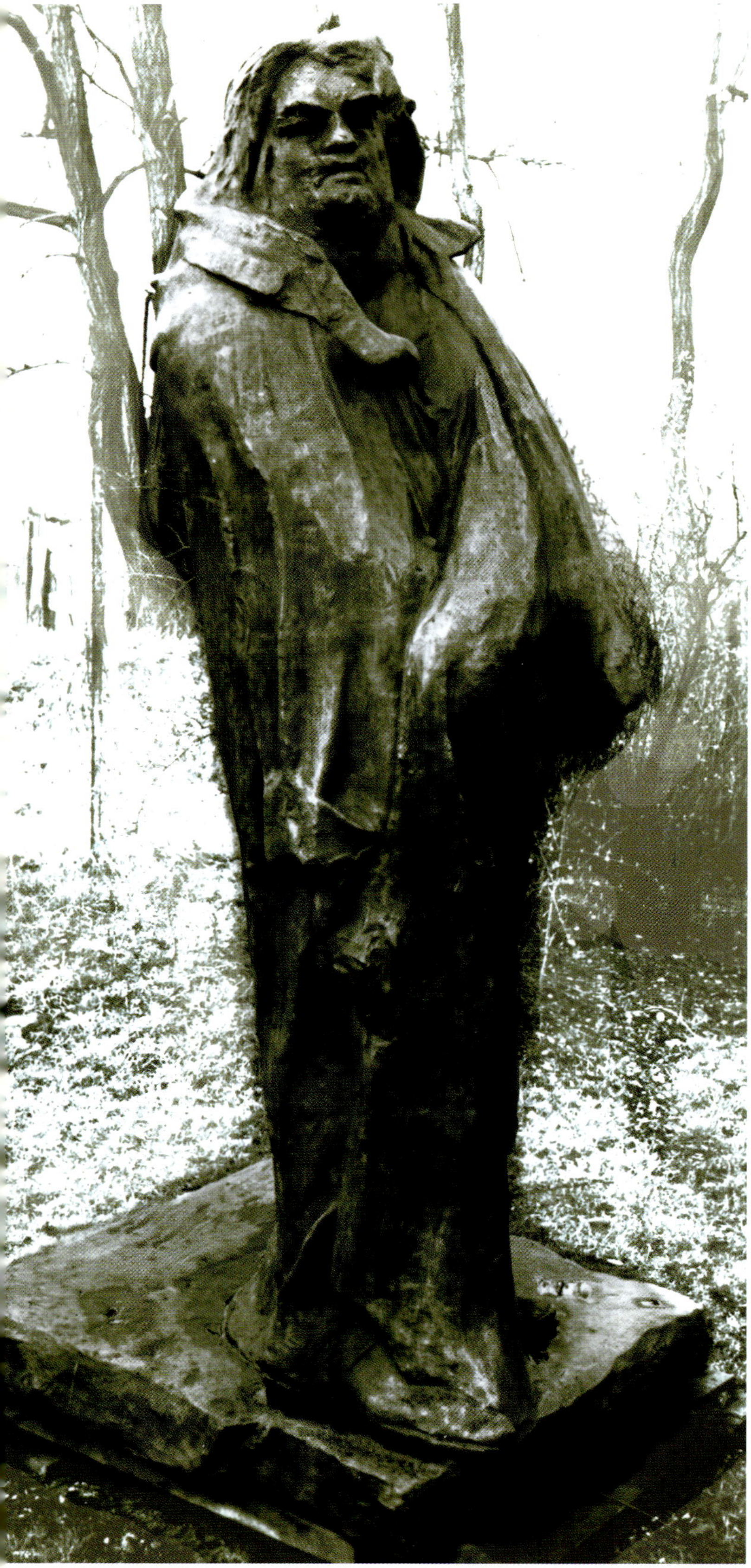

Balzac, *by Auguste Rodin. An atmospheric picture of a famous powerful image, typical of Rodin.*

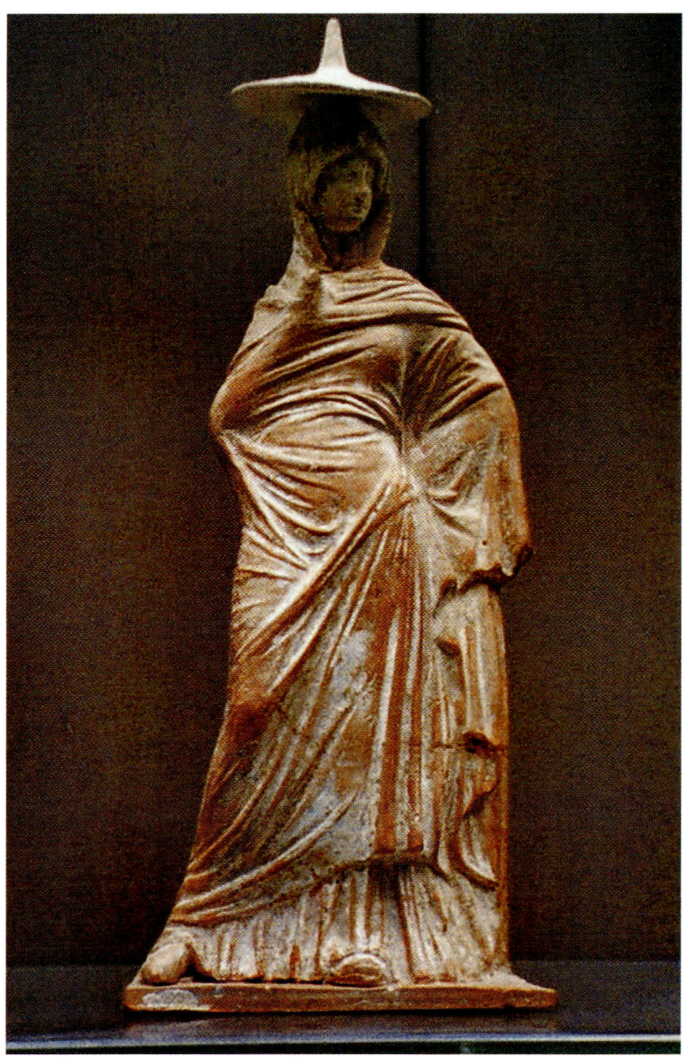

A woman in terracotta, made in Boeotia, 300–200 BC. *This elegant figure is beautifully realized. (The British Museum, London)*

observed reality. Of course, trying out something apparently new that is found to be stimulating is a necessary response to the multi-influential part of the rich world tapestry, but it is important not to adopt contemporary idiom too quickly. Fashion is fickle at any time, and by its nature transient. Trying a new expression or idiom will plant it in the memory, and it might prove in the long run to be a strong and useful experience. Observing mankind in all its manifestations will be rewarding and will constantly refresh and stimulate the imagination.

A great number of sculptures and sculptors have had some influence on my own work, and you should also carry out your own pursuit for sculptural influences. It is a particular pleasure to wander through a museum or a great collection of painting and sculpture in a random manner, ignoring chronology, allowing your attention to be attracted and distracted, encountering for the first time many different objects and images; it is an experience that contains the thrill of personal discovery.

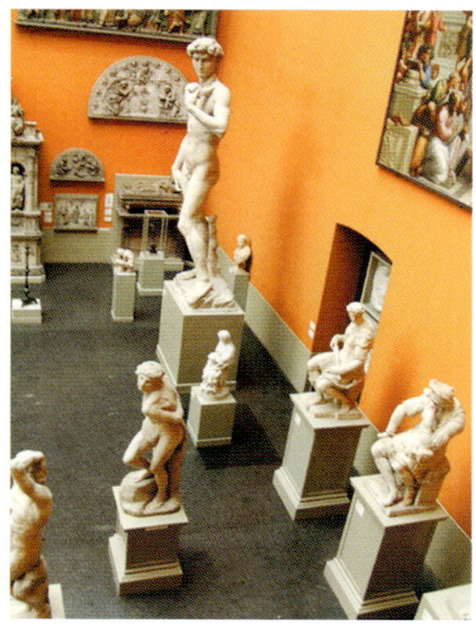

ABOVE: *The Plaster Courts at the V&A Museum, London, a store house of sculpture that is an essential port of call for every student of the art.*

RIGHT: *Cycladic figure, from Ancient Greece, made by abrading the stone, which gives it a uniquely hand-made feeling. (The British Museum)*

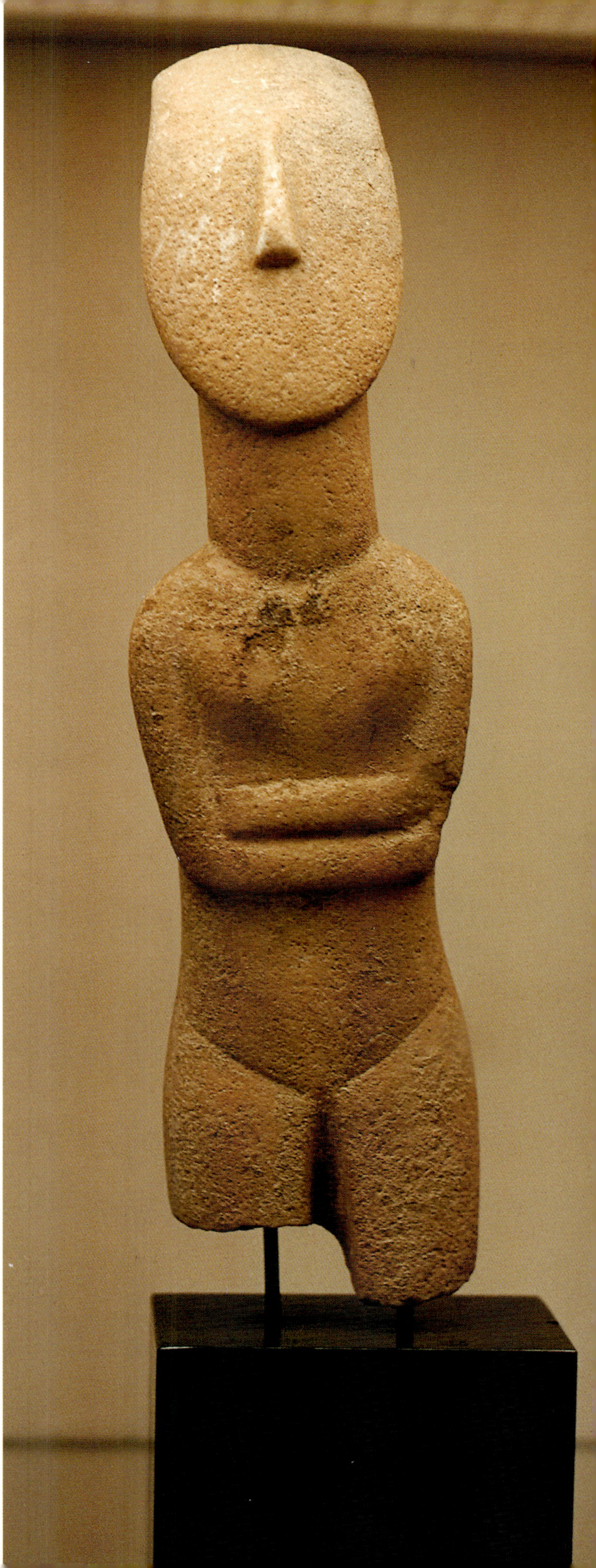

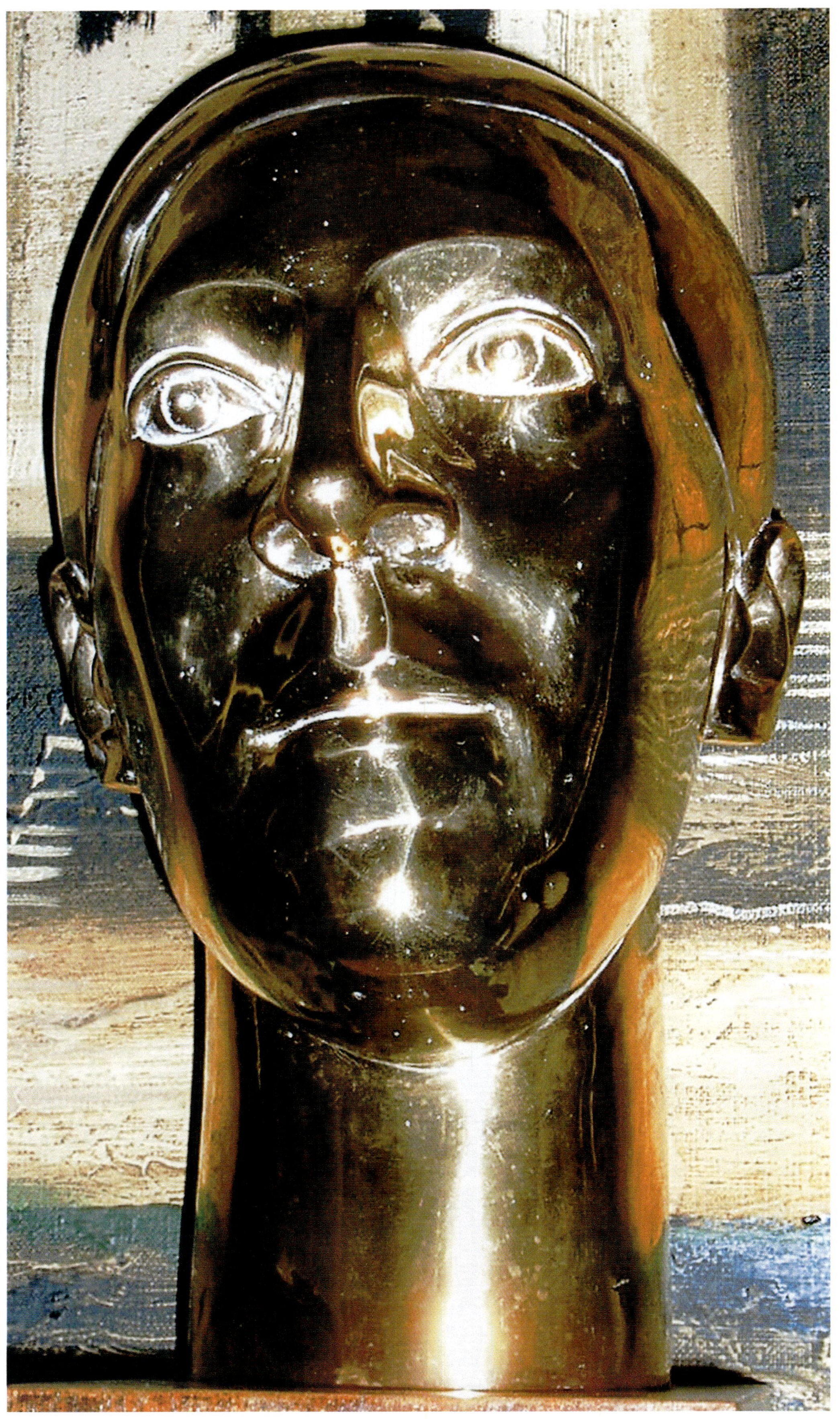

Portrait of Osbert Sitwell, *by Frank Dobson, in polished bronze. (The Sitwell Collection, Renishaw Hall)*

OPPOSITE: *Damaged carvings on the old BMA building, London, by Jacob Epstein.*

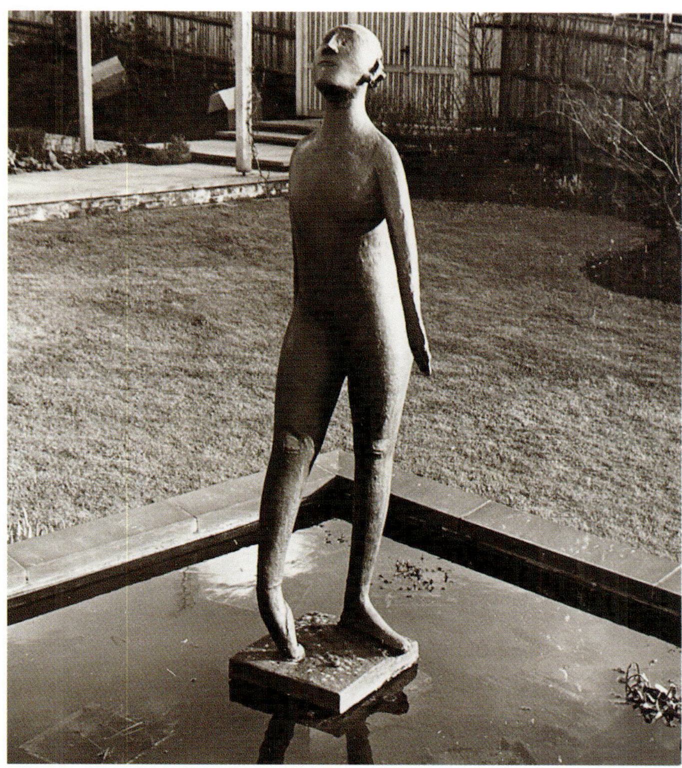

A selection of works by Marino Marini: (ABOVE) Dancer, *well presented by the owner, Mr M. Goldman, who designed the setting; (RIGHT)* Pomona, *in bronze; (BELOW RIGHT) Judith.*

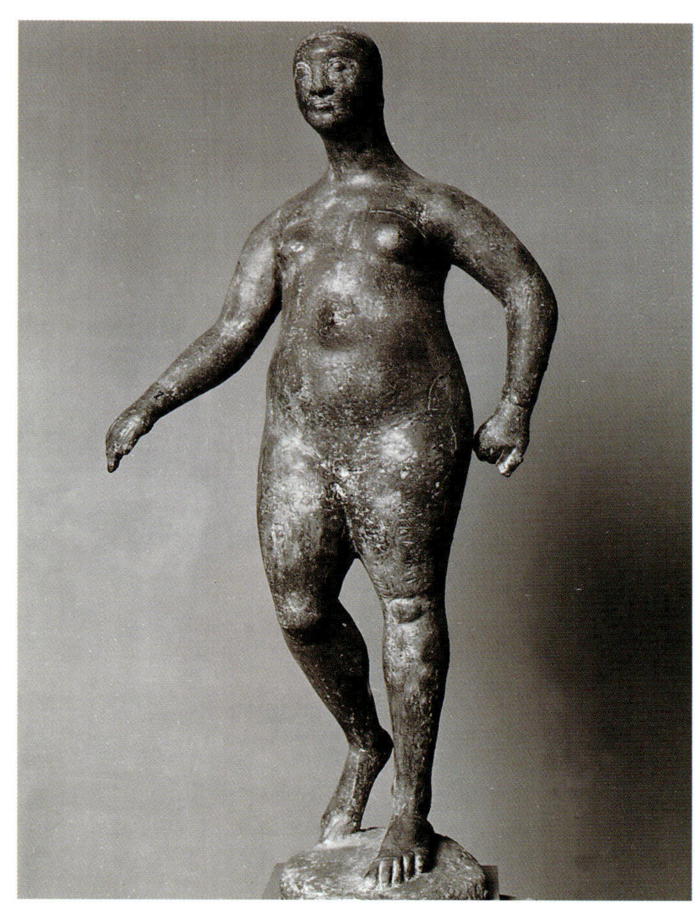

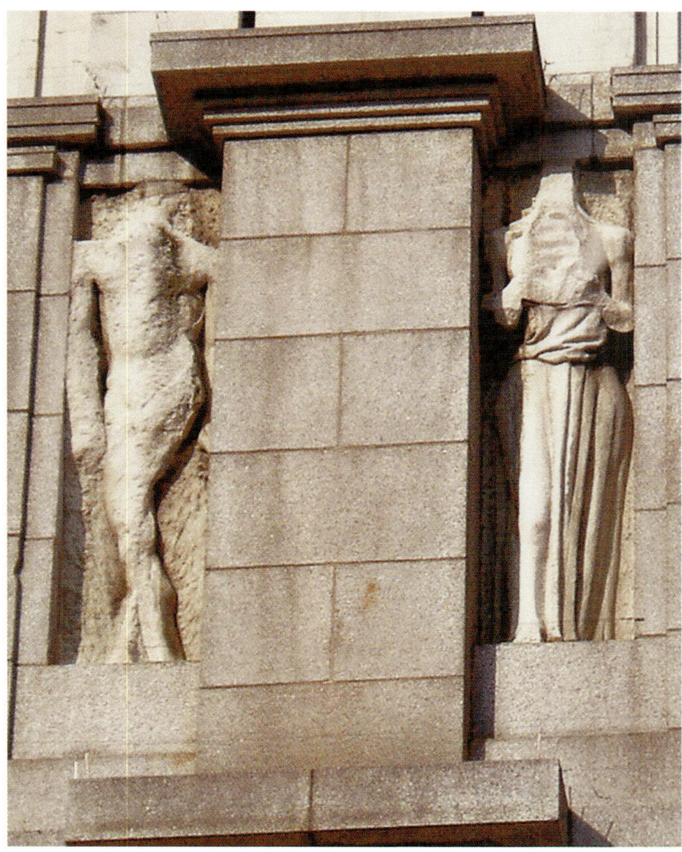

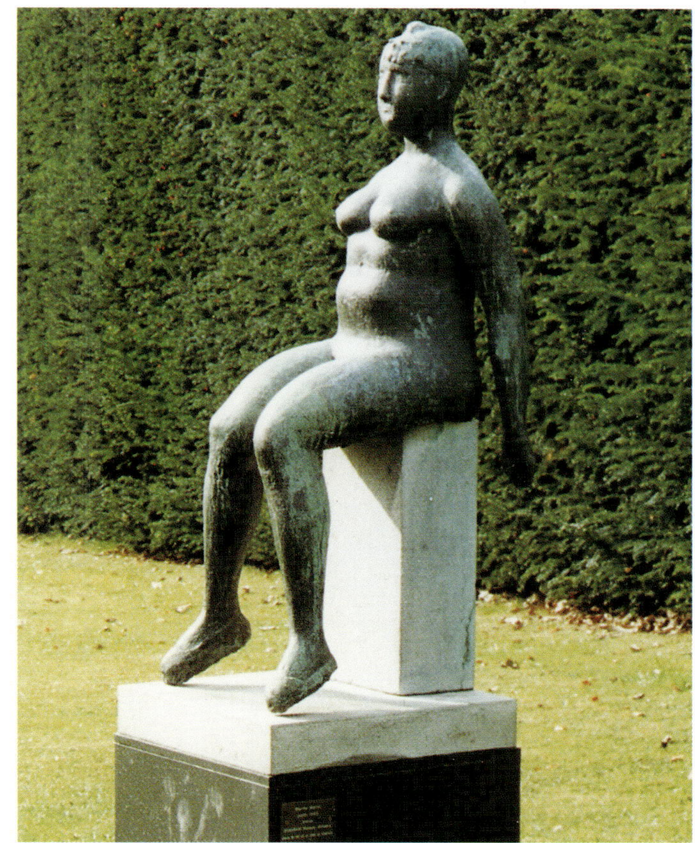

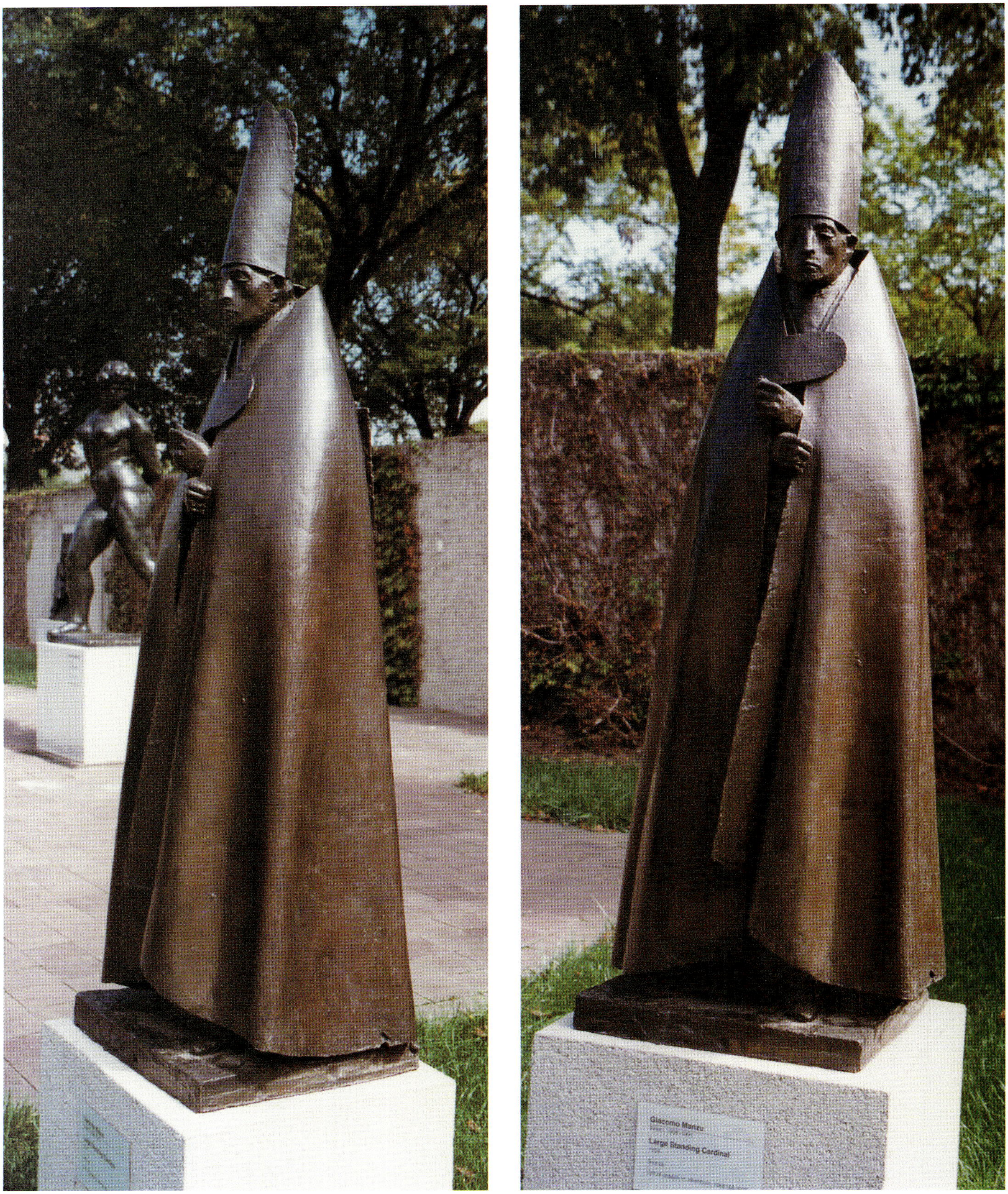

ABOVE: Cardinal, *6ft-high bronze, by Giacomo Manzu. (The Hirschorn Collection, Washington, USA. Photo: John W. Mills)*

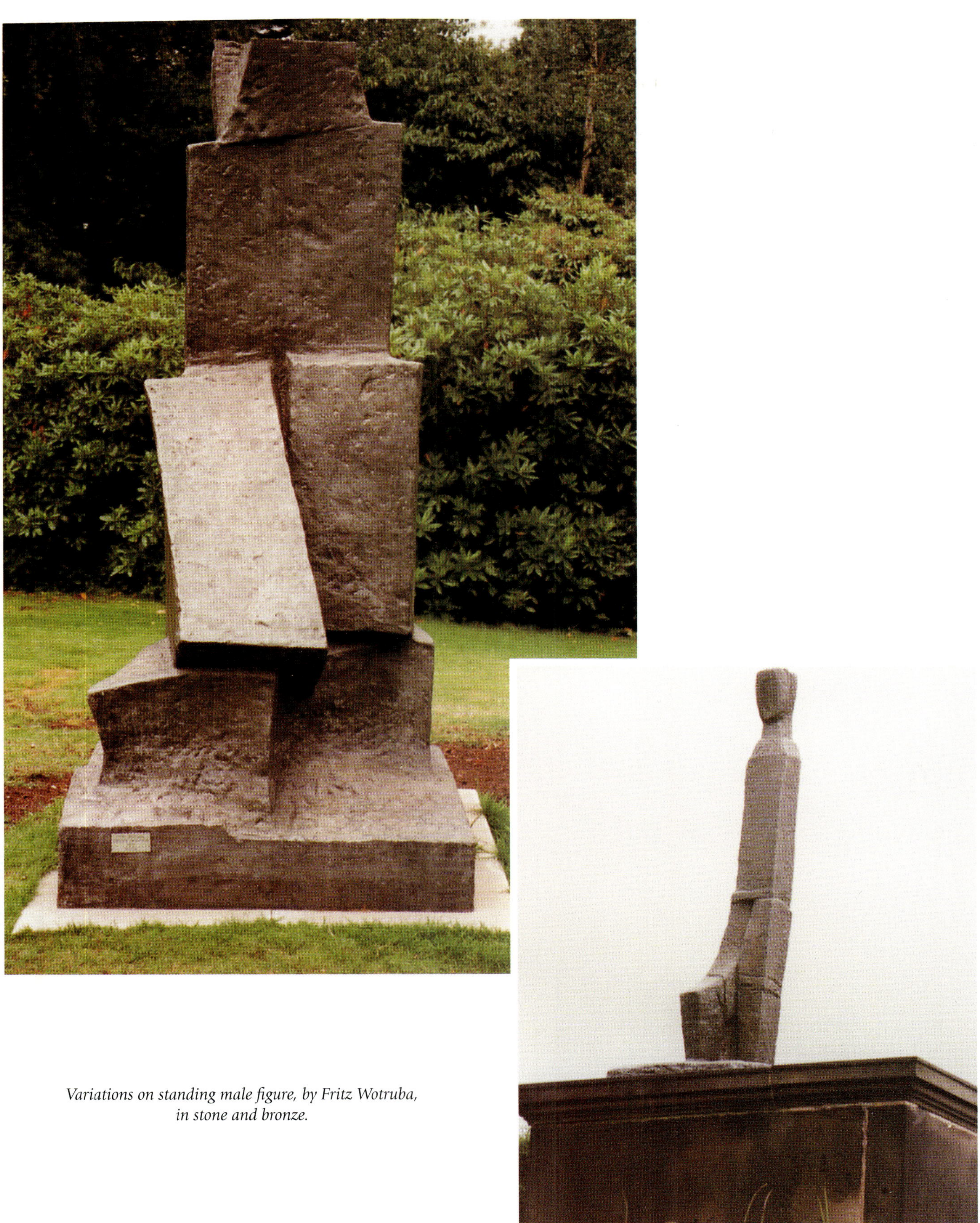

Variations on standing male figure, by Fritz Wotruba, in stone and bronze.

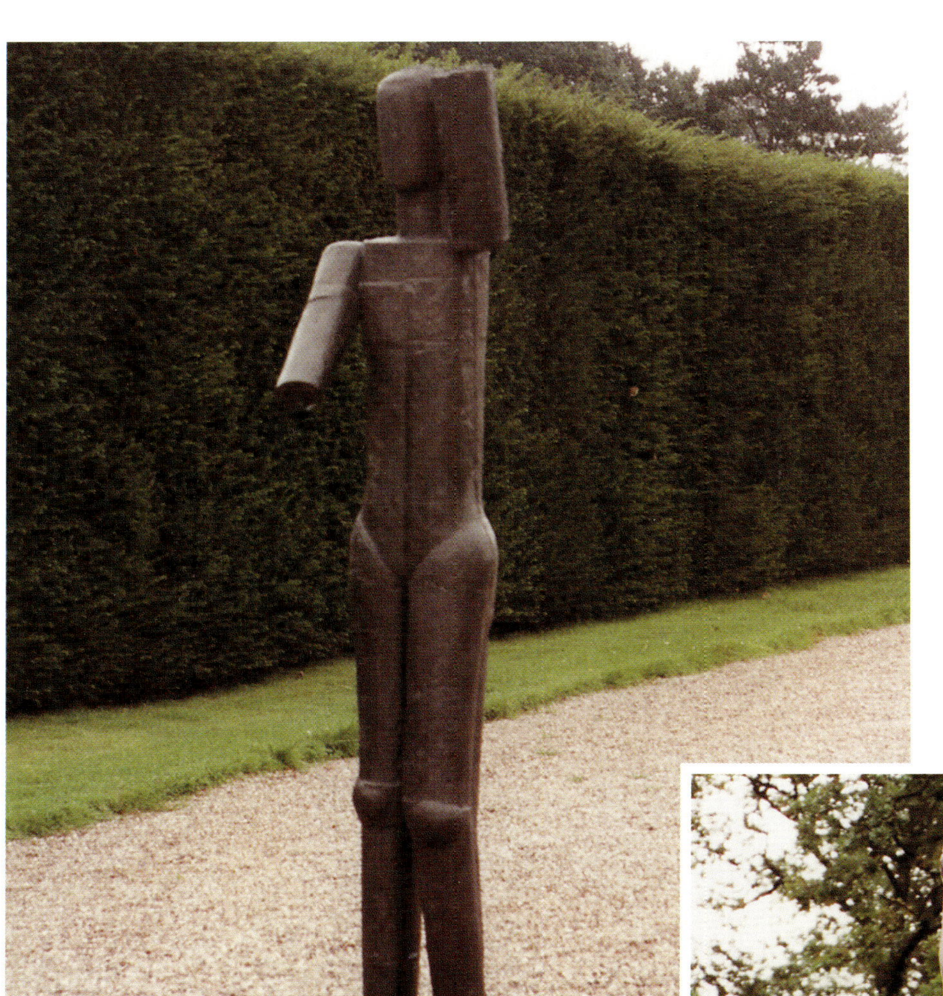

Variations on standing male figure, by Fritz Wotruba, in stone and bronze.

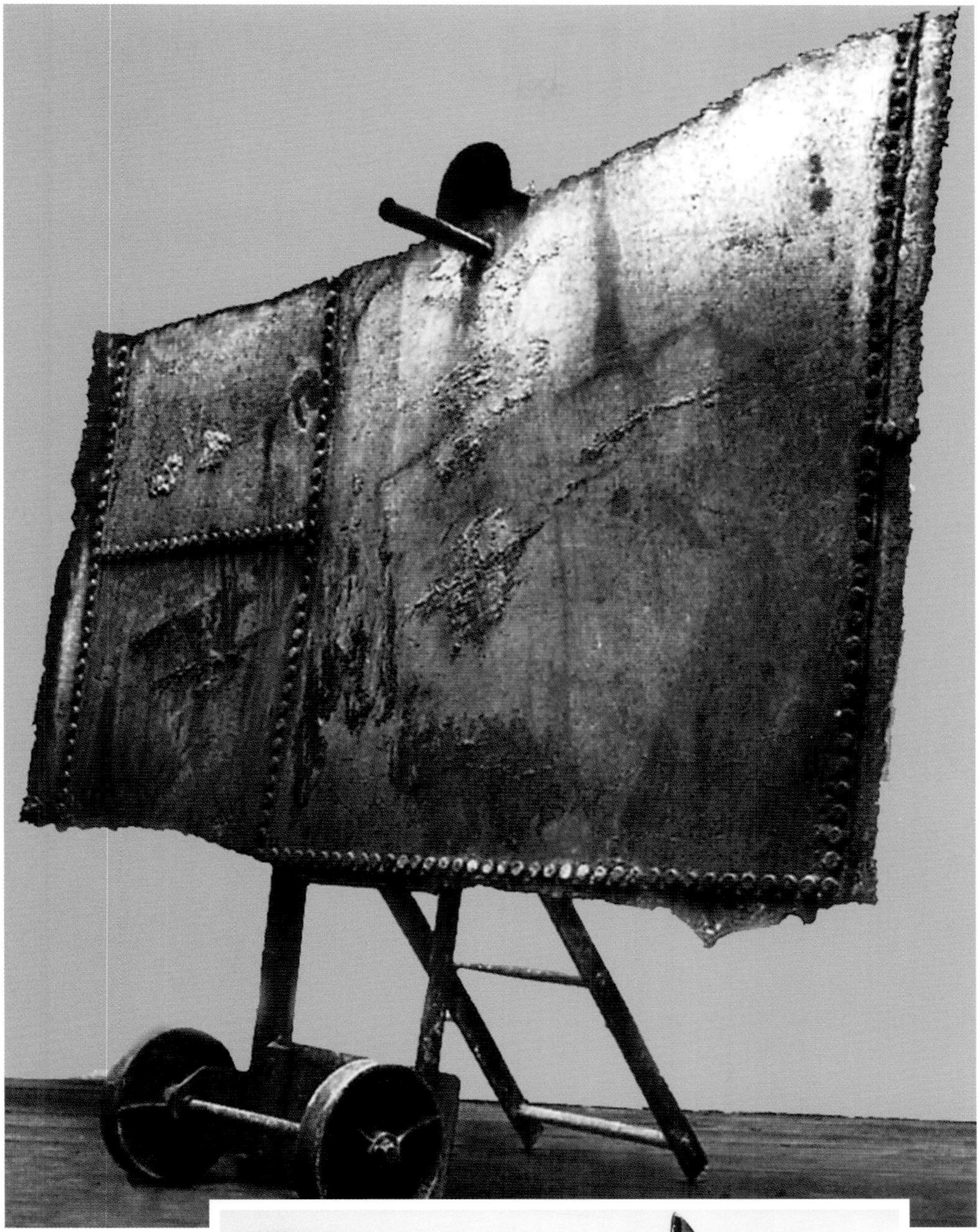

Various found metal objects assembled and welded together to make a powerful image, War Ghost, *by George Fullard.*

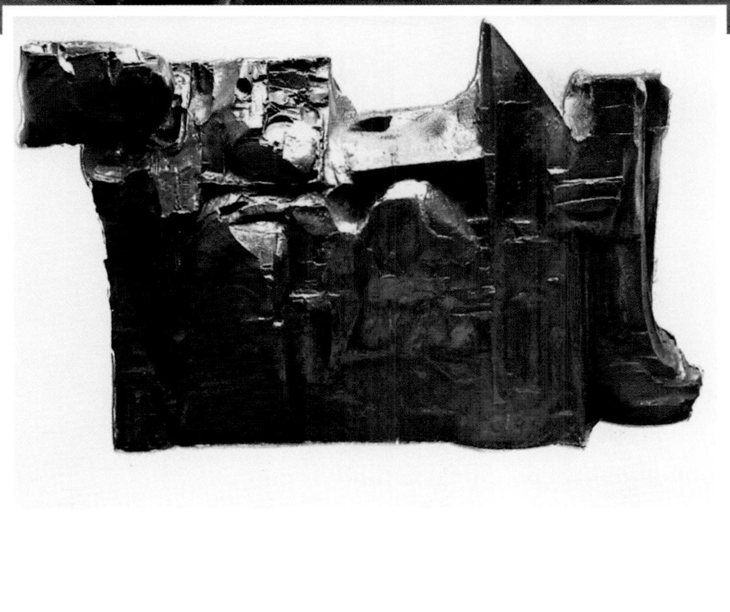

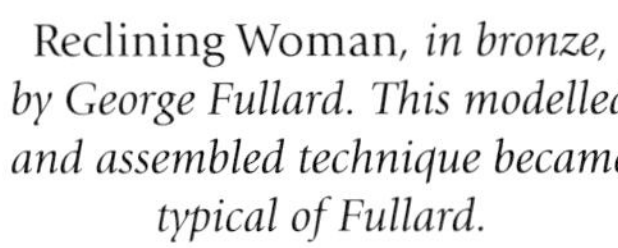

Reclining Woman, *in bronze, by George Fullard. This modelled and assembled technique became typical of Fullard.*

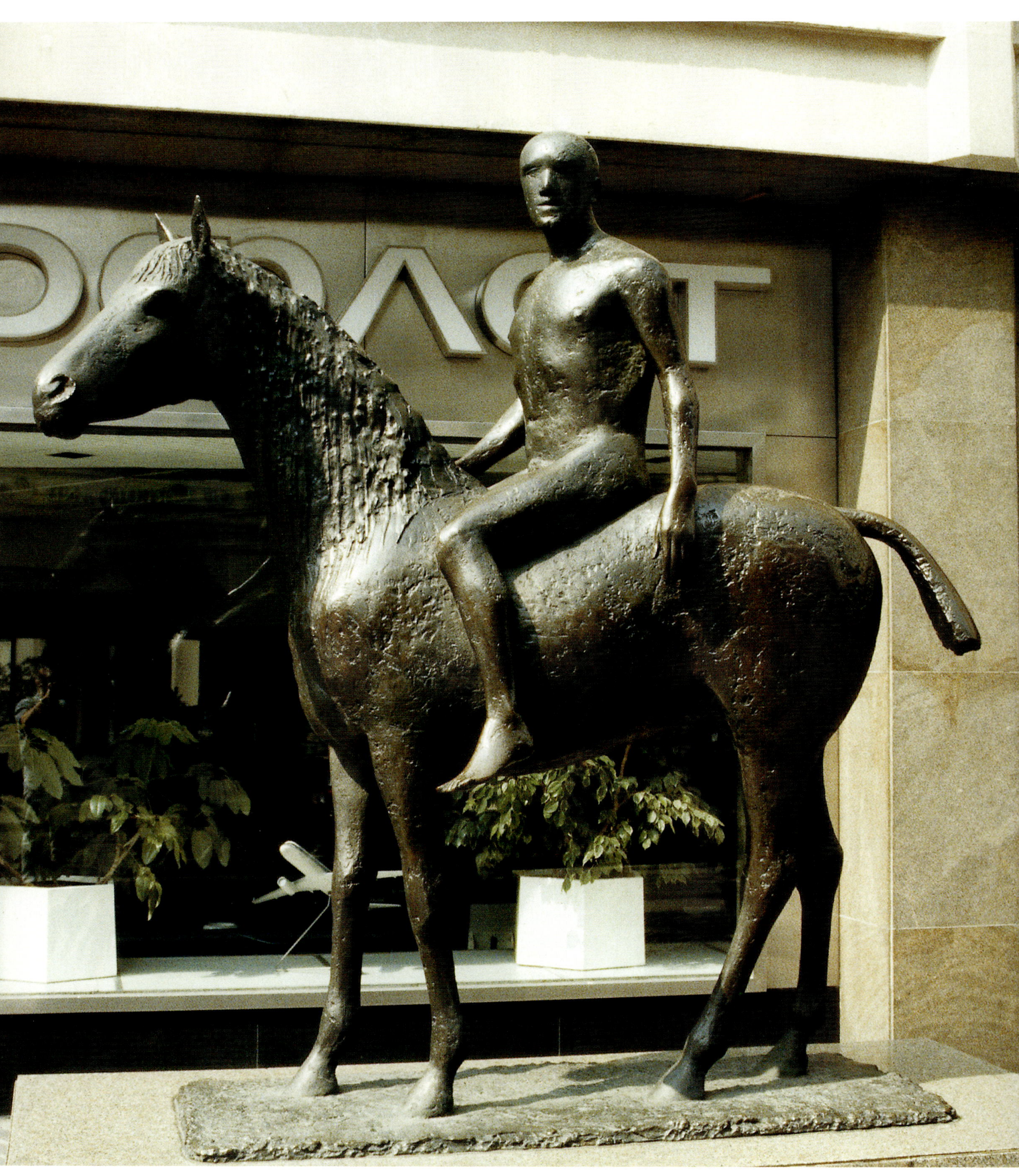

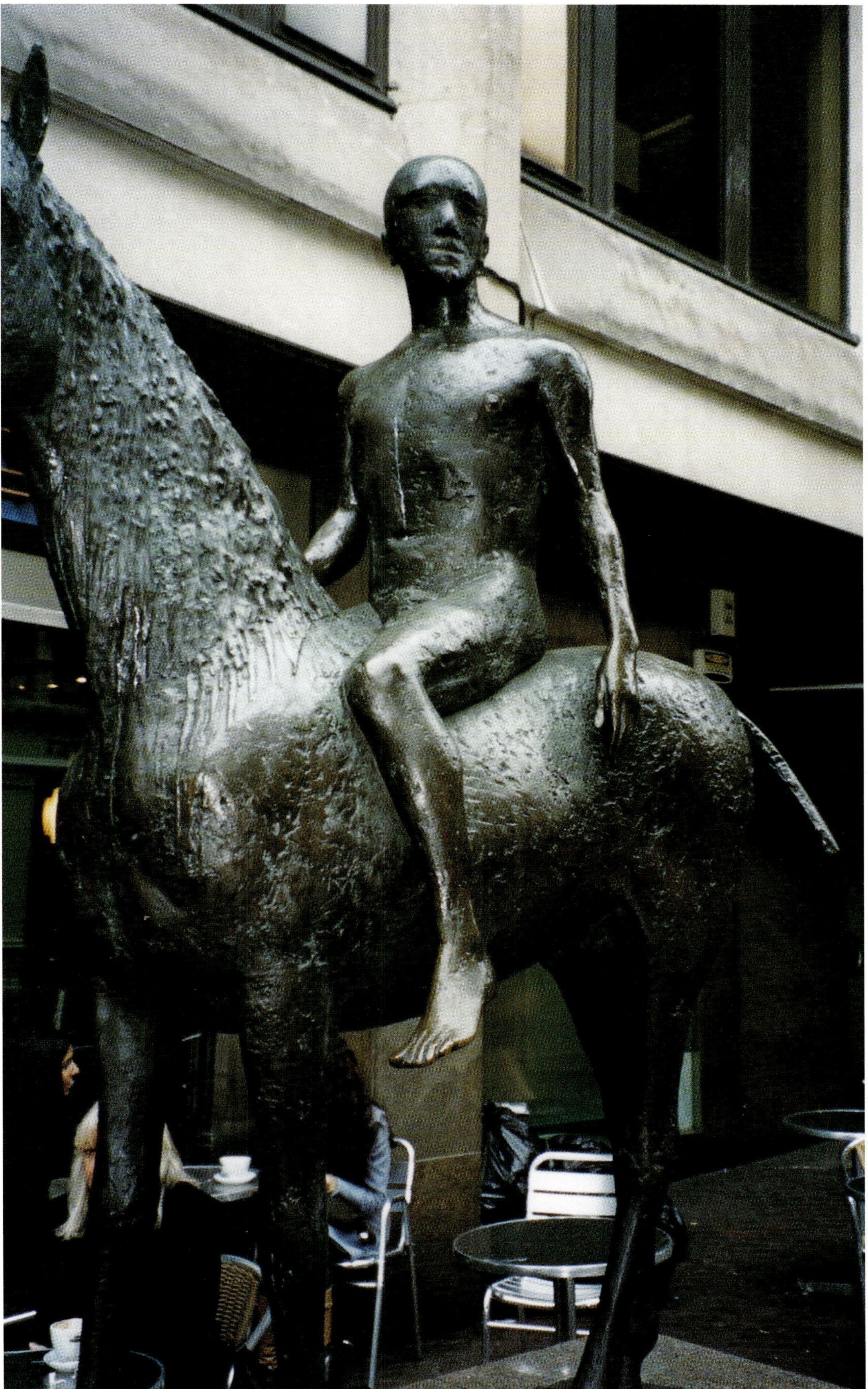

THIS PAGE AND OPPOSITE: Horse and Rider, *Elisabeth Frink. This bronze figure shows a very interesting interpretation of the male form.*

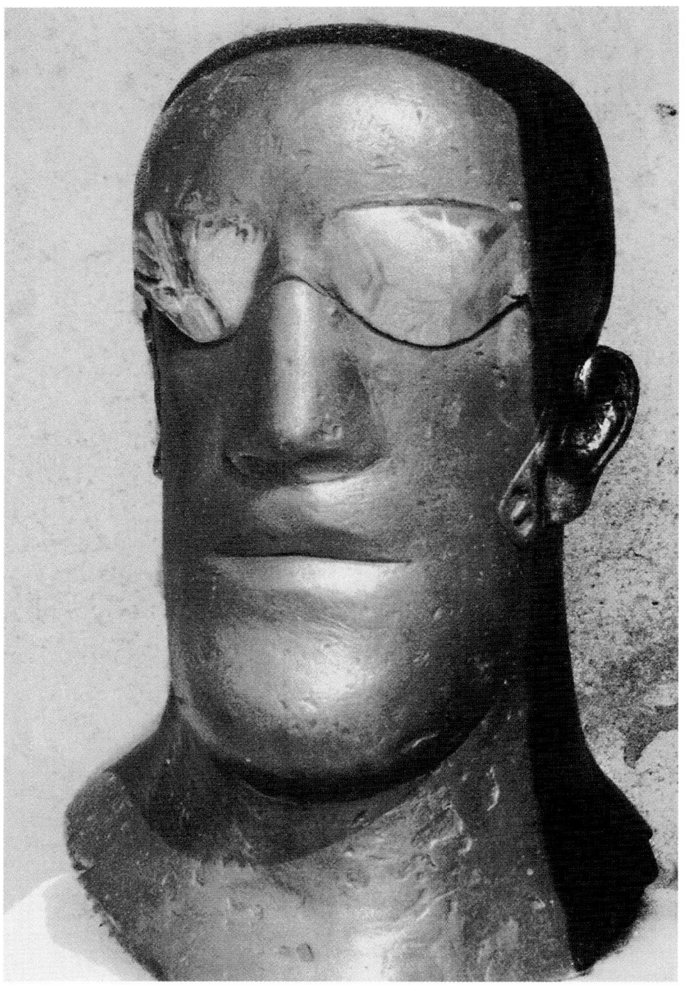

Goggle Head, *Elisabeth Frink. This powerful image in bronze expresses the active imagination of the artist. (Private collection)*

Seeing a beautiful thing for the first time, or suddenly seeing an object familiar from other experiences and finding it still enthralling, elevates the spirit and lodges that image firmly in the memory.

For me, finding sculpture in public spaces as well as in galleries and museums has always provided this kind of jumbled experience. My earliest conscious encounters were with public sculptures around London. The various soldiers, politicians and kings, memorials and celebrations, were not sculptures to me at that time, but merely people standing there. I did not question why they were there, how they were made or why, but they did intrude on my subconscious to become an important part of my cultural heritage and subsequent influence. Later at art school I learned that a large number of these sculptures were made by sculptors working in Great Britain at the end of the nineteenth century and well into the twentieth, who came to be known as the 'new sculptors'. They were influenced by trends emanating from Paris at that time, before the fascination with the exotic finds from tribal cultures took hold. These sculptors concentrated on the close study of and concern for the real in their everyday world. French sculptor Auguste Rodin was a major influence then, and, indeed, remains so today. His is the more familiar name, but his friend and colleague Jules Dalou actually taught for a few years in London. He became an even greater teaching influence than Rodin, having an impact on the new generation of sculptors in Britain, and as far afield as the USA, Canada and Australia.

Studying at art school in London shortly after the end of the Second World War, we were required to attend serious drawing classes in all the city's great museums. We enjoyed daily encounters with wonders of sculpture from all over the world, in all styles, idioms and materials, and this surely influenced my choice of sculpture as a profession.

London is rich in public sculpture – indeed, I later learned that it has more pieces than Paris. It was also rich in private art galleries, which brought to the public notice much of the new work that was tumbling out of artists' studios at the time, possibly as a result of the blessed release from the deprivations of war. Saturday-morning tours of these galleries became almost a ritual and a very interesting learning ground, allowing us to look at painting and sculpture, good, bad and indifferent, but full of experiment and excitement. I was prompted by those visits to experiment with abstract forms as well as figurative subjects. The lead was given by sculptors such as Jacob Epstein, Henry Moore and Barbara Hepworth, but we also admired such artists as Kenneth Armitage, Reg Butler, and the Italian sculptors Medardo Rosso, Marino Marini and Giacomo Manzu, and there was always the continuing presence of Rodin. They all used the real world as their source, coupling it to their imagination and skill to make unique sculptures.

The private galleries gradually began to show sculpture by younger artists and a continuity of influence was detectable in the work, including that of George Fullard, Ralph Brown and Elisabeth Frink, among many others. The same pattern was obviously repeated in other major cities around the world with different but identifiable national characteristics; it was relatively easy to pick out the French, Italian, German, Spanish and American identities. The 'airmail culture', as described earlier, had yet to happen and it was still possible to identify the countries of origin of the sculptures shown in these galleries.

OPPOSITE: The Ox Carriers, *in bronze, by Ralph Brown. (Harlow Arts Trust Collection, Essex. UK)*

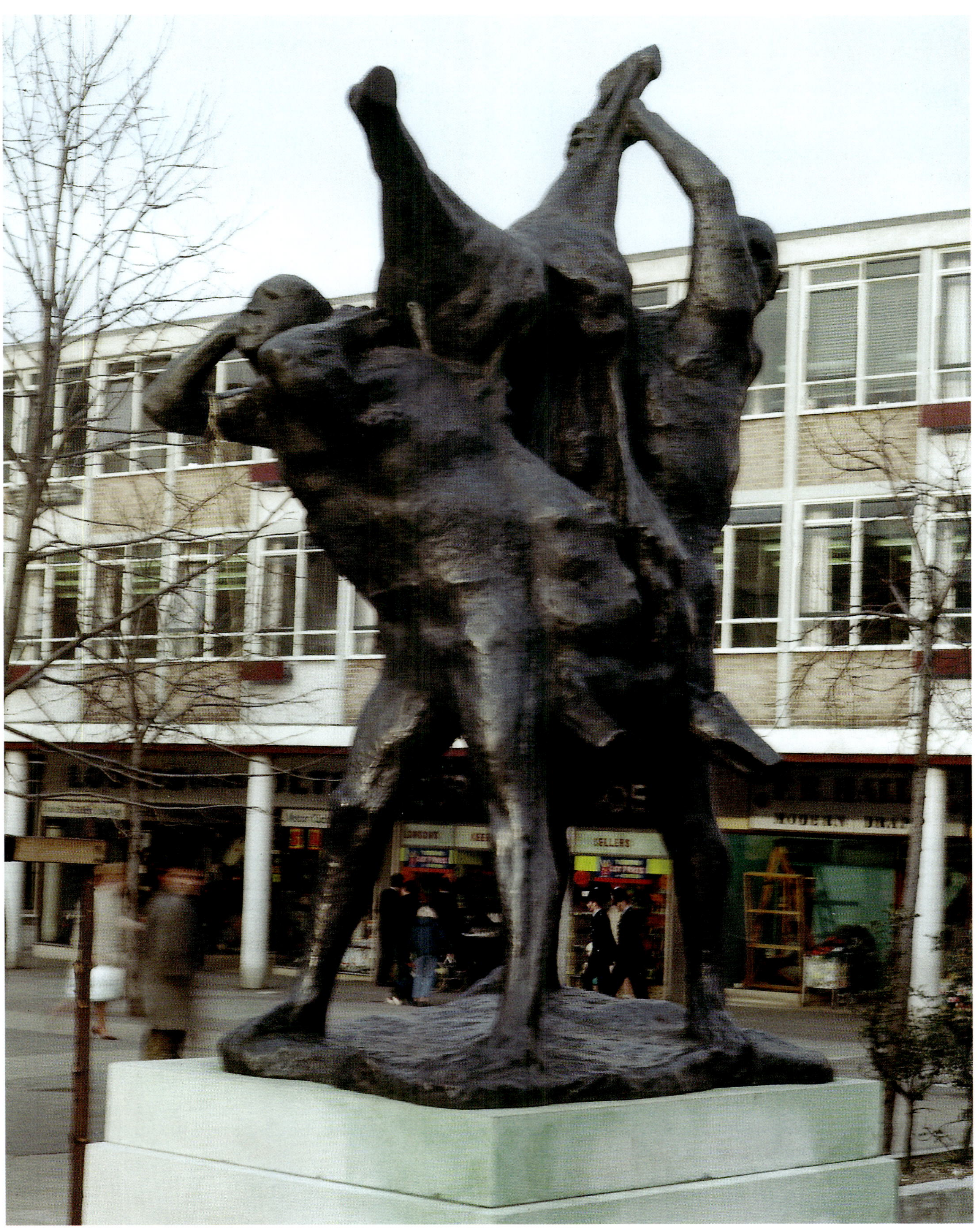

Materials and Tools

The idea for an image can be sparked off by almost anything but the sculpture it leads to will be resolved according to the blending of the idea with the chosen material, plus the tools and processes used to work it. All tools leave tell-tale marks and identifying them on completed sculptures can be a considerable aid in the study of sculpture, leading the diligent student through a maze of interesting materials and techniques, from the very softest substance to the hardest.

Clay is common to almost all civilizations and tribal cultures, either in its most basic condition of wet soil/mud, or in any number of sophisticated developments of fired clay, from terracotta bricks, vessels and images, to delicate intricate porcelain to adorn princely palaces. Where clay was abundant it influenced not only what is now recognized as sculpture but also, more fundamentally, domestic life, including the nature and character of the dwellings and subsequently architecture. This is as true of mud hut (wattle and daub) dwellings all over the world, particularly in hot dry climates, as it is of adobe and brick-built castles and palaces.

The materials to hand have always defined the style and character of the built and decorated environment, and the evolution of technical procedures peculiar to those materials affected their use in all applications. This influence of materials on the built world can be seen all over Britain, from the golden-coloured sandstone of the Cotswolds to the dark limestone of Derbyshire, which contrasts, for example, with the pale clunch stone architecture of Cambridgeshire. In addition, the same materials were employed in different ways in different regions; for example, the wattle and daub of Dorset is not the same as that used in East Anglia, and so on.

The stone-building practices of the Incas of Peru in South America, which are now widely known and admired, provide a significant example of the importance of local materials. Special masonry skills developed because of an abundance of granite, which became the preferred building material. It created a very sophisticated stone culture – with structures fitted miraculously together block by block, without mortar – which still seems marvellous today and reflects a breathtaking quality of craftsmanship. Clay was available to the Peruvian Incas but it was used predominantly in figurative pottery. With no written language, the Incas chose to depict most of their social history on their pots, from the most intimate couplings and everyday domestic affairs, to the placation of deities. As far as sculpture is concerned, the Incas left extraordinary examples of work, both of hard granite carving and of soft earthenware terracotta.

Wherever there were forests and a plentiful supply of timber there developed woodcarving and building techniques that were easier and quicker than those to do with clay. Nomadic tribes could build and leave a dwelling or shelter, in the safe knowledge that they could quickly make another somewhere else; clay was made into transportable precious vessels, and images endowed with more significant domestic and often spiritual meaning, which were closely guarded by the families. The technical handling of respective materials was often controlled or dictated by the use of the item made and sometimes by the hierarchy of the social order for which it was destined – the higher up the social pecking order, the more sophisticated the material and the techniques used to manufacture the object. This was prevalent in all societies; wealth and status play important roles in all the arts and in the technical developments pertaining to materials and expression. The more difficult the demands of a substance, the higher the value placed on items made from it, and this is reflected today in the various fashion industries of art and design.

The making of sculpture using similar materials is a more intimate affair than building (with the possible exception of the manufacture of colossal sculptures, from those of Ancient Greece to the gargantuan Buddhas of Asia). Sculpture more often than not is the product of single individuals working in private, this is especially true today with artists living away from regular gathering places where materials, techniques and ideas can be discussed and mulled over. The practice of apprenticeships and the dissemination of workshop skills went along with such communal gathering in the past, and sadly this does not happen very often today.

The sculptor relies on acquired skills, limited of course by training; personal dexterity and opportunity to experience a wide range of materials and processes, but his or her most basic and useful modelling tools will be the hands, fingers and thumbs. These are considered by the majority of sculptors to be the best equipment, especially for modelling malleable materials. Manufactured modelling tools are simply aids to these natural tools. Hands, fingers and thumbs leave unique human identities in clay and wax, and some sculptors like to see their fingerprints recorded on the finished work. This is simple when dealing with terracotta and its direct route between the soft clay and the final fired material, but some sculptors expect to see their prints on the cast surface, even on bronze after the many procedures involve in such castings.

Despite the importance of the hands, manufactured modelling tools are important items in the sculptor's arsenal of equipment. They are often personalized, perhaps given a serrated edge to facilitate scraping, which leaves a kind of crosshatching on the clay. Wooden mallets with patterns cut into the striking surfaces can also be used to consolidate and texture the clay. Pitted and crosshatched textures help to break up the play of light across the surface of the form, making it easier to read and therefore to model.

Inca terracotta representing fecundity. (Private collection, Lima, Peru)

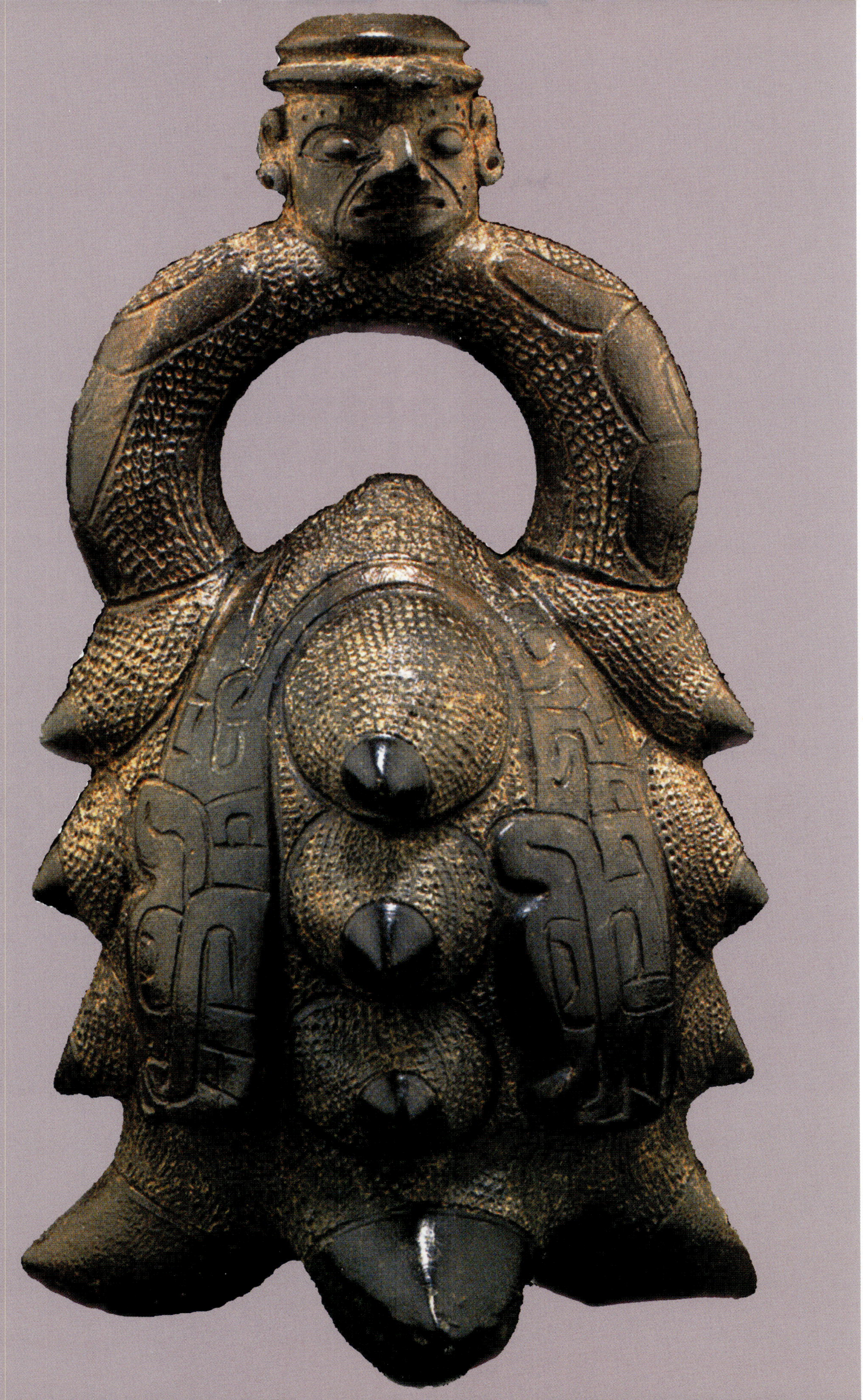

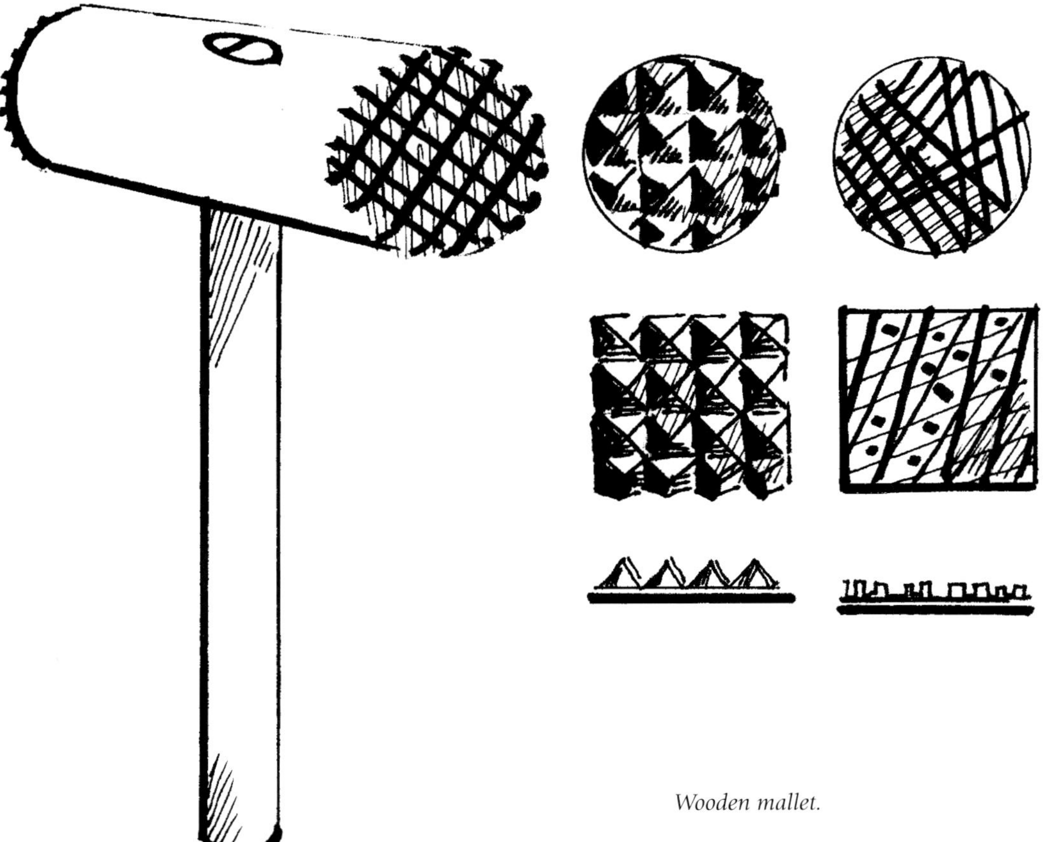

Wooden mallet.

A similar effect is achieved on stone using a hammer called a 'bouchard' or 'bush hammer'. This is a carving hammer with rows of points on the striking surface, which leaves a slightly pitted and matt surface on the stone. As with crosshatching and texturing on clay, this pitted surface breaks up the play of light on the surface of the stone, making the form clearer to read and adjust. This hammer does have other uses for shaping a stone form, but its role in creating texture is a significant feature. The claw chisel also leaves a kind of crosshatching on a stone or marble surface that can help the sculptor to read a form more clearly.

There are fewer tools in the woodcarver's kit that leave such helpful marks, apart from the various rasps that are used to remove wood. These leave scratch marks on the surface, which help to clarify a form. All the carving tools leave marks that can be detected – some more obvious than others – and finding them and defining their function is an interesting and useful study.

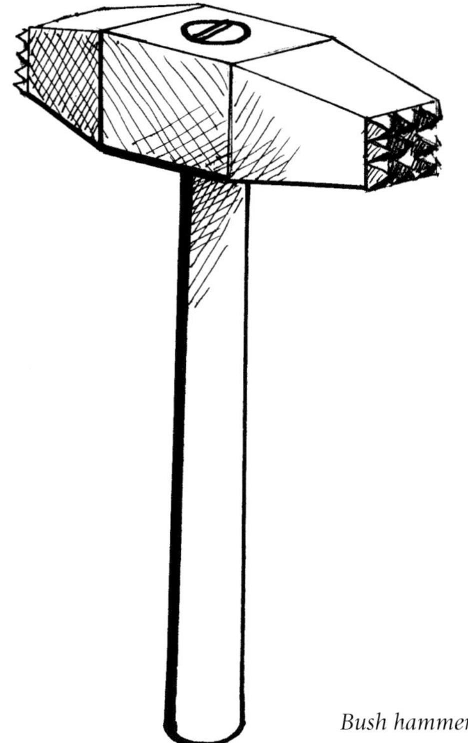

Bush hammer or bouchard.

1

Basic Techniques

There should be no secrets in the nature and use of materials for sculpture. Advances in technology have led to new materials being developed, some of which may prove to have useful applications in sculpture. In the main, however, apart from the electronic media, the technical processes remain the same: cutting, carving, modelling, casting and gluing.

CUTTING Involves making shapes of all kinds, both flat and in the round, using tools that have a sharp cutting edge that is harder than the material being cut.

CARVING Carving differs from cutting only in that the material being carved is usually bulky, like stone, for instance, and has a much harder resistance, requiring the aid of a hammer or mallet to deliver the required power to the arm and hand to remove waste material. Modern electrical and pneumatic tools do provide a range of power sources to aid the sculptor, and these include cutting and carving tools that have been highly developed, but the principles of carving are the same.

MODELLING Probably the most easily understood of all sculpture techniques are those associated with soft and pliable substances because of the natural tendency to squeeze and knead all sorts of materials, from bread dough to clay and wax. When baked in an oven or simply left to dry, most soft, pliable substances become hard, forming a basis for artistic as well as culinary expression, and enabling the buildings of vessels and food and sculptures and homes.

CASTING This process has evolved from the discovery of materials that can change from a liquid to a solid state, either hot or cold, from liquid clay to liquid metal. This element of change extended the thinking associated with modelling, leading to mould making, which is the making of a negative copy of the modelled subject from which a positive copy, the cast, can be made. This casting procedure allows vessels and images of utility and beauty to be made and reproduced in great number – a useful feature that has served artist and artisan for many centuries.

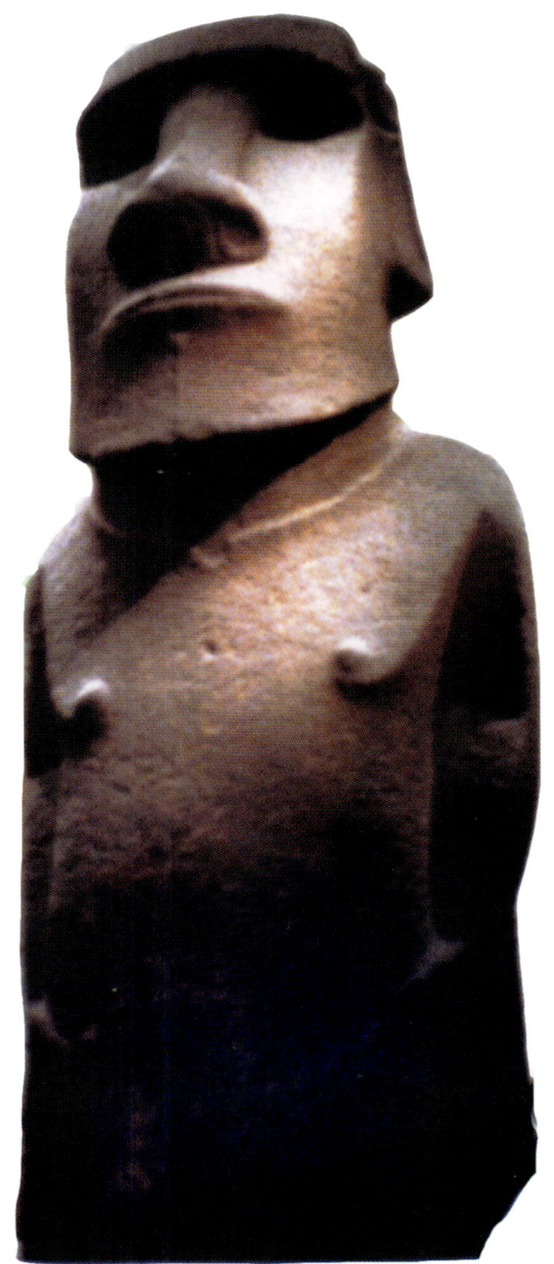

Heroic-scale granite head. (British Museum)

GLUING The sticking together of objects developed from the discovery of substances that change from a soft or liquid condition to a hard solid state, thus becoming a bonding agent (glue). Gluing is used in all walks of life in the widest possible combination, from igloos to mud huts and paper chains, to the complexities of soldering for jewellery and the welding of ships. The principle of attaching one object to another by means of a liquid that becomes a solid is the same in all these applications.

The Studio

A studio, somewhere private to work, is a basic need, especially if you are planning to work from the naked human being. The traditional life-modelling studio evolved over a long period, finally adopting a particular pattern that is still favoured. The room should be large enough to house the model (and keep him or her warm), plus the sculptor and equipment. A revolving turntable for the model to pose on is useful, as it is easier to turn the model than to move the work, especially as it gets heavier during the modelling process.

Sufficient suitable storage space is required to keep enough material, clay, plaster of Paris, armature materials and tools, to complete the modelling and casting task. Washing facilities may be a luxury but in an ideal situation they will be as important as adequate space to store the work or works in progress. The floor needs to be strong enough to bear the weight of the wet clay equipment, which is deceptively heavy, plus the human beings. Professional studios develop to accommodate the needs of an individual sculptor and can be vast and lovely, or small and cluttered accordingly. Storage is a perennial problem – you need enough room for both works in progress and completed works, together with all the required materials, both wet and dry, as well as all the paraphernalia that is required and accumulates over time; so if you are able to make a choice, go for the largest studio space available and affordable.

Natural moving daylight is preferred, east-west rather that north-south, with windows high up so that you are not viewing your work against the light. Artificial lighting is another personal choice, but beware of fluorescent lighting, which tends to flicker and provide an almost non-directional light that makes for poor shadows. Modern cool halogen lighting can be close to daylight in effect and cast good shadows; some experimentation is necessary. Electric, moveable heating to keep you and model warm is an essential feature in such a studio; it is vital always to keep your model warm and happy.

Clay work in progress can be kept in the best damp condition for as long as possible by using modern plastic sheeting, so the studio needs to allow for storing this, plus cloth to made wet to be placed over the clay under the plastic. If this wrapping up is done correctly, so that the work is sealed and in an airtight condition, the work can be kept in good condition for many weeks. In the past, when other means (some good and some bad) were used to protect wet clay, many a master work was lost due to the clay drying out and disintegrating. (Many more of Auguste Rodin's early works would have survived if he had been able to use plastic sheeting or any of the modern synthetic clays, but sadly none of these were available at the time.)

The storage of completed work, plus all the moulds that result from the manufacture of cast sculpture of all kinds of materials, is another constant headache, requiring space, or some difficult decisions to abandon them. Some sculptors have managed to acquire sufficient land to display their completed work, and thus created a collection. One famous example is Henry Moore, and The Henry Moore Foundation in the UK today guards and administers the collection that grew from his foresight. Other such artists' foundations now exist all over the world and offer not only the work but also some insight into the working ambience of the artist.

Private studios are of course a modification of the ideal and custom-built studios are a rarity for the average artist, but dreams feed the creative process, so dream on and keep working.

Modelling from Life

Using the Living Model

Following the European Renaissance in painting and sculpture in the fourteenth century, drawing and modelling from the naked human figure became a tradition in art schools all over the world. The belief was that working from the living naked model on a regular basis would enhance the student's understanding of form and proportion. This may or may not have been the case, but over time such study became an examinable subject and therefore truly 'academic'. It became bound to the art school studio and its usefulness as an aid and means to personal expression was brought into question. Gradually, 'life drawing and 'life modelling' – that is, gathering together as a group to model or draw, for no apparent good reason, an unclothed person who was posing without movement – existed only as an art school subject. Eventually, it was dropped from most curriculums, to the dismay of many older artists. Why did this happen? It was once considered to be the backbone of art school study, but it was no longer in favour. Perhaps the answer lies in the fact that, in this modern age, the human

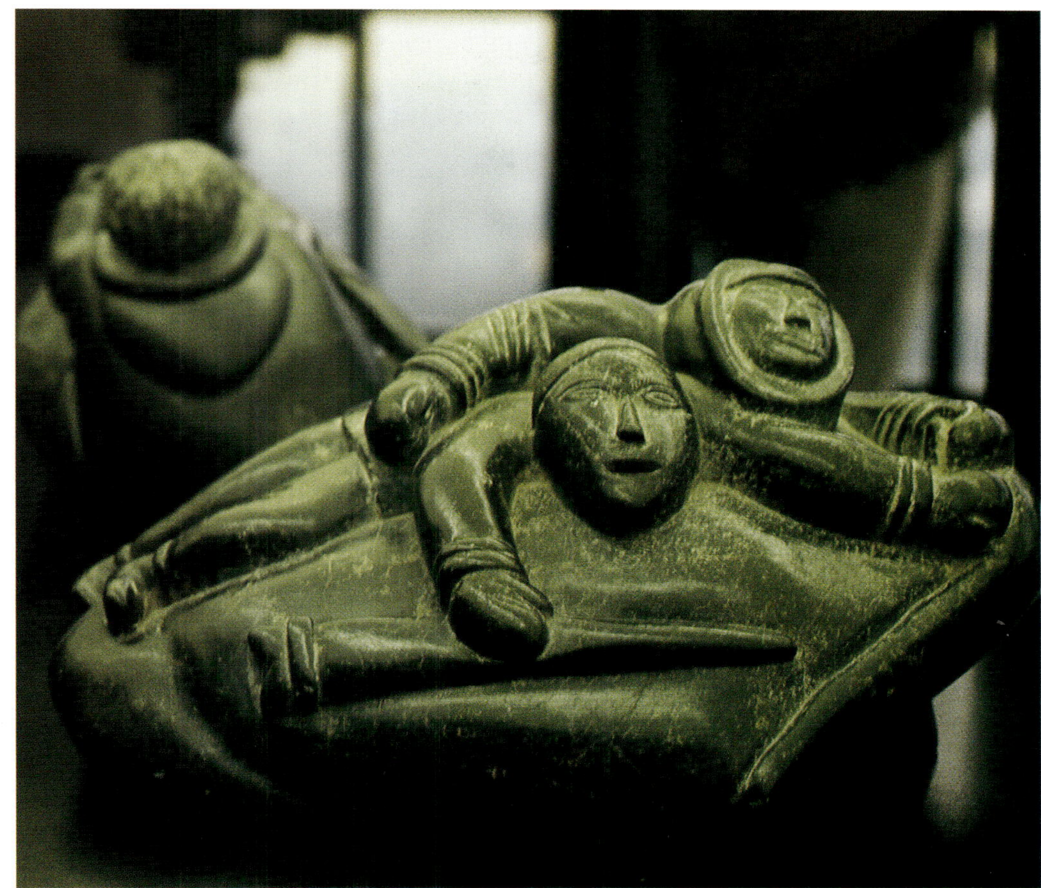

Inuit carvings made from rare and precious stone and ivory. (Toronto Dominion Collection, Canada)

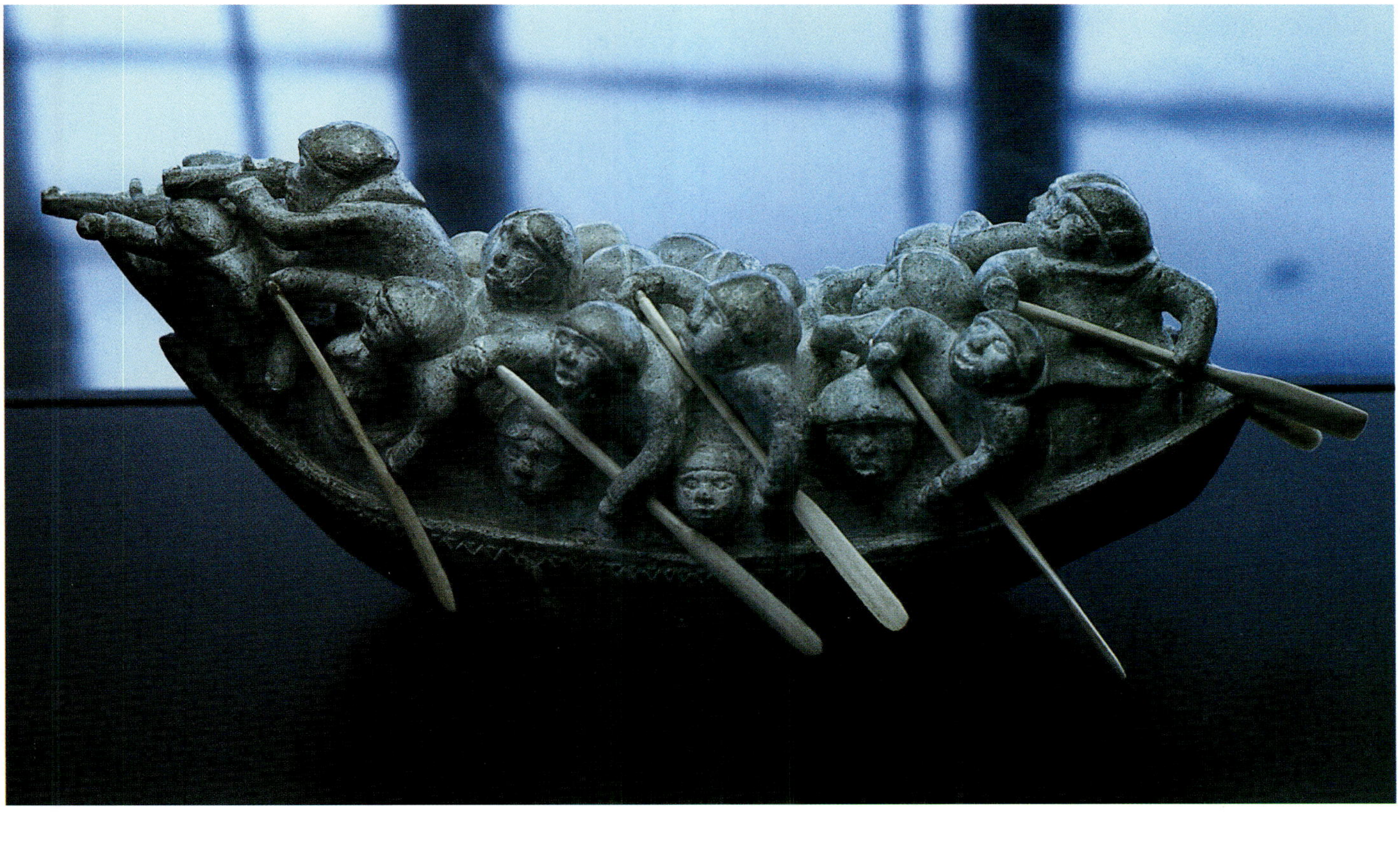

figure is easily accessible; it can be seen everywhere, lightly clothed or unclothed, on film, in books, on athletics fields, in the theatre and on the fashion catwalks. Contemporary dress can be very revealing and the human figure, which was previously covered and mysterious, can be studied in all its manifestations – healthy or sick, slender or gross, beautiful or ugly; or perhaps expression based only on the self has become a dominating self-centering factor.

There is a view that nudity, especially between artist and model, is best experienced privately and not as a group activity. Proper life study actually takes place outside the art school studio. The studio model is useful in the same way that a reference library is useful, but the student of art will learn more in the everyday world. The artist will develop in the best way by using the human faculty of the visual memory, taking on the ever-present wealth of inspiration and information in the real world.

Practise training yourself to have confidence in your ability to recall specific shapes, characters and incidents, so that the stimulus of the ever-changing real world provides your source material, and such inspiration will stay with you for ever. Train your memory to help you develop your work and accomplish drawings and three-dimensional sketch models (maquettes), which will lead to a selection of images that you may wish to resolve at a larger scale. In turn, this will become your unique self expression. Developing and enlarging an image will inevitably reveal gaps in your knowledge about the human figure and this is where specific 'life study' comes in. Your reference library – that is, the living model – becomes necessary at this stage, to provide the opportunity for specific research and the study of anatomical factors that have been identified according to a particular image or set of images. This is not a group activity, but when used correctly it will lead to unique and special sculptures.

The traditional view was that a course of 'life study' would lead to a greater understanding of the figure. However, most people from a very early age learn to use and live successfully with a complete set of human bits, male or female. Such learning is so thorough that it is taken for granted, unless the body malfunctions. Every student comes to art school already knowing a great deal about the figure from his or her

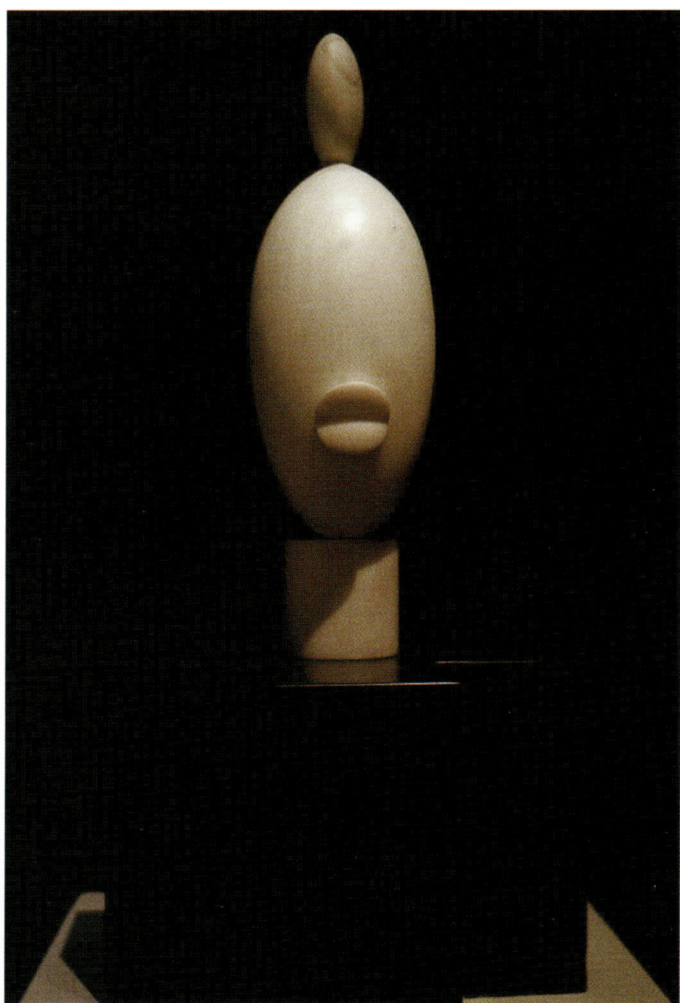

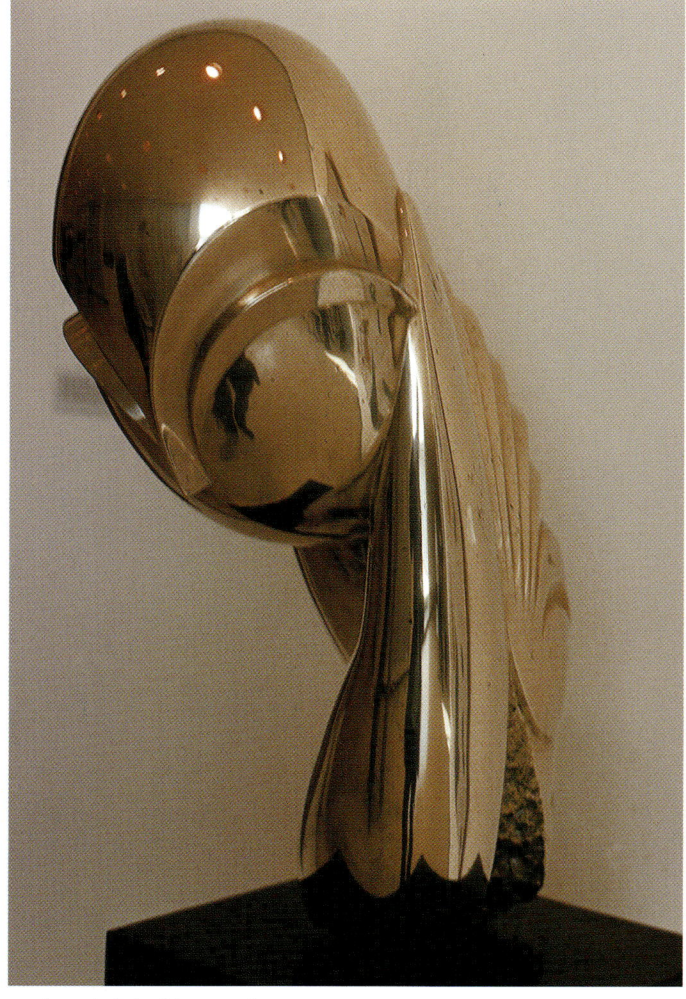

The Princess *(LEFT), in marble, and* Mlle Pogany *(RIGHT), in polished bronze, by Constantin Brancusi.*

own personal experiences – although such knowledge may be subliminal. Everyone subsconsciously acts on such knowledge, for example, not putting their arms or legs in a position of hazard, and protecting their physical selves instinctively, but such inherent learned understanding tends to be forgotten when 'art' lurches in to the equation. Every student possesses visual and physical empathy to a greater or lesser degree – this enables them to function and interact with others on a daily basis. For the artist working figuratively these faculties need to become more conscious and developed, by not only carrying out certain movements and actions, but also by thinking about them as they are done. Knowing how a certain action or posture feels will help to add truth to an image and provide even more specific points of reference and research. Again, this is where the living model becomes an important source of information.

Materials

Modelling materials are most commonly used for making studies from life because of the relative ease with which they can be handled. Clay is the most widely used material for modelling, either over an armature for eventual casting, or by building up purer clay to be fired to make terracotta. Clay is also one of the cheapest and most versatile materials.

Wax in its various forms can be used to make studies from life but it is usually restricted today to fairly small items. It was widely used in the past and led to the process of metal casting known as the 'lost wax process, but often it became the final material, to which colour was added to make a life-like replica of a human being. Typical sculptures of this kind are those that featured in Madame Tussaud's exhibitions, and the tradition continues today using both coloured wax and resins.

Making life studies in more durable materials is not a common practice – flying chips of stone or wood are uncomfortable for the model – so sculptures are usually worked directly according to shapes suggested by the bulk of the material. For the more literal works, they may be carved using a modelled study (sketch model/maquette or working model) as a guide.

Making a replica of the human figure, like those on view at Tussauds, as well as those works that are simply cast from life to make a reproduction, is questionable as sculpture. Such work requires a wide range of skills but it represents an art of deception, and it is the art of interpretation that imbues great sculpture with the qualities that impress. Reality is filtered through the sensibilities of the artist and this, according to that artist's dexterity and control over the chosen material, results in a personal statement that is unique to the individual. The interpretation of reality in response to a concept or an idea leading to a specific image is the

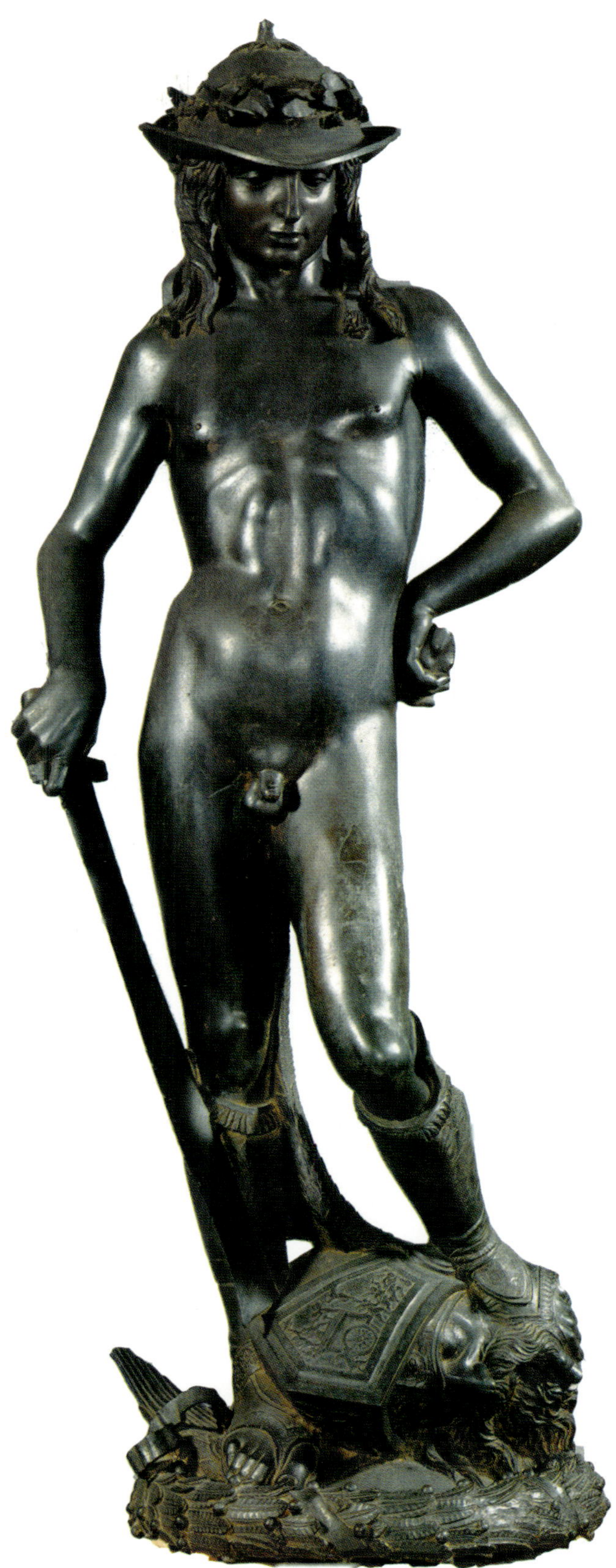

David, *by Donatello, in bronze painted plaster. This is reputedly the first free-standing nude figure of the Renaissance. (V&A Museum, Plaster Courts, London)*

factor that helps to create sculptural entities, sculptures that sometimes seem to open the doors of perception augmented by the viewer's sense and observation of reality. Such images may be admired and accepted in their global diversity and appreciated as sculptures, being equivalent to but not replicas of human beings.

It is an inescapable fact that the artist's cultural background will affect his or her works of art, no matter how hard he or she tries to change it. The characteristics of sculpture from Southern Europe that Kenneth Clark described as 'ecstasy' reflect the sensual nudity of the warmer clime; work from the colder north reveals a certain nakedness that seems to have seldom seen the sun, thus creating a completely different sexuality. Such differences make it interesting to study, for instance, the work of sculptors who come from all over the world to Rome under the auspices of the 'Prix de Rome' competition. The opportunity is offered in most countries to graduates in art, architecture and engraving, and, although some reveal themselves to be profoundly affected by the Eternal City, their inherent cultural references remain.

Carving

The act of carving in either stone or wood is a subtractive process, so it is important to remember that the final volume of the sculpture will be less than the material you start with. Although this seems obvious, it does confuse some beginners. It means that what you present yourself with at each visit to the studio will be heavier in fact and in feeling than the image you are striving to achieve. If you are not constantly reminding yourself of this fact, that heaviness may remain in the work, resulting often in rather dumpy, thick-legged figures, with arms to match. This is very much a problem when carving stone, when the hard physicality of the work makes it difficult to retain in the front of the mind the image that is in development. Retaining a grasp on the developing image is always a problem in sculpture because of the various lengthy processes involved, regardless of the materials you use, but it is a discipline that must be practised and understood, and well-designed sketch models are a great help in this respect.

The perception of volume is affected also when the carv-

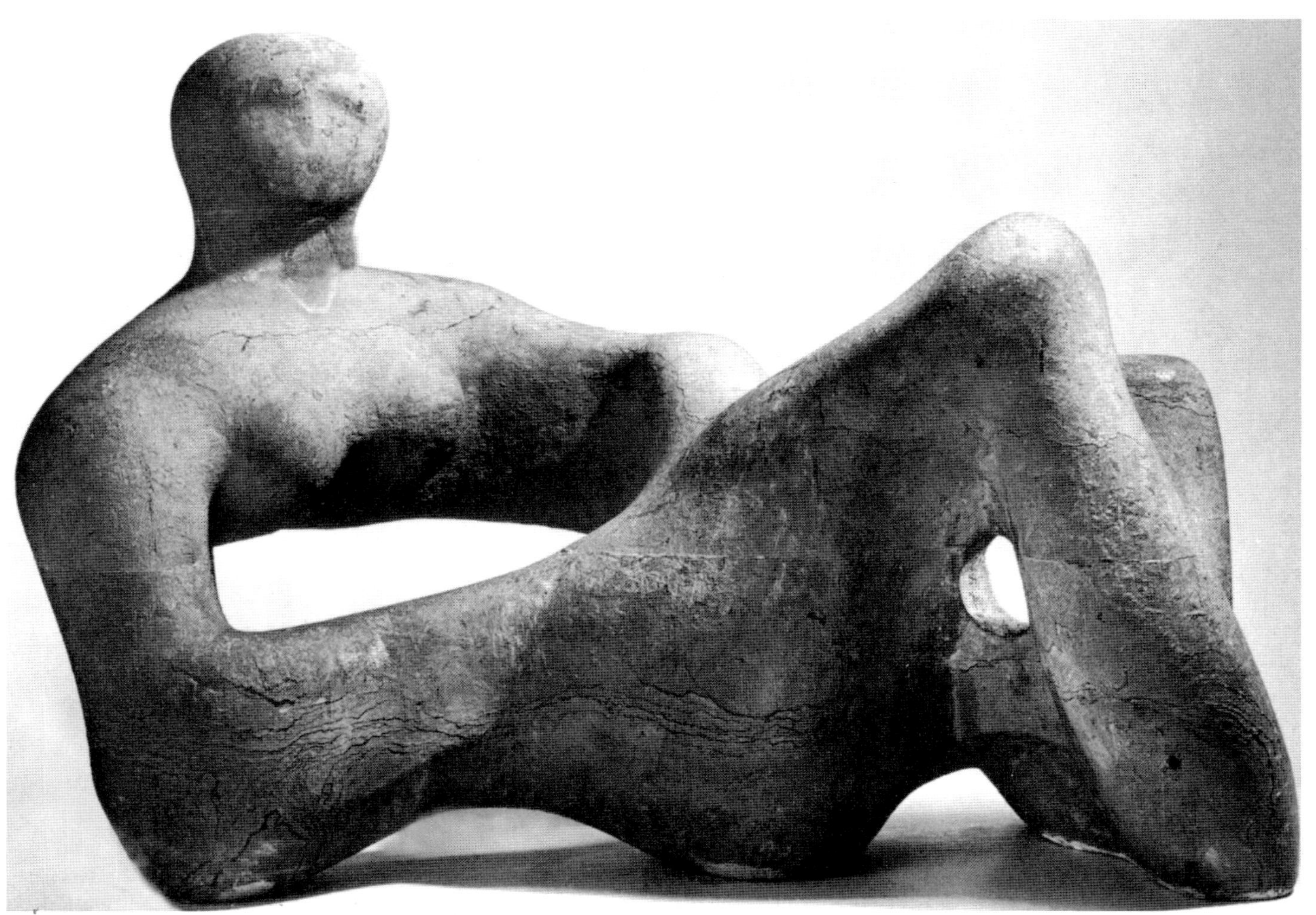

Henry Moore's Recumbent Figure *in Hornton stone. Done in 1938, this sculpture is an early example of Moore's exploration of the hole as a positive form. (Tate Gallery, London)*

ing is opened – that is to say, when material is cut away to pierce the block, stone or wood. It is tempting to do this soon into making the sculpture, but be warned – 'be sure before you pierce'. Once a hole has been made, the forms around it can only get smaller in volume whilst the hole will get larger, often resulting in slender shapes with very large spaces in between. The error often occurs in woodcarving because this particular material can be cut and drilled relatively easily. It occurs less frequently with stone, because the sheer physical effort tends to make for second thoughts, but with this material even greater care must be taken as the work progresses not to weaken its inherent strength. Once you are sure it is right to pierce the wood or stone (and this is a decision best made using well-considered maquettes), then you can enjoy the carving. If you are uncertain, it is wise to keep stone in reserve by not opening it. Henry Moore is credited with introducing the hole as a positive form in sculpture; some say it was a result of finding pierced stones on a beach and after close inspection declaring that a hole was a form of equal importance to that of solid matter. Whether or not this was the case, it is worth studying what he and his contemporaries did in this respect.

The elements of balance and stability are always important in sculpture, and should be considered very seriously when setting up the material to be carved. After the block has been selected and received in the studio, its bottom face needs to 'made true', that is to say, it needs to be made flat so that the block stands correctly according to the design established with maquette or working model. This process is best done as the first part of the project as an integral part of the setting-up procedure, assuring not only actual stability but also a visual stability to be encountered whenever the work is approached.

These points will be covered again in each of the chapters to do with carving the head and the figure, as it is vital to understand such basic techniques.

Stone

Being able to exploit the quality and special character of stone is an important part of a carver's life. Time and experience will bring knowledge, but it useful to have some idea of the geology of the natural formation of stone as a starting point. The three basic groups are igneous, sedimentary and metamorphic rock.

Igneous rocks are formed by the cooling of subterranean masses, and the rate of cooling plus their depth affects the nature of the stone. Those cooling slowly at great depth, such as granite, are usually coarser-grained. The finer-grained stones are those that cooled nearer the earth's surface and include basalt and obsidian. Colours vary according to the minerals present when the mass is formed and absorbed as it cools. This also traps harder minerals that give the granites their speckled quality and adds to their hardness. These harder stones are often pink, brown-red and dark green, and quite difficult to carve. The finer-grained granites are less colourful, being usually in the range of light and dark grey to dense black; although these stones are also very hard, their carving quality is better because of the finer grain.

Sedimentary rocks, sometimes referred to as stratified rocks, are formed by the deposition of sediment, by water or from the atmosphere, which then gradually hardens with time. The deposits are of varying coarseness and are intermingled with organic matter, which is similarly deposited. These include skeletal remains of various kinds, which contain calcium carbonate, the main ingredient of limestone. Limestone is probably the most widely used stone in all its varieties for sculpture and building. The denser limestones can often be polished to an attractive surface. Sand and grit stones are often coarse and gritty, as the name implies, and contain large amounts of silica (sometimes as much as 98 per cent). They can be as hard as steel, making them tricky to carve. The silica imparts durability and such stone was commonly used as paving in many cities, providing a lively export trade for English quarries in the past. The stratification of sedimentary rock dictates its use: the stone is best used as it was formed, with the layers horizontal. If it is used upright, the layers will eventually part due to the action of water and frost, becoming like the leaves of a book on edge.

Metamorphic rock is either igneous or sedimentary rock that has undergone dramatic changes since its original formation, usually volcanic in nature. The rock has been subjected to intense heat, great pressure and strong chemical reactions. This activity of heat and pressure causes a recrystallization of the original stone. The resulting materials, which include all the variations of marble, are among those most favoured by sculptors and architects because they offer a wide range of colour and textural qualities. There is great pleasure to be had from carving marble.

Wood

There are two varieties of wood – hardwood and softwood – and the designation of a particular wood does not depend on whether it is hard or soft, but whether it is from a deciduous tree (hardwood) or from a coniferous tree (softwood). Generally, the grain of the wood depends upon the tree variety and it can differ widely in both softwoods and hardwoods. The nature of the grain needs to be studied because it affects quite dramatically the carvability of the timber. The close-grained woods are the most rewarding to carve, allowing for fine surface and intricate detail, whilst the coarse-grained timbers are more difficult to carve because of the stringy grain, which also produces very strong markings. The hardwoods are generally the most durable.

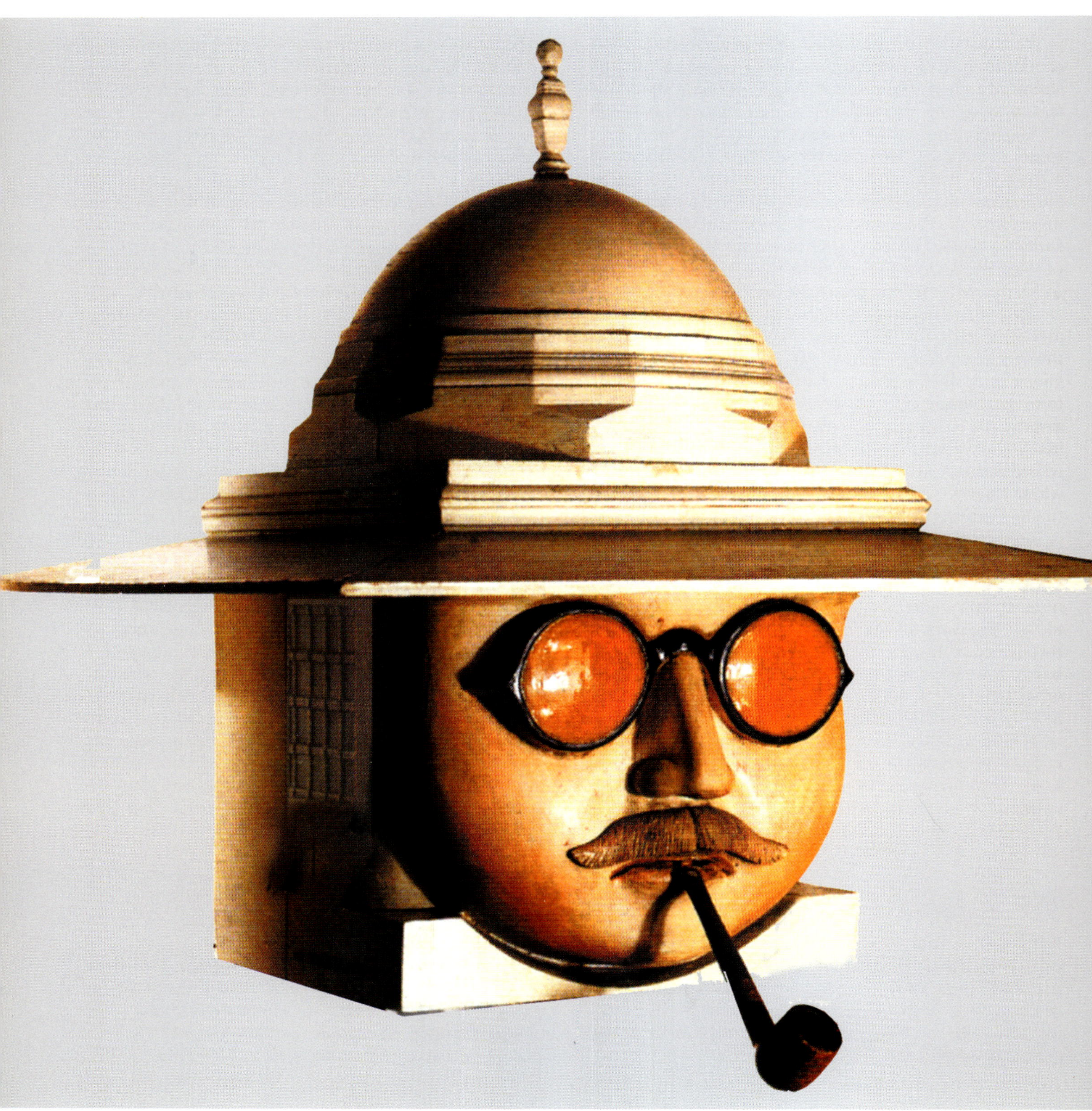

An eccentric but fond portrait of the architect Edwin Lutyens, made by artisans working on the buildings of New Delhi, which were designed by Lutyens. It is an an assemblage that makes amusing use of wooden offcuts.

All timber objects are subject to changing atmospheric conditions, swelling when the atmosphere is damp, and shrinking in dry conditions causing the wood to split, and this is the eternal problem for the woodcarver. Well-seasoned wood will be less subject to splitting and sculptors go to extreme lengths to season timber. This can be done by stacking it in such a way as to allow air to circulate freely around, covering the tops of standing logs to prevent water ingress, and keeping it out of direct sunlight. Properly seasoning a large log can take anything up to six or seven years, or even more. The objective is to allow the natural moisture in the timber to dry out evenly and slowly, trying to control and minimize the resulting shrinkage. The wood will shrink around the log centre (the heart) and some sculptors take the precaution when it is feasible to drill out the heartwood, giving space for the timber to shrink. There are many ways to season timber and traditionally wood yards often carried a stock of well-seasoned wood. Today, the procedure is to kiln-dry timber to get it to the market sooner, but this is mostly done for the building and furniture industries, where various kinds of planking rather than large bulks of timber are required.

Resourceful sculptors cut down their own trees or buy freshly cut trees to season or to carve green (unseasoned). The notion of carving holes through sculptures to make a negative form a feature, therefore reducing the volume, can aid to some extent the shrinkage of green timber as it dries. If the image is to be placed against a wall or in a niche, the back can be hollowed out; this was the practice in the past when carving religious subjects for specific sites in churches and cathedrals.

Timber scores over stone in that its tensile character enables the artist to make long slender forms that are self-supporting. Wood is also more easily joined, by the careful use and design of joints and with modern glues. A combination of these two practices extends the range of possibilities for the sculptor, including laminating sheets and planks of timber to create very strong large forms as an alternative to a felled log, as well as the most slender items with good strength.

One recent carving technique involves the use of a chainsaw as a carving tool, a method that imparts a certain excitement and adventure to the business of wooden images. At first, the chainsaw simply represented a speedy means of getting rid of waste material that was not pertinent to the image. It was much faster than a handsaw, axe or adze, and it was not long before it replaced the older tools. It is difficult to carve with any finesse using a chainsaw (some sculptors do not appreciate the crudeness of the technique and refer to it as 'wood-butchering'), but it does allow for a robust attack on the log, and sometimes leads to sculpture of power. It is best used on very large logs, and has also been applied to unfelled stands of timber in the UK after Dutch Elm disease swept through the country. The disease left in its wake many dead trees, but the timber was perfectly good for carving.

A chainsaw can be dangerous to use and care should be taken to ensure good practice, including using protective clothing and equipment, and practising good tool maintenance. Detailed safety information can be acquired from the tool manufacturers and health and safety advisors. There are a number of chainsaw off-shoots on the market that utilize the same basic chain-link blades attached to grinding discs. Some of these smaller tools can be used with fine control and have proved to be useful additions to the sculptor's repertoire of carving tools.

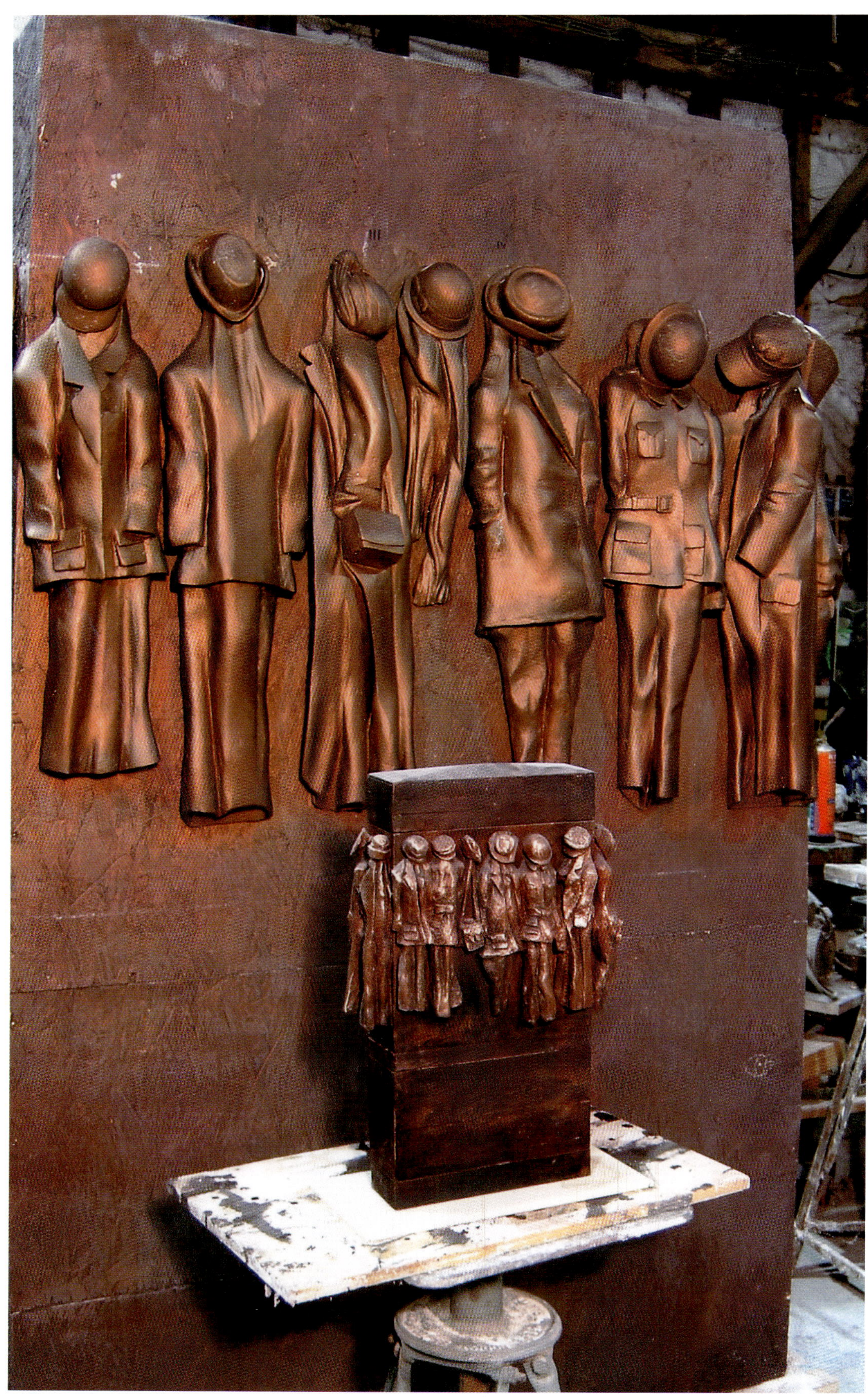

The maquette and the working model for the monument The Women of World War II, *by John W. Mills.*

2

Sketch Models (Maquettes) and Working Models

Thinking in the Round

The sketch model, more often referred to worldwide by the French term 'maquette', plays a vital role in the making of a sculpture. It helps to establish an image in the sculptor's mind and has been described as 'thinking in the round'. It is often remarked that sculptors think in the round because they encounter and use solid materials of all kinds to make sturdy images, as distinct from simply alluding to three-dimensional form and space on a two-dimensional surface (although these skills are valuable and necessary to all artists). It is also common for sculptors to create free-standing images in the round using a single figure or by designing a compilation of figures that make a single element. This may be a consequence of history and the survival of single-element imagery in stone and bronze affecting the notion of what sculpture is. More romantically it could be that the final siting of the sculpture, which will complete the picture, is lodged firmly in the mind of the artist. As the sculpture develops, this will include considering the orientation of the site as well as the surrounding countryside or urban landscape. However this single-element factor has developed, the sketch model helps to resolve problems brought to mind during the design process.

The sketch model/maquette is usually quite small, from 2–10in high (50–250mm), and is a rough approximation of an idea that is made as an aid to thinking and not as a finished sculpture. (Interestingly, the three-dimensional thoughts of the great masters have become very collectable

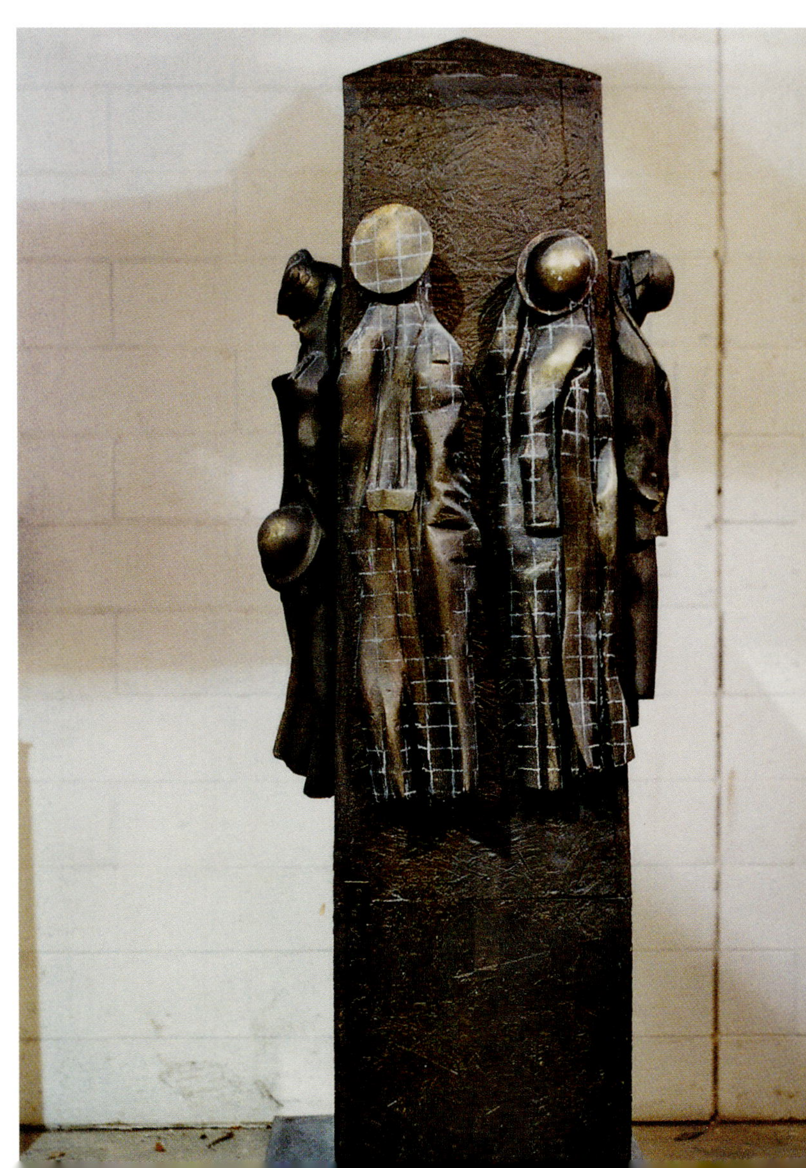

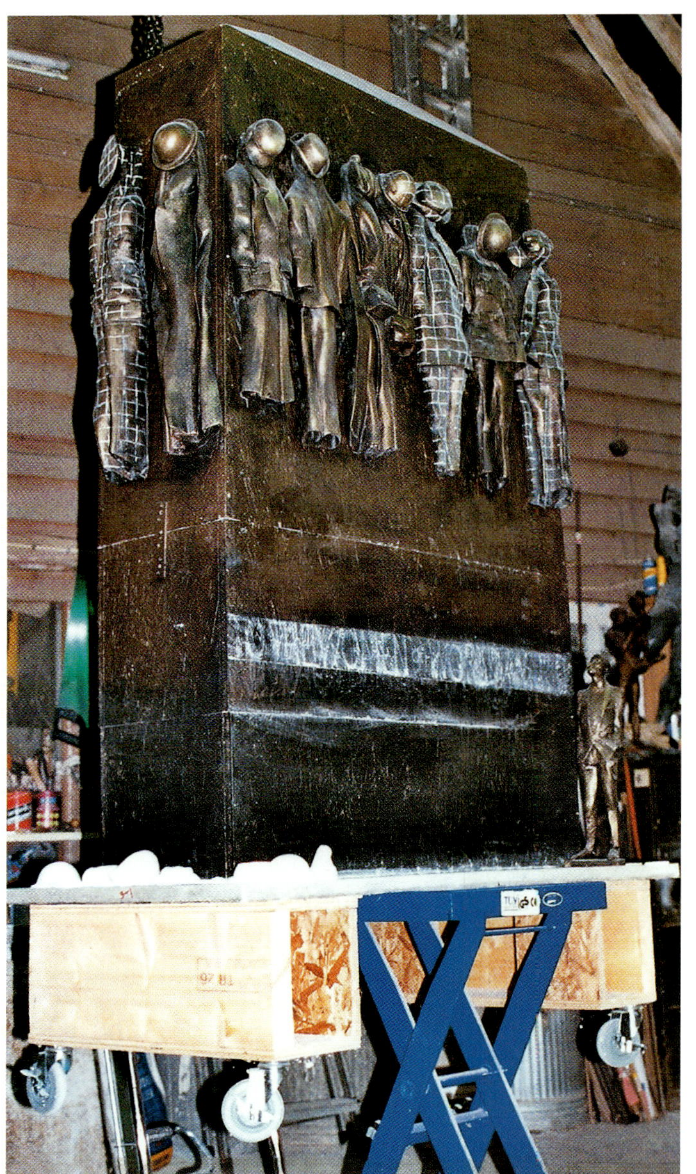

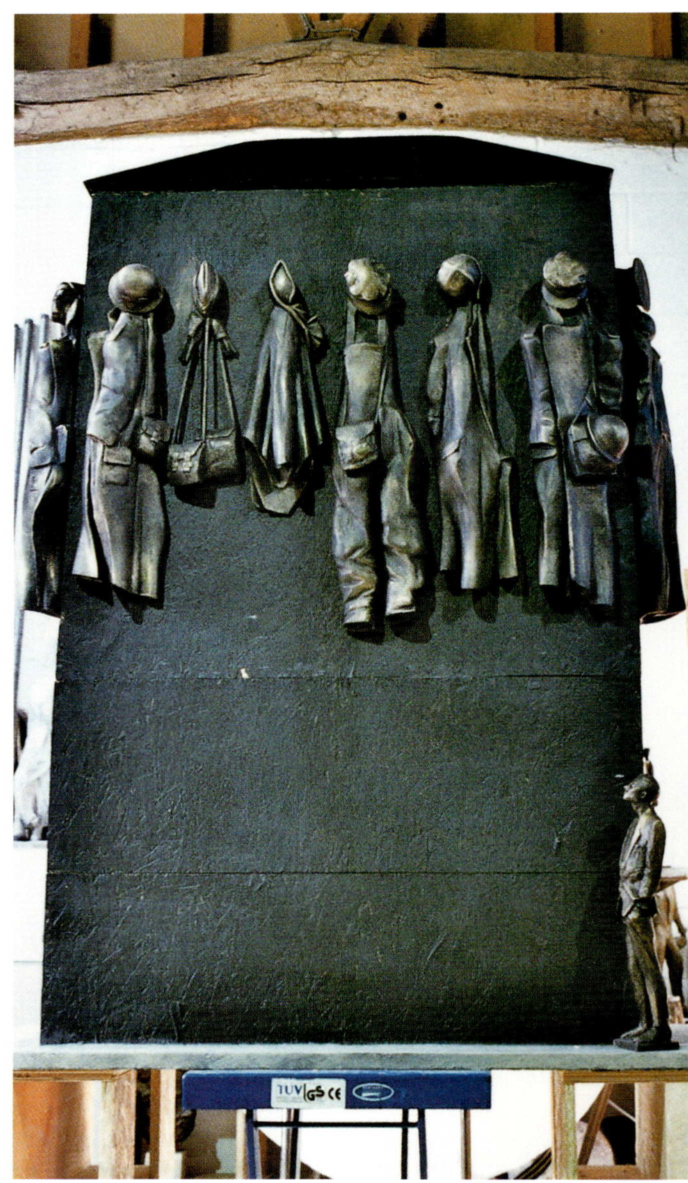

THIS PAGE AND PAGE 41: Working model for The Women of World War II, *by John W. Mills. The visible grid drawn on the surface was used to aid the process of enlarging to scale.*

items and are represented in major collections throughout the world.) It is good practice to make a number of small sketch models exploring different configurations of the planned image, testing all the variants of gesture and posture that come to mind; great detail is not a factor at this stage and is therefore unnecessary unless it emphasizes a specific feature that is vital to the image. If such a feature does occur, latch on to it and repeat it so that it will always spark off a prompt to the memory of the source of the image – it is vital to retain this uppermost in the mind as the work progresses.

When making sketch models/maquettes, investigate interesting silhouettes, significant actions, and the larger physical characteristics of the subject. These are the important features at all stages of development but they will be more easily exploited at this early stage. When composing a sculpture that includes more than one figure, the sketch model becomes even more valuable. This is the time and place to work out the interaction between figures, to explore their differing characters and study the disposition of form, weight and balance of the composition as a whole. It is useful to repeat and modify a proposed image as often as possible so that the idea can be assessed and re-assessed, and accepted or rejected, and all the essential factors can be firmly planted in the mind.

My own practice is to repeat an image for as long as alternatives to my first thoughts occur to me, until no more present themselves. At that point, that particular subject or image may be exhausted. Alternatively, it may be so firmly implanted in my mind that I may confidently proceed with the final sculpture, with only infrequent reference back to the sketch model studies. I do this regardless of the size of the final sculpture, using maquettes, drawings and enlarged works (working models).

It is most frustrating to embark on a large sculpture and then to be compelled to make major changes because a better alternative comes to mind. Always explore alternatives at a stage when making changes and adjustments are a pleasure rather than when it becomes a chore and a hindrance to progress. And if your creative energy and imagination are stimulated to such an extent that an alternative does continues to impinge on your thinking, then make the intruder as well, if you have all the materials to hand.

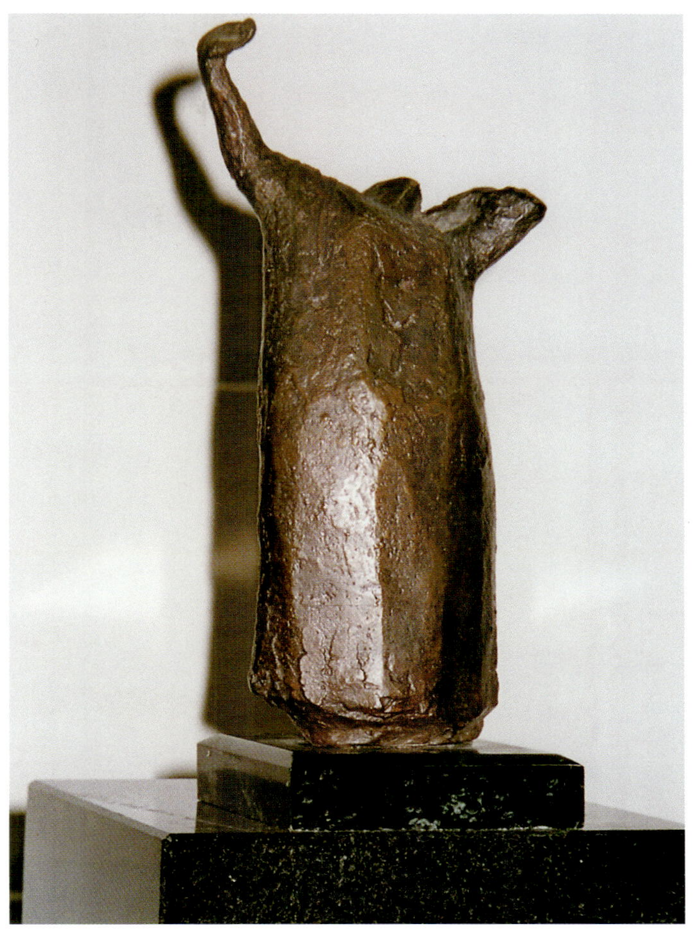

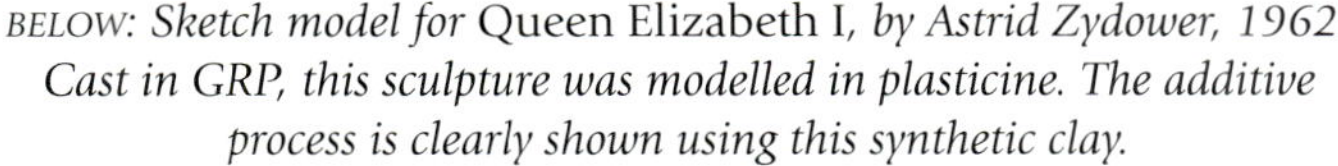

RIGHT: *Bronze maquette.* Stretching Girl, *by Betty Rea.*

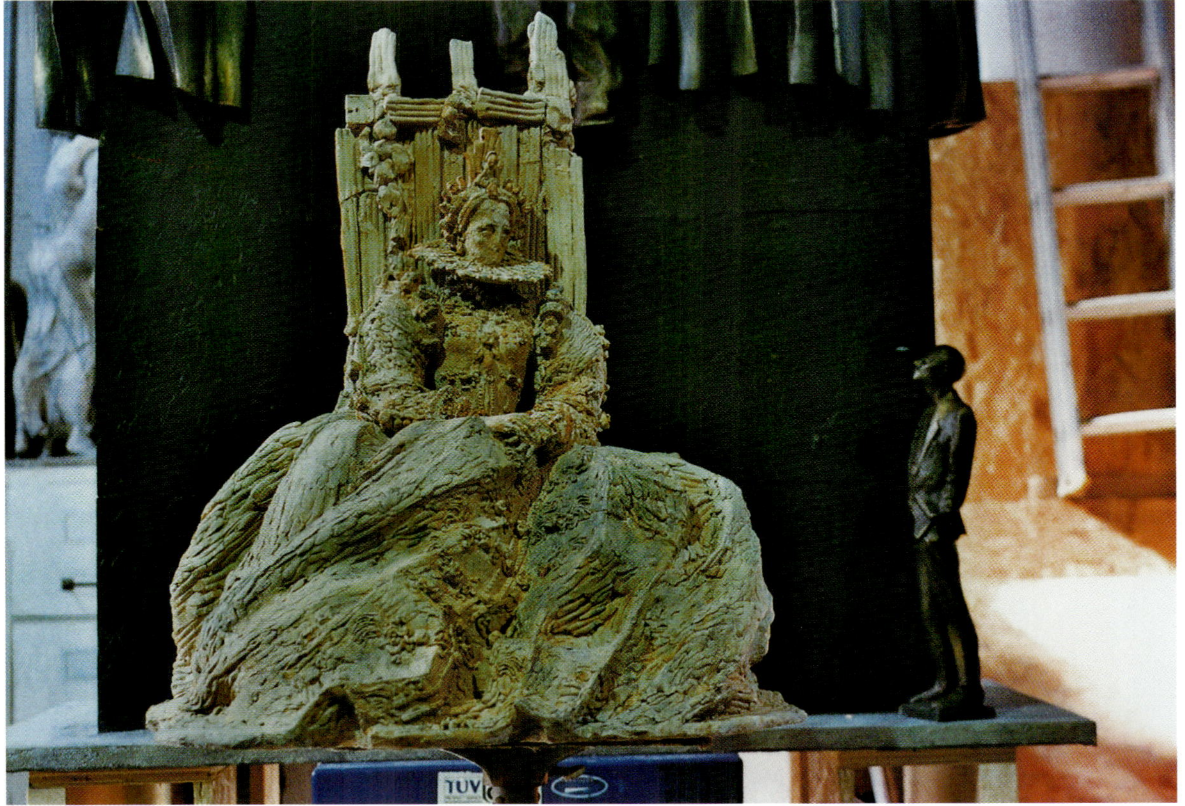

BELOW: *Sketch model for* Queen Elizabeth I, *by Astrid Zydower, 1962. Cast in GRP, this sculpture was modelled in plasticine. The additive process is clearly shown using this synthetic clay.*

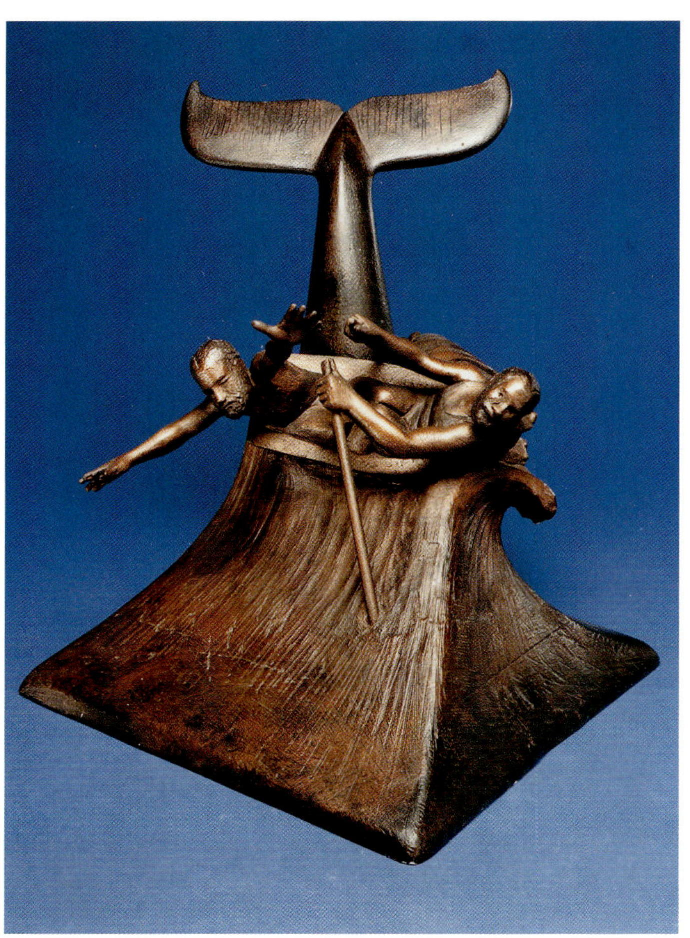

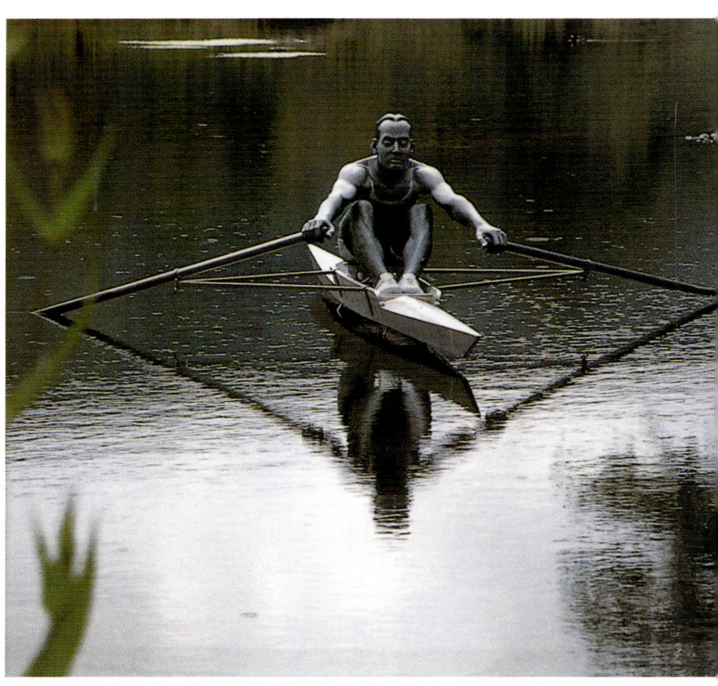

The wit and humour in these sculptures by John Clinch are carried through with great skill: (RIGHT) and (BELOW) two maquettes for Jonah and the Whale, *in bronze and painted bronze; (ABOVE)* The Sculler, *in steel, glass fibre and wood.*

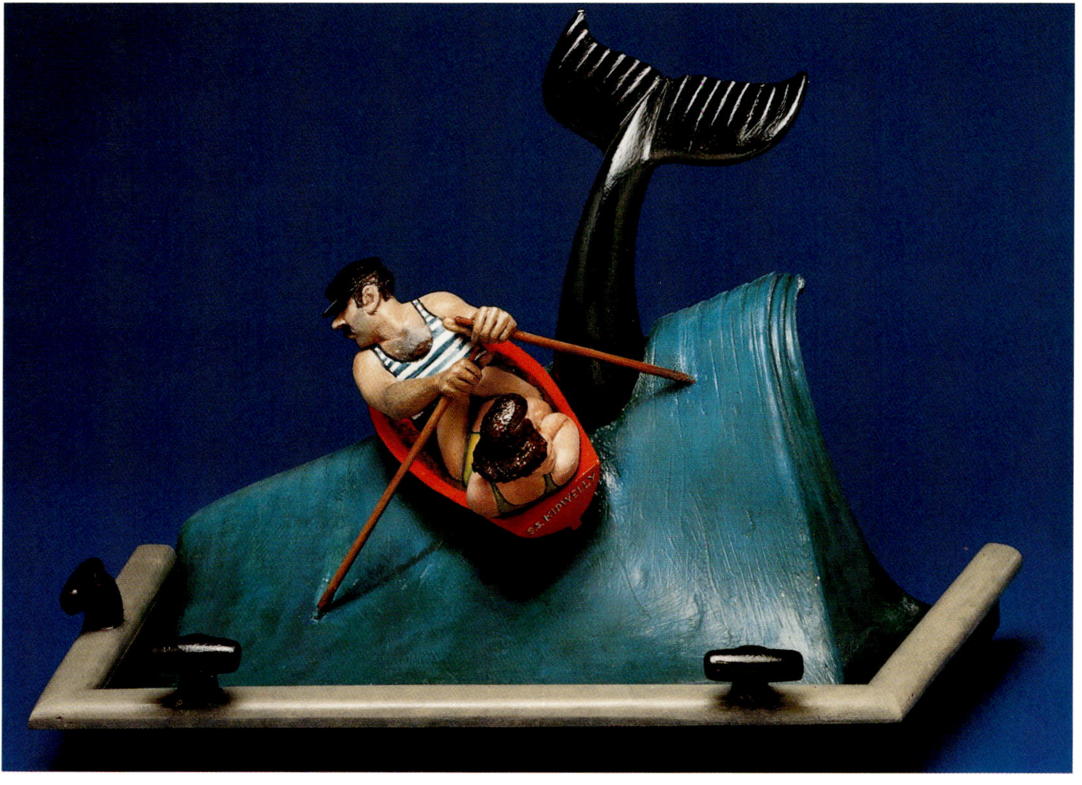

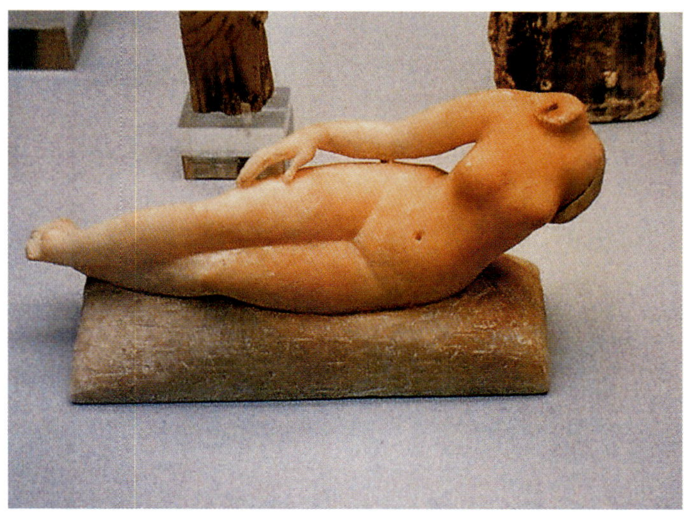

These Minoan terracotta figures – possibly dolls – are fine examples; they are similar to maquettes in their style and detail. (British Museum, London. Photo: John W. Mills)

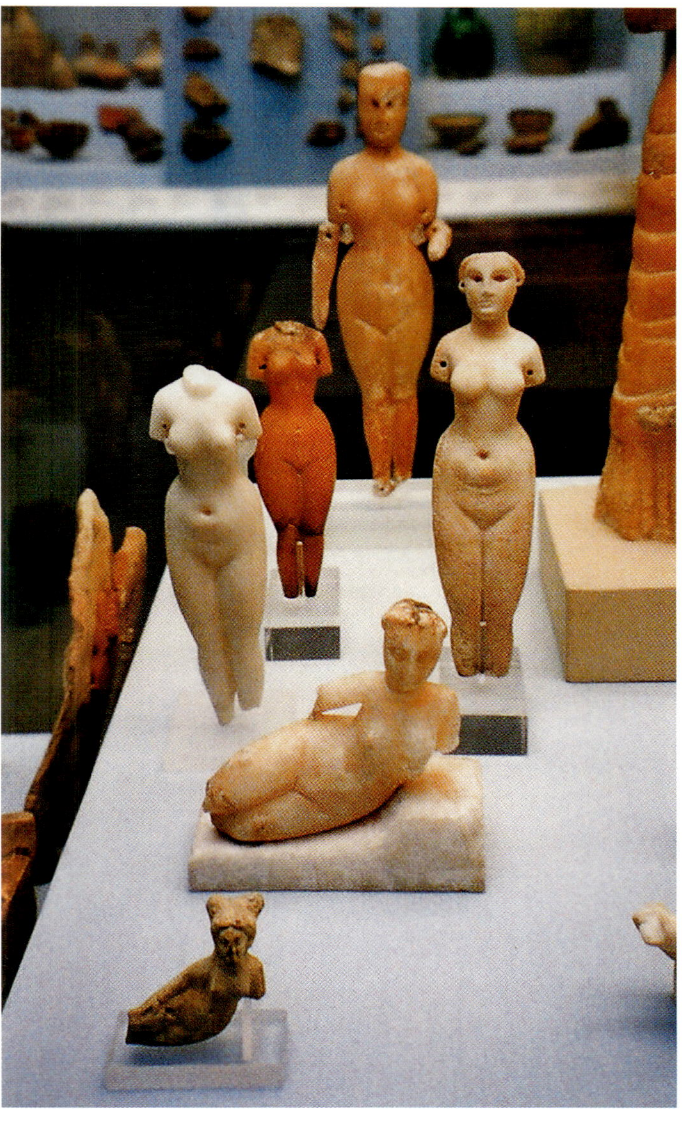

Making the Maquette

Materials

The maquette is best made using a material or process similar to that of the proposed final sculpture. Sculptures to be modelled and cast are more comfortably explored using a modelling medium such as wax or clay. At an advanced stage in a sculptor's career and as skills progress, modelling with wax gives the added advantage of enabling small sketch models to be cast directly in bronze. This is always a pleasure and one for the beginner to anticipate and use as a distinct target of achievement. If the sculpture is to be assembled, for instance if it is to be welded, then often soldering or welding techniques can be employed to make the sketch model in keeping with the final sculpture; in this way there will be fewer surprises when making the final version. Procedures for other assemblage materials can be explored to good effect using similar processes to those envisaged for the final work – these may include cutting and gluing card, foam board (a useful model-making material), wood, found objects, and so on – to gain an affinity with the larger image.

If the sculpture is to be carved, clay enables cutting and carving to some degree. This has the advantage of allowing changes to be made if necessary by addition, but this temptation should be avoided if possible, because it does not truly reflect the subtractive carving process. When using clay to design a carving it is best modelled with a greater volume than planned. It should then be allowed to harden, then cut and carved, employing subtractive techniques, as it goes through the drying and hardening processes, from leather-hard to very dry.

Carving a harder material is probably a better solution to exploring an idea to be resolved by subtracting (carving) waste material. A soft stone may be used if it is available at a suitable size. Aerated concrete blocks can be used to good effect, or even plaster of Paris as a last resort. Plaster allows the artist to make a rough approximation to the larger stone or block of wood by modelling and casting and leaving it for a while to dry and harden off before carving, but it has no intrinsic quality, and presents a poor carving experience. Aerated concrete also offers a poor quality, but it is cheap and readily available in block form from most building suppliers. It is a little more durable than plaster and is therefore sometimes useful for practising. Some teachers use this material to give young beginners an affordable carving

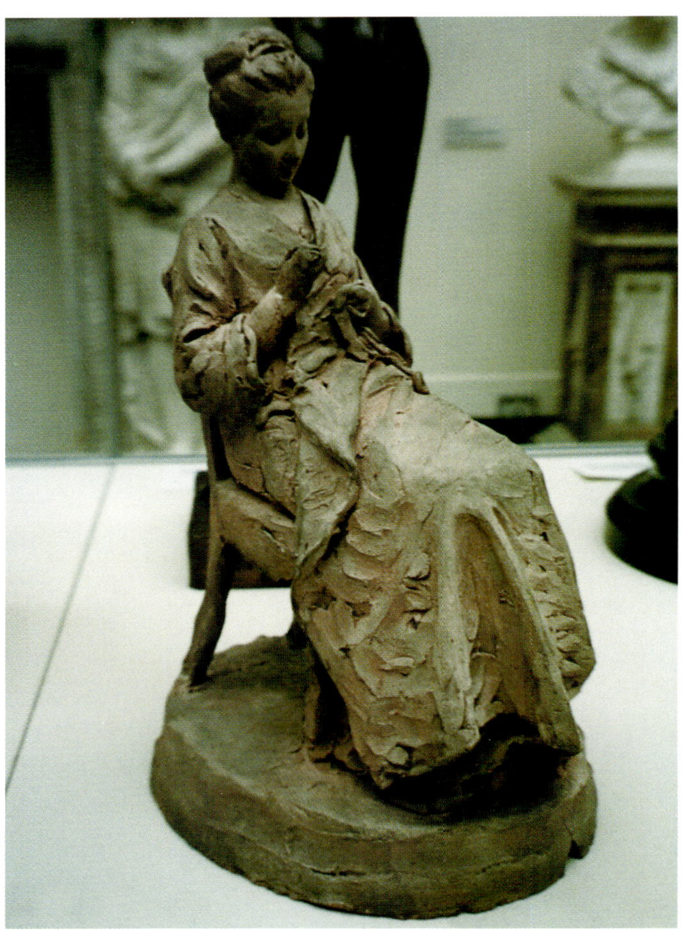

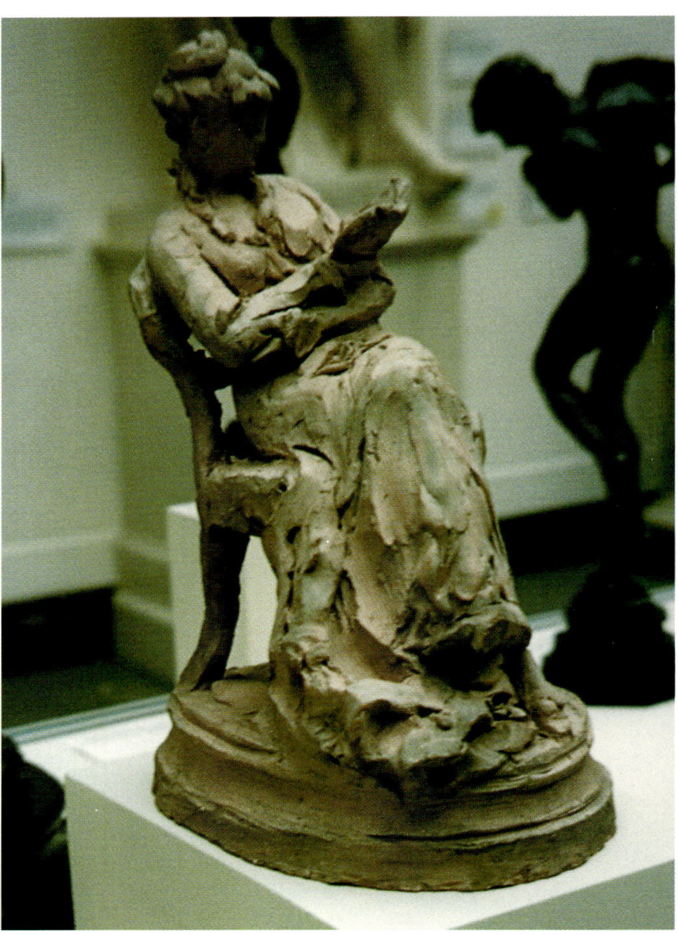

Two terracotta maquettes by Jules Dalou: (LEFT) Girl reading *and (RIGHT)* Girl sewing. *The modelling is very free and lively. (V&A Collection, London. Photo: John W. Mills)*

experience, getting them acquainted to thinking in the round and familiar with the subtractive process.

Polystyrene (Styrofoam) in its solid form, either as blocks or sheets of material, can also be cut and carved. It provides very quick results, allowing for a large number of alternative solutions to a given idea to be explored rapidly. However, although it has its uses, polystyrene is another substance with very little intrinsic quality. It can also be quite hazardous in practice, and great care must be taken not to inhale any foam dust or particle; a protective mask should be worn at all times when working with it.

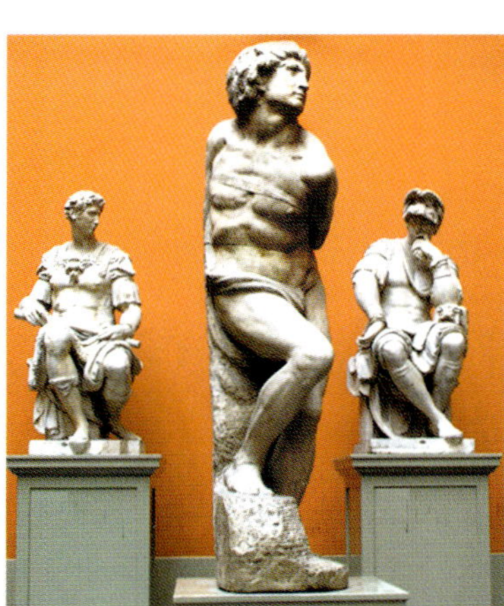

Heroic Captive *(foreground) and* Giulliano and Lorenzo Medici *(background), by Michelangelo. (V&A Museum, Plaster Courts, London)*

Experienced sculptors who are familiar with their chosen materials will seem to break assumed rules and use whatever is to hand to sketch and investigate an idea. Their technical knowledge and experience allows them the freedom to explore the basic concepts of their subject matter in all kinds of ways, because they know what can be resolved in the final material. The great Italian Renaissance sculptor Michelangelo claimed to dislike bronze and, therefore, by association, modelling using clay or wax. However, he often used both of these materials to explore, on both a small and sometimes a large scale, ideas and anatomical detail that he planned to carve in marble, which was the material he loved best. He used sketch models as a means of honing his thought and resolving the greater compositional elements of the form and image, fixing essential features in his mind, and planning their place in the marble block. This allowed him to conserve the marble as he roughed out the larger sculpture and retain any possibility for change as the image matured. Michelangelo was the acknowledged master carver of his time and the main inspiration for the carvers who followed in his footsteps.

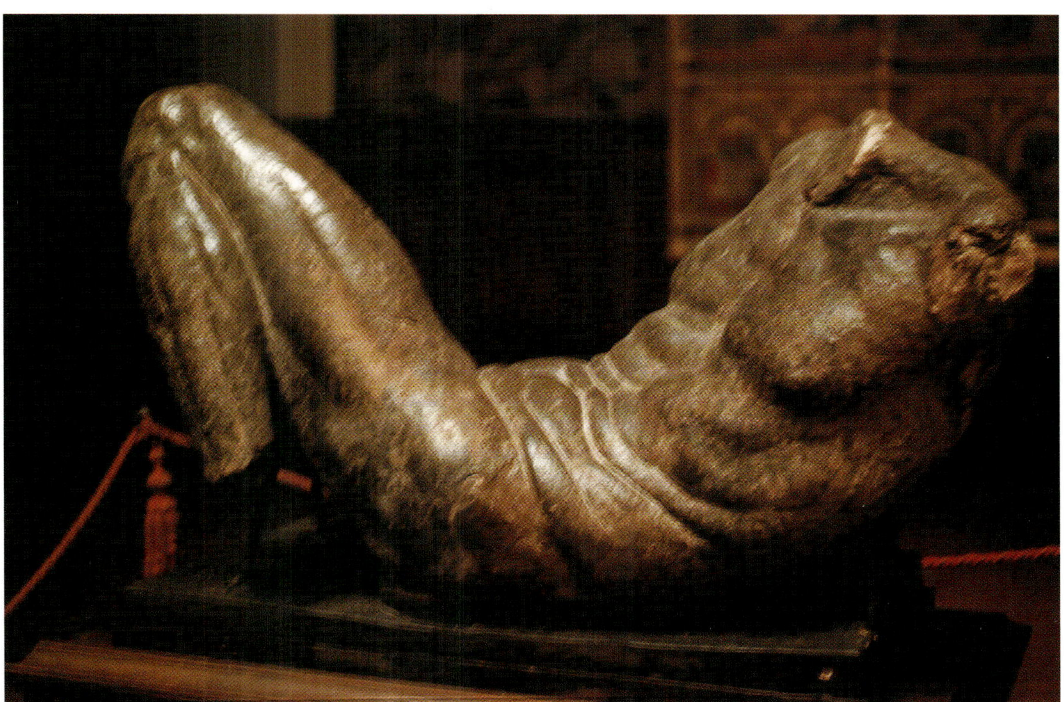

Michaelangelo sculpture: (TOP RIGHT) River God, clay figure, (BOTTOM LEFT) Young Giant and (BOTTOM RIGHT) Boboli Giant. (Accademia, Florence. Photo: John W. Mills)

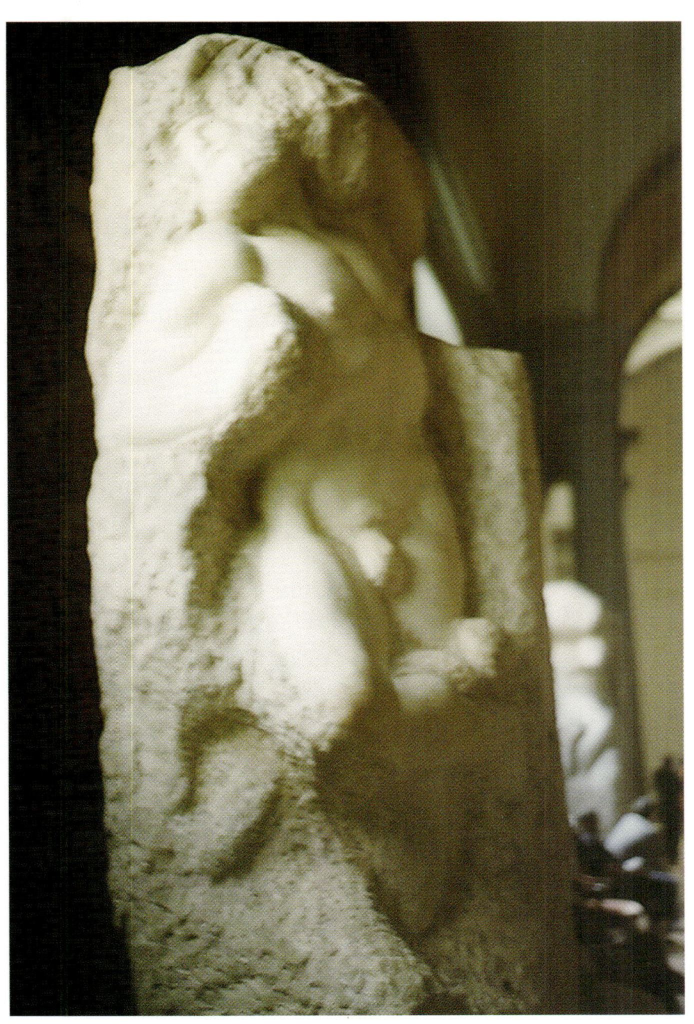

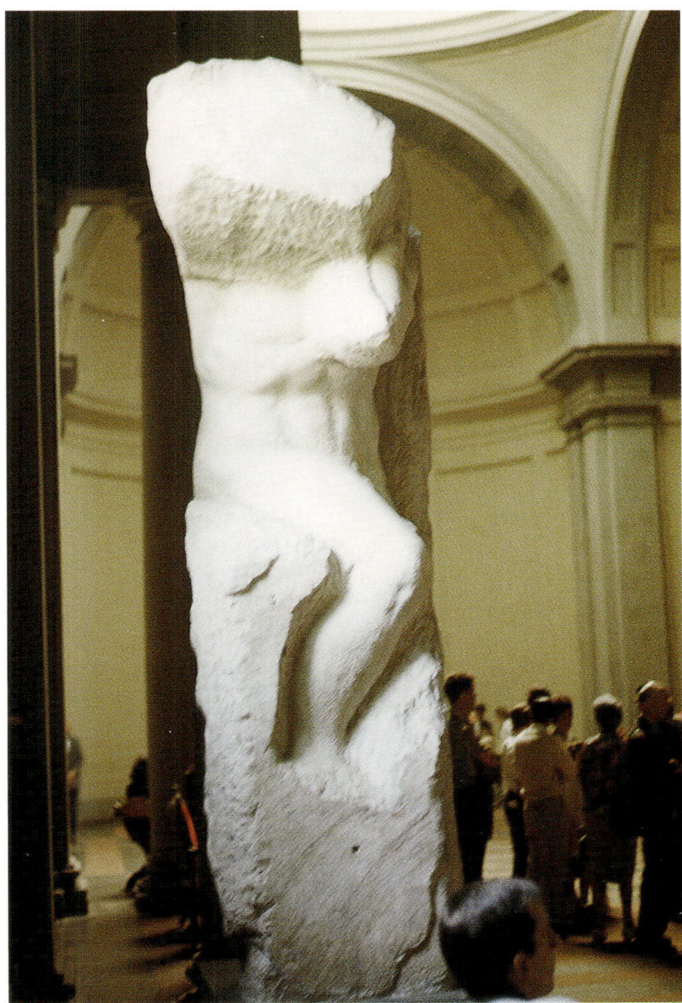

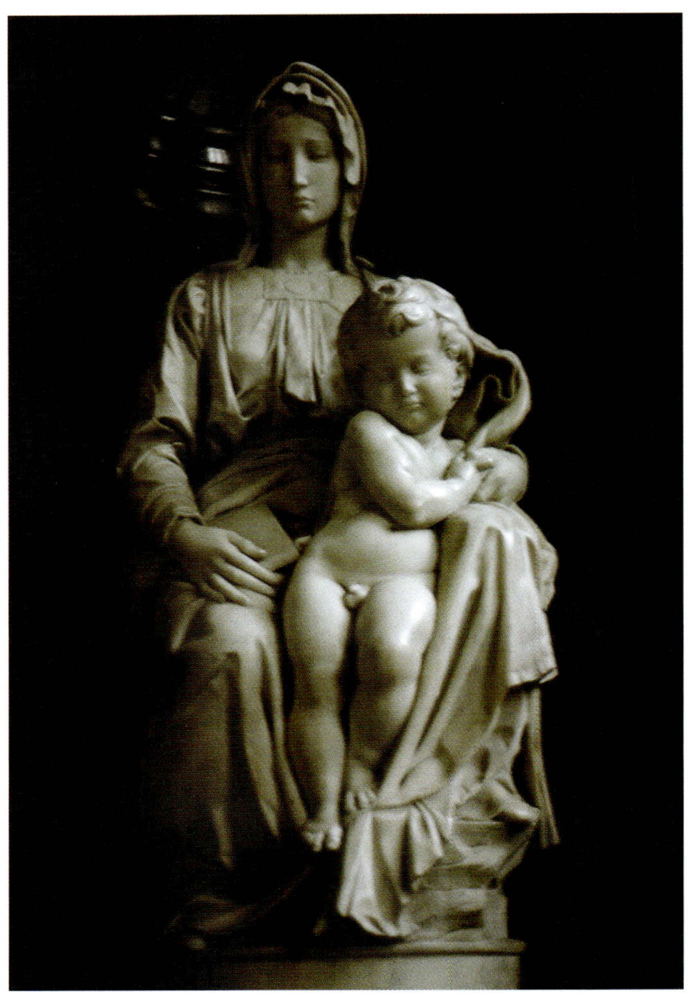

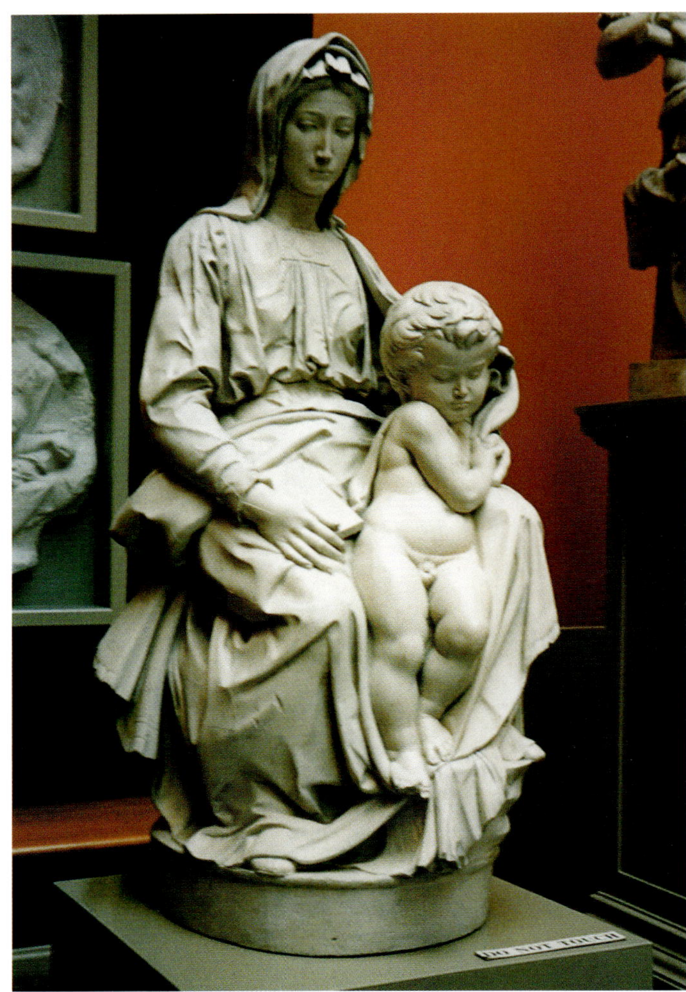

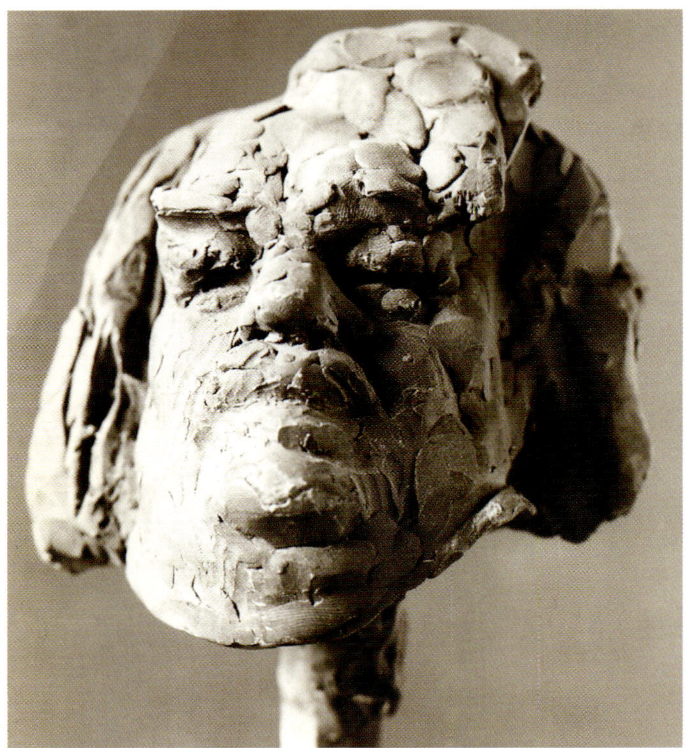

Notre Dame *by Michelangelo: (*TOP LEFT*) in marble in Bruges, Belgium, and (*TOP RIGHT*) the plaster cast in the British Museum, London. (Photo: John W. Mills)*

LEFT: Maquette for the Figure of Balzac, *by Auguste Rodin. The modelling is free-hand. (Rodin Museum, Paris. Photo: John W. Mills)*

Modelling or Carving

It is a fact that some sculptors are naturally inclined towards carving – the art of subtracting or cutting away to reveal an image – while others are predisposed to modelling, the technique of using the additive process to build up an image. These two apparently opposing attitudes to making sculpture are revealed in the two extreme cases of Michelangelo the master carver and Rodin the master modeller. Michelangelo's only bronze (which he hated working on) was melted down to make a cannon, while Rodin's attempts to emulate the marble carving of Michelangelo merely served to prove his superior talent for modelling bronze figures. Their strongest works were achieved when they were most relaxed, working with the materials they knew best, and that were probably closest to their hearts.

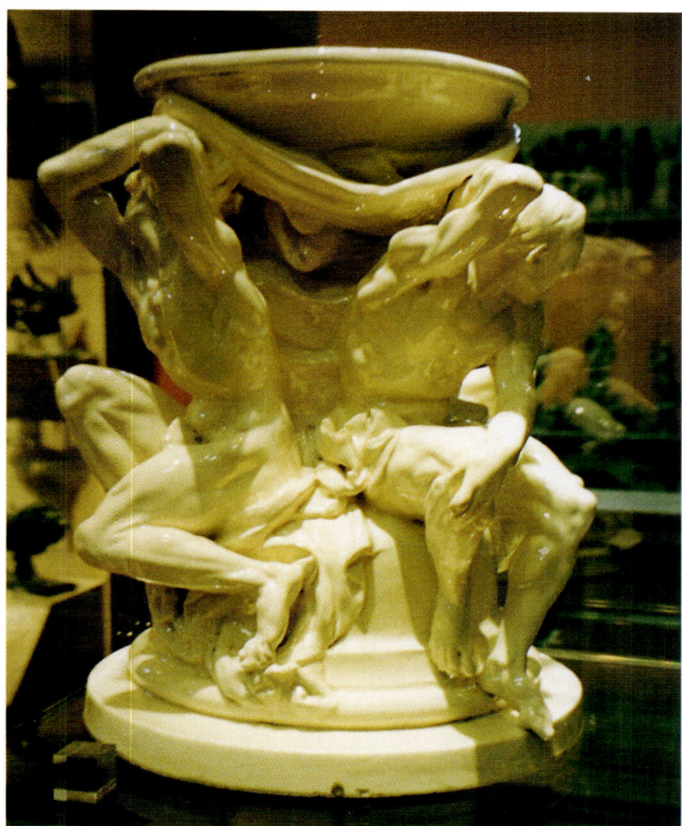

Caryatids, *by Auguste Rodin, in porcelain. (V&A Collection, London. Photo: John W. Mills)*

A more modern example of this predisposition to either carving or modelling is evident in the work of Henry Moore, whose work dominated English sculpture for so long. A study of his work reveals the change between the earlier sculptures, which were mostly carved directly in stone or wood and are very strong in form and composition, and the later, middle-period sculptures, which were mostly bronze and often modelled by assistants prior to casting. These later sculptures were at their best when they reflected Moore's natural affinity with carving and the subtractive process. I think Moore was aware of this to some degree because he mostly used plaster of Paris as his modelling medium, which allowed him to combine the additive and subtractive processes in his working method. He even made his maquettes modelling and carving plaster in this way and was not relaxed when modelling with clay. Polystyrene was introduced to his studio towards the end of his working life, which brought back the subtractive process to him, albeit in a much faster carvable version. The sculptures he made in Italy, and in particular those made during the twilight of his career, enabled him to return to marble and stone by directing the fine-carving skills of the artisans of Pietrasanta in Northern Italy. This area has a long history of carving stone, and marble in particular, and Moore came to have a great affinity with it.

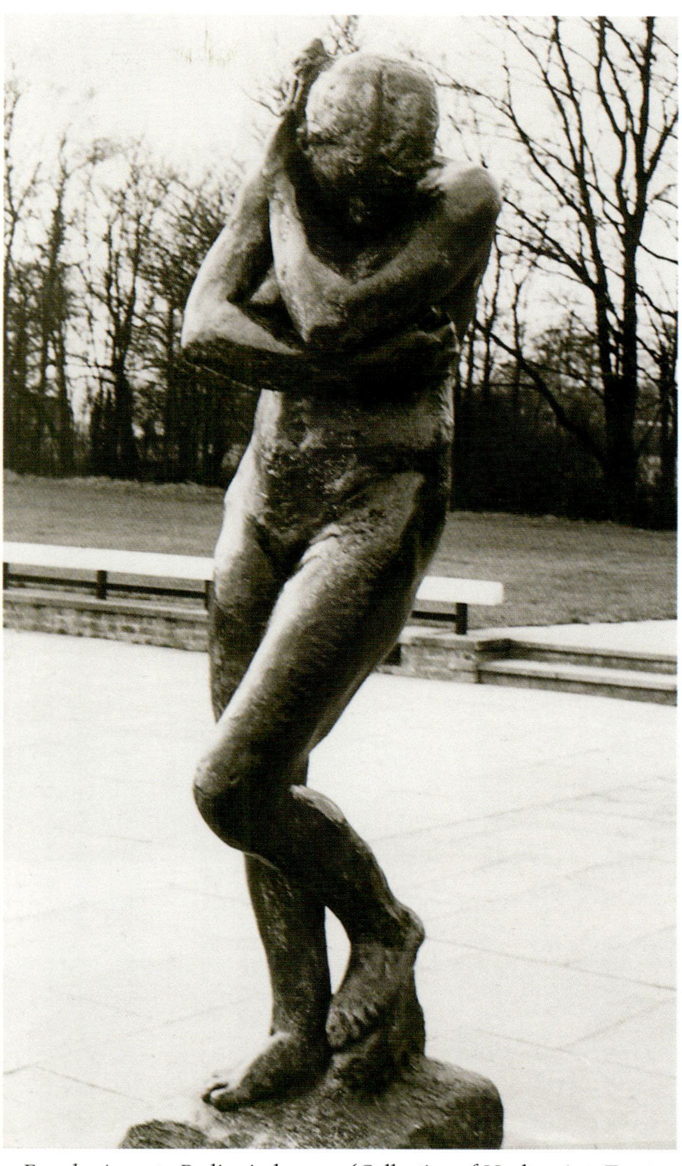

Eve, *by Auguste Rodin, in bronze. (Collection of Harlow Arts Trust, UK. Photo: John W. Mills)*

Sculptures that result from the opposing processes of modelling and carving are usually easily distinguished, and this can be gleaned from visits to museums that have a strong archaeological department as well as an historical cultural survey. The forthright stone cultures produce work that could only be carved, retaining the fidelity and integrity of the stone that was so deeply embedded in their cultural background. Those cultures that relied predominantly on clay to make terracotta produced sculptures that could only have been resolved in that material. And so on. Although it is possible to imitate one process with the other, it is not usual and when it occurs it is often criticized. A modelled form should not resemble too closely that of a carving, and vice versa. Unless the quality of cut clay is essential to the idea and the desired image, it is best avoided, and finishing

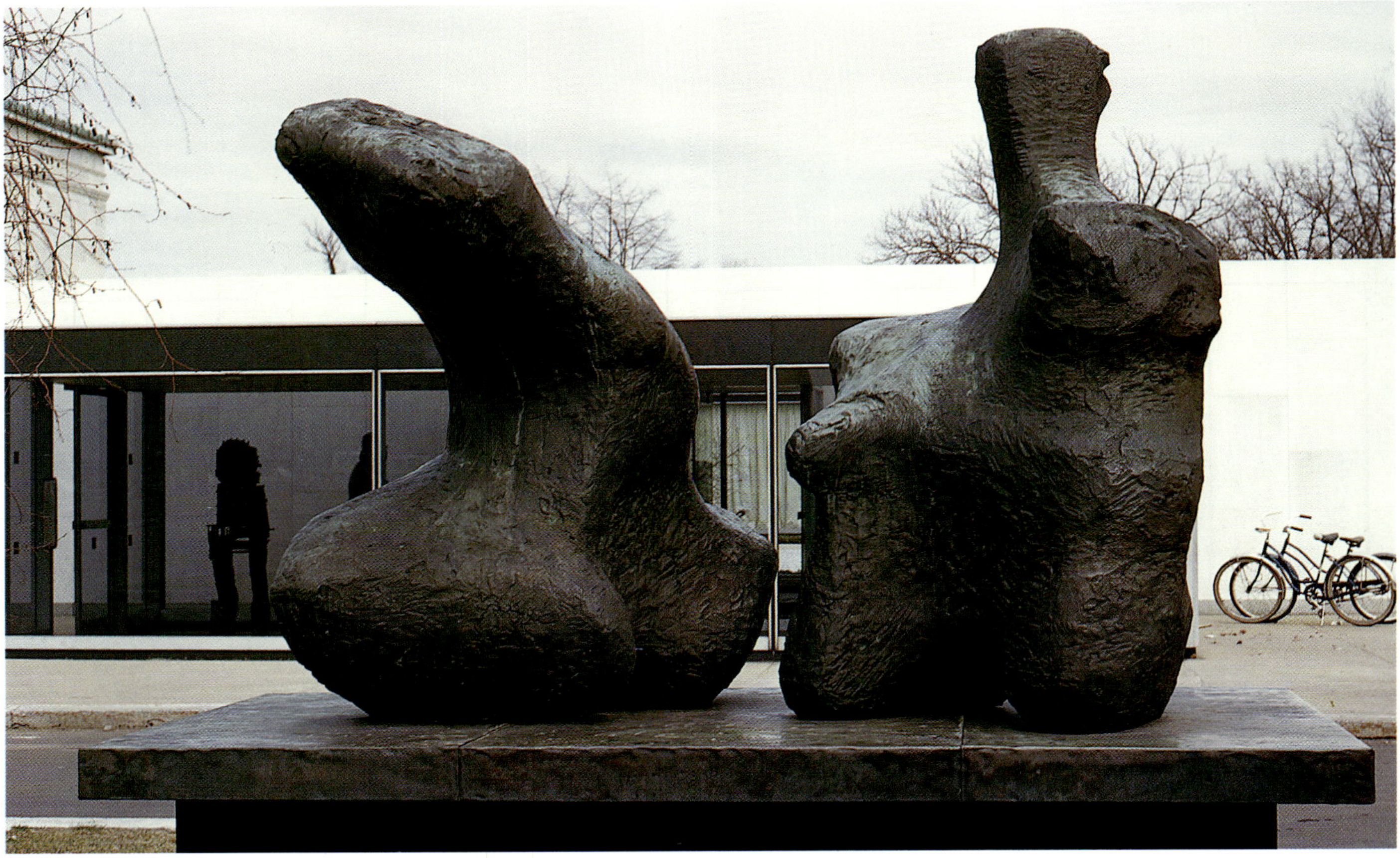

Reclining figure, *by Henry Moore, in bronze. (Albrigh Knox Gallery, Buffalo, USA. Photo: John W. Mills)*

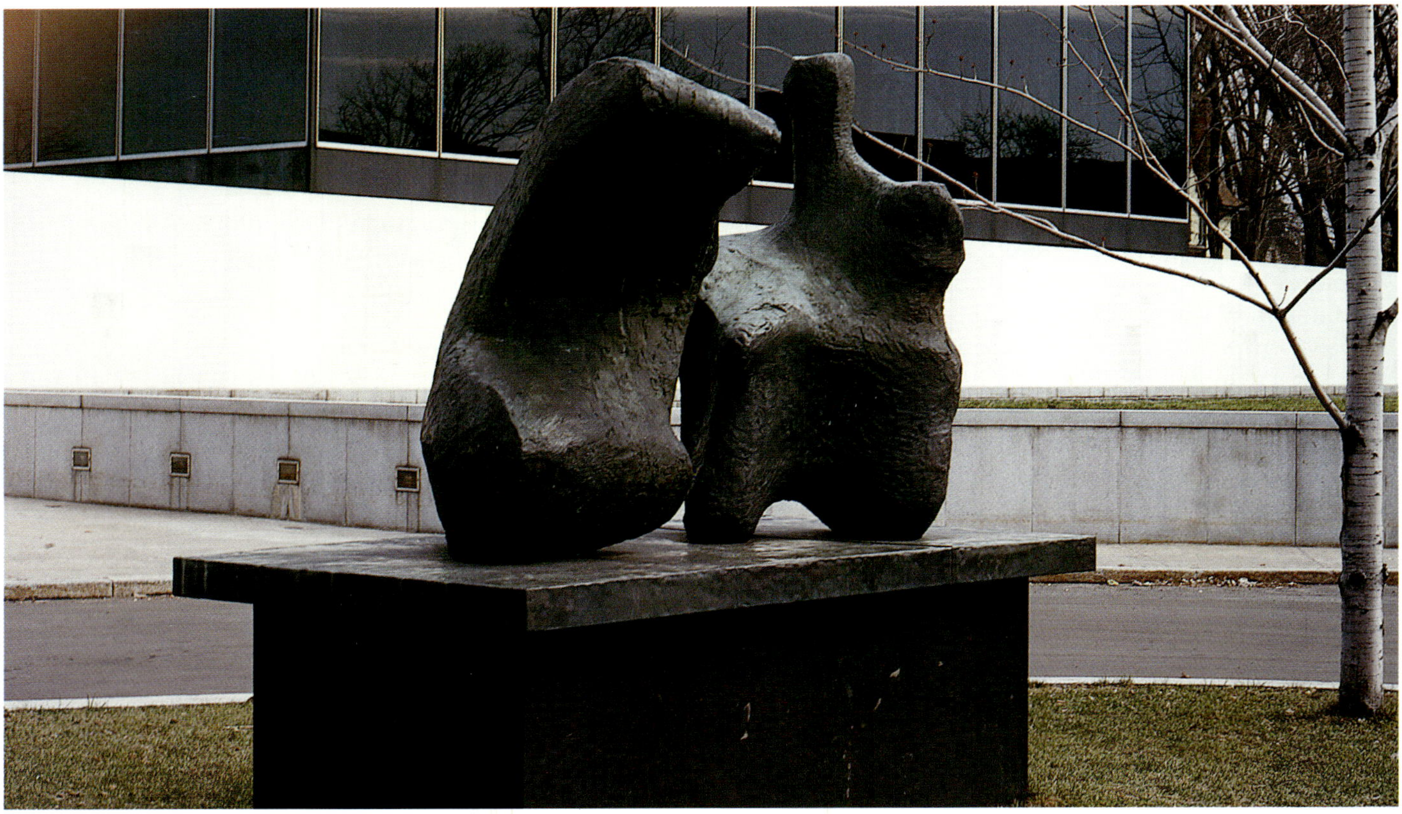

a carving with the appearance of a modelled form is another cause for criticism. However, such rules may be seen to be the last refuge of the purist. Perhaps they are there to be broken by the brave or the ignorant, and the maxim that 'a successful end justifies the means' can sometimes be employed with some justification.

Working Models

The sketch model (maquette) is very important in the development of an idea for sculpture, encouraging 'thinking in the round' to explore an image, but it should not be confused with the working model. This is just as important in the developmental process of a sculpture, but it usually appears much later in procedures. The maquette is a rough approximation of the final sculpture, whereas the working model is made to be proportionately accurate in all respects to the final work. It is most useful if not essential, when the sculpture is to be of a heroic size, which means anything over one and a half times life size. Some sculptors also like to work using a working model at much smaller dimensions. It is, of course, a matter of choice and experience.

A working model can play a very useful role when negotiating a commissioned work, by conveying an accurate picture of the final sculpture to a client, and to any architect, engineer or committee who might be involved. It has become a common practice today to use a photograph of the working model in a montage of the proposed site, in order to convey scale and character.

The working model is commonly made at a quarter of the scale of the final project, but can be made at almost any size, as long as it is accurately scaled in all proportions to the planned work. The procedure is often referred to as scaling up (or, when the reverse is called for, scaling down). This is the stage at which all form, detail and expression are established, so that the sculpture can be simply enlarged. It is also the stage at which engineers can make accurate calculations that might be needed for constructional and installation purposes – an essential factor in the logistics when planning the building and placing of a large sculpture on a public site.

Enlarging

In the past, the work of enlarging a sculpture was a very common practice in sculpture studios, being done traditionally by skilled studio assistants. Their task was to enlarge from both the maquette and then the working model, scaling up to the chosen size, carving or modelling

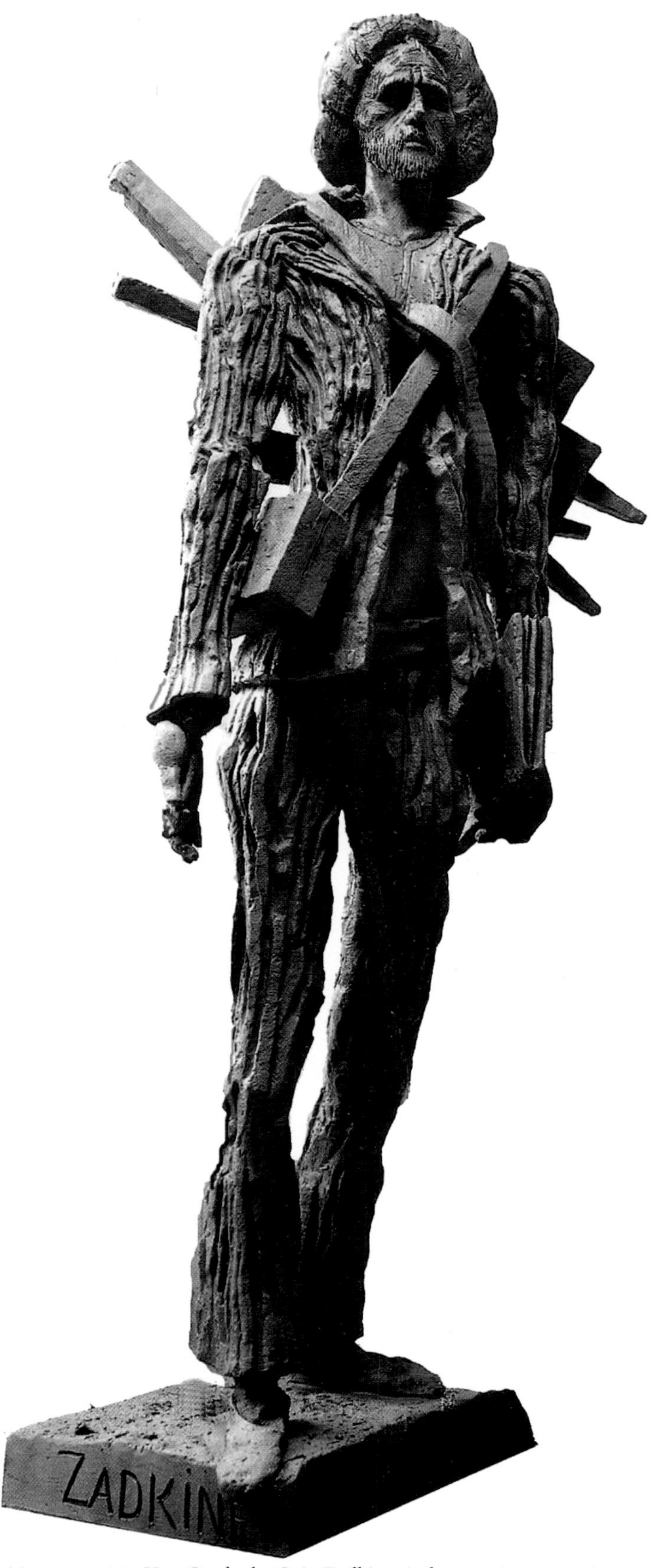

Monument to Van Gogh, *by Osip Zadkine, in bronze. An eccentric but powerful image.*

the sculpture to within about a half-inch (12mm) of the final surface. At this stage, the master sculptor would take over to apply the final touches and flourishes to establish that specific personal identification. This practice also provided a useful training ground for young apprenticed sculptors and allowed those with some basic skills to learn more from the master. This of course was dependent on the master/studio practice that became almost defunct between the wars. It was initially replaced by art school studios, which did provide some training but was not an ideal alternative to apprenticed experience. Sadly, today, there is no provision for proper apprentice-type training.

The current welcome demand for more public sculpture, and the manufacture of large sculptures for display in sculpture parks and important collections, has brought about a kind of renaissance in the skills of enlarging, which have become available again as specialist services. This scaling-up process is aided mechanically using a wide variety of apparatus, from simple home-made devices to complex traditional instruments called pointing machines; the choice is obviously controlled by cost and the availability of complex equipment. Some of the larger art bronze foundries now include enlarging services and some have installed expensive pointing machines to provide the most accurate scaling-up. In this way, the cost of such machinery is shared, and it may also help the foundry to gain the commission for the complex casting work. Many specialists have also set up workshops to carry out an enlarging service independently, making a range of expensive mechanical equipment available, supported by the necessary manual sculpture skills.

Retaining Control

Those artists who enjoy the possibility of developing the sculptural image as it builds up, and who want to produce more than just an accurately enlarged copy of the maquette or working model, will get some pleasure from working in a free and easy manner without undue pressure to be very precise. Simple technical aids that can be hand-made in the studio are accurate enough for the accomplished working sculptor – someone who has a trustable eye for shape, form and balance. (For more on such devices, see Chapter 10.) It is a common practice among sculptors working to commission, especially on sculptures to be finally executed at a very large scale, to develop their ideas using a combination of both sketch and working models. In this way, they gain greater peace of mind for themselves and their client, or committee if there is no client. It also gives further opportunity for any serious engineering consultation. Even more importantly, it allows the sculptor to retain control over the developing sculpture. The creative mind is given the chance to take advantage of any enhancing possibilities that present themselves as the work progresses; such possibilities can occur at all stages as the image advances through the various materials that might be needed, and techniques that go with them.

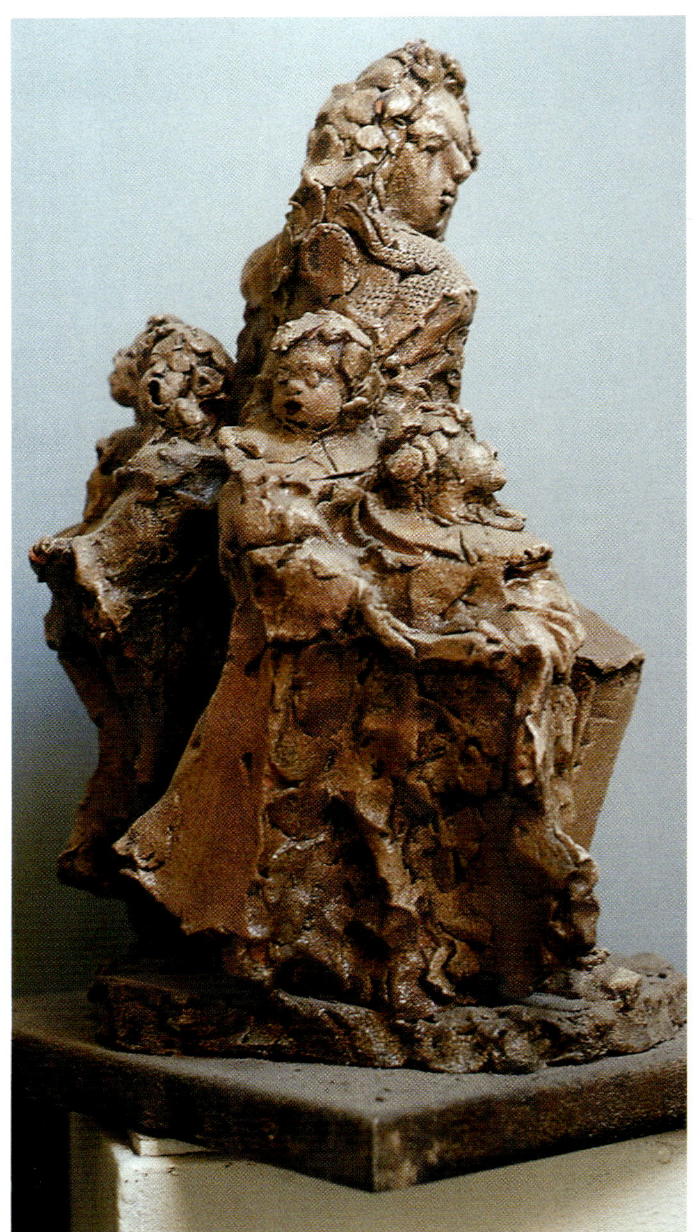

A maquette for memorial to Purcell, by John W. Mills, in terracotta.

3

Armatures

Support system

The most widely used modelling materials, such as clay, wax and plaster of Paris, have little or no integral strength. It is possible of course to build up an image with clay if the mass is retained, but if a slender shape is attempted without support it will eventually collapse. Similarly, wax, although a little more self-supporting than clay (depending on the type of wax employed), is restrictive in the size it can be manipulated to make a sculpture when used on its own. Plaster of Paris, like clay, will allow a build up in mass, but it is very brittle and cannot be made into slender shapes without support.

Because of the nature of the materials used, therefore, it is vital to understand how to support a sculpture. All sculptors need to acquire the basic skills to make the armature – the internal support system required for a sculpture that is to be modelled using any of the modelling media. In many respects the armature functions like the skeleton of the human body, which gives almost unlimited complex support to the body's bulk in all motor functions, although it will not do as an armature for a modelling project to try to imitate the human skeleton. The job of the armature support system is to hold the modelling material securely in place and in the correct position, while enabling adjustments to be made whenever necessary as work on the sculpture progresses. The armature must be stable, constructed in such a way as to give firm support without trembling or moving as the modelling material is built up, and allow for alterations.

When designing the support system, it is important to take into account the nature and weight of the material to be supported. An inexperienced sculptor will often make an armature too quickly. It may seem to be strong and stable but, as the modelling material is built up, a construction that is too flimsy will bend and quiver under the pressure of modelling until it eventually collapses under the weight. French painter Edgar Degas, a formidable artist in most respects, made some fascinating sculptures, the most famous being Young Dancer Aged Fourteen Years. However, he could never grasp the importance of making a suitable armature; if he had had the necessary skills, it is certain that many more of his sculptures would have survived. There is one account of him trying to provide support for the arm of a portrait bust by balancing pebbles one upon another; using the clay as a kind of mortar. Some modelling progress was made but, inevitably, the whole assembly collapsed, much to his disgust.

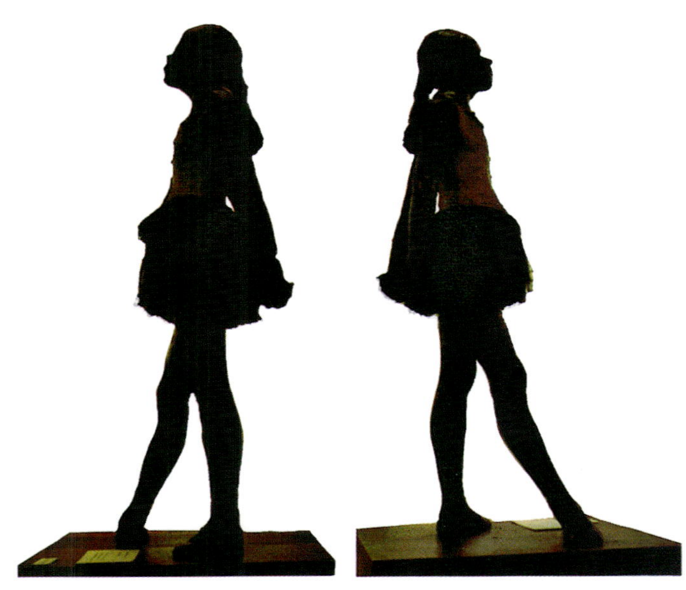

Young Dancer Aged Fourteen Years, *by Edgar Degas, in bronze. The strong and interesting silhouette is emphasized in this picture. (Albrigh Knox Gallery, Buffalo, USA)*

An understanding of the significance of armatures and all kinds of support systems, and a knowledge of their design and manufacture, will bring rewards. The sculptor will have a greater freedom for modelling with all materials, being able to work with the least frustration, concentrating on the sculpture and not having to fight poor construction.

Planning the Armature

Because of the physical activity associated with making sculpture, the work needs to be well planned so as to conserve both energy and ideas. This fact becomes most evident when preparing an armature for modelling, no matter what material is being used. The work should be planned remembering at all times that modelling is an additive process, and that the final volume of a modelled sculpture is achieved only when the last layer of material is applied. If an internal supporting armature is to be sufficiently strong and solid, it is essential to use the heaviest-gauge metal and timber, judging this according to the final height and volume of the sculpture. One tutor of mine used to test the armatures made by his students for life-size figures by the slightly risky method of swinging on them. If the structure moved at all it had to be taken apart and made stronger.

Considering Materials

CLAY

Clay, either natural or synthetic, is an extremely heavy, inert material and, therefore, a dead weight. It needs a supporting armature that will cope with this. Natural clay, for example, when it is fresh and therefore wet, and built up in proportion to a life-size figure, will weigh approximately twice that of the equivalent human body. This may change slightly as the clay dries out and hardens a little, but not much.

The moisture content of natural clay can be an aid to making a sturdy armature, especially if timber is incorporated in the construction. Timber will absorb some of the moisture and will swell, causing any bindings made of wire or string, holding the various components together, to tighten up and become more secure. Natural clay becomes hard and tougher as it is allowed to dry and its hardening bulk will become another slight aid to strengthening the armature – but this is not a reason for making a weak or skimpy structure.

The modelling surface needs to be kept soft and pliable while it is being worked and this is achieved by regularly spraying the clay with clean water; time and experience will allow the sculptor to judge the degree of softness required at any time; too much water will cause the clay to soften and fall off the armature, but too little will make it impossible to model.

Synthetic clay has no water content and therefore cannot help to make a structure firmer. It does not harden either, except in very cold conditions, and so requires a particular kind of armature. This usually means that more armature material is used to give the thickest support evenly over the whole structure.

PLASTER OF PARIS

Because it can be carved as well as modelled, plaster of Paris needs the kind of support that will allow for a variety of activities, some of which will be hard-hitting. Modelling this material as it quickly sets and hardens can be quite a heavy-handed process so a very rigid and strong support is required. It will also need to deal with robust carving using heavy blows with an axe or mallet and chisel.

OTHER MATERIALS

Armature supports for other materials need less forward planning because in most cases the support can be added to as the images progress, but they will still need thought before and during construction so that the work can proceed as smoothly as possible. The diagrams on pages 55–61 illustrate the difference in the armatures required for various modelling materials; clearly, the armatures for clay and plaster of Paris need the most careful planning.

George Fullard, a sculptor for whom I had the greatest respect, was an accomplished modeller and unique observer of people, who became also a subtle practitioner of assembled imagery. He produced a fascinating range of sculptures using a wide range of found objects. The rule to which he worked when making this kind of sculpture was that 'the identity of the final image must dominate its assembled parts'. The parts become the whole and also their own integral support system. There is a subtle difference in such an assemblage and a sculpture modelled over an armature.

Making the Armature

Armatures for Clay

An armature for clay must be made of suitable sturdy materials, strong enough to support its dead weight. Metal rod or bar of a gauge appropriate to the size of the sculpture to be modelled is the material most commonly used for this, and can be relatively easy to work with simple tools. There are many kinds of metal rod, ferrous and non-ferrous; the choice is down to personal preference and experience, but the most commonly used today is mild steel (ferrous). Rod or bar of mild steel with a diameter of up to about half an inch (12mm) diameter can be easily bent and shaped cold in an heavy-duty engineer's vice; the thicker rod may require the aid of a long steel pipe to apply greater leverage (see the illustration opposite). Heavier-gauge mild steel will need to be heated to a bright red colour at the spot where the metal is to be shaped, so that it will bend easily and accurately, using a heat source such as a forge, a gas torch, propane or oxyacetylene.

The objective is to make a strong rigid basic structure. This will support more flexible materials, which can then be shaped according to the gesture and expression of the figure to be modelled. The strong basic structure must provide the rigid load-bearing factor for whichever clay is used (natural or synthetic), while at the same time allowing scope for more pliable metals to be attached, to be manipulated to conjure up the more specific gestures and character of the figure or group of figures.

In the past, lead in various forms was used to provide the bendable additions; today it is more likely to be square-sectioned malleable aluminium wire, which is not only safer but also lasts longer. It is widely available, easier to use and can be purchased in coils by weight, and in sizes that range from 3mm to 25mm. If only round-section aluminium wire is available it is wise to hammer it, to make facets to help secure one piece to another. This malleable aluminium may on occasion prove to be too pliable, having a low tensile strength, but this can be rectified by twisting the wire along its length, increasing the surface tension of the material. This will make it stronger and better able to support the clay.

The bulk of a form can be taken up by adding lightweight substances, such as wood, cork or expanded plastic foam of any kind, to the basic structure. Providing these are firmly tied to the basic support, and designed to stay well inside the proposed final volume, they will lessen the load and aid the build-up of material.

Galvanized or plastic-covered wire (binding wire) is the best means of fixing pieces of armature together, and for attaching other bulking materials as and when they are required. The best method for making strong attachments using binding wire is to use a tourniquet configuration (see the illustration right). These can be made at almost any size and gain their strength by being twisted from both ends, to squeeze the items together and tighten them securely. Simply winding wire around components will not provide a strong fixing.

Binding thin lengths of wood (lath) to the metal will provide additional rigidity to the armature for natural clay; some moisture in the clay will migrate to the wood, causing it to swell and tighten the structure, adding strength. The lath and its bindings will also provide a key to which the clay will cling. Such keying is important, to prevent clay simply sliding along the wire or rod, and can also be provided by other means, such as twisting galvanized or aluminium wire about the basic support. The spiral created by twisting a length of aluminium wire for additional strength also makes a good key for clay.

Thin strips of wood cut and formed in a cross formation with binding wire (called 'butterflies') are a most effective means of giving additional support to a mass of clay, where armature material close to a working surface may prove to be a hindrance. This method can be used to good effect with both natural and synthetic clay (the latter will require many more of these 'butterfly' supports). Butterflies prevent the clay slipping and, depending on their size, provide good efficient support for bulky forms. They need to be hung from the metal supports and placed at the centre of the planned volume; hanging them in clusters is good idea if the volume is slender or long.

Like cheese, clay can be quite easily sliced with a wire, and gravity and the weight of the material can cause the clay to be cut through if the support is too thin. It is vital, therefore, to design, plan and build the armature according the intended bulk of the sculpture, and the kind of clay to be dealt with.

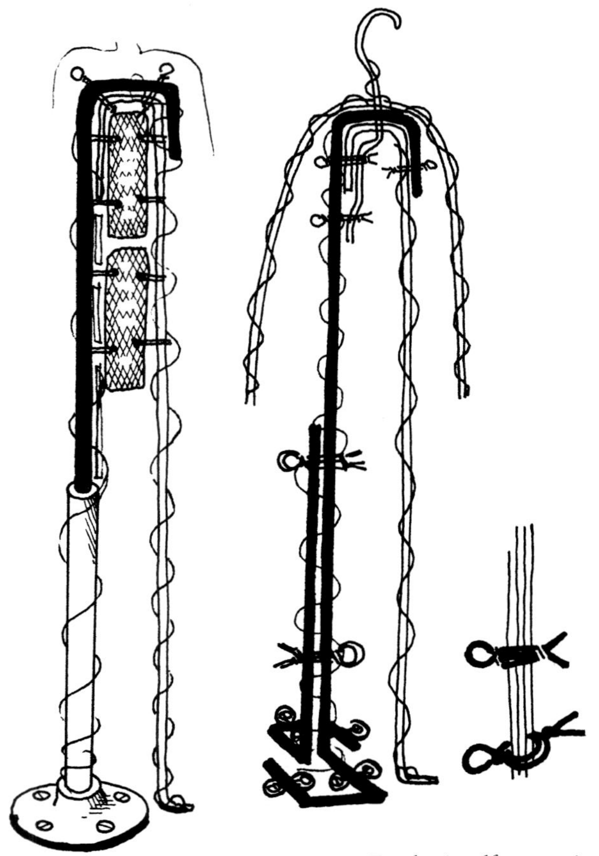

Two basic self-supporting armatures showing tourniquet fixing.

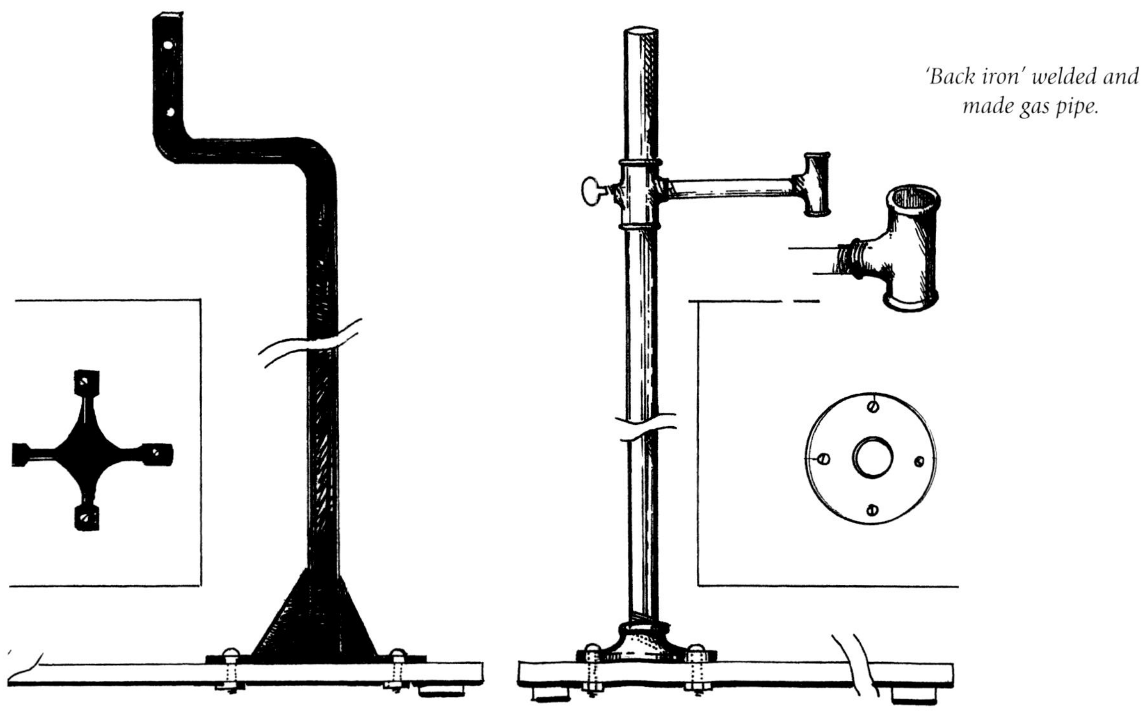

'Back iron' welded and made gas pipe.

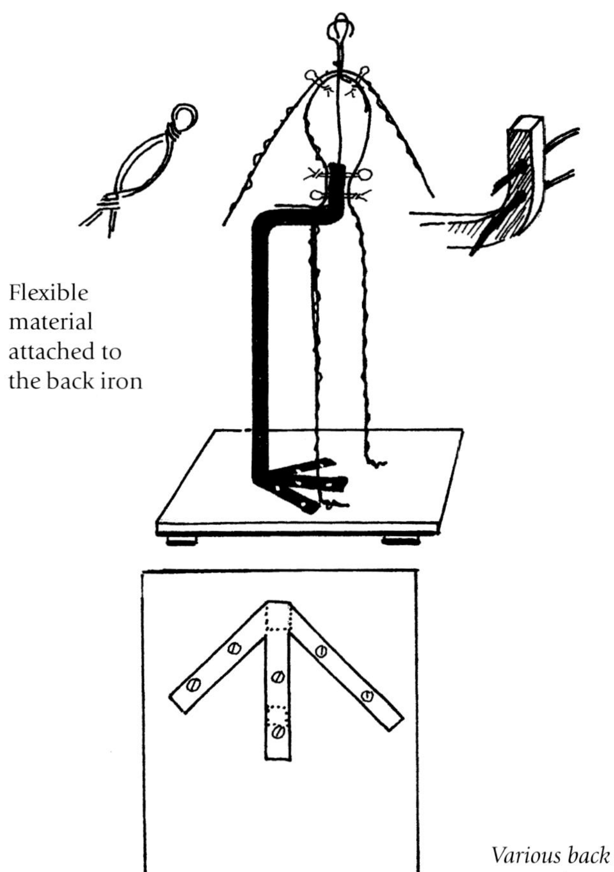

Flexible material attached to the back iron

Various back iron external supports.

The mild steel used to support all the elements of the armature and the clay can be designed and made to provide good internal support (see the illustration on page 60); although this is more difficult to make, it is the preferred method. Before this steel became available, an external supporting structure was the studio norm. Known as a 'back iron' (see opposite and above), it is a vertical column of iron approximately 2in (50mm) thick, usually of a square section with a splayed foot to be securely bolted down to a suitably strong baseboard. The column has a double right-angled shape projecting at the top. Flexible skeletal material plus any timber or laths, together with any butterflies forming the armature, is hung from the projection (see the illustration opposite). When securely fixed with strong binding wire, this will support the clay. The legs of the armature are free at the place for the feet and not fixed down. The metal is bent at right-angles at these points to be buried in a clay base, to prevent the limbs pulling away as the figure is being modelled. A strong back iron allows freedom to move the limbs as desired.

This kind of support can be made in the studio by anyone who has the right welding skills and equipment, but they are also made and sold in a wide range of sizes by suppliers of sculpture equipment. They are useful for beginners who have difficulty in making complex structures and also allow an armature to be made quite quickly. The drawback of such supports is the visual disturbance they cause to the perception of the sculpture being made; there is a constant vertical element, which interferes with the visual apprecia-

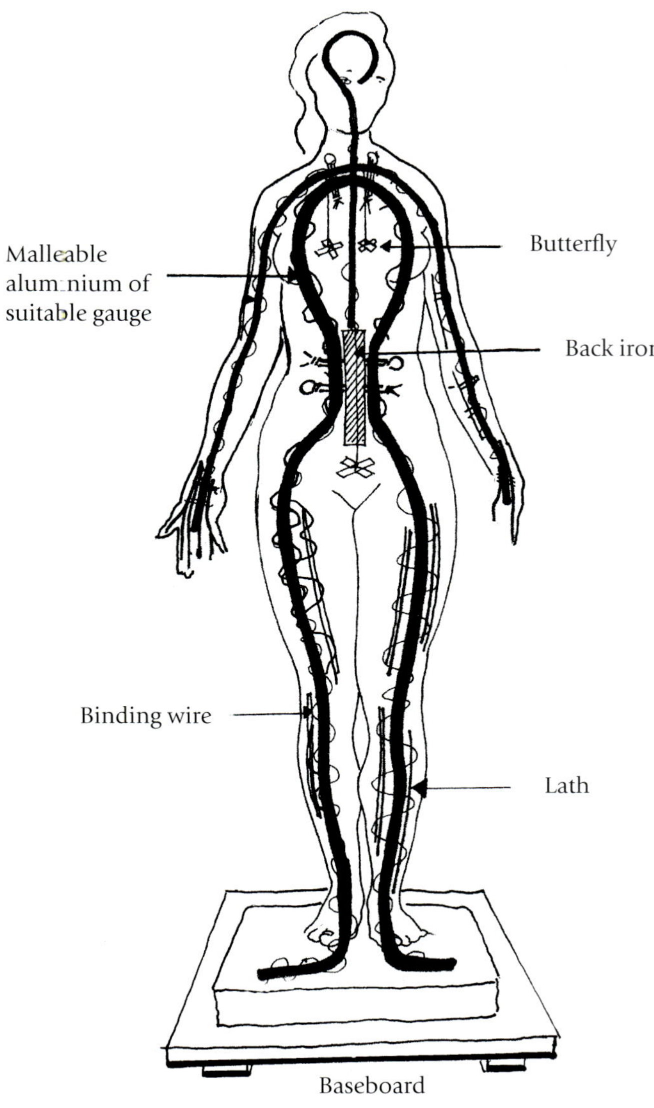

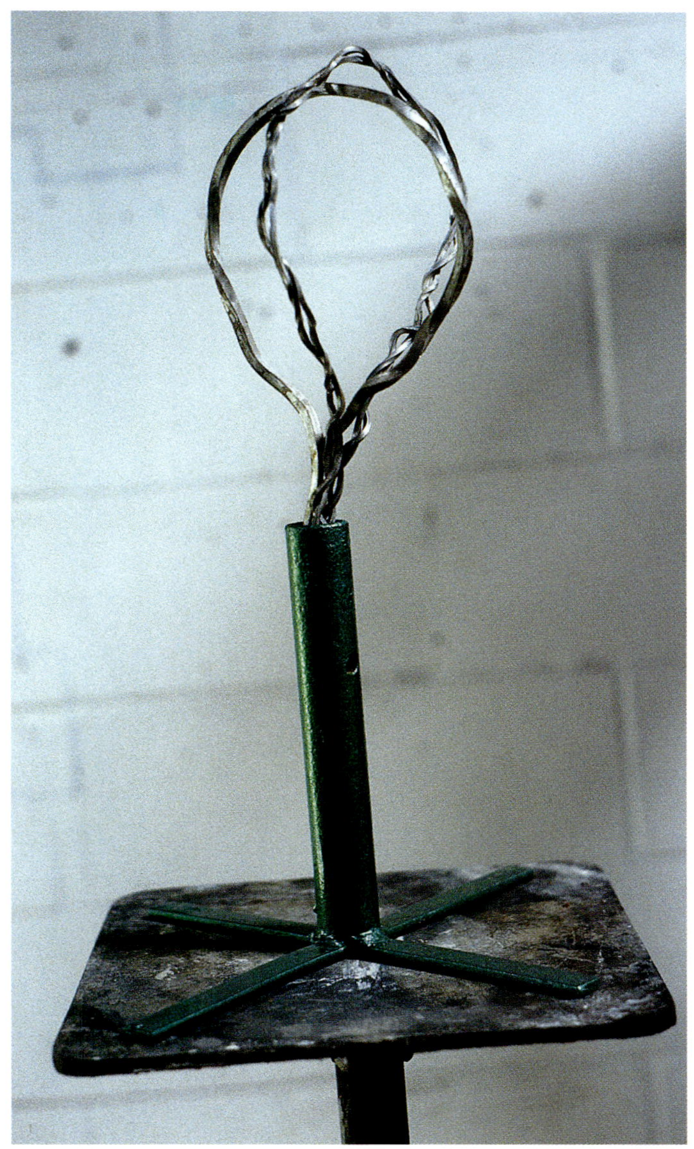

Head pegs.

tion of angles. Because of this, a well-constructed internal support will prove to be worth the effort in the long run, despite taking more time to make.

For examples of both kinds of support, external and internal, see the illustrations above. It can be seen that the stable internal support is given to only one leg – preferably the obvious anatomically supporting limb – while the other leg is made free-moving, to give greater selection of movement as the figure is developed. This leg can be fixed down when its final position has been decided upon.

The sculptor's choice of armature will depend upon his or her skill and modelling preferences, but it is important to be familiar with both systems. Generally, what is used is a compromise of the two, plus anything that occurs as the artist's skills progress. Rules are made to be broken – but only when the rules are known.

The armature required to model a head is commonly called a 'head peg', and these range in size. Some allow the modelling of a simple head down to the neck, while a full-scale head peg and armature will allow the modelling of a full bust down to the waist including arms. There are a number of variations of head peg design (see the illustrations on page 58). For a simple head, down to the neck or shoulders, the best system is made using a tube into which two crossing loops of aluminium wire are inserted (see the illustration above). The value of this design is proven at the moulding stage when part of the tube below the modelling is included in the moulded seam edge. This element in turn becomes the register for correctly placing any fixing in the subsequent cast, to make a support that will allow the finished cast to be attached to a base at the correct angle. Thinking ahead to the cast is always a good idea.

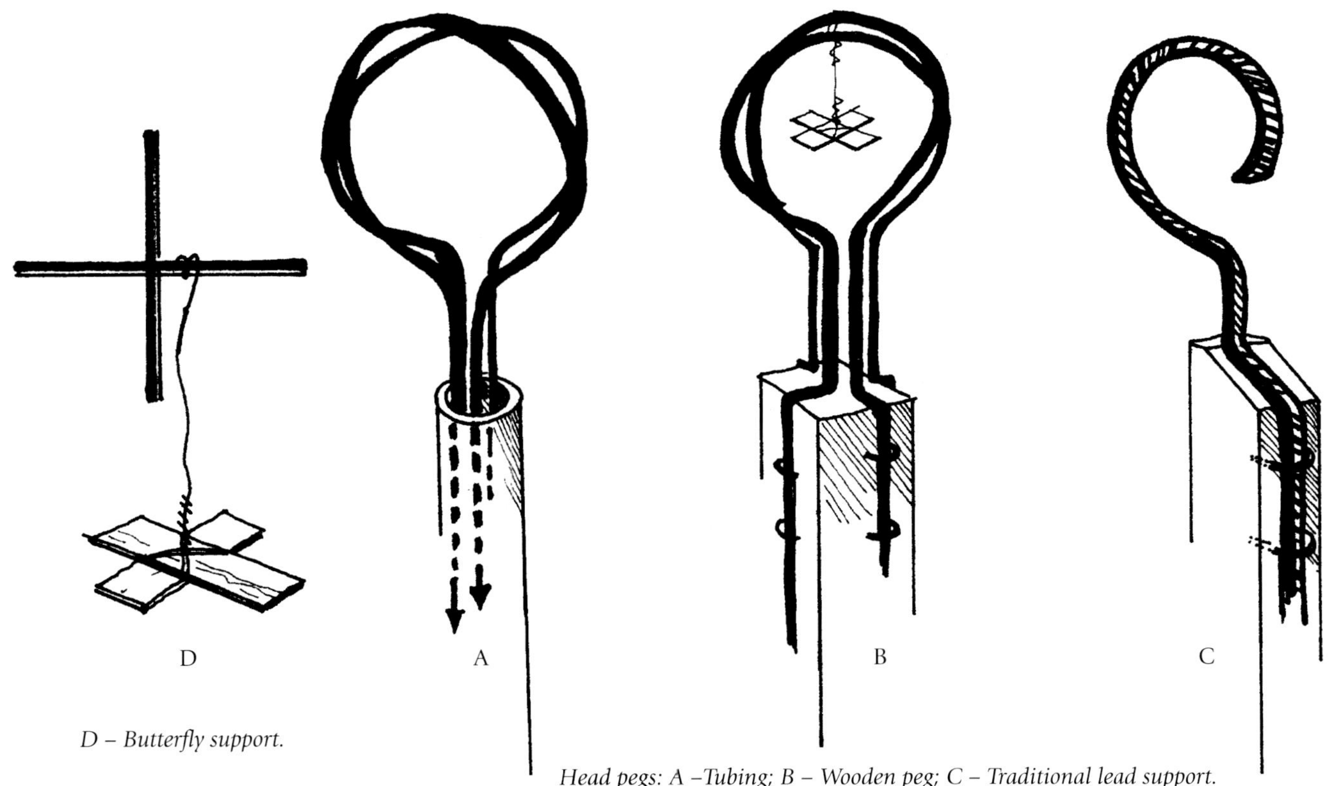

D – Butterfly support.

Head pegs: A –Tubing; B – Wooden peg; C – Traditional lead support.

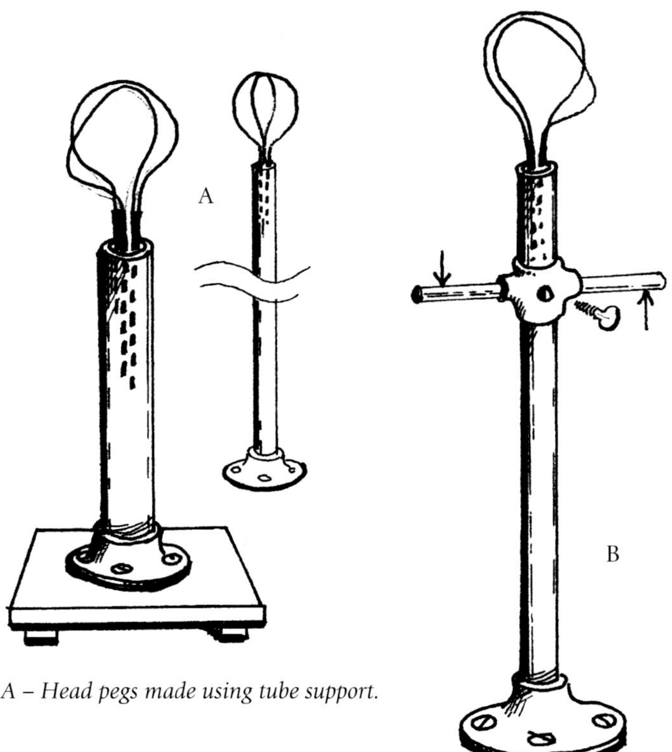

A – Head pegs made using tube support.

B – Head pegs for a full bust.

Supports for both natural and synthetic clay must be designed with the processes of mould-making in mind. The kind of mould most commonly used is the waste-mould, using plaster of Paris. When it is complete, this type of mould will encase the finished clay entirely, so provision must be made in the design of the mould for it to opened up so that the clay and its supporting armature can be removed. The armature therefore must be demountable. This is another important factor in its planning and construction. Unless it is very carefully planned, a welded armature, for instance, can prove to be very difficult to remove, so it is best avoided when using clay to be waste-moulded. It is more practical to design the armature so that any fastenings can be easily undone and its component pieces removed without recourse to heavy cutting equipment. This will also prove to be thrifty, as the materials will be able to be recycled.

Armatures for Plaster

Plaster of Paris is one of the basic materials of a sculptor's studio. When the powder is mixed 50/50 with water, it becomes a liquid with a consistency of cream, which then gradually thickens and hardens to become a dense, brittle solid. This material may then be model or carved by the

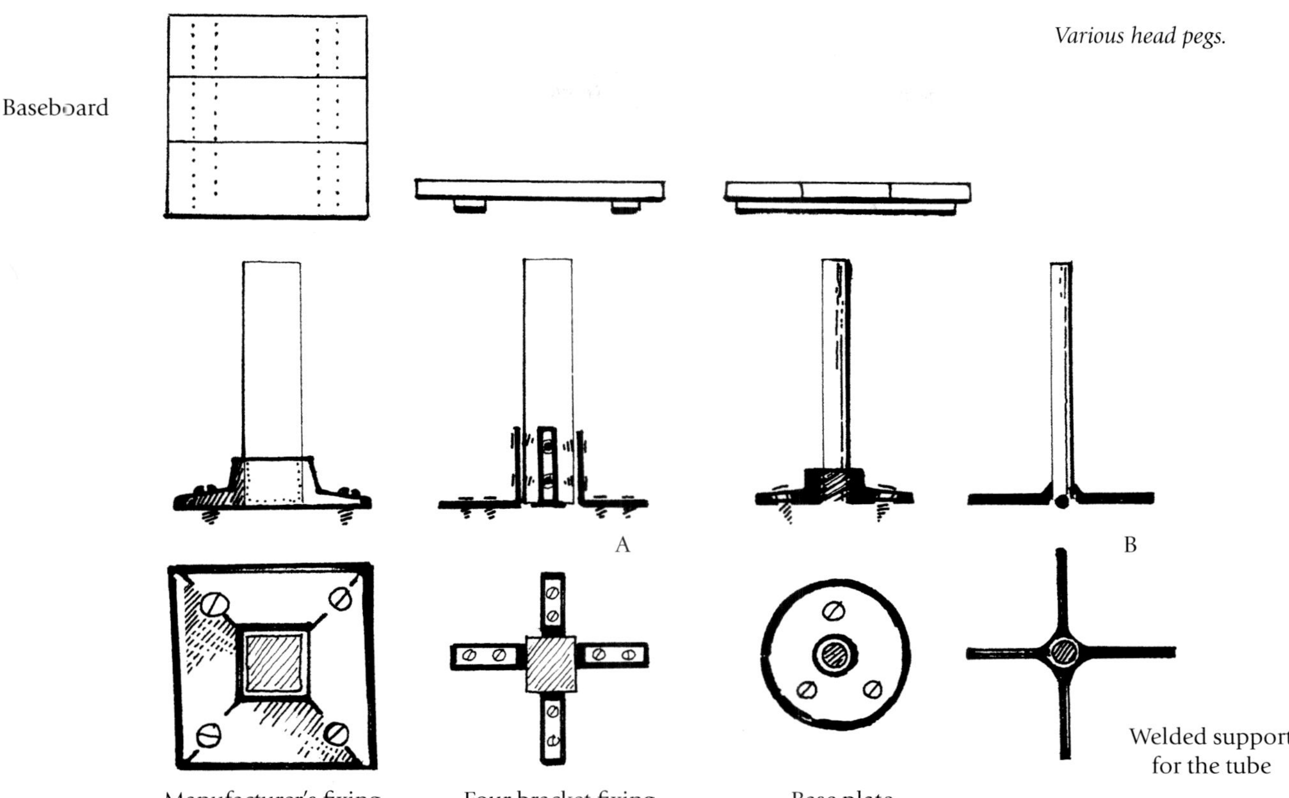

Various head pegs.

sculptor. Modelling when the plaster is at the thickening stage and carving when it has hardened, the process is called the 'direct plaster' method.

Because of the carving, hammering and rasping aspect of the working process, plaster requires an armature that is particularly strong. It will remain as an internal support to the sculpture and therefore can be welded, and this is often the best solution to providing a particularly strong armature. If welding is not an option, an internal armature construction should be used, as for clay, but using mild steel in place of malleable aluminium, which will not be strong enough. All the mild steel should be painted with an anti-rust paint. The moisture in the plaster will cause untreated mild steel to rust and contaminate the plaster, leaving unsightly brown stains that not only harm the sculpture visually, but also will cause the plaster to crumble and eventually disintegrate.

Tensile strength is given to the plaster by adding jute scrim, which is a fibrous material and improves the workability of the otherwise brittle solid. The scrim dipped in plaster of Paris is used first to bind the plaster to the armature and in this way can be used to attach other items securely, to add bulk or strength as required.

Polystyrene foam (known as Styrofoam in the USA, and now fondly referred to by its studio name of 'Poly') is the most favoured material used to bulk out a form working with plaster of Paris. Its lightweight bulk enables large forms to be made quickly. It can be cut into strips and used with

Armature for plaster of Paris.

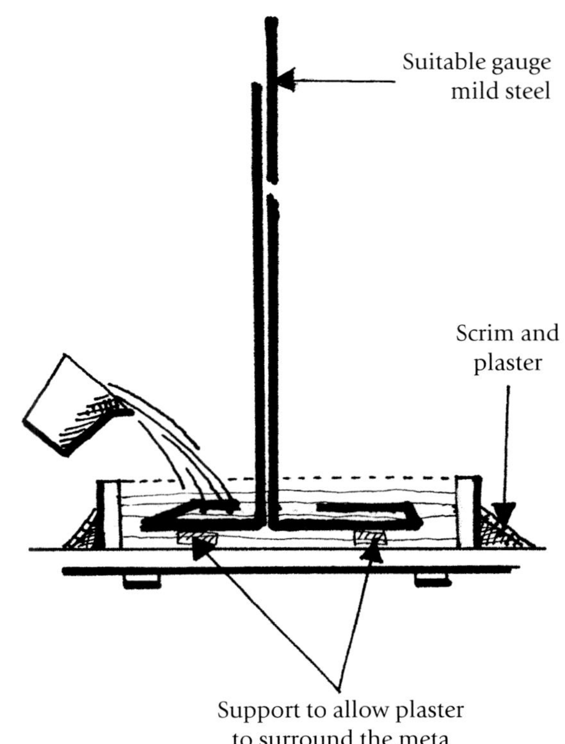

plaster of Paris as the sculpture is built up over a metal armature on top of the plaster and scrim layer. In this way it adds strength to the support but, because it can be easily cut away, it also allows for changes to be easily made to the image. This is the best technique to use when making large figures quickly. Poly has the added advantage that it can be easily measured, cut, glued and constructed, which makes it an extremely useful material.

Polystyrene (Styrofoam)

In film studios, poly is used to make film-sets and props of bewildering variety, it is now a useful practice for sculptors to make images from polystyrene by using a variety of assemblage and carving techniques. Even though this material has very little intrinsic aesthetic quality, it is possible to make sculpture using only polystyrene because, according

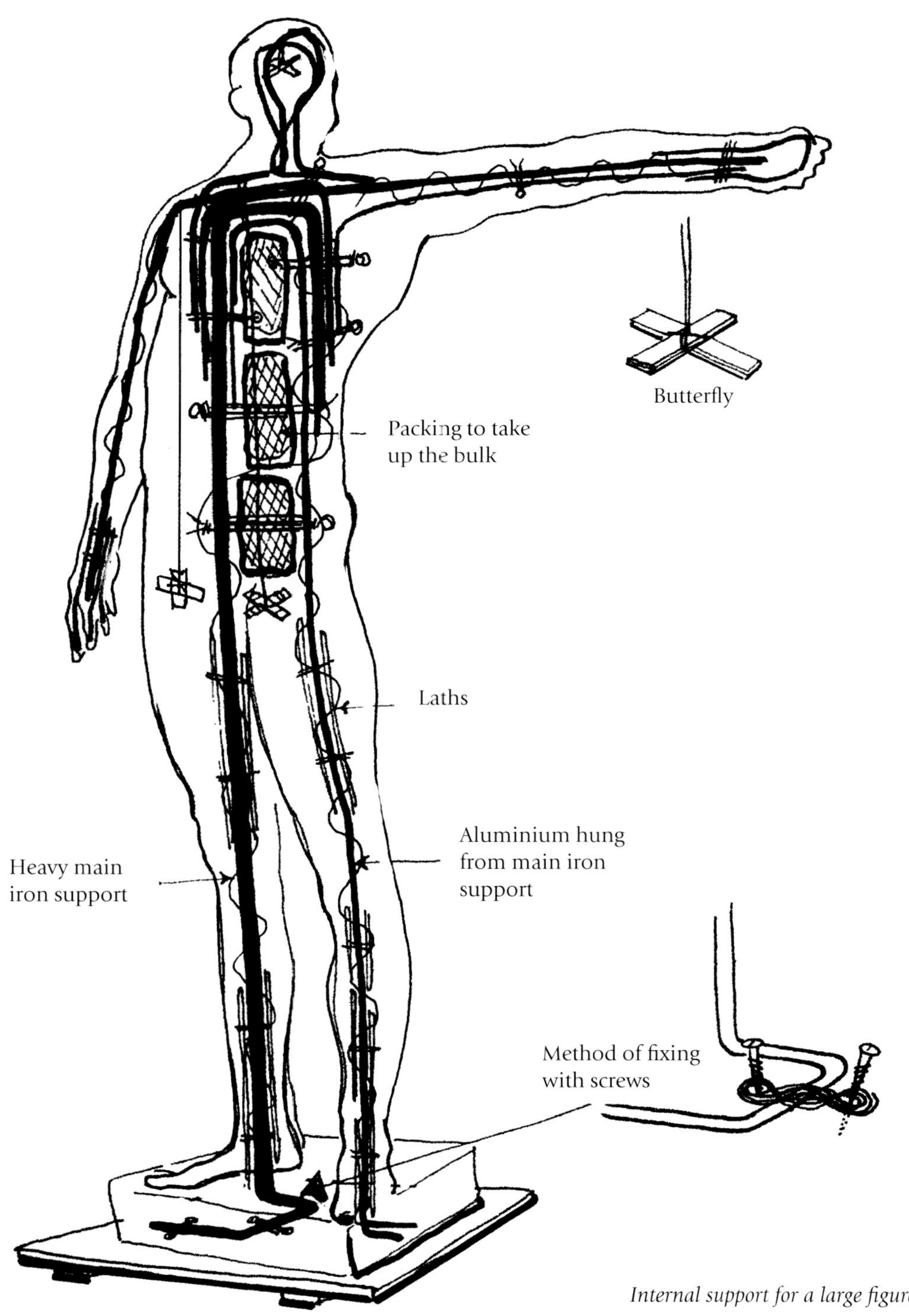

Internal support for a large figure.

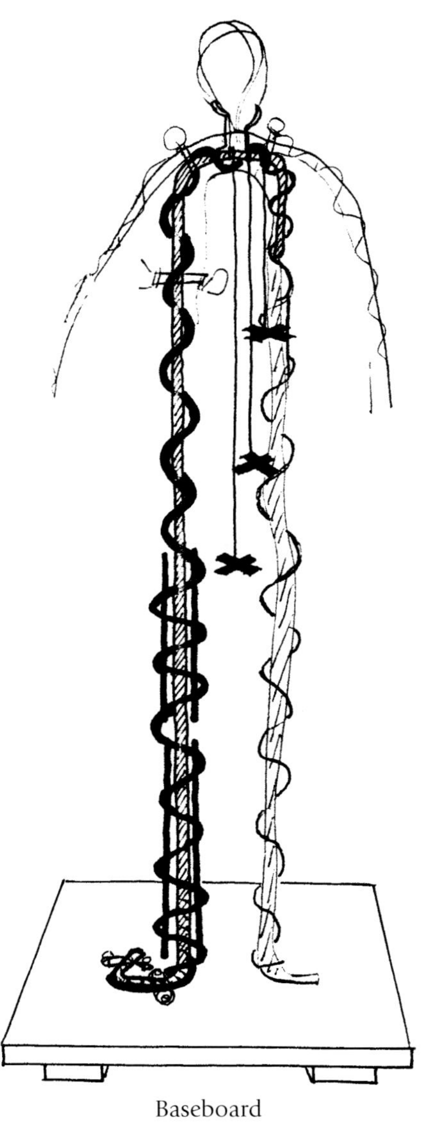

Internal support for a small figure.

to the density of the material, it will also allow fine surface detail. Detail can be cut and refined using very sharp knives of various size and shape; it is essential to keep the knives sharp so that they cut and not tear the material.

Poly has also become for the sculptor a modern alternative support system, replacing in certain cases a constructed armature even welded, or other structure. If a slender form is to be made, this can be achieved by roughly carving the poly to make the form, then with a sharp knife or, ideally, a hot wire, cutting the form in half along its length. A support of metal or timber (whichever is appropriate) is designed and made, to suit that configuration, then a groove is cut into the cut surfaces and the support is placed in the groove, and both it and the cut surfaces are glued in position at the same time, using a specialist glue made for polystyrene (usually a foam). Whole figures and groups can be made using this method.

If a finer surface is required, the polystyrene can be coated with plaster or some other water-based filler and allowed to harden and dry. The surface can then be filed, cut, rasped and sanded, as with any plasterwork. If this method is chosen, the initial carving needs to be made smaller in volume than the finished sculpture, to permit the application of plaster and any build-up required.

The Baseboard

The baseboard to which an armature is fixed is an important element in preparation for the modelling process. It needs to be made so that it will not warp or deteriorate, so it is best made of boards of planed timber of a thickness chosen according to the size of the work to be made. The boards are placed side by side and attached securely to battens running across their width; this will prevent warping and make the handling of the work easier by providing a grip. The degree of carpentry employed depends upon personal skills and time, but the better the job, the longer-lasting the baseboard will be. Although modern laminated boards are useful, they do have a tendency to disintegrate over a relatively short period of time so the sculptor must judge their suitability according to the sculpture to be made (see page 59).

Fixing metal parts securely to a baseboard in such a manner as to allow easy dismantling is a point to be emphasized. The most adaptable method is to place two screws on either side of the items to fixed down and make them firm by turning them just two or three threads. Bind a long piece of galvanized or plastic-coated wire in a tight figure-of-eight clockwise around the screws, over the item being secured, then drive the screws all the way in. This will pull the wire tightly down over the armature, making it very secure and unlikely to be pulled out during the modelling process, but it will be easily removed from the mould and may be used again on another modelling project.

This kind of fixing down should not be done carelessly (see the illustration on page 60). Other methods, such as driving in nails and then bending then over to fix armature components, or hammering staples of various dimensions to do the same job, may be quick but they will inevitably loosen and be in danger of collapsing, especially on larger work. Such simple methods of fixing down should be kept for very small items that carry little deadweight, and must be avoided on important jobs.

It is not possible to anticipate every individual's particular requirements in relation to armatures, and it is best to develop a personal style and attitude towards the sculpture's basic supports.

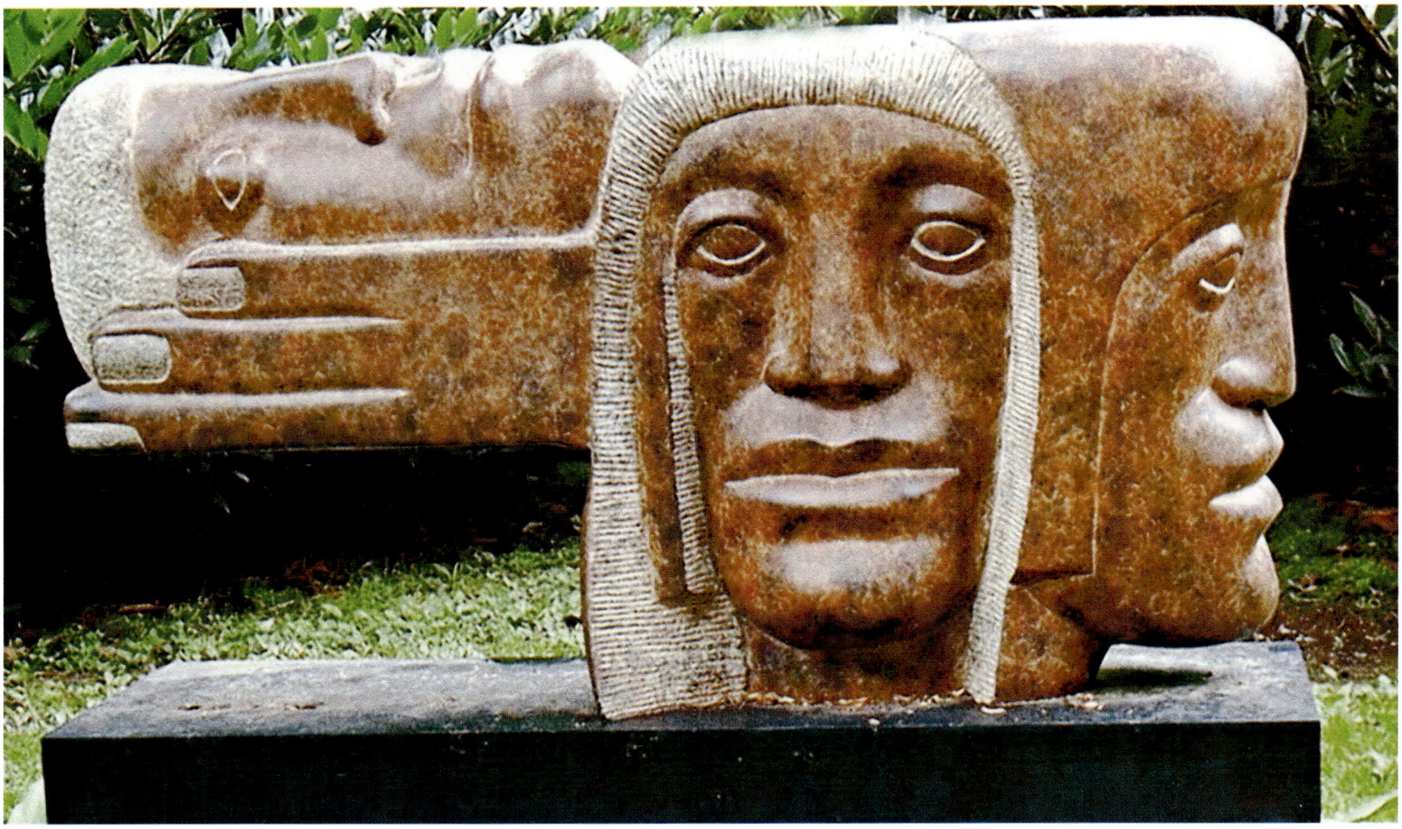

An emotional year, *by Dawn Rowland, in alabaster.*

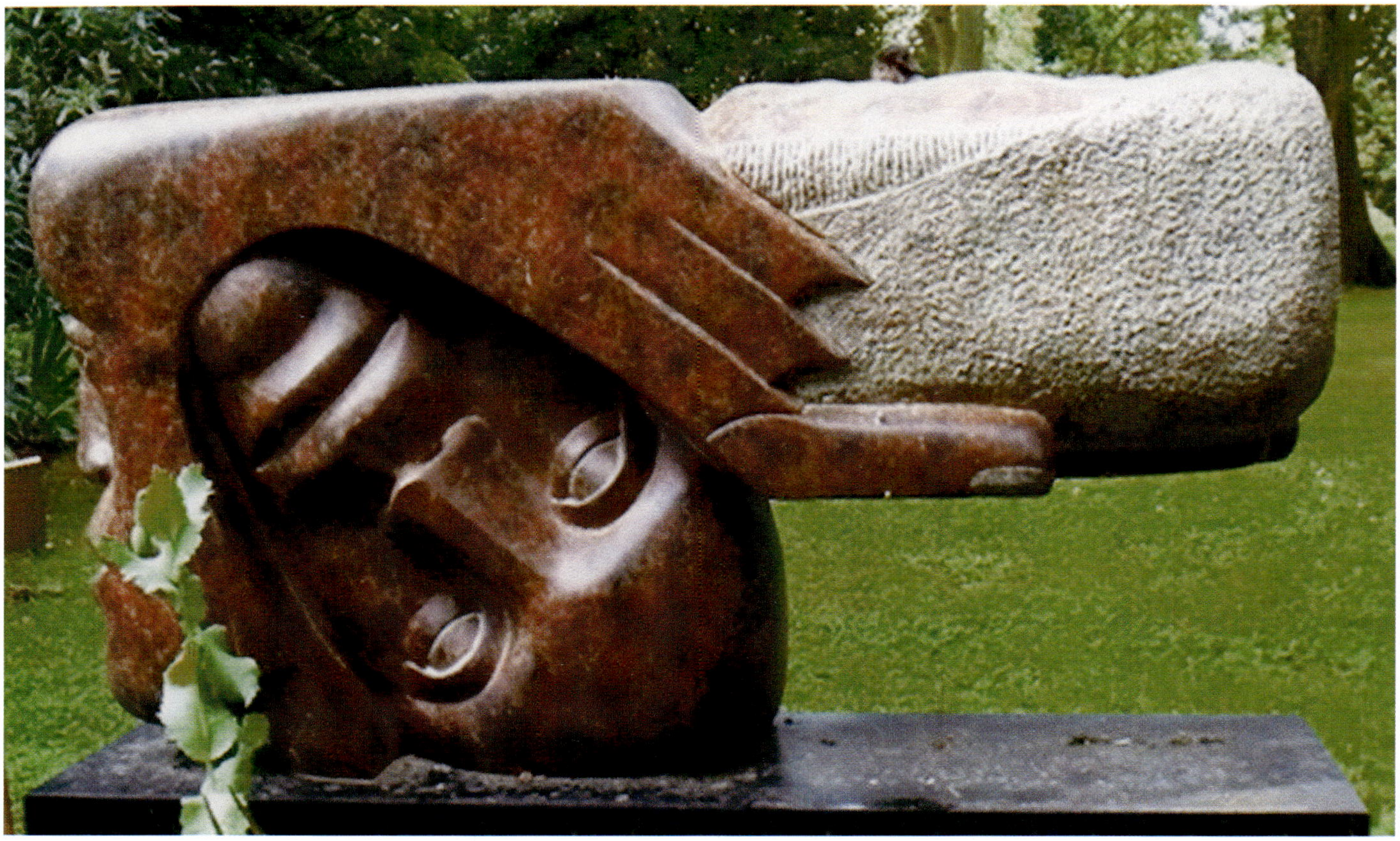

4

Modelling the Head

Handling clay of any kind or quality often seems to activate a basic human instinct to fashion a head, either human or of some other animal. The head, and in particular the face, is the human feature with which we communicate most closely, and is also the means by which we try to read expression in almost all other creatures.

For sculptors and painters who use the figure in their work, making a portrait is a serious challenge; it tests both their skills of observation and their use of their chosen medium. Making a replica of a human being is not necessarily the objective when producing figurative sculpture and this pertains as much to the head as it does to the whole figure. The sculptures illustrated (see the illustrations on pages 63–5) are examples of heads rendered in clay (terracotta), bronze, stone and wood, which have been simply conjured from the imagination of the artists. A detailed knowledge of human anatomy, although implied, is not a dominating factor in this kind of sculpture; it is, instead, a testing ground for the artists' imagination. Making a head or figure entirely from imagination gives the sculptor the

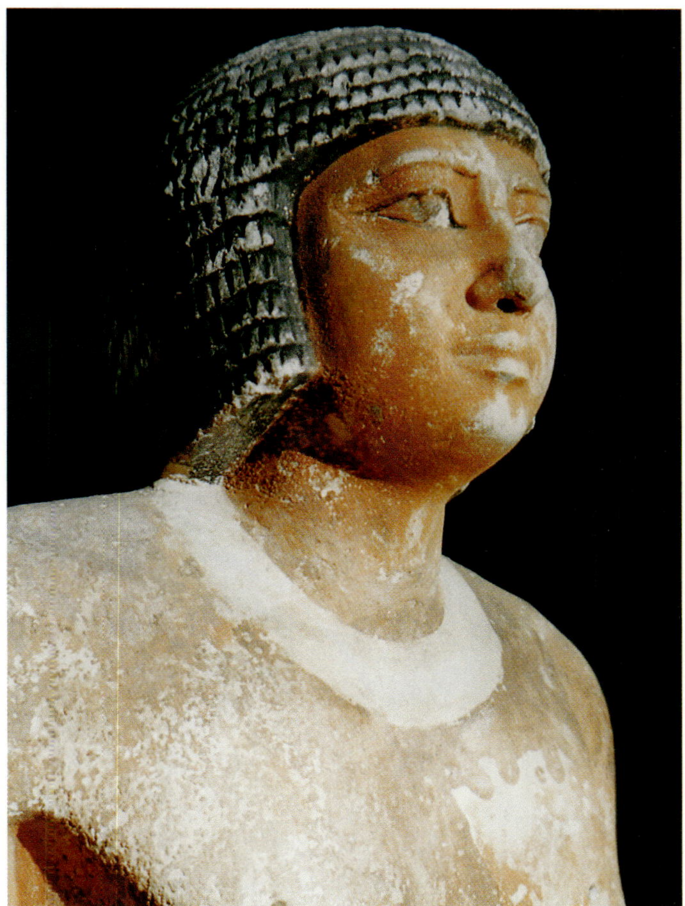

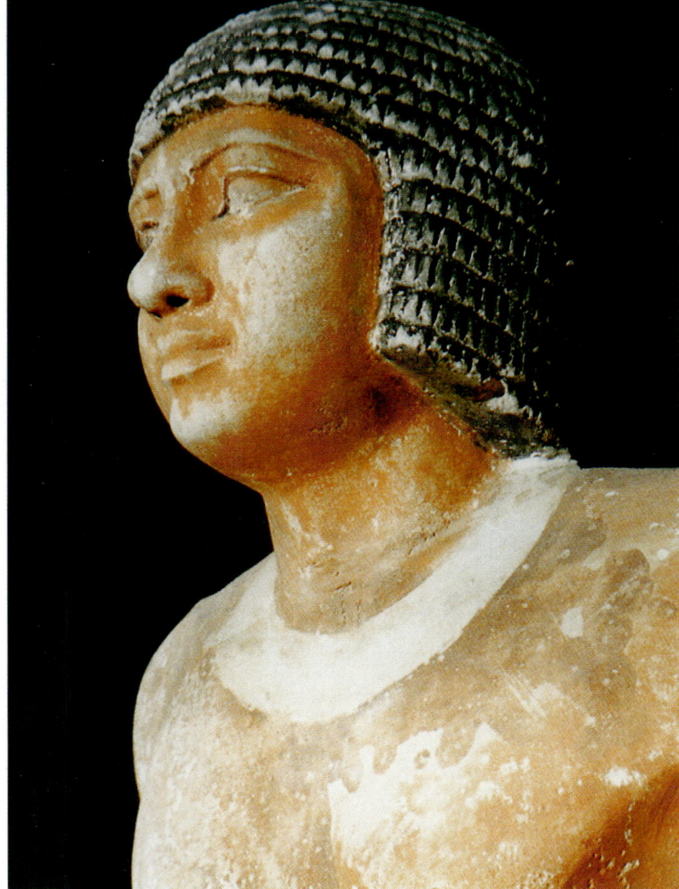

Painted limestone carving from Ancient Egypt. (British Museum, London. Photo: John W. Mills)

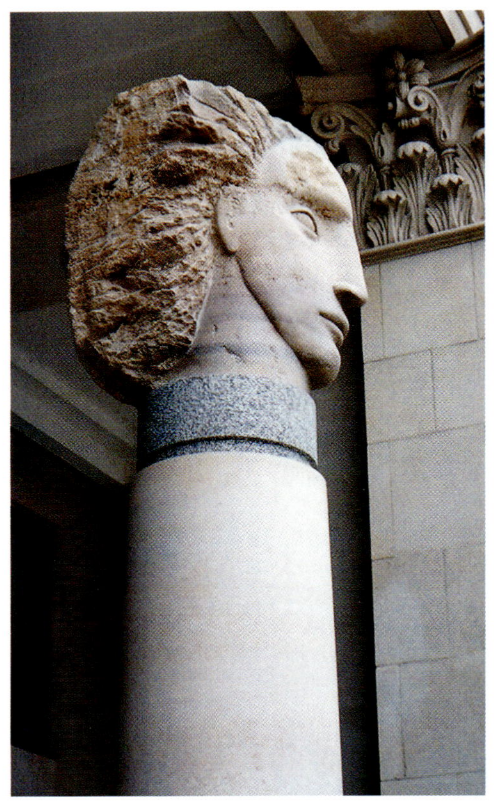

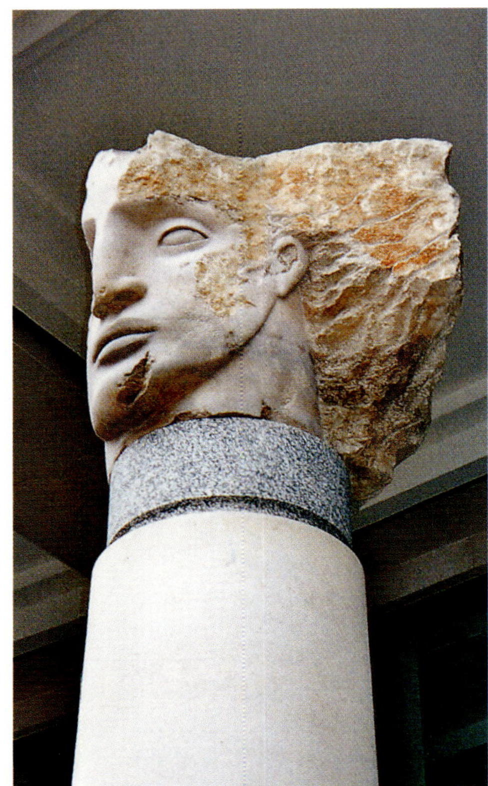

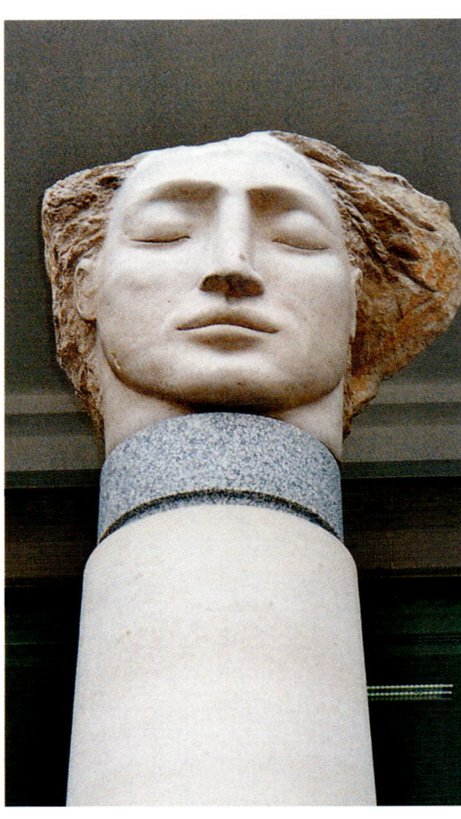

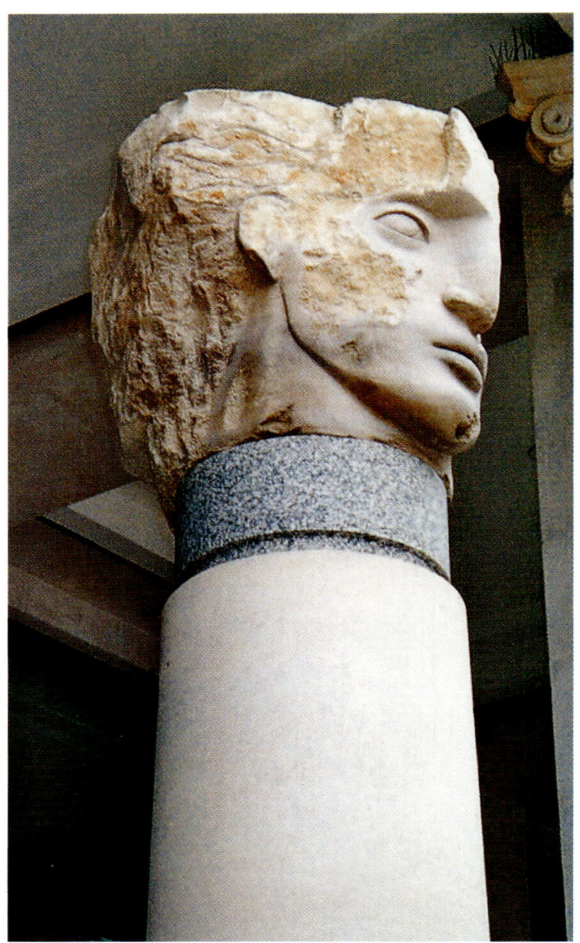

Heads, *by Emily Young, in marble. A very interesting collection of directly carved images. (St Paul's, London)*

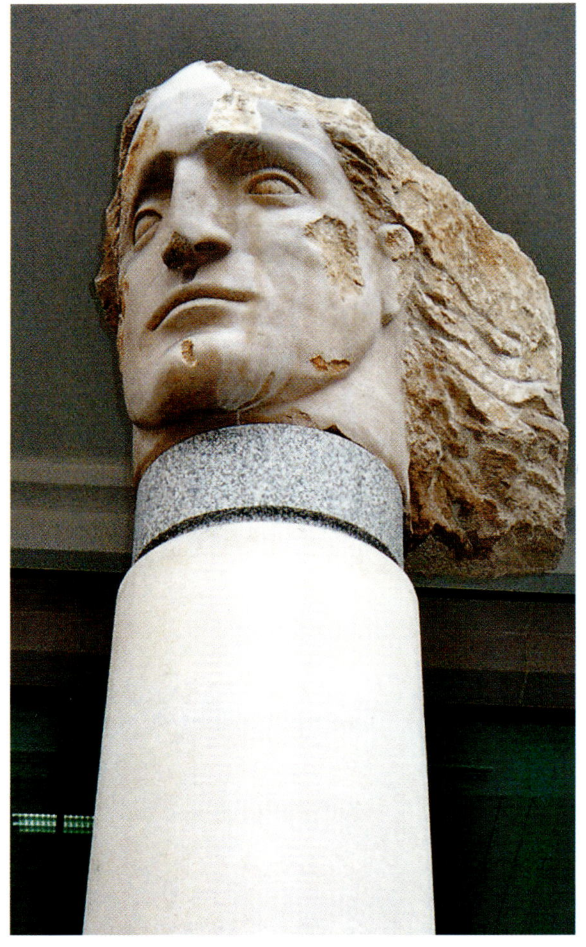

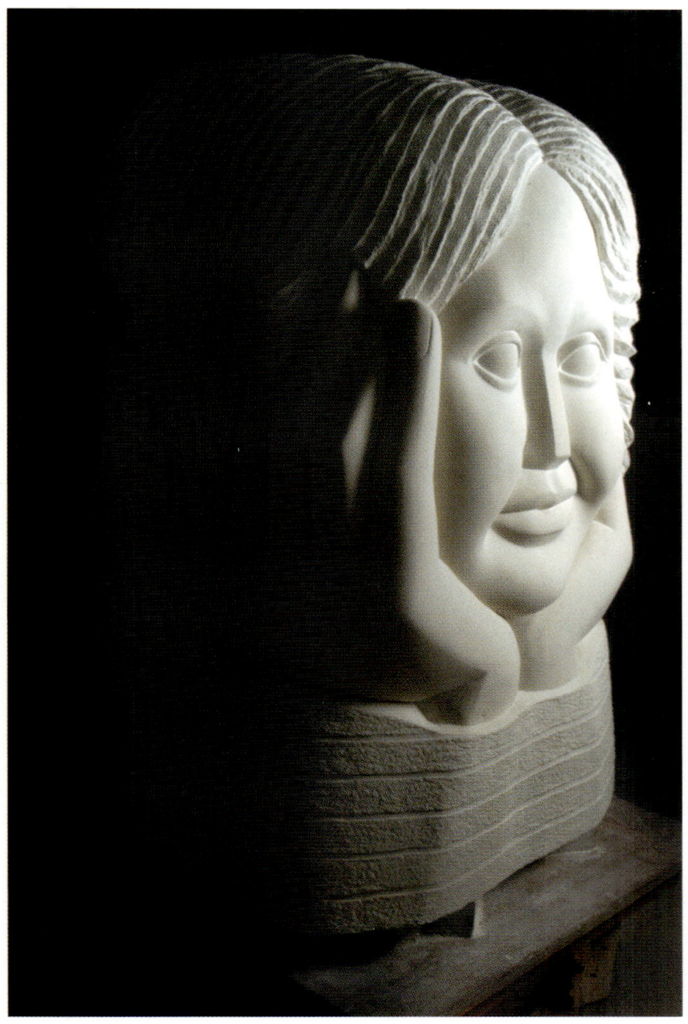

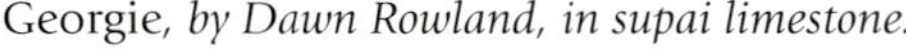

Georgie, *by Dawn Rowland, in supai limestone.*

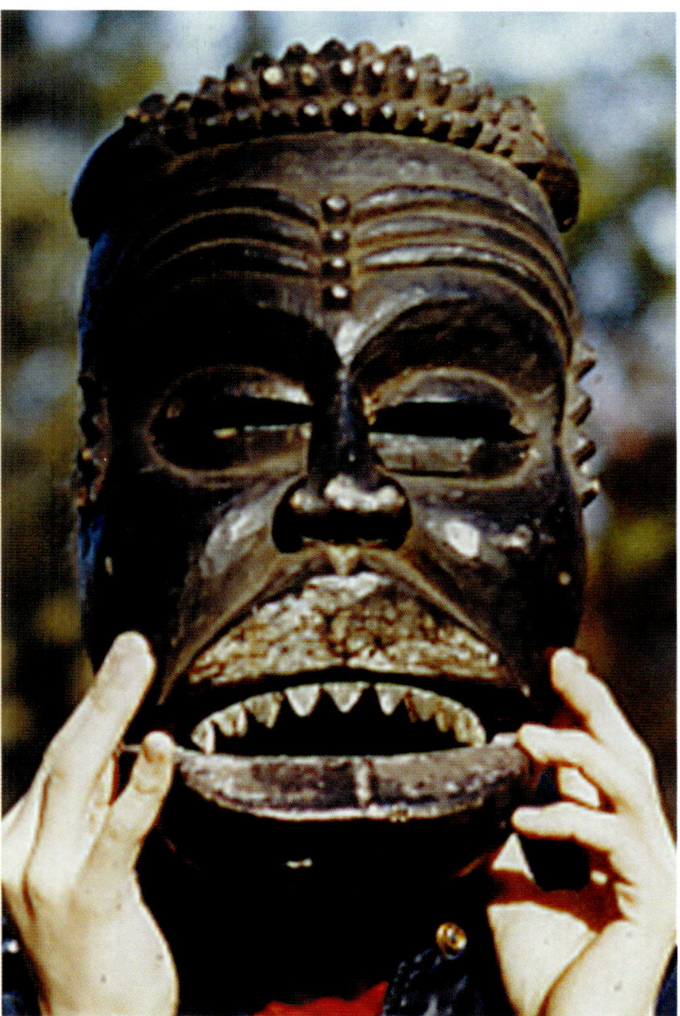

African mask, woodcarving.

opportunity to experiment with materials and tools, texture and techniques, while providing a certain freedom from the close observation of a living model. This liberation allows for invention and the chance to build and test a personal vocabulary of form. Reference to reality remains, however, constant in everyday life; it helps to create and increase that personal reference store in a sculptor's memory, of forms to be employed later to stimulate the creative imagination in all kinds of ways.

Making a Portrait

The demands of portrait sculpture are different, in that the personality and character of the subject need to be expressed. Obviously, making a near replication of features might seem to be the means for doing this quite powerfully, but the risk in this manner of working is that the artist, particularly the beginner, can become preoccupied with making a likeness rather than with identifying the unique structure of the subject's physiognomy. It is the anatomy that dictates the appearance that underlies the beauty or the beast of the model. Strong structure is the basis of all good sculpture and, in the context of portrait sculptures and when embarking on the modelling of a portrait head, 'structure leads to likeness'.

The structure of the head is governed by its hard anatomy and by the skull in particular. However, the skull should not used as it has been seen in forensic reconstruction on television. The sculptor should be looking for the visual evidence of the skull as presented by the living, breathing subject. Such evidence is more obvious in a very thin and hollow-eyed person than in someone with more flesh or more hair than normal, but the skull is certainly always there, protecting and supporting as nature intended. The importance of the skull in nature – its function, volume and shape – is echoed by its equal importance to the sculptor, but only in so far as it is common to all living human crea-

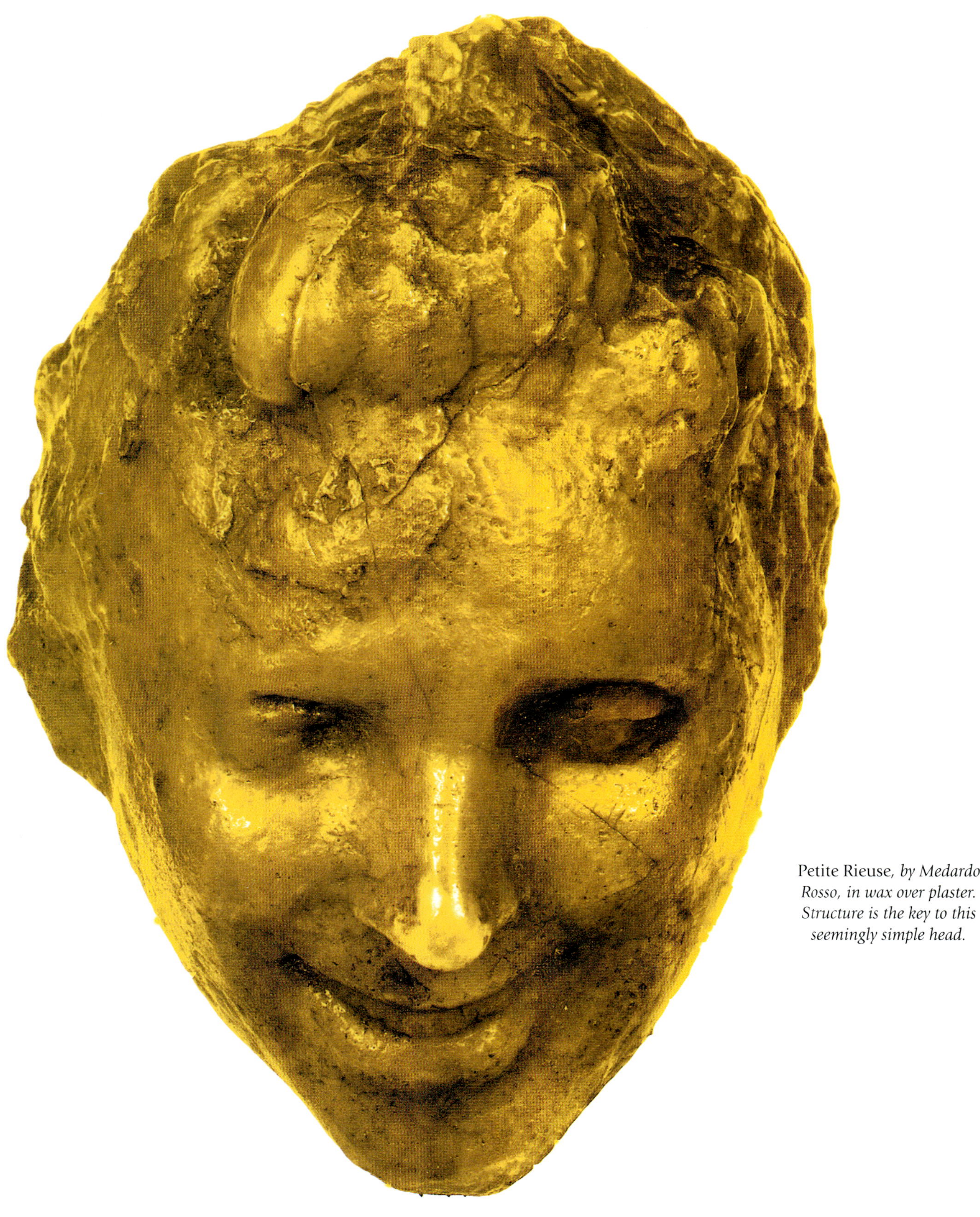

Petite Rieuse, *by Medardo Rosso, in wax over plaster. Structure is the key to this seemingly simple head.*

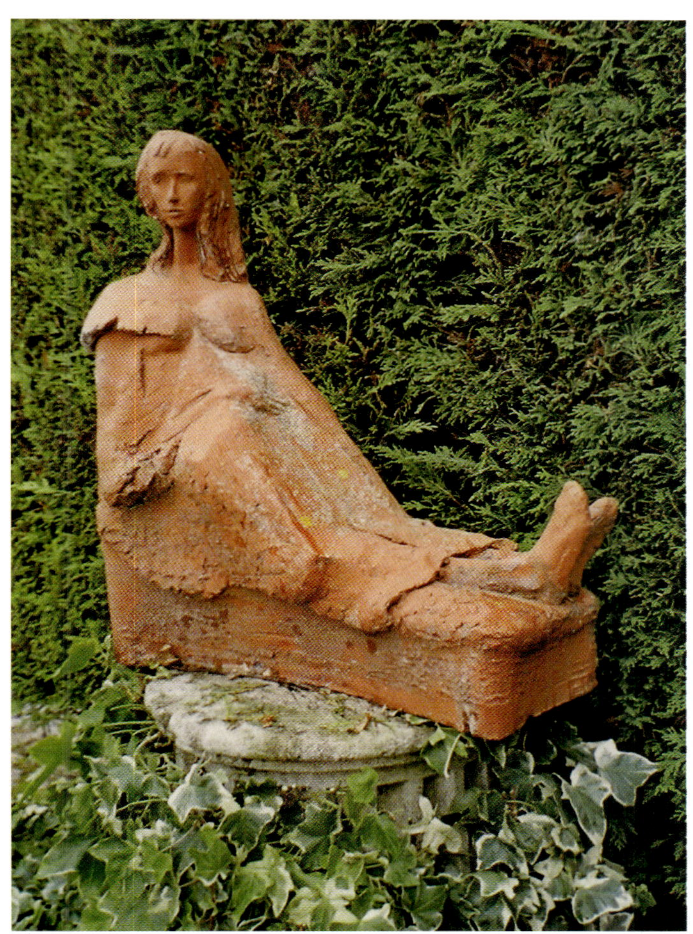

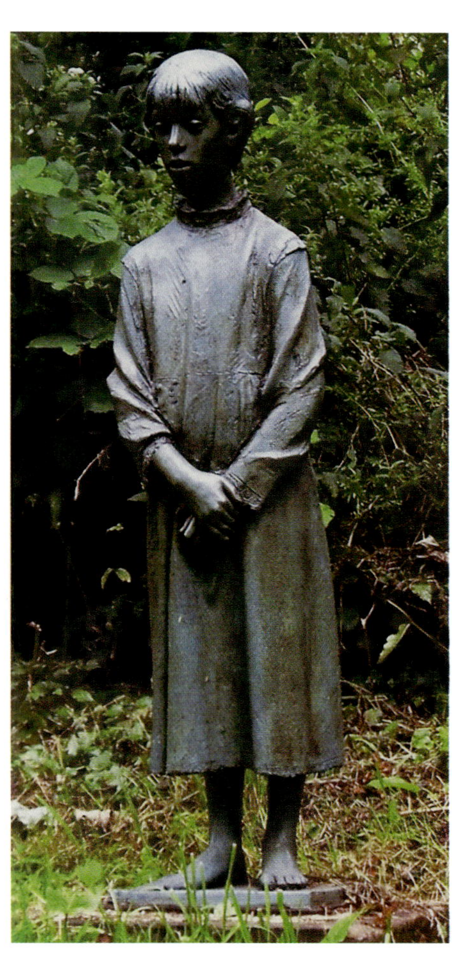

LEFT: Jo *(1962), by John W. Mills, in terracotta. This is a portrait of an event as well as of the person.*

RIGHT: Kate, *by James Butler, in bronze. A very sensitive full-figure portrait of the sculptor's daughter. Exhibited at Renishaw Hall, 1904.*

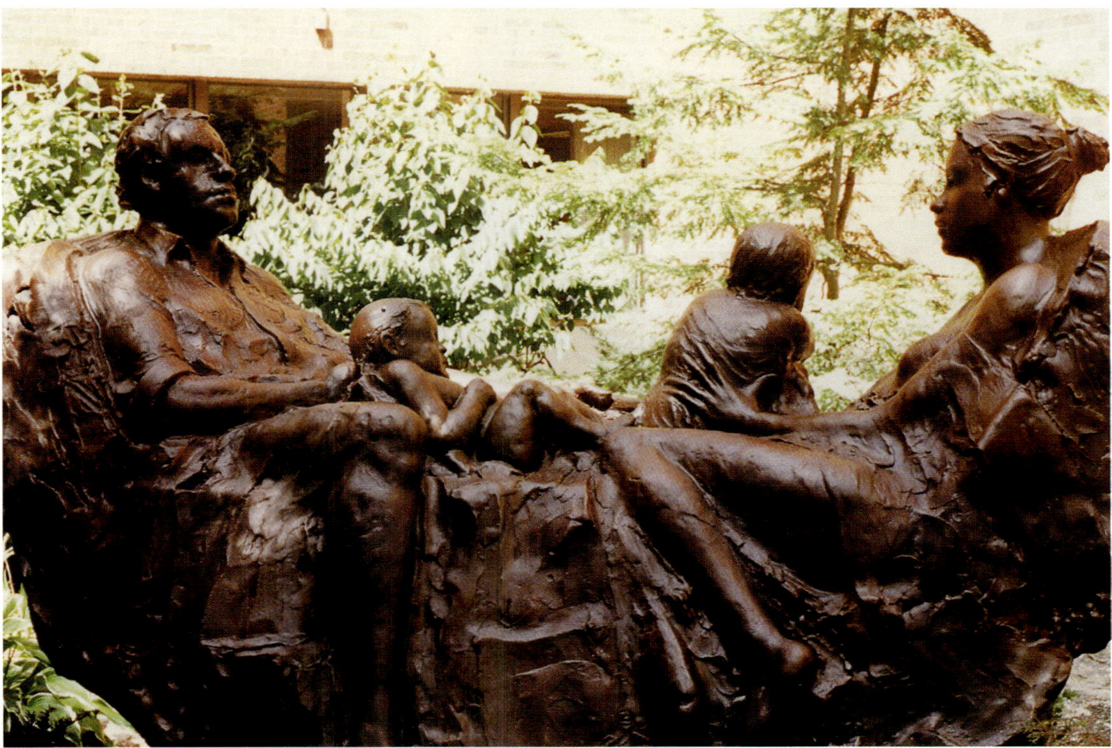

Family group, *by John Pappas, in bronze. A fine example of free 'gestural' modelling, as well as portraiture of a family group. (Michigan, USA)*

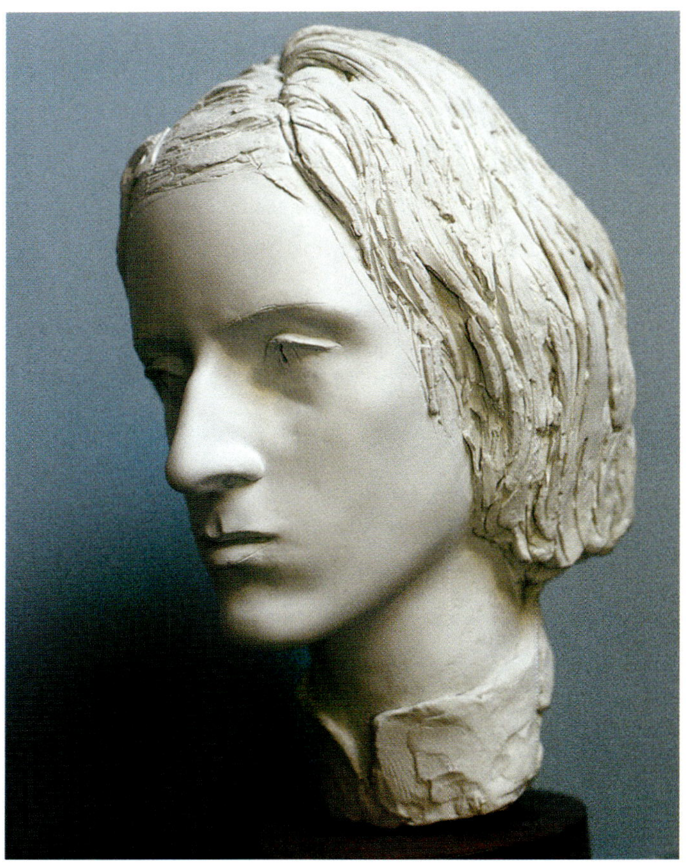

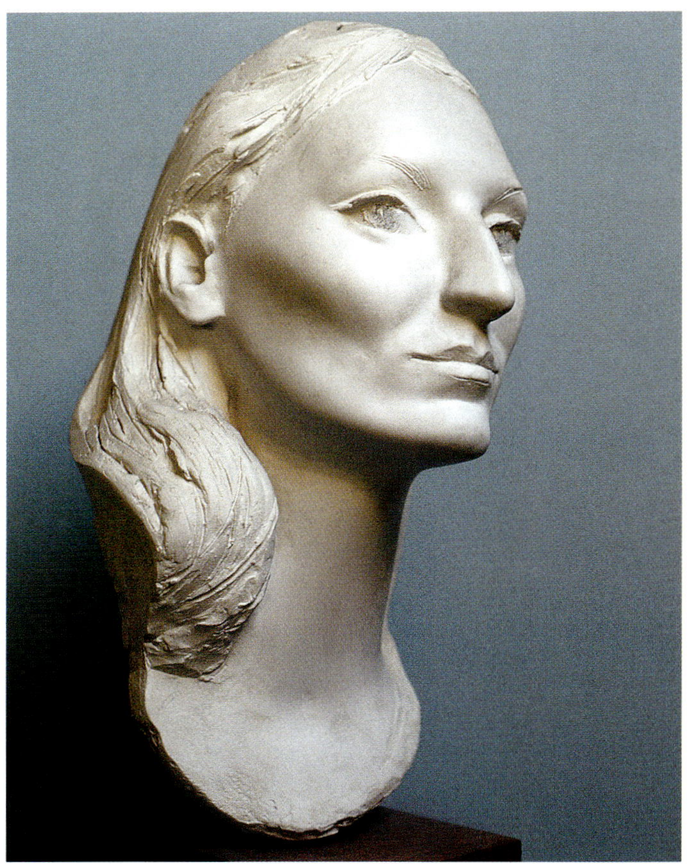

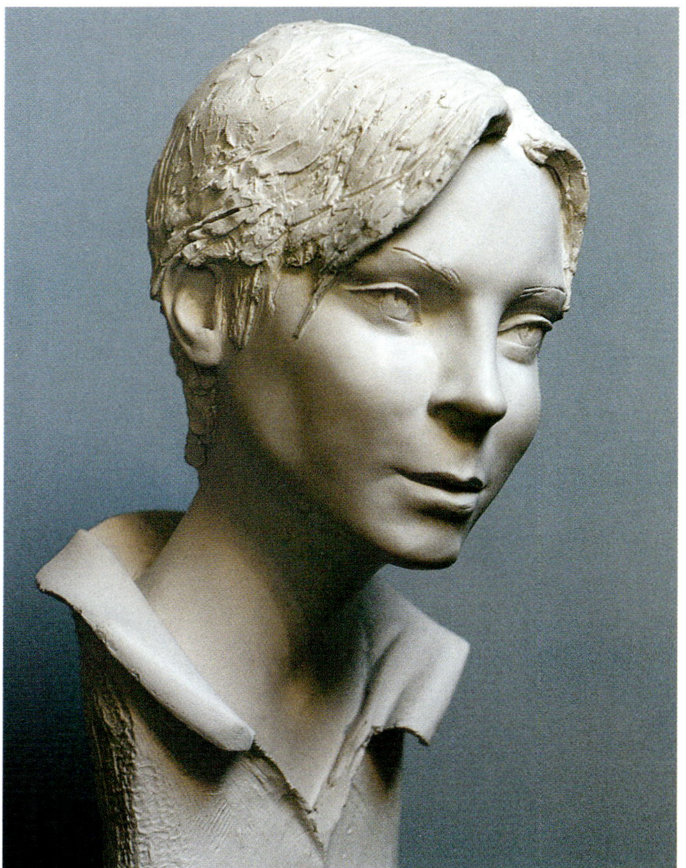

THIS PAGE: *Portrait sculpture by John W. Mills. Clockwise from top left: Charlotte; Collette; Sinead.*

tures and provides racial, individual and genetic evidence pertaining to the subject and his or her background. Sometimes, a sitter will declare during the modelling of their portrait, 'It reminds me of my father [or aunt or grandparent].' This means that the family structure has been identified and that the genealogical base is good enough for the individual likeness to become the focus of attention, allowing the sculptor to concentrate further on the idiosyncrasies of the particular subject's facial features and expressions.

The search for anatomical structure will proceed alongside the attention to and study of facial expression and detail as the sculptor becomes more experienced. For the beginner, however, it is wise to think separately of structure, starting from the premise that the skull must exist and then concentrating on seeking out the visible evidence of its presence. A head that is bald is always a gift to sculptors, and it can be a most useful subject for the inexperienced to begin with, to become familiar with detecting the vital evidence of the skull. Such evidence is there to be found in all subjects, no matter how much hair they have, but it will differ from individual to individual. It is most likely to be discernible on the cranium, of course, but also on the forehead, the back of the head and behind the ears (particularly in a male subject), as well as in the cheekbones, the bridge of the nose and the teeth in the upper jaw. These are all fixed points that

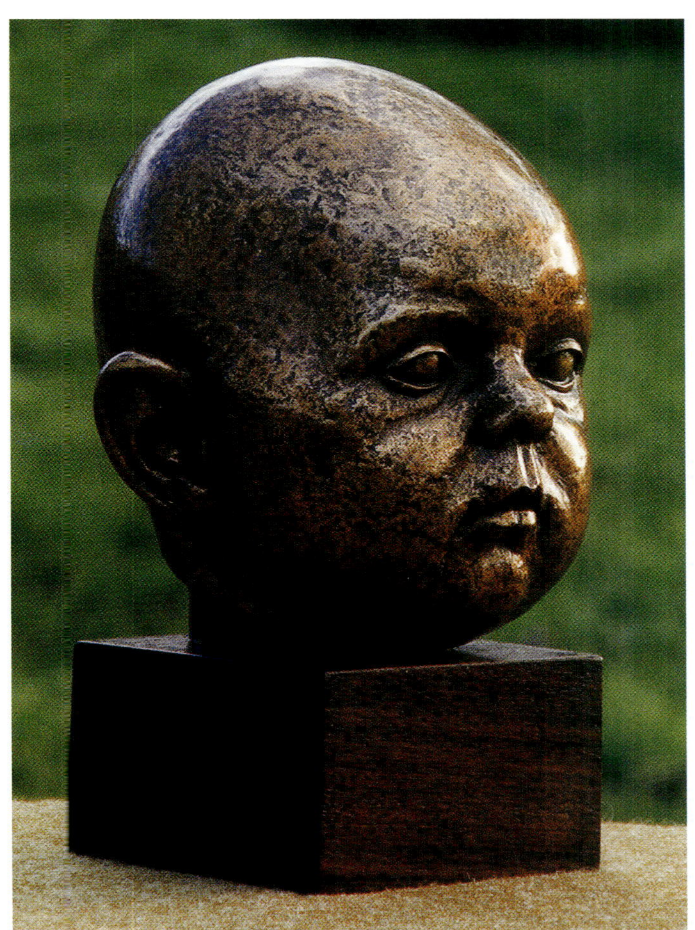

A Portrait of a Baby, *by Sally Arnup, bronze. (Private Collection)*

do not move as the subject becomes animated. The lips, eyes, cheeks, lower jaw and chin do alter as the subject moves and talks; encouraging the model to talk and move during a sitting, and watching the animation of the different parts, will give the sculptor the freedom to create an expressive head, based on accurate observation.

The disposition of the hair about the head is influenced to a large degree by the shape of the skull as well as by fashion, and can provide another welcome aid to an image. The features of the face, particularly the eyes, nose and lips, tend to be the focus for the beginner searching for a likeness, but without studying and stating the basic structure the likeness will be elusive. How does the eyeball fit in the socket and what is the evidence? What shape are the teeth under the lip, and how is the bony bridge of the nose constructed? What relationship does the ear have to the hole in the skull? These are questions that should lurk in the mind as the subject is investigated to make the portrait sculpture. The sculptor's personal skills of observation and modelling obviously affect the final portrait; such skills, whatever the level of expertise, will provide the personal filter of information that leads eventually to an individual statement and an interesting interpretation of reality.

Materials and Procedures

Clay

Clay is a moist tenacious earth that can be shaped and fashioned with comparative ease; it is the most common material in sculpture and will be found in nearly all sculptors' studios. It is employed in a myriad of uses as well as modelling, but more importantly here it is the modelling media most frequently used to make portrait sculpture of just the head, the head and the shoulders, or the whole figure. It is usually modelled as an intermediary to be cast in another material, such as plaster of Paris, concrete, resin, bronze and other metals, but in its purest form clay can be baked (fired) to become terracotta (literally, 'baked earth'). This process provides the most direct contact between the finished material, the sitter and the artist, and is unique in the tenets of sculpture: only baking the clay (firing) comes between the actual modelling process and the completed terracotta sculpture. Two French sculptors Jules Dalou and

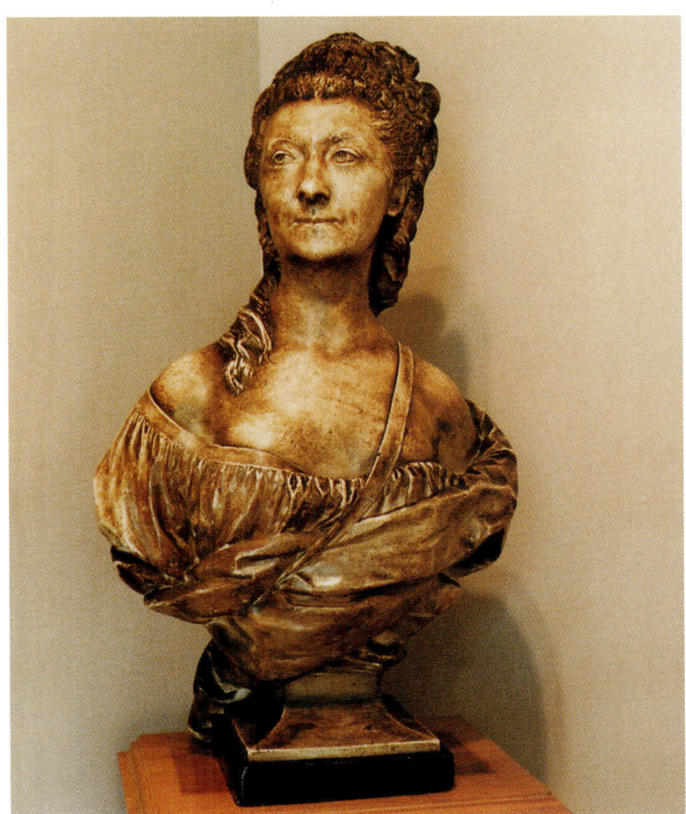

Madam His, *by Jean Antoine Houdon, the plaster master pattern, used by the marble carvers as the pattern for them to copy in the same way as a terracotta pattern. (Sterling and Francine Clark Collection, Williamstown, Mass., USA)*

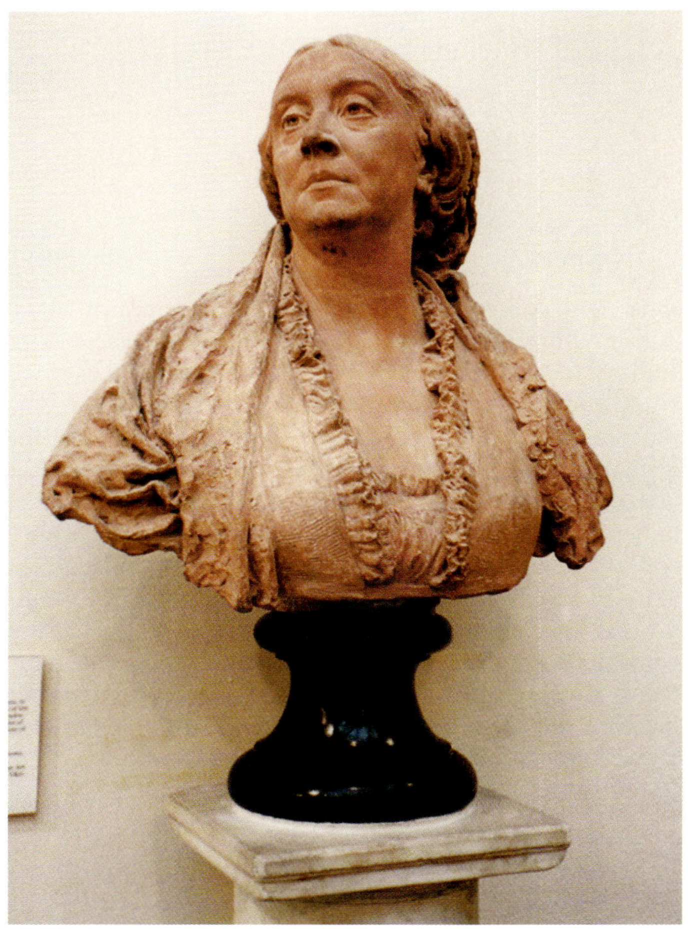

Eugenie Maria Wynne, *by Jules Dalou, a very fine example of terracotta portrait sculpture. (V&A Collection, London)*

Antoine Houdon are illustrated here, but many more such terracotta and plaster portrait heads from many cultures are to be found in most museums. Baking clay is one of man's oldest activities, featuring in almost everything made for domestic and spiritual needs, and terracotta is still a fascinating medium for sculpture.

The basic modelling procedure of kneading, pushing, pulling, adding and generally exploiting the malleability of the clay is common to all its uses, no matter what material the final sculpture incorporates. If the end result is planned to be terracotta, however, the clay must be clean, well consolidated and free from trapped air pockets and foreign bodies, which will corrupt the quality of the clay causing it to bake unevenly. Air pockets will expand and may cause an explosion; foreign bodies may do the same thing, or contaminate the pure clay by releasing chemicals as it heats up, which will affect the appearance of the finished sculpture. Although this might be seen as an enhancement, reflecting the mysteries of the firing processes, and the unexpected changes that can occur when clay is submitted to fire, clean and thorough preparation is recommended. To facilitate the baking procedure the clay image is made hollow, with as even a wall thickness as possible. This will allow an equal shrinkage of all parts of the image as the clay slowly dries ready for firing, and any residual moisture will be driven out during the slow baking process (see the illustration below).

When clay is used as an intermediary material it need not be so clean or so precisely prepared, but it should none the less be free from grit or the grog (ground ceramic) that comes in some proprietary ready-prepared clay. These addi-

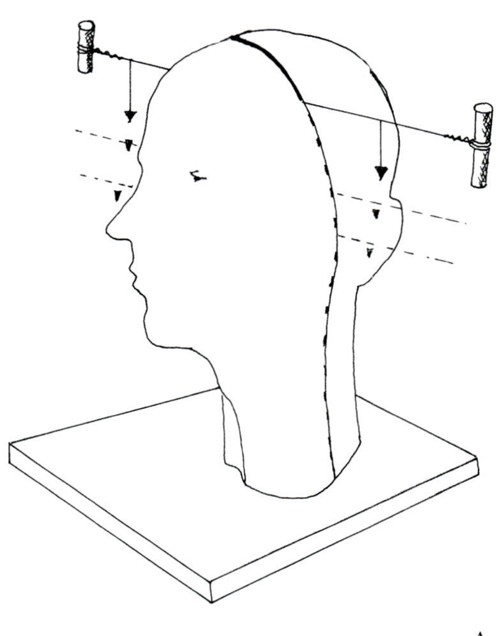

A

Cutting the clay head with a wire prior to hollowing.

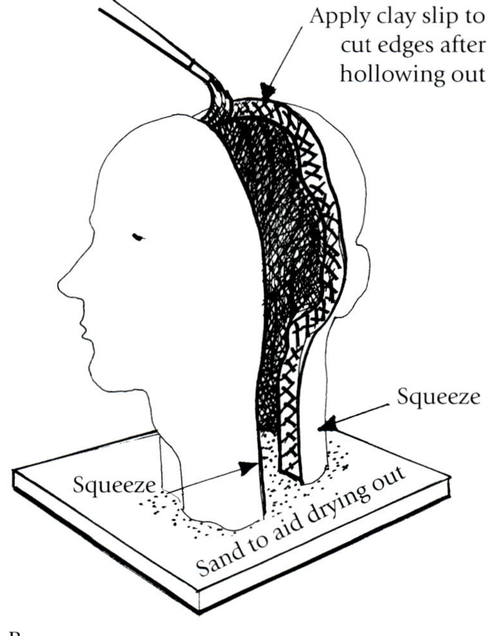

B

Applying clay slip to fix the two halves after hollowing out.

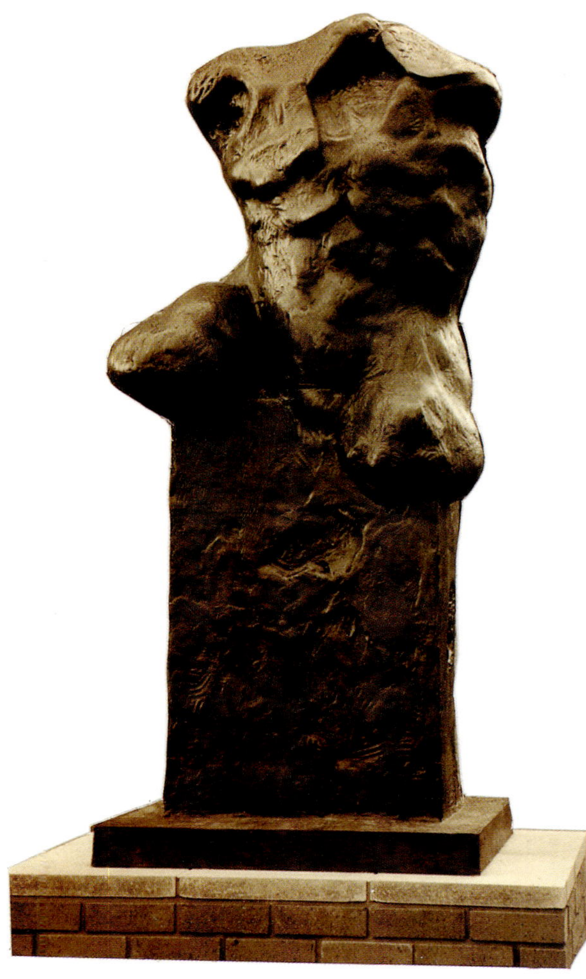

Torso, *by John Pappas, in bronze. (Detroit Private Collection, USA)*

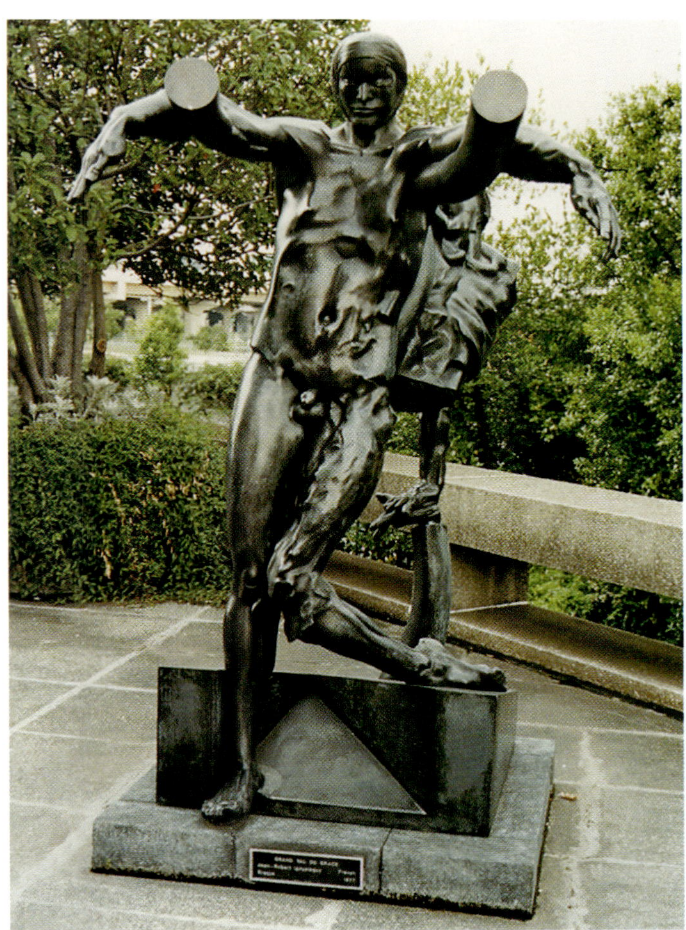

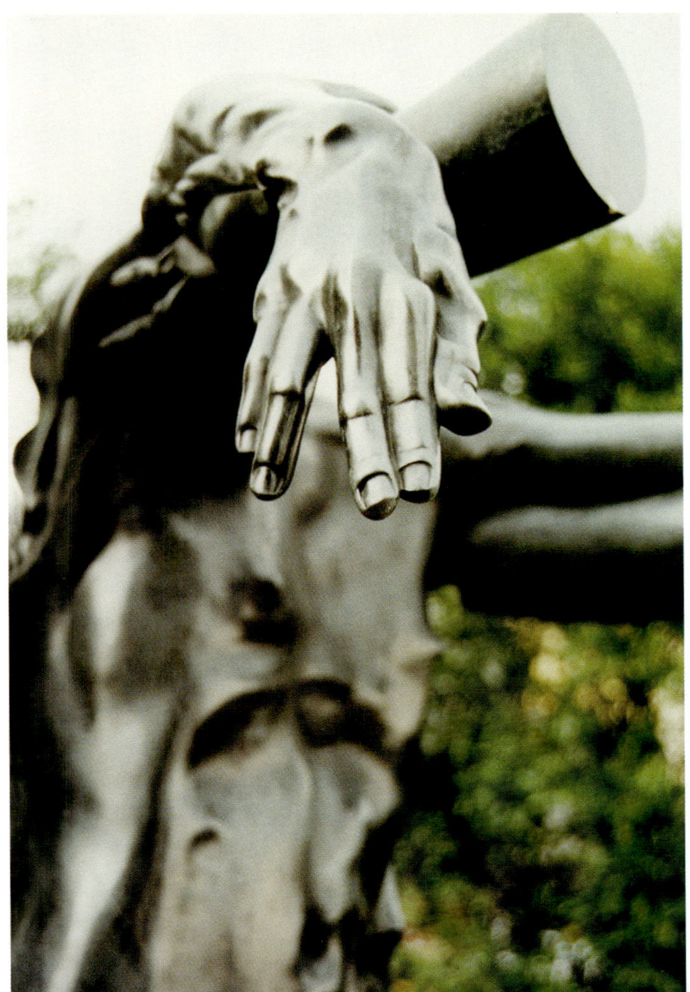

tions tend to inhibit some casting processes. It is always a pleasure to model with well-prepared clay and, as the basic modelling stuff is recyclable, care must be taken in its preparation. Any foreign bodies – bits of wire, splinters of wood and chips of plaster – must be removed. Such debris will inevitably get into the clay over time, especially when it is used over an armature and undergoes the complexities of casting. If it is left, it will inevitably appear on the surface of the sculpture being modelled and impede the visual perception of the work as it progresses; this can be very annoying, no matter how small the offending speck.

With every project, the act of modelling starts by pushing the clay into the basic shape to be achieved, whether the image is designed to be self-supporting or built up over a suitably supportive armature. Remember that this is an

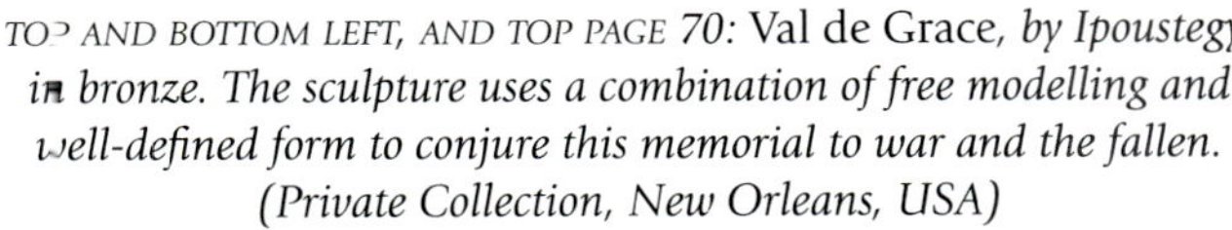

TOP AND BOTTOM LEFT, AND TOP PAGE 70: Val de Grace, *by Ipoustegy, in bronze. The sculpture uses a combination of free modelling and well-defined form to conjure this memorial to war and the fallen. (Private Collection, New Orleans, USA)*

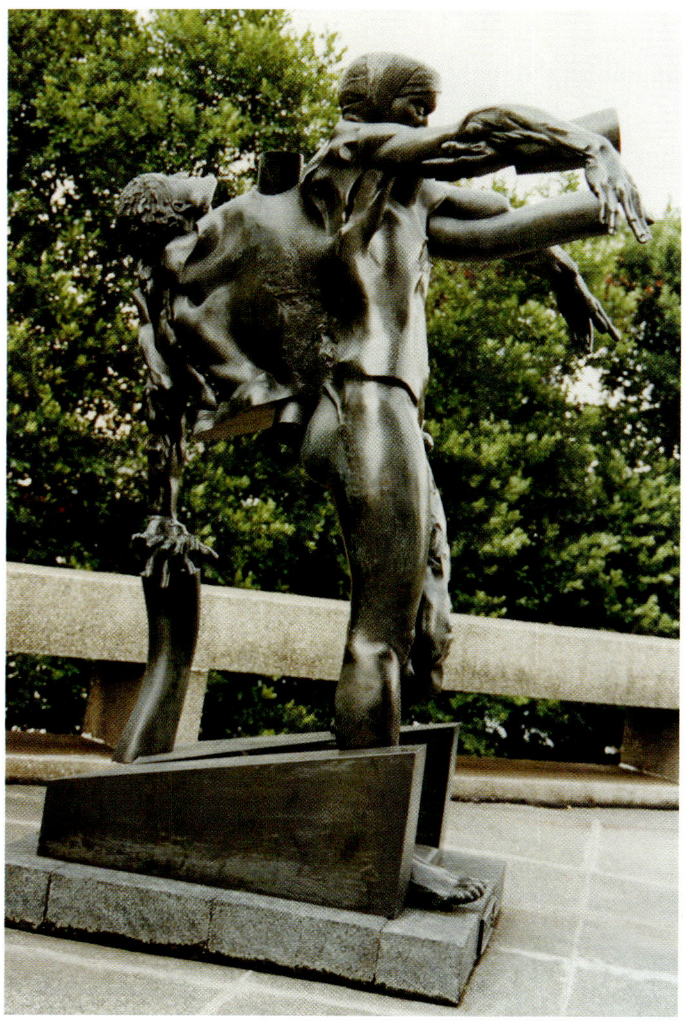

Val de Grace, *by Ipoustegy*

additive process and that the final volume of the sculpture will be determined by the last application of clay, which will also create the final surface. This surface is determined by the sculptor's personal preferences, and may have various finishes, from a roughly or freely handled (gestural) texture to a finely worked, smooth, tight effect. The sculptor will encounter a whole range of intermediary effects and textures that become available as the work is built up, according to the predominant use of the hands, of modelling tools, or a combination of both.

The initial blocking-out process usually accounts for the enjoyably free, sweeping applications of clay that will excite not only the artist but also any visitors at the studio. This period of élan is best followed by a period of consolidation – a moment of calm after the excitement of beginning the work, during which the mass needs to be considered relative to its compositional elements of balance and volume, plus the careful juxtaposition of forms and figures. Now is the time to decide if some clay needs to be removed or merely compacted. The dynamics of the composition must be considered. For instance, diagonals and spirals at an early stage in the build-up help to indicate movement and giving these features an upward dynamic imbues the sculpture with a living force. If this is done early on in the blocking out, that dynamic is likely to remain, even if it is modified as the sculpture progresses. It is much more difficult to achieve such vibrancy at a later stage. The importance of a good maquette is made even more clear at this stage, especially if the task at hand is a portrait of the whole figure.

This interval of deliberation is important because it leads to the drawing stage, when particular forms and features are stated in greater detail; this is the considered build -up to the final image, warts and all, and to its final volume. It also allows the clay already in place and built up to harden a little; the extent to which it is left to harden is a matter of preference, but the drawing stage is best carried out by placing layers of soft clay over slightly harder layers. Roll some fresh clay in your hands to get acquainted with its consistency and keep doing this until you find just the right feel relative to what you wish to draw. The resistance from the harder layer will give greater control over this drawing technique and the same principle applies to all successive layers of clay. If the final surface is to be fine and detailed, each layer will be similarly fine and getting finer, until the ultimate surface is arrived at and the job done.

There is real modelling pleasure to be had in using real (natural) clay that hardens as it dries on exposure to the air. Spraying or covering the clay with damp cloths can control the surface hardness to maintain a suitable modelling quality. Some sculptors like to leave the clay exposed for a longer period to let it get to 'leather hard'; in this condition, the surface can be refined by burnishing – rubbing the clay with a clean wooden spatula that almost polishes the surface. These niceties are down to personal choice, but decisions relating to them can only come from experience. Model some clay and then model some more clay and then model even more clay. Practice might or might not make perfect, but it will build confidence and lead to a greater knowledge of the chosen material.

Terracotta

The pleasures of working with real clay are particularly intense when modelling clay for terracotta, which can retain for ever evidence of the direct touch of the sculptor's hands. Fingerprints burned into the surface of the final baked clay are one obvious feature, but anything done to the clay image – textural modelling, cutting and scraping the surface, or burnishing it to a sublime finish – will all be preserved when the clay is fired and baked. It is possible to bake solid clay items, for example bricks, but the kind of clay that allows this has a coarse and open texture, and the baking process needs to be slow and very long, which leads to a particular heavy muscular form of sculpture. If finer pieces are to be successfully baked, they need to be made hollow, with as even a wall thickness as possible.

There are several ways to achieve hollow forms, the most ancient and direct of which is to model a solid shape, either over a simple support or not, but being sure to consolidate the clay so that no air pockets remain in the build-up. The clay is then allowed to harden until it is firm and unlikely to collapse; this will happen naturally and gradually as the image is modelled. At a stage just prior to completing the modelling, the mass is cut in half using a wire (see the illustration on page 70). The next task is to hollow out the two halves using suitable wire loop tools, trying to make a wall thickness of about half an inch (12mm) and as even as possible. Of course, the character of the modelling will determine how well this can be achieved; some variation in the thickness is inevitable and acceptable to a degree. It is essential to keep the cut edges of the clay as clean and accurate as possible as the form is being hollowed out, as these are the seams that will be glued together when the whole sculpture is being reassembled.

When the required thickness is achieved, the next task is to glue the two halves together using clay slip (a slurry of clay and water), making sure that the seam edges are firmly pushed together and modelled over. Final surface modelling can be carried out to finish the work.

The hollow form is then placed on a board sprinkled with dry sand or newspaper, which will allow movement as the clay shrinks on drying. The sculpture is ready to be baked (fired) only when it is thoroughly dry and the drying process needs to be very slow. Some sculptors cover the finished clay with newspaper to prevent complete exposure to the atmosphere, as this will cause the clay to dry too quickly and unevenly, making it liable to cracking. When the clay is completely dry it is ready to be baked (fired).

One alternative to modelling solid and then cutting to hollow out the shape is to model the clay over a substance that can remain in the clay, becoming a kind of core. This core needs be soft enough to compress as the clay shrinks and of a material that will burn at a temperature lower than that required to fire the clay. When the image is complete the whole assembly can be left to harden and dry and then baked. The core can be made of loosely packed paper (newsprint is the best) or fine straw held in shape with cotton or string; it simply needs to be easy to handle and have a low combustibility.

Other ancient methods for making hollow shapes include coiling and slab building; the terms are self-explanatory. Coiling is done by rolling or cutting clay into long strips, which are then coiled over each other to build a wall; slab building involves building up a structure using slabs rather than long lengths of clay. The volume and shape of the planned terracotta sculpture dictates to a large degree whether coiling or slab building is chosen. The rolling and cutting of the clay should be done on a clean porous surface such as a wooden board or a marble slab. As a cheaper alternative to marble, it is possible to cast a thick slab of plaster of any size, perhaps to fit a workbench. When it is thoroughly dry, the slab provides a good surface for processing the clay, and it can even be made with indentations that might help in creating the image.

The thickness of the clay wall will depend upon the size of the sculpture to be made. This will also determine the thickness of the rolled and cut slabs or lengths of clay. The shape of the object being made, whichever method is being used, can be adjusted as it is constructed, by cutting and squeezing the clay as it is laid one piece upon the other to build the hollow form. Practice is required to gain experience in judging the quality and strength of the clay as it dries, to enable complex shapes to be made. A sparing layer of clay slip is painted on the abutting surfaces of the strips, slabs or coils as they are assembled, helping to consolidate the wall as it is built. The clay can be blended and consolidated as it is applied, to make a homogenous clay wall and the surface modelled at the same time to achieve a particular character and detail, using the wide range of fingers and modelling tools.

Another fascinating technique for making hollow figures – also an ancient one – is that of press moulding, which involves pressing clay into a dry plaster mould to make elements that are subsequently stuck together using

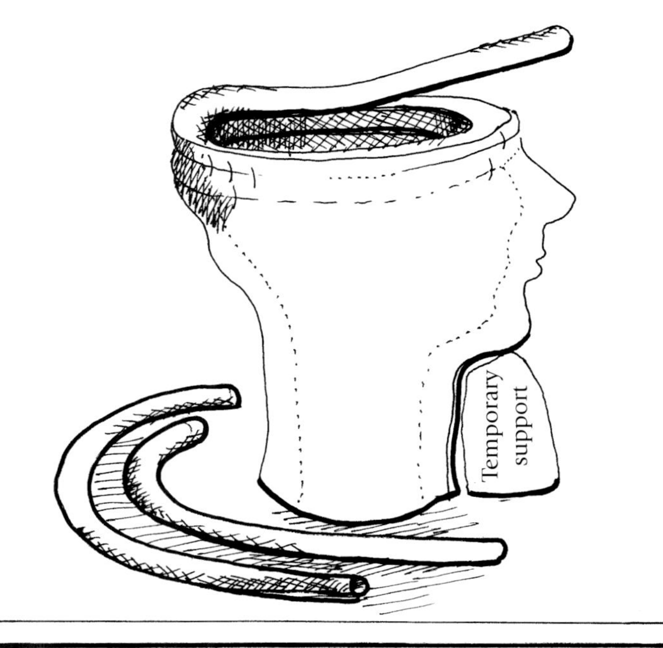

Coiling.

clay slip to make a figure. Even though this skill has been practised for centuries by all clay cultures, it is an advanced technique and one that will grow in sophistication after practice and experience of the moulding and casting processes.

Synthetic Clay

Synthetic clays are now widely available, sold by most sculpture suppliers, and offer a very different modelling experience from natural clay. They are made of various inert fillers mixed with plasticizers and some oils, and each proprietary make differs, so some research will be needed to find one that suits. The old oily plasticine familiar to most people from childhood was probably the first of such synthetic materials; it was useful, but it had a limited life and a tendency to harden too quickly. Unlike these (and real clay), the synthetic clays available today do not harden in the short term, as there is no moisture content to dry out. They are affected only by changing temperatures, being usually soft in a warm atmosphere and hard when it is cold. They can be left uncovered for long periods of time, permitting a sustained working time. (Indeed, I have left certain figures, both large and small, uncovered in the studio for up to five years without a problem; the only slight flaw is the build-up of dust.)

Because synthetic clay stays soft, it does not allow the 'soft clay over hard clay' interaction that can be carried out with real clay. Sculptors need to work out their own resolution to this, but therein lies another kind of modelling fun.

It is important to remember that there is a difference in the support structures required for synthetic clay and real clay; see pages 55–61, on armatures.

Plaster of Paris

Plaster of Paris is the other most commonly used modelling material. It is used to make moulds and castings, and has a myriad of other common studio uses. The basic material is made from gypsum, which, although ancient uses occur in almost every civilization, was first mined and marketed commercially at Montmartre, then just near Paris, hence the common name. The gypsum is mined in a solid crystalline form that is broken down and heated partially to dehydrate and de-crystallize before crushing with steel balls contained in large revolving cylinders. It is then further ground down to a fine powder. When this powder is mixed with water it re-crystallizes to form a solid. The re-crystallizing process generates exothermic heat almost equal to the heat employed in its manufacture as plaster and the resulting solid is as hard as the original gypsum. The powder needs to be stored in dry conditions, because it is hygroscopic and

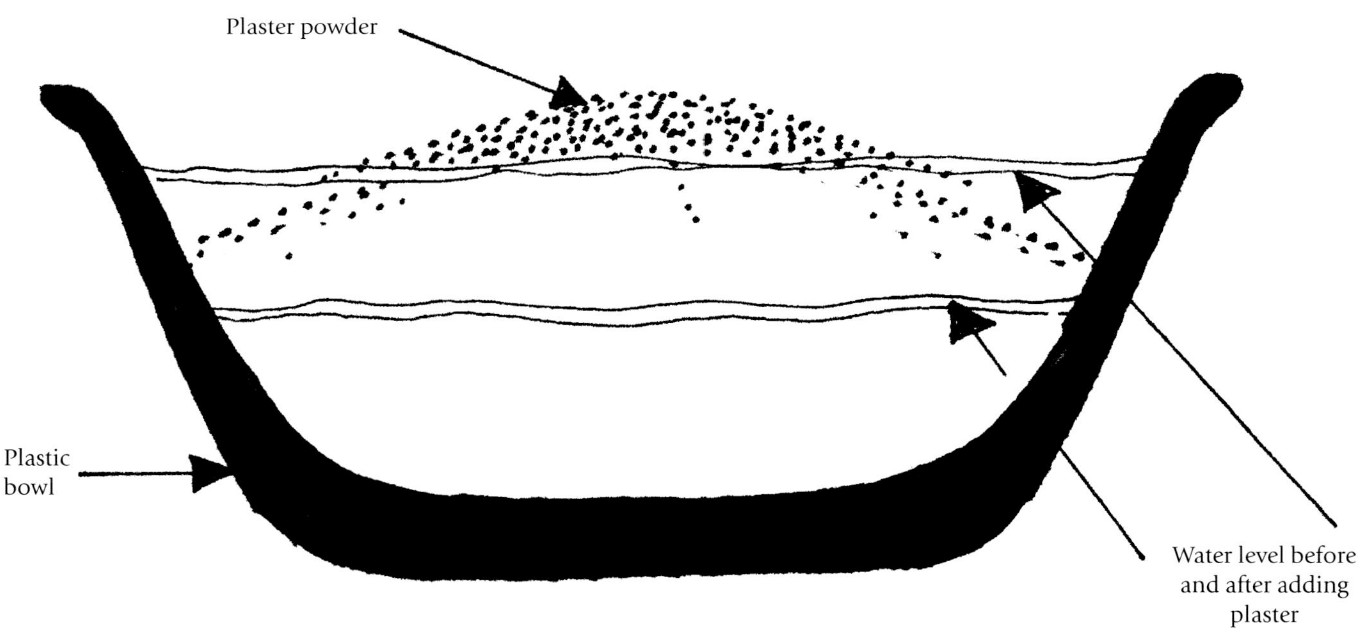

Mixing plaster of Paris.

any dampness will cause it to go hard; a large plastic dustbin with a well-fitting lid is ideal.

When it comes to mixing, the powder should first be stirred to aerate it and make it ready to be easily mixed with clean water in equal volumes. Aerating the powder does two things: it makes each particle free to dissolve in the water and in turn this prevents lumps of coagulated plaster forming that will spoil the quality of the mix, which should have the consistency of cream. Plastic or rubber mixing bowls and buckets of varying sizes are useful for mixing, and can be easily cleaned, preferably as each application is finished. If some plaster is left to harden in a bowl or bucket, which can happen in the haste to get work done, it can be cracked out by simply flexing the vessel. Powder should always be added to water; this can be done by measuring but after some experience it can be judged from the appearance of the powder in the water. As a rough guide, the measure of water should be about half the volume of mixed plaster required for the work in hand. Add the plaster to the water by letting it filter through the fingers and continue to add the powder until it is just covered by the water, with a small mound showing above the surface in the mixing vessel (see the illustration on page 74). Add one more handful at this point for good measure. Leave the mix to stand for a few seconds; some plasters can be left at this stage for ten to fifteen minutes, and it is important not to stir the mix as the powder is added. The plaster does not set and harden until it is thoroughly mixed and then will become a solid in about ten to twenty minutes.

The slow change from liquid to solid gives plaster of Paris its unique modelling and casting qualities. Experiment by making small samples to gain some experience of the action of the material before starting on a sculpture. Never mix too much; small amounts can be easily handled, while large quantities can be somewhat scary, and panic is not a good studio assistant.

Modelling Tools

Tools for Clay

The best tools for modelling clay are the hands, fingers and thumbs, but manufactured modelling tools are none the less an important part of a modelling sculptor's kit. These tools come in two types: spatula-shaped and loop tools. The first are usually made of wood, and the best are made of boxwood, although fruit woods provides a good second best. The gracefully curved spatula shape preferred by most sculptors provides a useful means of applying clay to a surface and of burnishing it. The loop tools are made of loops of wire firmly attached to a shaped handle, often with a loop at each end of the handle.

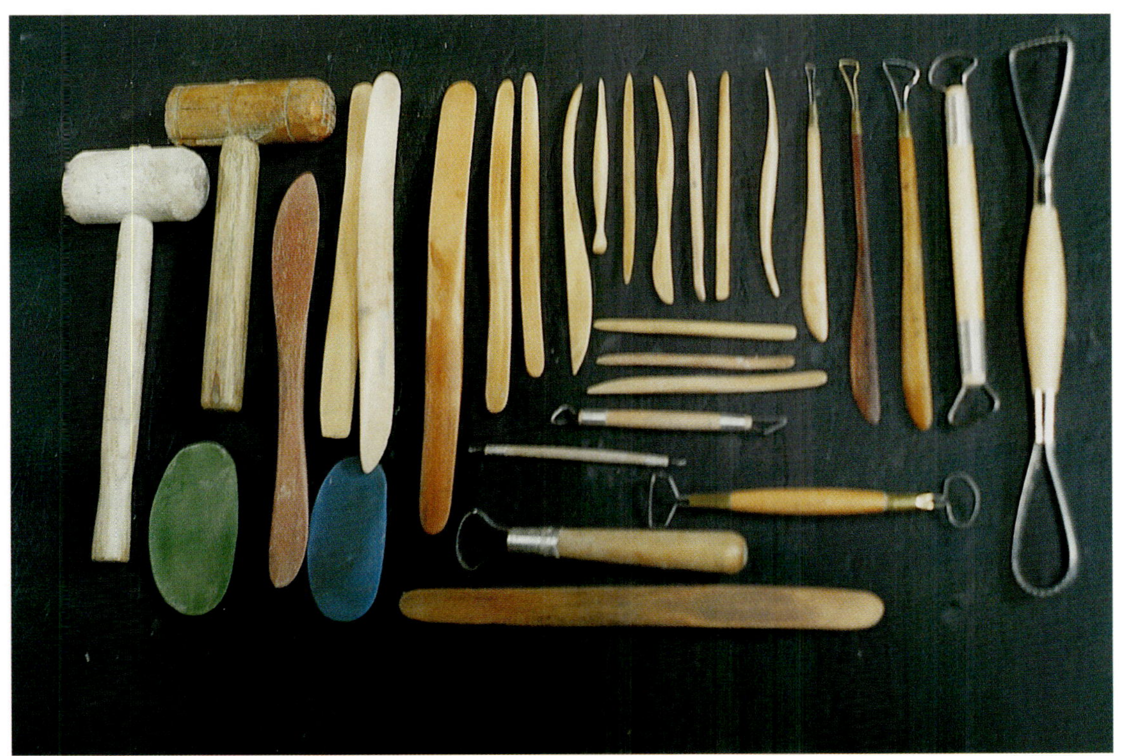

Mallets and boxwood spatulas of various shapes and sizes.

Some of the finest manufactured tools come from Italy, which exports very sophisticated shaped tools of both types that have evolved over centuries and come in a variety of shapes and sizes. The average art supplier sells a range of tools that are poor in shape and in quality of material; some are even made of cheap plastic. These are best avoided, but if there is no alternative it is possible to modify them, polishing with a very fine wire wool and trying to make them fit comfortably in the hand. It is also possible to make modelling tools from scratch. Use the best box or fruit wood, study the shape of old implements, and make tools of various kinds that are a pleasure to handle.

The right tools only come to hand over time. Good tools are not cheap and wooden tools, which are the best for working clay, should be treated with care. They should not be washed, but any dry and hardened clay should be carefully scraped from the surface. This should be followed by polishing with a very fine steel wool and then an application of a little thin lubrication oil.

Wire loop tools are used to scoop out clay, leaving marks according to the shape of the loop; these have evolved over time to help deal with specific shapes. Some loops, which are used to aid the actual modelling technique, mostly for scraping a surface, are often given a serrated edge or are wrapped around with fine wire. The scraping leaves a kind of crosshatching, a useful texture that helps to clarify the form. The crosshatching breaks up the play of light over a form, showing up any discrepancies to be modified.

Tools for Plaster of Paris

The tools required to model plaster of Paris have evolved in large part from some of the tools used to work stone. They are metal and take the form of steel spatulas, rasps and rifflers, sharp knives and chisels. They are of course employed on other materials that need to be scraped, cut, rasped and sanded, chiselled and carved; unlike wooden tools that are practically useless for working plaster and are therefore kept exclusively for modelling soft and pliable substance.

Hands are again the most useful basic modelling tool and are used to apply large quantities of mixed plaster in building up the sculpture, over a properly designed and manufactured armature. The hands will also detect the gradual thickening of the plaster mix, which allows the build-up and a certain degree of fast modelling. It is wise to protect hands with a suitable barrier cream treatment to prevent dehydration of the skin and avoid possible infection. In some extreme cases, heavy-duty latex gloves might be a better option.

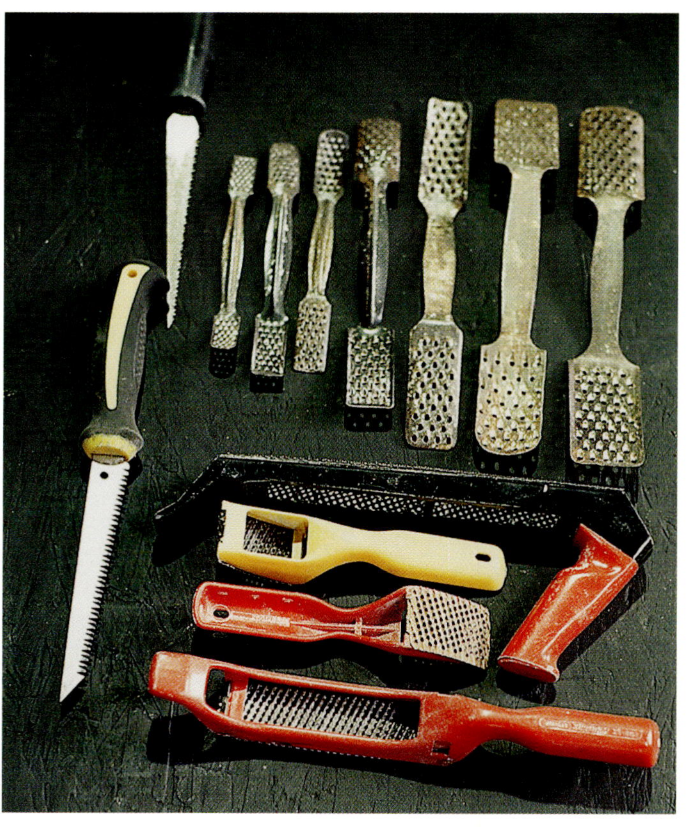

Plaster rasps of various kinds, sizes and shapes.

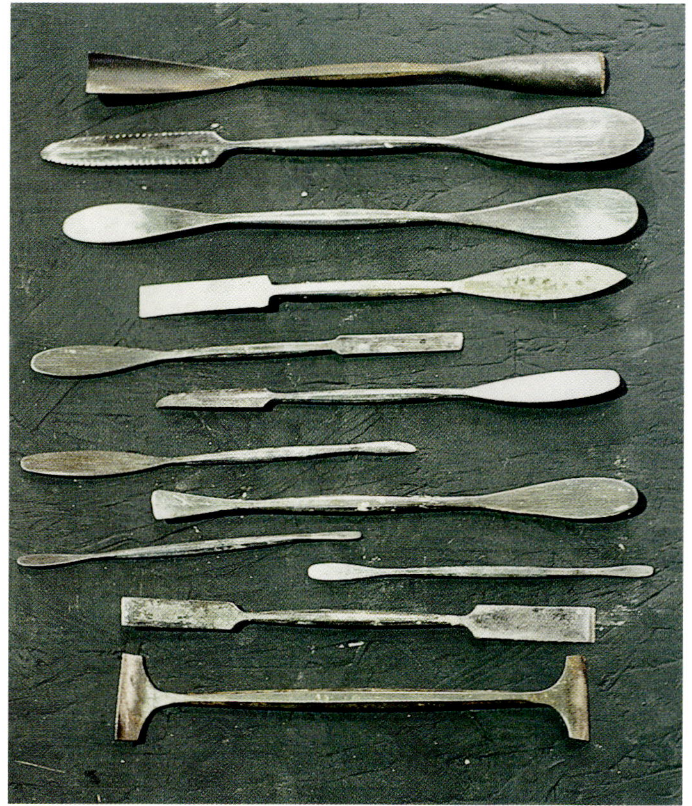

A selection of steel spatulas.

Steel spatulas are used to apply the plaster in a more controlled manner, usually working with a mix of plaster in a small rubber or plastic bowl. The size of spatula used depends on the size of the work or the nature of the detail being modelled. Wash the spatula as you finish the mix if this is feasible, and certainly scrape off any plaster left to harden before using it again on another mix, as new plaster will quickly build up on the old residue and make the tool almost useless.

Rasps and rifflers (smaller, finer-toothed versions of rasps) are employed on a hardened plaster surface to draw form and render a fine surface; this can be done on both fresh and old dry plaster. When tools are used on fresh or damp plaster, the teeth will clog up quite quickly so a wire brush is essential to clean this off regularly while work is in progress. Plaster rasps are made especially for working plaster, and are rather like a domestic cheese grater, from which they have evolved. The grated material passes through holes in the rasp, making it possible to rasp fresh plaster more easily and for longer periods. The wire brush will be needed on these too, as there will eventually be a build-up of plaster residue. A modern tool called a surform is a very sharp version of the cheese grater, designed originally for use on wood and plastic materials. They are available in various shapes and sizes and are extremely useful for working plaster of Paris.

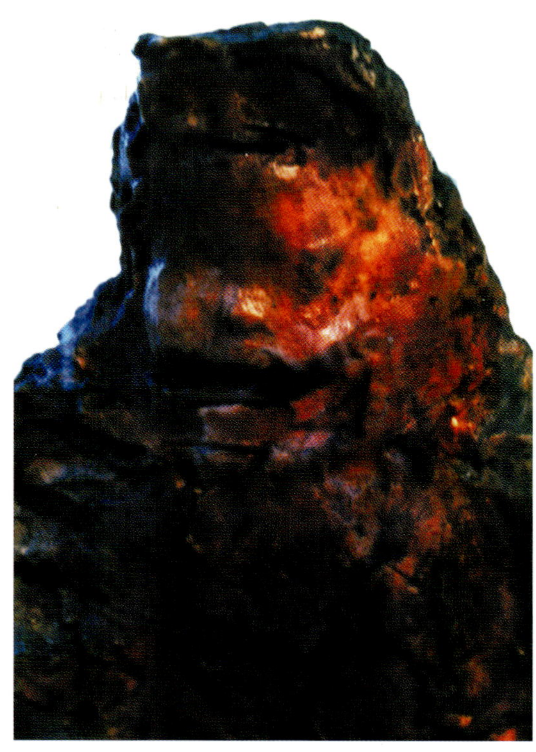

Portrait of a child, by Medard Rosso, in wax over plaster. A freely modelled, subtle impression of a sleeping child, using wax to explore the melding nature of the material.

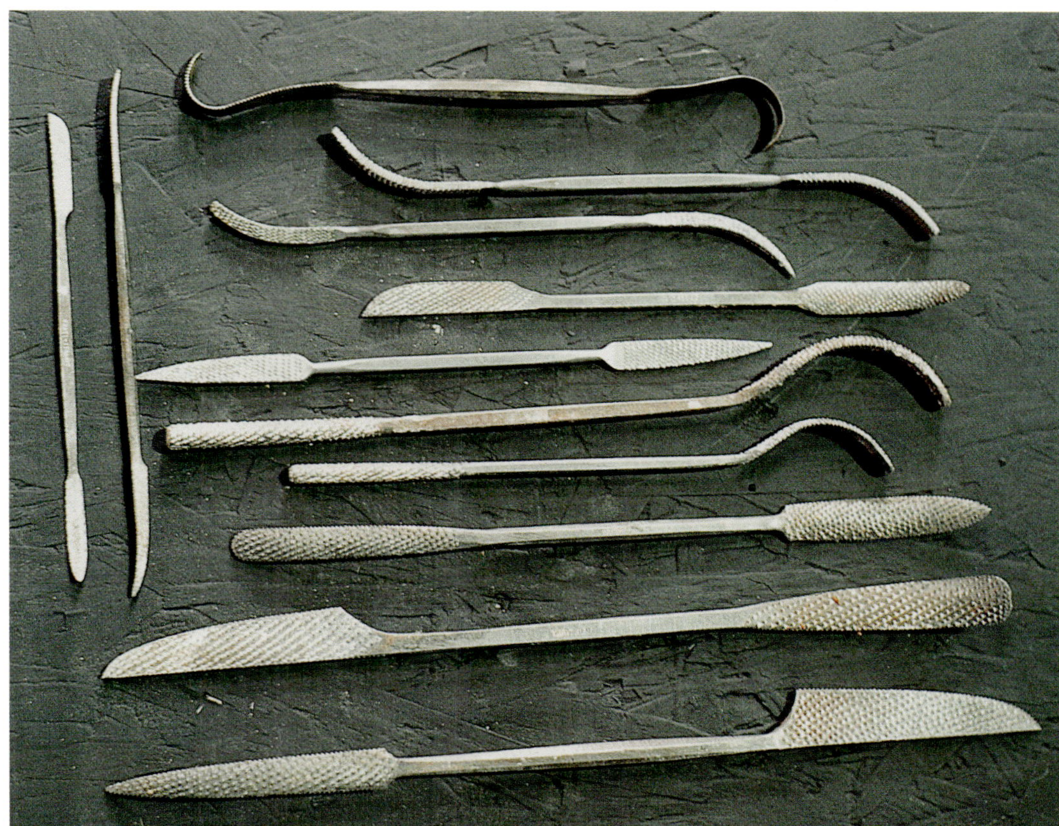

Small rasps and rifflers.

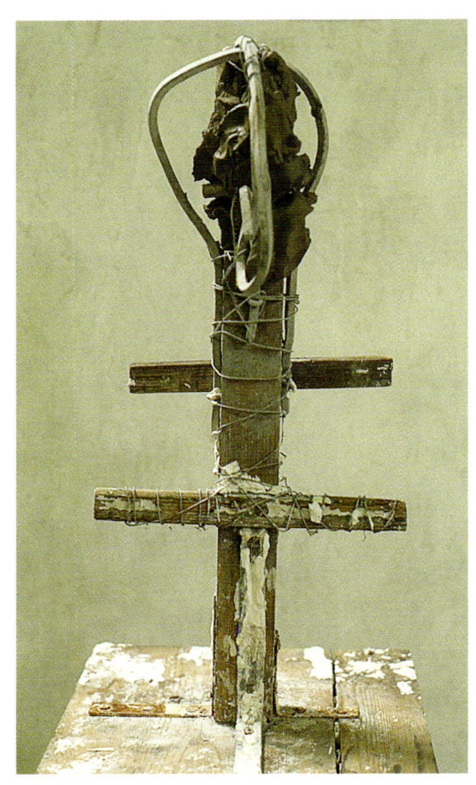

THIS PAGE AND THE NEXT: *Anthony Hawken showing stages in the modelling of a portrait head, from head peg to final clay.*

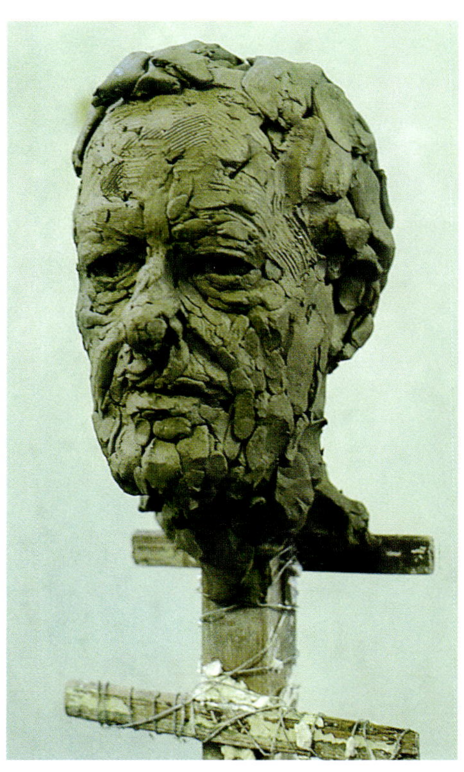

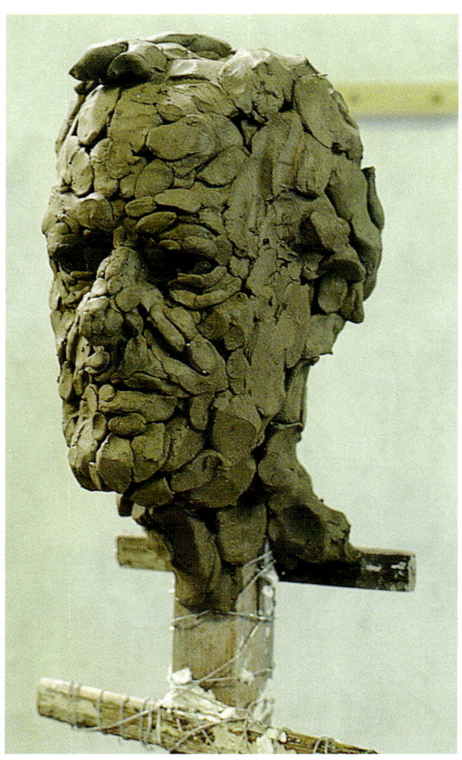

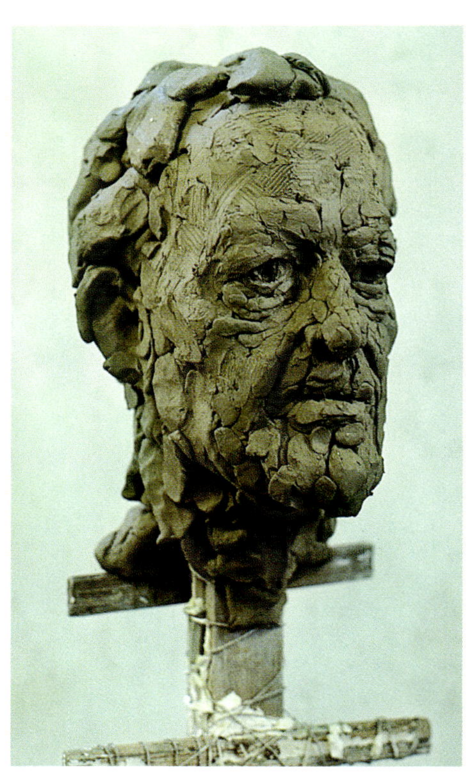

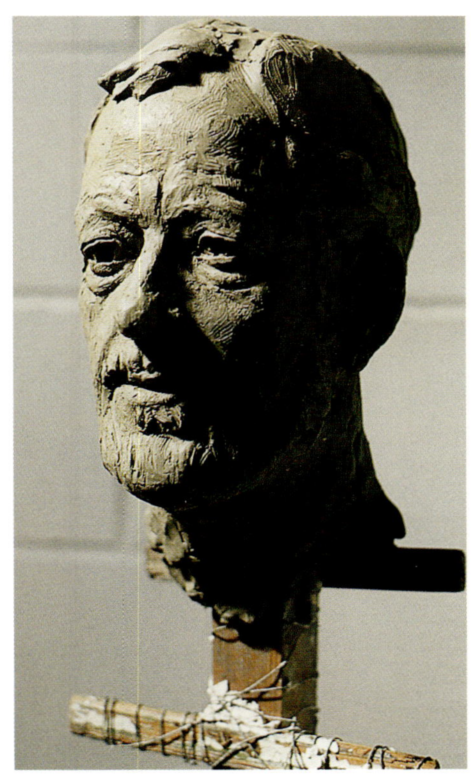

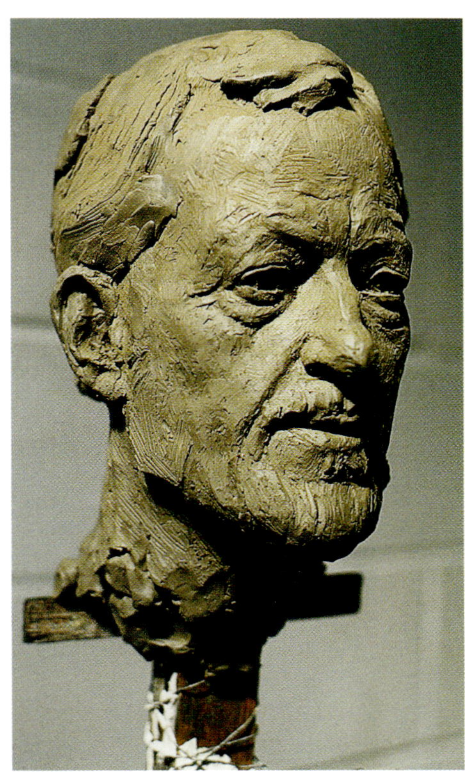

Chisels, knives and other cutting tools have obvious uses, and are generally available in a good working studio.

It is good practice to clean tools at the end of a working session, to keep them sharp and give them a longer life. A very thin application of oil will help but too much is not a good idea. Tools that are well cared for develop a shape and character that make them a pleasure to use. It can be a sad moment when a favourite implement comes to the end of its working life and a new one has to be broken in. It is a good idea to collect old quality tools whenever they crop up, as they can be a joy to handle from the first time you pick them up.

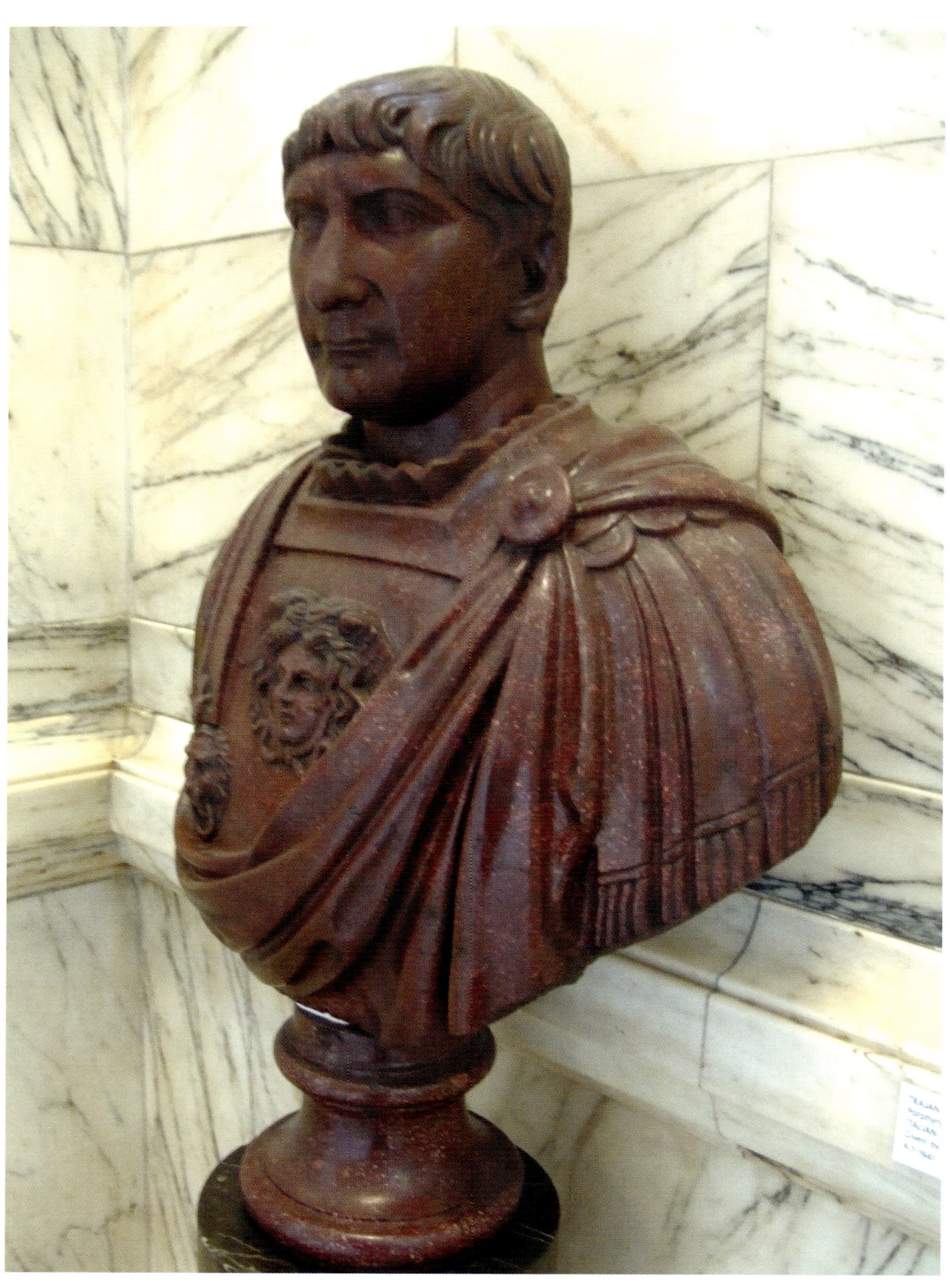

Roman Emperor Trajan in a portrait carved from porhyr, a stone as hard as granite, demanding a broad treatment.

5

Carving the Head

Procedures

It is very unusual to carve a portrait directly from the sitter. Flying chips of stone, marble or wood make life very uncomfortable for the model and, although it is not impossible, it is not common practice. Until very recent times, it was usual in carved portrait sculpture to make a very accurate life-size modelled study of the sitter, often using terracotta because of the directness afforded by this kind of modelling. This time-honoured practice provided a pattern for the marble or stone carver to copy.

The Working Model

Making a working model is still the sensible way to work a carved portrait sculpture. A modelled portrait study of the subject, which is to be copied or interpreted in marble, wood or stone, provides a static readily available reference from which to carve. Whether the sculptor intends to carve the sculpture personally and keep the possibility of modifying the image as work progresses, or plans to engage the services of a professional carver, who will make an accurate copy of the working model, this pattern will prove to be invaluable. As a result, the better it is, the better the carver will be served.

The practice of making a life cast – a casting taken from the living or dead human body – to provide a pattern from which artisans could work to produce a portrait has been evident in all European cultures. It is an expediency that suits a particular need, especially funereal. The use of a life or death mask casting is not easily identifiable in the best of sculptured portraits because of the personal interpretation of the subject's features by the sculptor or artisan, according to the materials used for their carving skills.

During the Roman Empire, portrait working models were prepared by whatever means, cast from the human countenance or modelled, and copies of these patterns were distributed throughout the Empire for local carvers and bronze

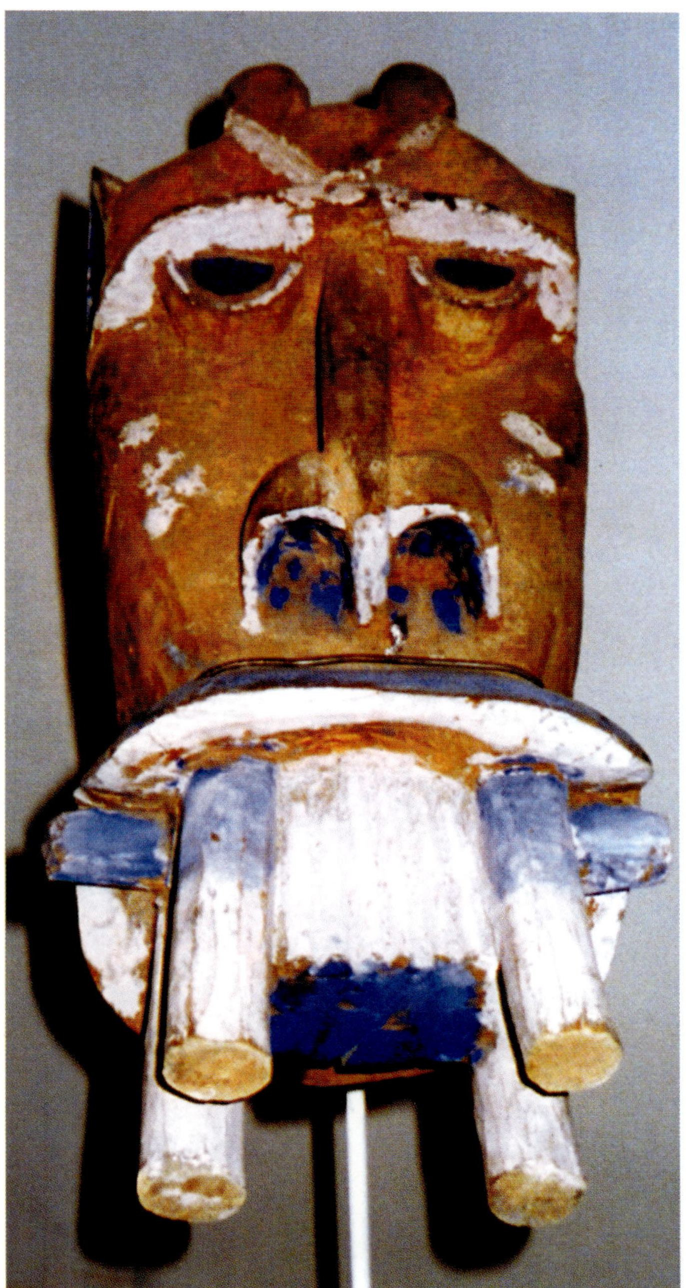

African mask, polychrome woodcarving. (Private collection)

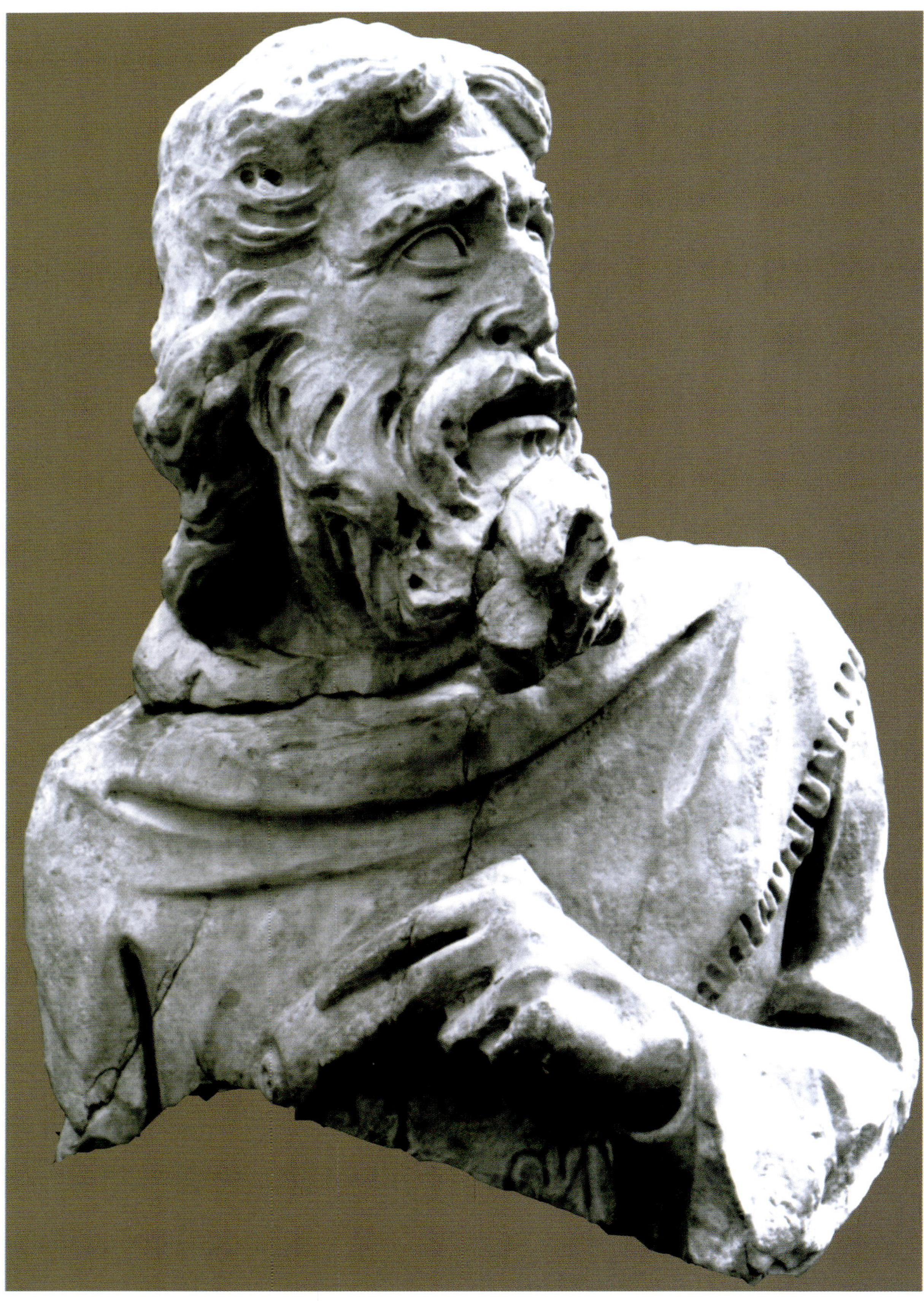

Head of Habbakuk, *by Giovanni Pisano. This carving is as close to free modelling with clay as it is possible to get. A powerful use of light and shade has conjured a strong character from the marble. (V&A, London)*

casters to copy. The range of differing but recognizable images of any Emperor based on the first working model is considerable, because interpretation was left to the local artisan to make of it what he could. The influence is tribal and geographical according to the part of the Empire where the representation of the Emperor was being made, and how far it was removed from the original working model. This accounts for the many variations on the likeness of many of the important personages of the Roman Empire, including Julius Caesar. It is a recognized fact that one of the great Roman contributions to world sculpture is the art of sculptured portraiture. Many fine portrait sculptures can be seen in museum collections in the western world, including many examples of the interpretation of the head into sculpture. This practice of interpretation is probably more easily achieved when the original subject has already been through many hands and therefore any number of filters.

Direct Carving

The complete opposite carving technique is referred to as direct carving. This requires not only an active imagination but also a strong personal vocabulary of form if it is to be successful, because it is the process of visualizing an image in the block and then carving directly into the marble, wood or stone to expose that image. Michelangelo apparently believed that the image existed in the block and simply needed to be revealed by removing the surplus stone. The shape of the block of stone or bulk of timber inspires the artist who, in the truest sense of carving direct, makes no intermediary studies but tackles the block directly, to release what is envisaged to be trapped inside.

The decision to dive straight into the carving is a brave one, requiring confidence and tenacity and these characteristics should be pursued as much as possible to retain the freshness and spontaneity that are offered by carving directly. The confidence necessary to tackle this kind of carving can be gained by making many drawings rather than maquettes of what is perceived to be in the block before taking up the tools, trying to fix the nature of the task in the mind. Repeated drawing should help to identify the main features and characteristics of the image so that, when the carving begins, the quickest route to the sculpture can be taken. In this way, the sculptor avoids the tedious process of the gradual reduction or whittling away of the block of stone or wood. This sort of plodding activity – repeated cutting of the image over and over again, gradually nibbling the material away until the final image is achieved – is one of the drawbacks associated with carving of any kind. It is a way of working that makes it difficult for the artist to keep the image fresh and dynamic in his or her mind. Too often, the final effect will be simply a tired reflection of the originally perceived form; as the volume is gradually reduced, the sculpture can lose the excitement and spontaneity that give it its life.

Studying the work of Michelangelo, who produced some of the finest examples of sculptures of their kind, offers some of the best lessons in carving with economy and control. He would give himself all the information he could, making drawings and small maquettes of the planned image, which helped to locate the image in the marble, and making close studies of the block of marble he proposed to use. He did this partly to ensure that the marble delivered to his studio was indeed the same block he had ordered from the quarry, but it also meant that he really knew and understood the block, with all its natural foibles and could tell where the image lay within it. He then would proceed to carve directly to reveal the image. As features of the sculpture were revealed, he made detailed research into the anatomy of the figure, so that he could resolve parts in greater detail. Sometimes, for example, he would take a knee to a smooth, polished finish, while leaving material around it almost untouched. This enabled him to carve the image just once, seeming to peel back the marble to reveal the subject. In the logistical development of the carving, he was able to see the effect of different surfaces to be exploited as he worked. It also gave him the possibility of altering a gesture if he needed to, having retained enough marble to make the change; indeed, there is evidence that he moved an arm from the front to the back of one figure. The sculptures often referred to as 'the unfinished marbles' illustrate this technique quite clearly. Unfortunately the effect of high finish and rough stone that was so important in his iconography has been imitated ever since, such that it has become something of an affectation. In the case of Michelangelo, those sculptures were as finished as he needed than to be. His main concern was the human figure as narrative sculpture and he achieved this in all his carving, while retaining the excitement of carving marble.

Materials

Stone

The nature of the carving material should have some bearing on the kind of form and detail to be expressed. Although it is possible to carve exquisite detail in both stones and wood, and such skills should be carefully practised, it is much more telling to resolve the image according to the nature of the chosen material. Granite is an extreme example that illustrates an important point. Carving a head in granite is more

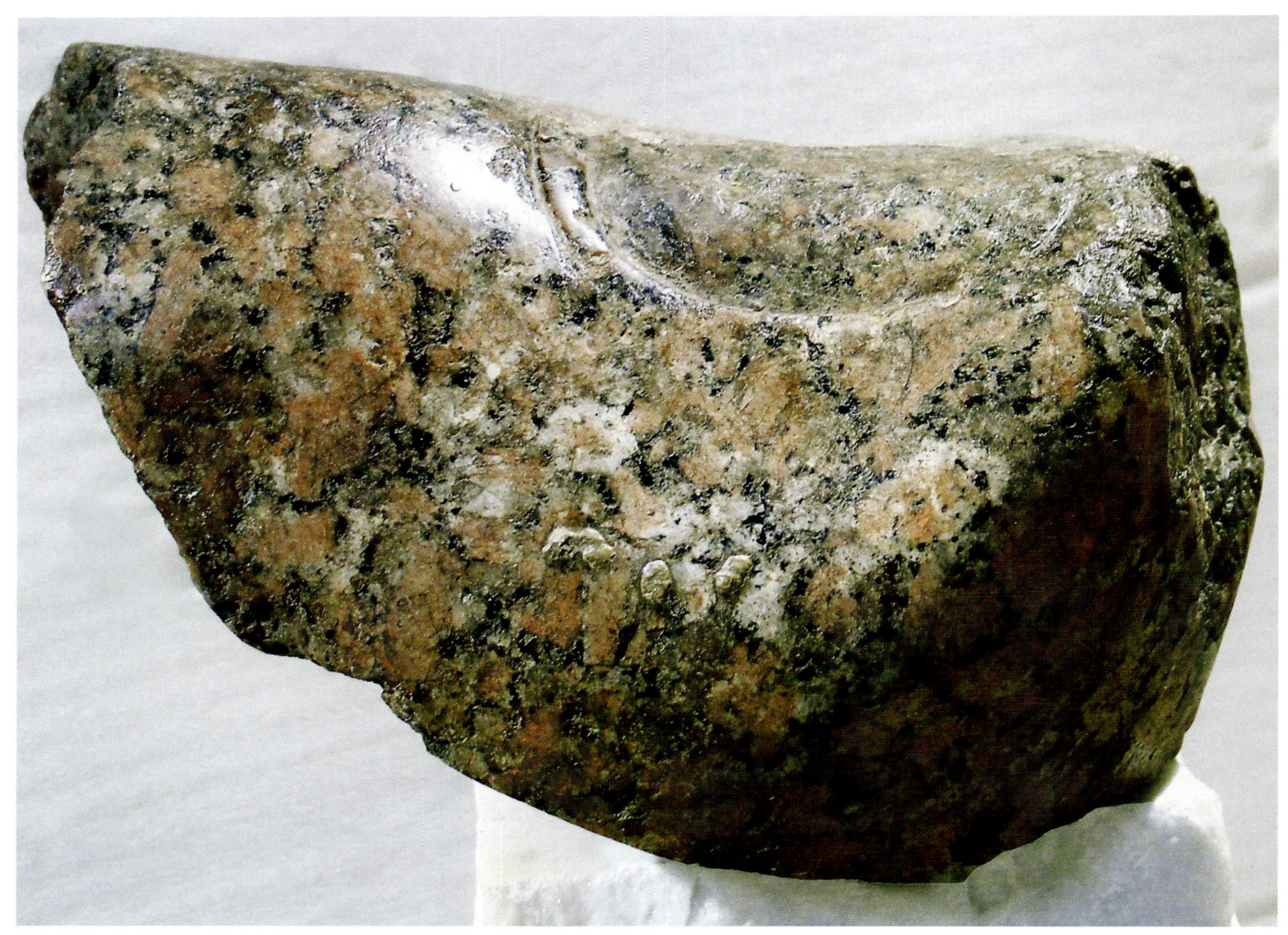

Granite Toe, *Ancient Egypt. A bold work that is typical of granite carving.*

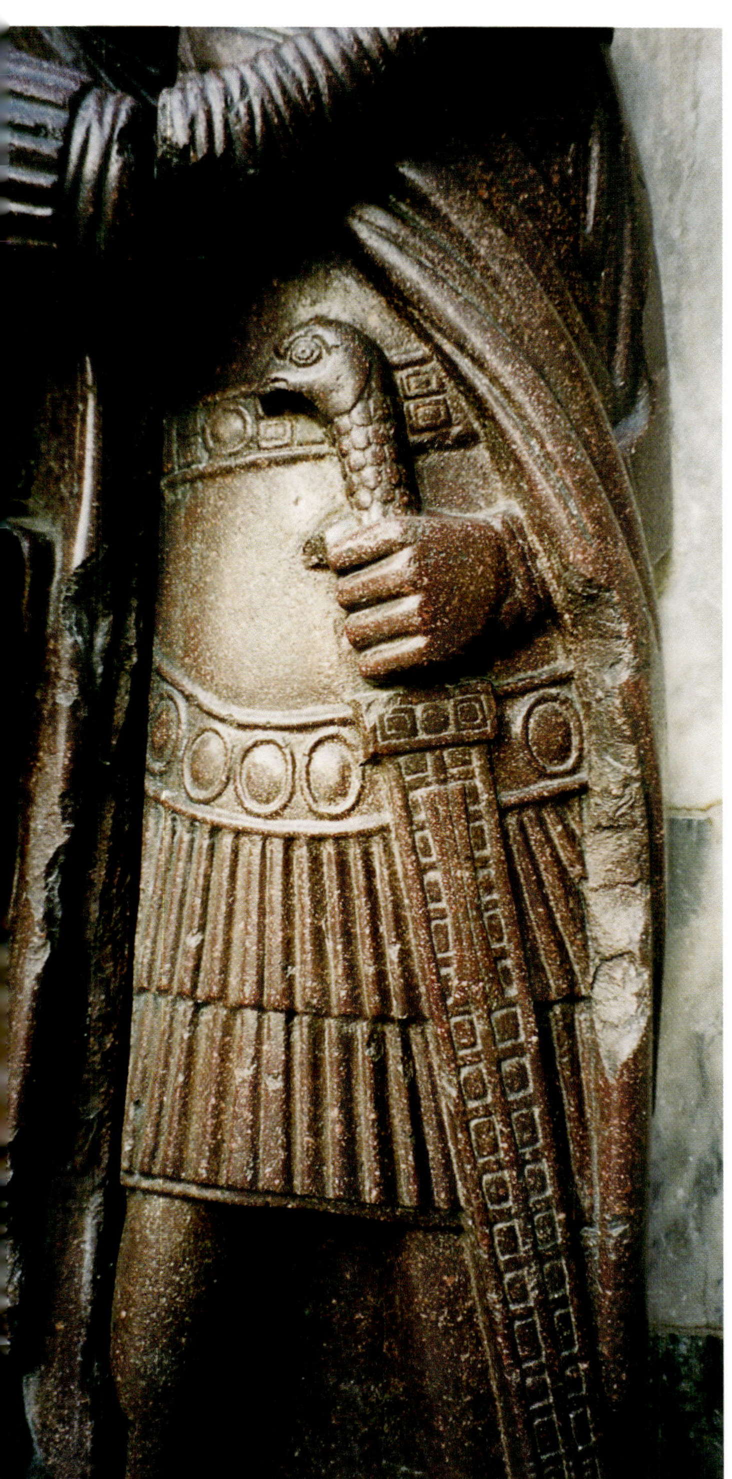

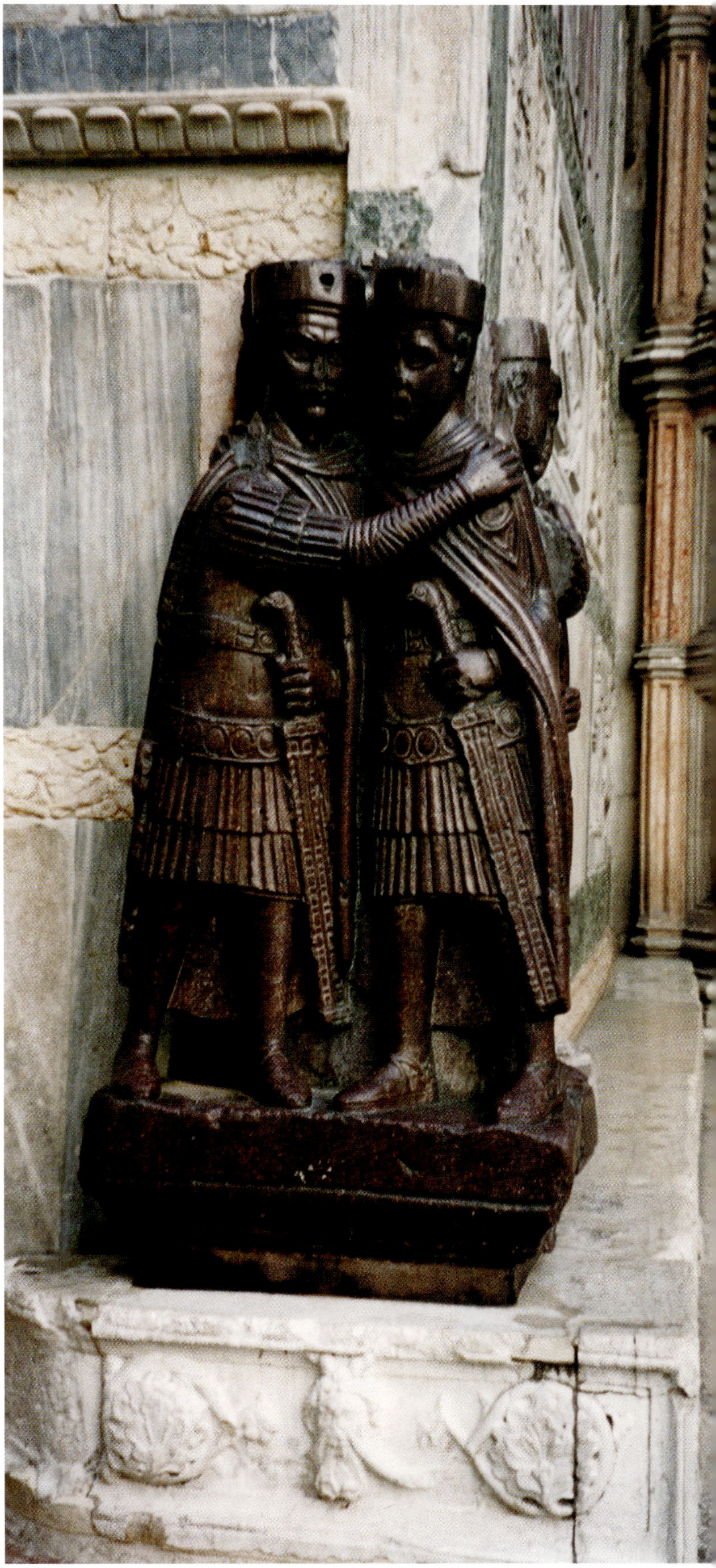

ABOVE LEFT AND RIGHT: The Tetrachs, *granite. (Venice)*

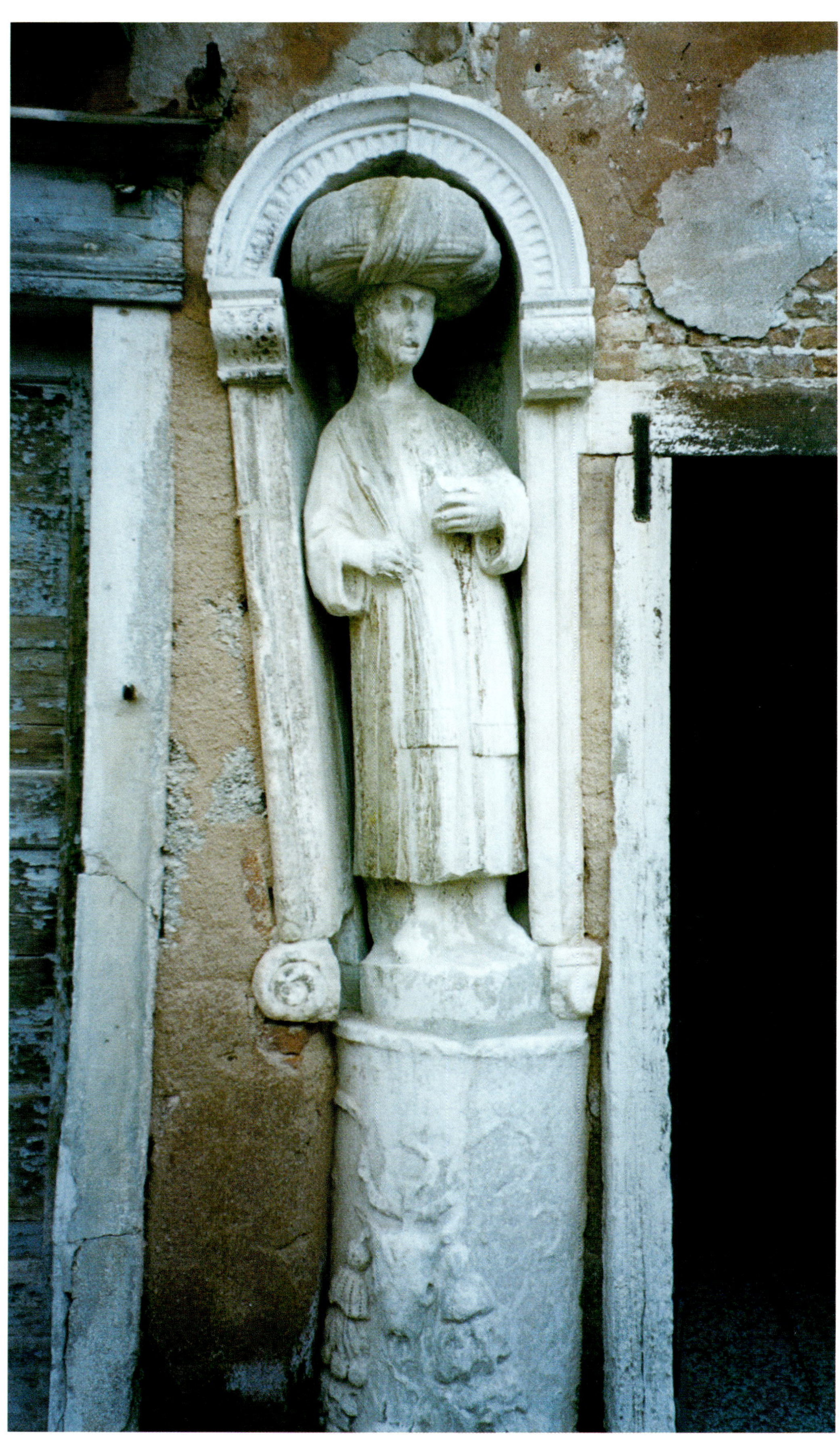

LEFT: Eroded limestone carving of a merchant at Venice, Italy.

demanding than making a carving using, for example, lime wood, the favourite material of most woodcarvers. Granite is one of the hardest of all stones, while lime wood is the softest, most crisp of woods to carve. Granite is not only very difficult and hard to work but, being a very dense material, it is also quite brittle, making it nearly impossible to make fine detail except in relief. Its very good compressive strength is useful for construction, but it can also lead to sculptures that are too bulky and sometimes ponderous. Slender limbs and delicate features are not possible in granite so, clearly, this material presents a difficult challenge to the creative thinking of the sculptor. Many sculptors do love to take up that challenge, and will try it at some time in their career; some even become devotees to the stone, despite its reputation for being a material that often hits back – granite chips that fly off during carving are sharp and can easily draw blood.

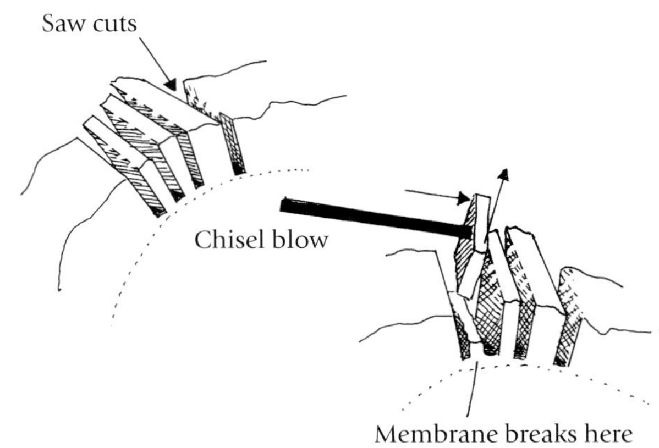

Cutting into the stone block to facilitate removing waste quickly.

Wood

In comparison, carving wood gives the impression of being quite a simple art; most boys have tried to whittle wood at some time, needing just a sharp tool, time and patience. Using the same sharp tool it is relatively easy to modify a driftwood find, for instance, but taking a log, visualizing the image within, and bringing it to light is a more sophisticated affair. Fine-grained lime wood has long been seen as the most friendly of timbers to carve; having no coarse fibre, it allows the sculptor to make fine detail. Other fruit woods are usually a little more coarse, but they can be satisfying to carve too.

Timber that has a long, coarse, fibrous structure, such as oak, offers greater resistance to carving; cutting across its grain requires very sharp tools and care in the direction of the cut. This sort of wood can be fashioned into large and powerful images, with the quality of the grain exploited fully. In the past, such timbers were coated with a gesso mix (a kind of plaster) filling the grain to make a smoother surface finish; the sculpture could then be treated in many different ways. Some cultures, particularly Spanish, favoured elaborately painted and decorated woodcarving, particularly to make evocative and highly emotional images of religious subjects. In other cultures, notably those of tribal Africa, the carvers utilized the inherent colour and quality of the timber, which was sometimes endowed with special spiritual qualities.

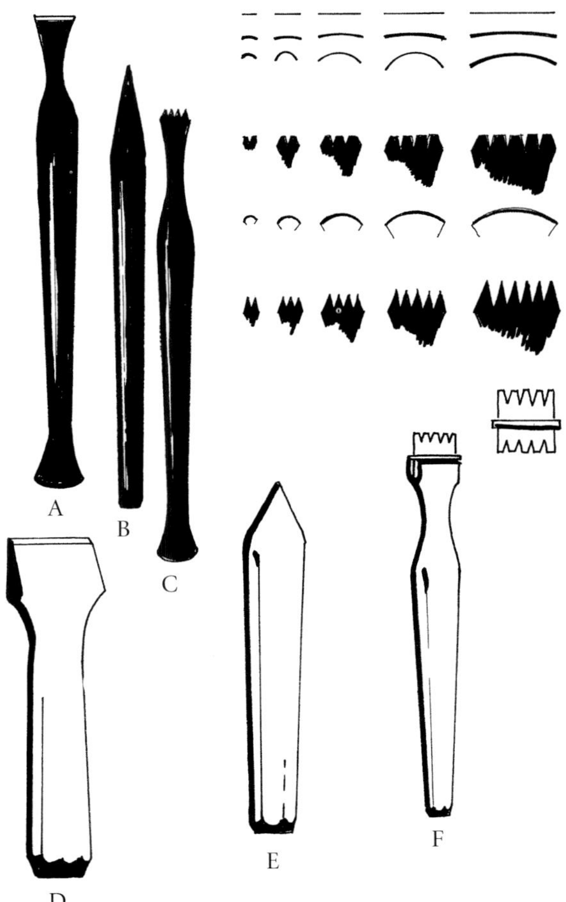

Carving tool profiles.

Cutting Away Waste Material

All the materials used have in common the subtractive process, and sculpture in any material is best accomplished if the image is quickly identified in the block and equally

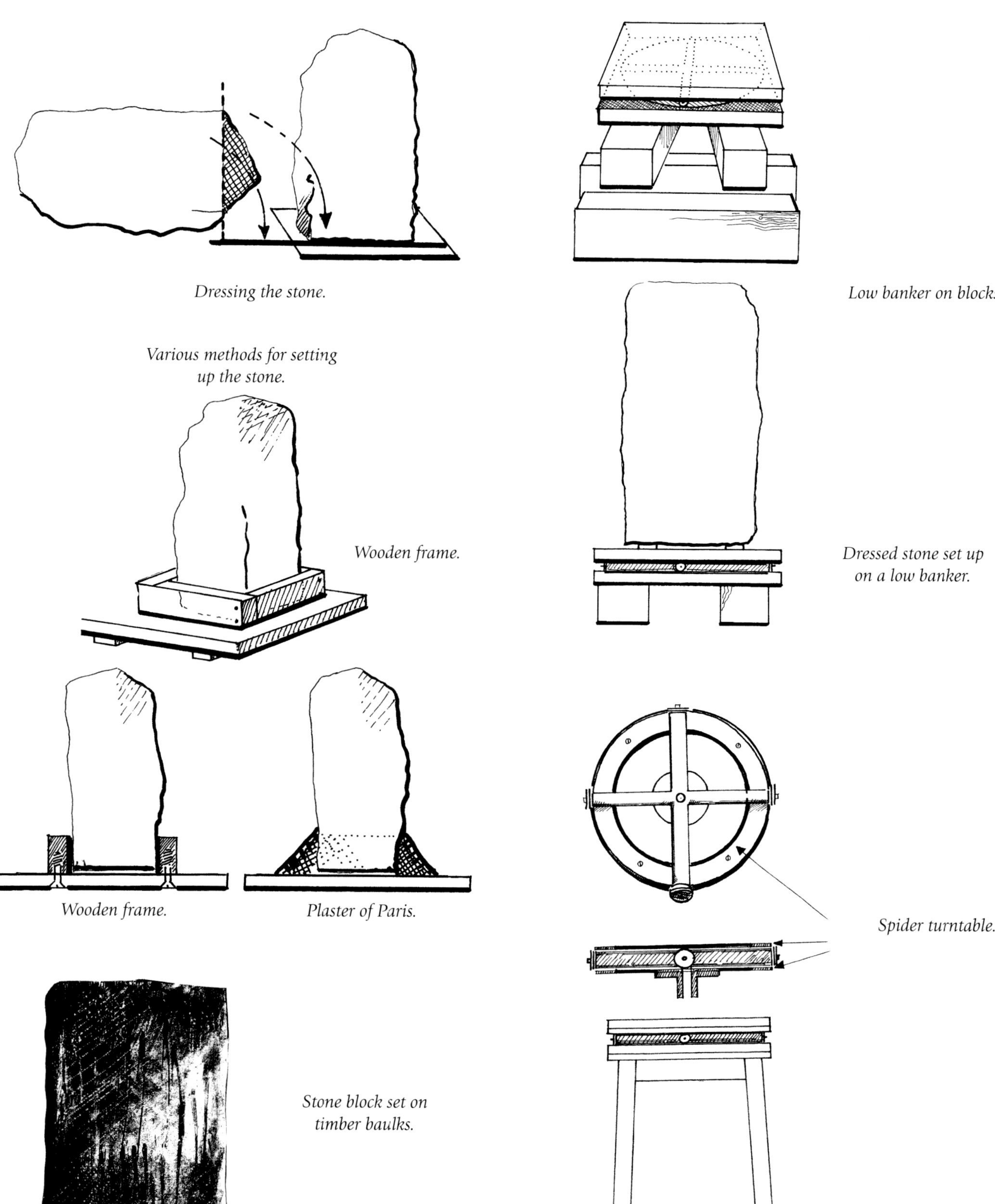

Dressing the stone.

Low banker on blocks.

Various methods for setting up the stone.

Wooden frame.

Dressed stone set up on a low banker.

Wooden frame.

Plaster of Paris.

Spider turntable.

Stone block set on timber baulks.

Banker and turntable.

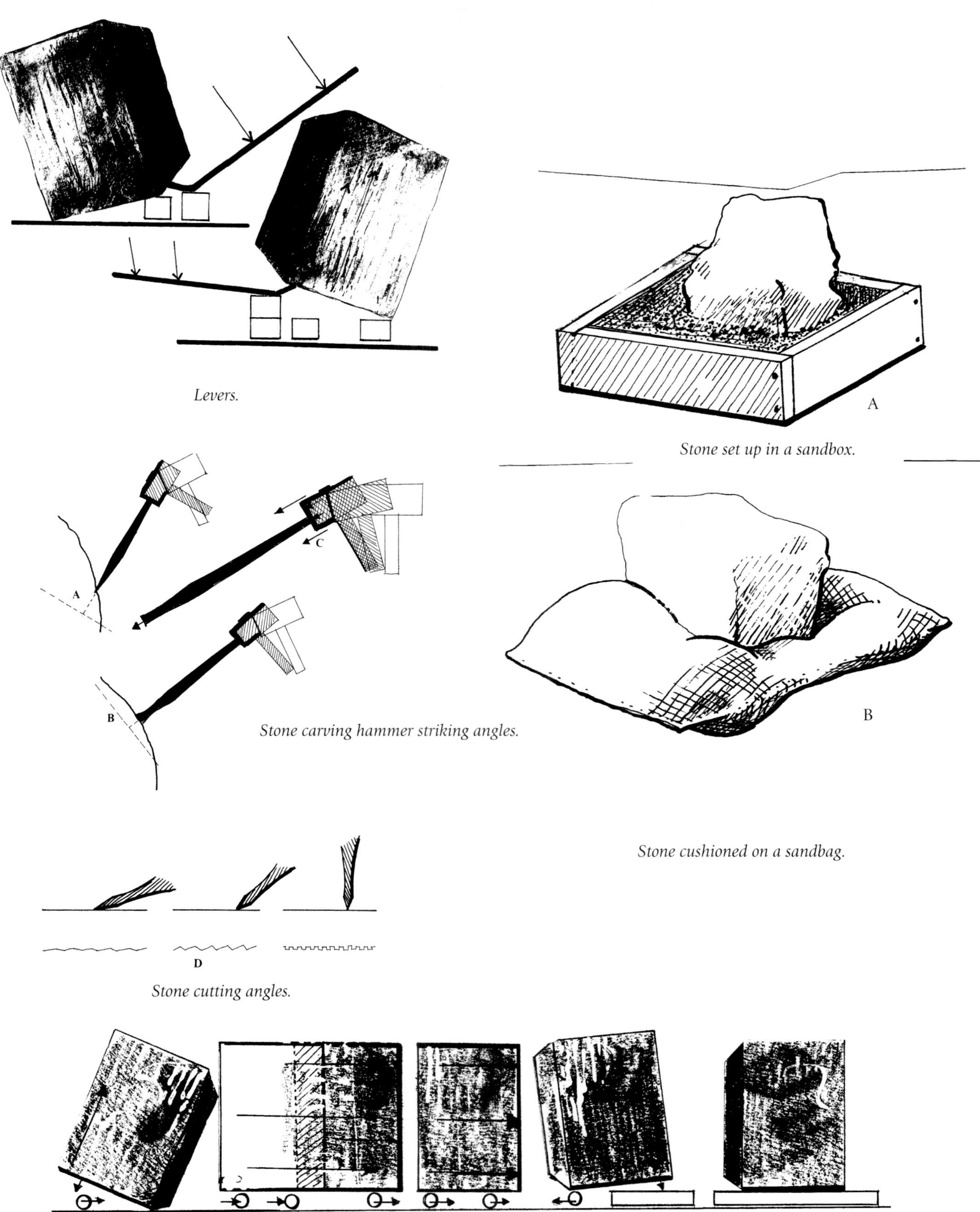

Levers.

Stone set up in a sandbox.

Stone carving hammer striking angles.

Stone cushioned on a sandbag.

Stone cutting angles.

Moving stone with rollers and levers.

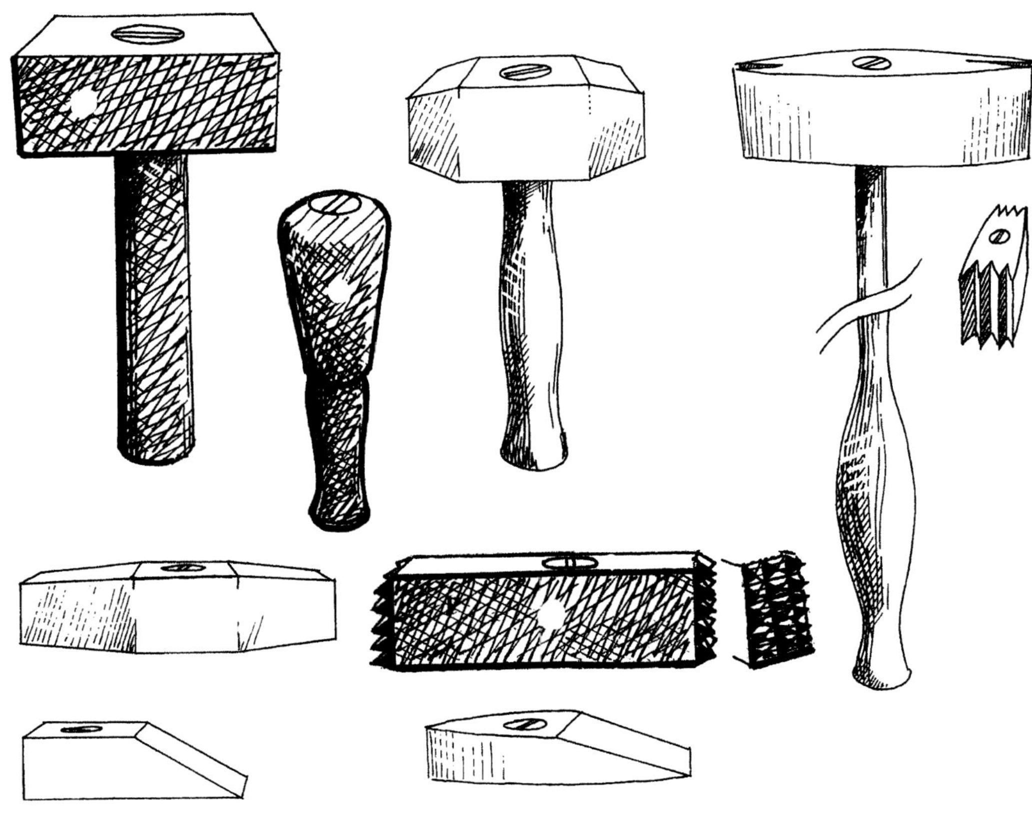

Various stone carving hammers.

quickly revealed. (Speed is, of course, a relative factor controlled by the size and scale of the work involved and the character of the material being used – its hardness or softness.) To save the whittling-down procedure, it is wise to cut away as much waste material as possible using the various cutting tools available. These will include traditional saws, which are now supplemented by various powered equivalents for use with both wood and stone, and almost any other material likely to be encountered in sculpture. It is a good idea to remove as much waste material as is technically possible and practical. This serves two purposes: it gets the sculptor close to the perceived image more quickly, and it may also provide useful off-cuts that can be used later for smaller projects.

Study the block you are about to carve and determine where you can make your cuts to best advantage. Sawing timber is a fairly familiar procedure using a sharp tool. It is possible to buy quite cheap handsaws with hardened tips to the teeth that can cut across and along grain of all kinds. Graduating to mechanical tools such as chainsaws should be done with some caution because of their inherent danger but with good training a chainsaw can be a most useful addition to any carving kit. Stone can be cut with a handsaw in much the same way as wood; use a saw with diamond- or tungsten-tipped teeth. Powered disc-grinding and cutting tools armed in the same way with diamond or tungsten edges are faster than hand saws, and with practice and care will probably become the most favoured of cutting tools.

It is important to understand the density of the stone being cut. If for instance you make a saw cut in wood it is relatively simple to make another cut at an angle to it, so that the waste can be removed as a block. Although this is also possible with stone, the density of the material gives the artist another choice, which is to make two cuts in roughly the same way as for timber but it is not necessary for them to connect; a lever placed in one cut and pressure applied will cause the membrane of stone left between the cuts to snap, allowing the smaller block to be removed (see page 87). It sounds simple on paper, but it is none the less a skill to be acquired; patience and practice will help in the learning process, as will seeking out good practitioners and watching them work, or, even better, getting them to teach you.

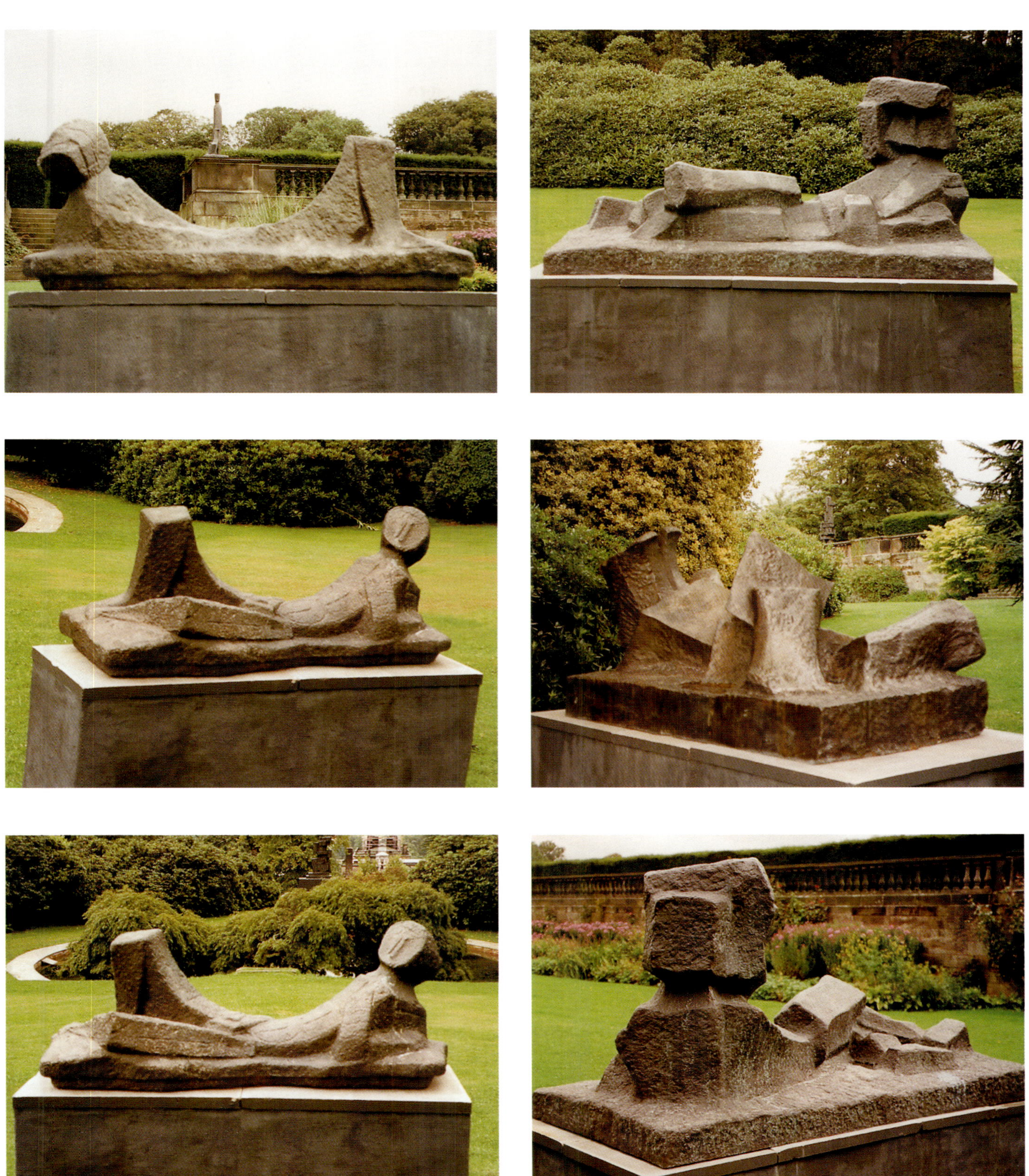

Reclining Figures, *by Fritz Wotruba, in limestone. These carvings illustrate the positive exploring of alternative interpretations of a theme.*

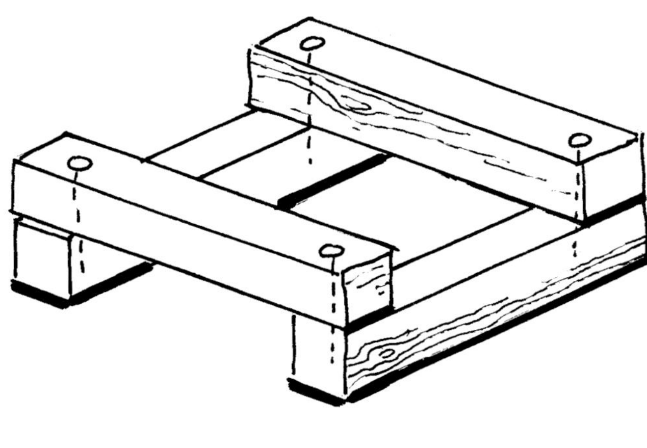

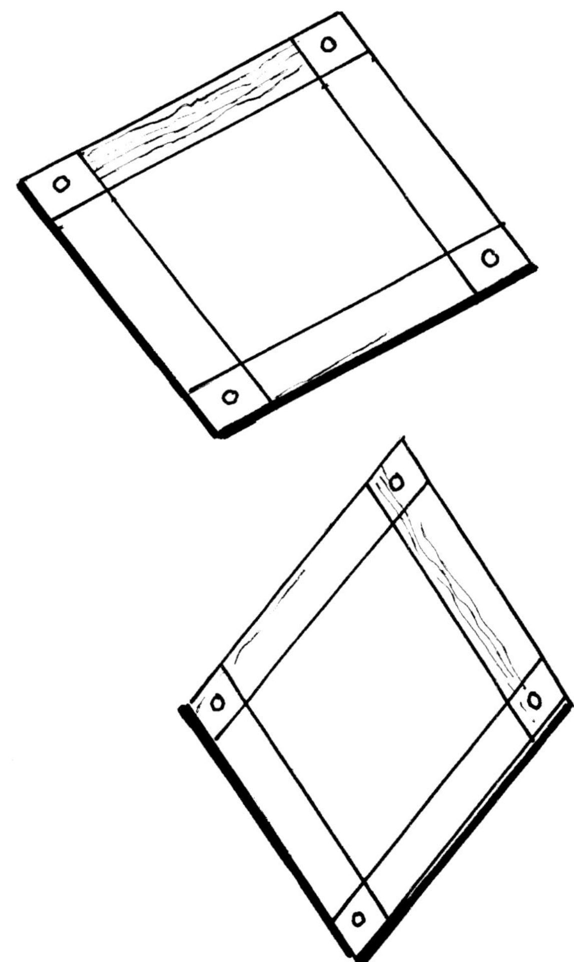

Wooden frame.

Practical Considerations

The following practical advice applies to all carving, whether of the whole figure or a combination of figures, heads, hands and feet. Equipment for carving except on very small items is usually geared to heavy lifting and a carver's studio will include heavy bankers. These are sturdy low benches, usually square, made of heavy-duty timber and often with a turntable top to allow the sculpture to be turned, viewed and carved from all round. Professional studios use a range of bankers, to cope with the smaller blocks of stone to the largest the studio will ever use. Very small stone blocks, and those with a soft surface, are catered for using a sand bag – a sack of hemp or some modern equivalent, three-quarters filled with dry fine sand, which will cushion the stone as it cut or carved. The sand will absorb the impact of the hammer blows while allowing the object to be turned over and around as the work progresses. A simple modification of the sand bag is a large deep tray filled with dry sand and used in the same way, by placing the stone into the sand to carve it (see page 88). The disadvantage of the sand tray is that the chips of stone collect in the sand and need to be sieved out periodically. It is essential when carving a portrait to have some device to hold the carving firmly, whichever way it is turned; in this way, the fine work can be achieved with safety both for the sculpture and the sculptor.

Another simple device is a wooden frame that can be made easily in the studio from four pieces of stout timber, nailed together to form a square. This frame will help firmly nestle the object being worked. Frames of varying sizes can be used to carve stone or wood with suitable cloth padding. They can be used also to work on casting of various kinds, particularly bronze, and are a common sight in foundries (see the illustration opposite).

Lifting heavy weights is very much part of the sculptor's world, no matter what processes or materials are preferred. Techniques for moving heavy objects with simple levers, rollers and blocks should be studied with care and attention, to avoid any injury or damage. There are many different machines available to help with lifting, and some are reasonably priced. The basic block and tackle can be used from a substantial beam or gantry, according to the poundage to be dealt with; those made for industrial use are capable of lifting many tons, but the final choice will depend on cost and requirements. Most heavy-duty gear can be hired. Whether it is bought or borrowed, it needs to be used safely and time spent learning about equipment and its uses will be time saved in the long run. Most manufacturers of industrial equipment will give advice and some even arrange training courses. The back is a vital part of the sculptor's equipment and protecting it will extend his or her working life, so always resist the temptation to lift heavy weights bodily if there is some other means of doing so.

6

Relief Sculpture

This form of sculpture has existed since mankind first scratched an image in the sand and depicted what were for him the important features of the world around him. All cultures worldwide practised this skill, and in all the materials now associated with sculpture, so this chapter applies to both modelled and carved relief sculpture, emphasizing the comparative freedom of the former and the limiting factor of using the harder materials of the latter. It can be very simple – just a scratched mark – but it can also be very complex indeed, combining at its most sophisticated level both allusion to three-dimensional space and actual three-dimensional figures, or other elements.

The term 'relief' refers to the relieving of the flat surface by cutting into it or by building up from it to create an image. Relief sculptures vary in the projection from the flat surface: relief cut into the surface is referred to as incised or intaglio; the lowest possible projection is called low relief or stacciato relievo. (The latter is often regarded as the most exacting trial of the sculptor's ability to draw, alluding to the three-dimensional space using line with the very smallest projection of volume.) Bas relief or basso relievo involves a projection that is as much as half the volume of the form, but without undercutting. The pattern of light across the surface of the bas relief is an important element in its design. Another type of bas relief is known as mezzo relievo; although this means half the volume, it is usually made with deep undercuts so the forms appear to turn from view, casting a shadow, which gives the impression of real form. Finally, high relief or alto relievo is the highest projection from the flat surface; it is almost fully in the round, and sometimes attached at only one or two points.

Relief sculpture is conceived and made to be seen from a single frontal viewpoint, working in much the same way as a painting but with discernible shadows, and is therefore affected by both artificial and natural light, sometimes to great dramatic effect. This single frontal aspect of relief can be altered to some degree by the shape of whatever supports the work, such as a curved wall or column. This will influence the normal viewing characteristic of the image and should be kept in mind when planning and making a relief. The actual point of view should kept in mind too when

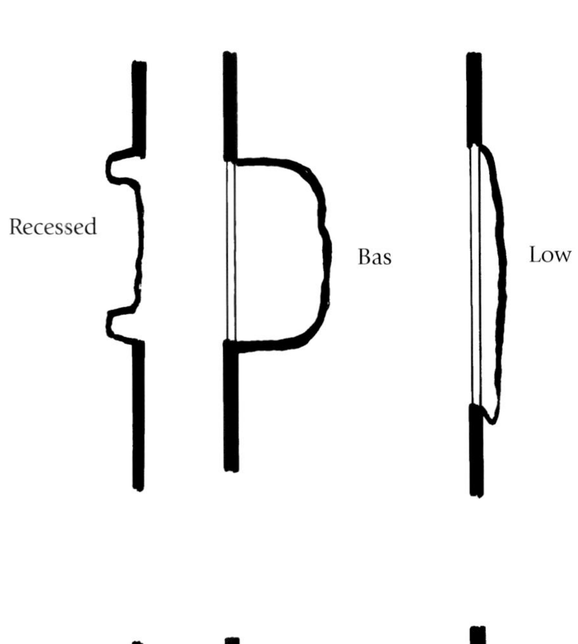

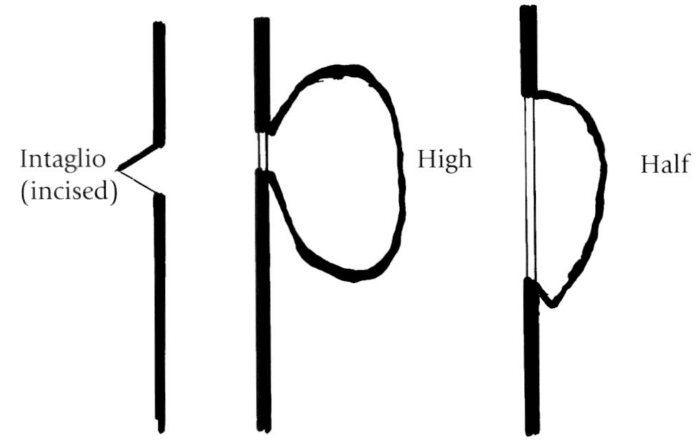

Relief.

looking at significant examples in museums and on buildings.

Reliefs range in size, from the smallest coin or jewel to the largest decoration embellishing a whole building. They are made in all materials associated with sculpture, from precious stones and metals and timbers of all kinds to all marbles and stone, and they have also been seen in some significant shaping of the landscape. Terracing of hillsides for farming purposes has provided some spectacular landscape relief, but mankind in many parts of the world has also made deliberate relief sculptures of great size on the earth's surface. These vary from the Natsca lines and images of Peru, which stretch for many kilometres, to the equally long sacred serpent of the North American Indians. Some sculptors today, sometimes referred to as 'land artists', continue this practice, effectively working in relief and sometimes using the human figure. Today, of course, such artists can use heavy digging machinery and can even view their work in progress from the air. In the light of this, the handmade achievements in landscape shaping represented by those ancient sites are even more awe-inspiring.

Apart from the straightforward scratched line made on or cut deeply into a flat surface, the other simplest form of relief is achieved by cutting material away from around a drawn image, leaving the image proud of its background and with vertical sides to the projection. The background can also be cut away completely to make a pierced screen thereby giving the artist the chance to make a two-sided relief. This basic technique is particularly suitable for carved relief sculpture and lends itself especially well to decorative architectural embellishment, as well as to narrative sculpture.

Searching for relief sculpture in the urban environment can lead to many valuable and unexpected examples, and will prove to be a useful experience. Looking above the modern shop fronts in any town or city will often reveal decorative panels let into surfaces, above doorways and windows, taking all forms, from simple decoration to elaborate figurative narrative reliefs. Keystones in particular were often made into a strong decorative feature, to emphasize their structural importance as the centre stone of an arch that locks all the components together. The variety of

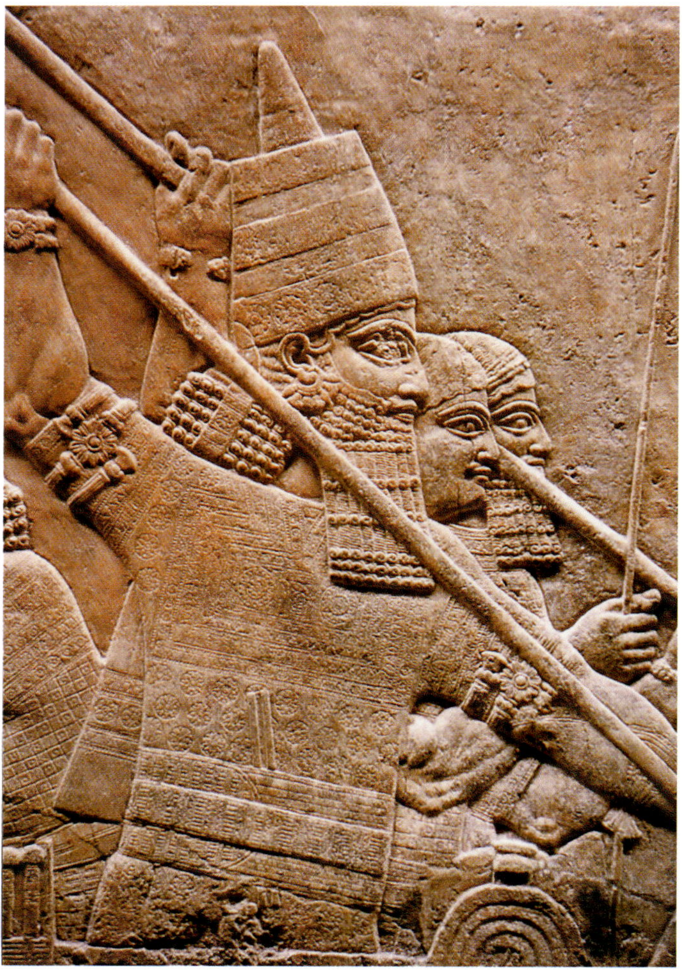

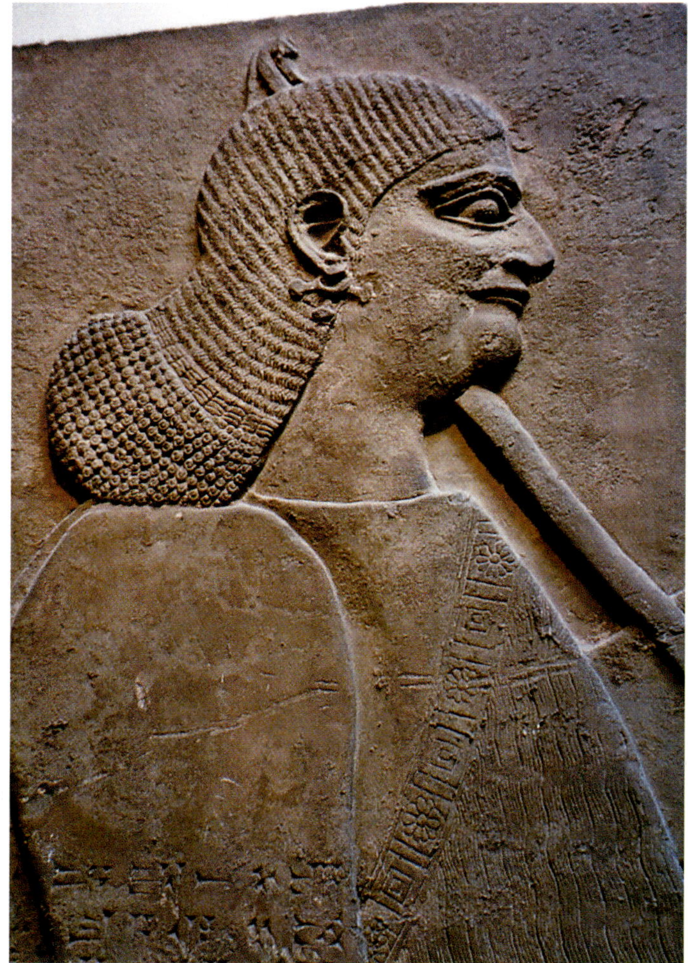

Assyrian Palace reliefs, in limestone. (British Museum, London)

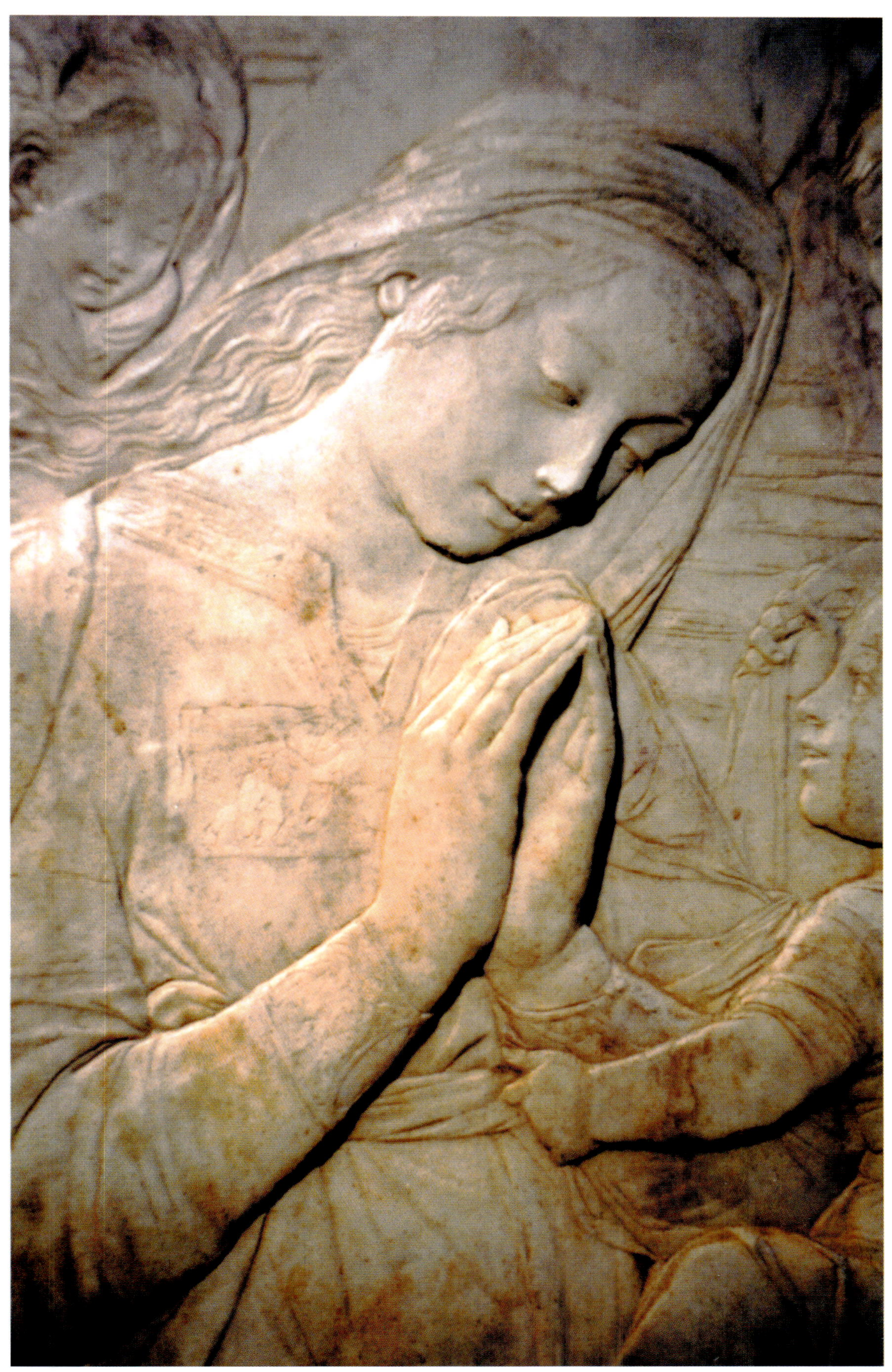

Marble relief of the Virgin Mary and Child, *finely drawn and carved by Desiderio de Settignano. (V&A Museum, London)*

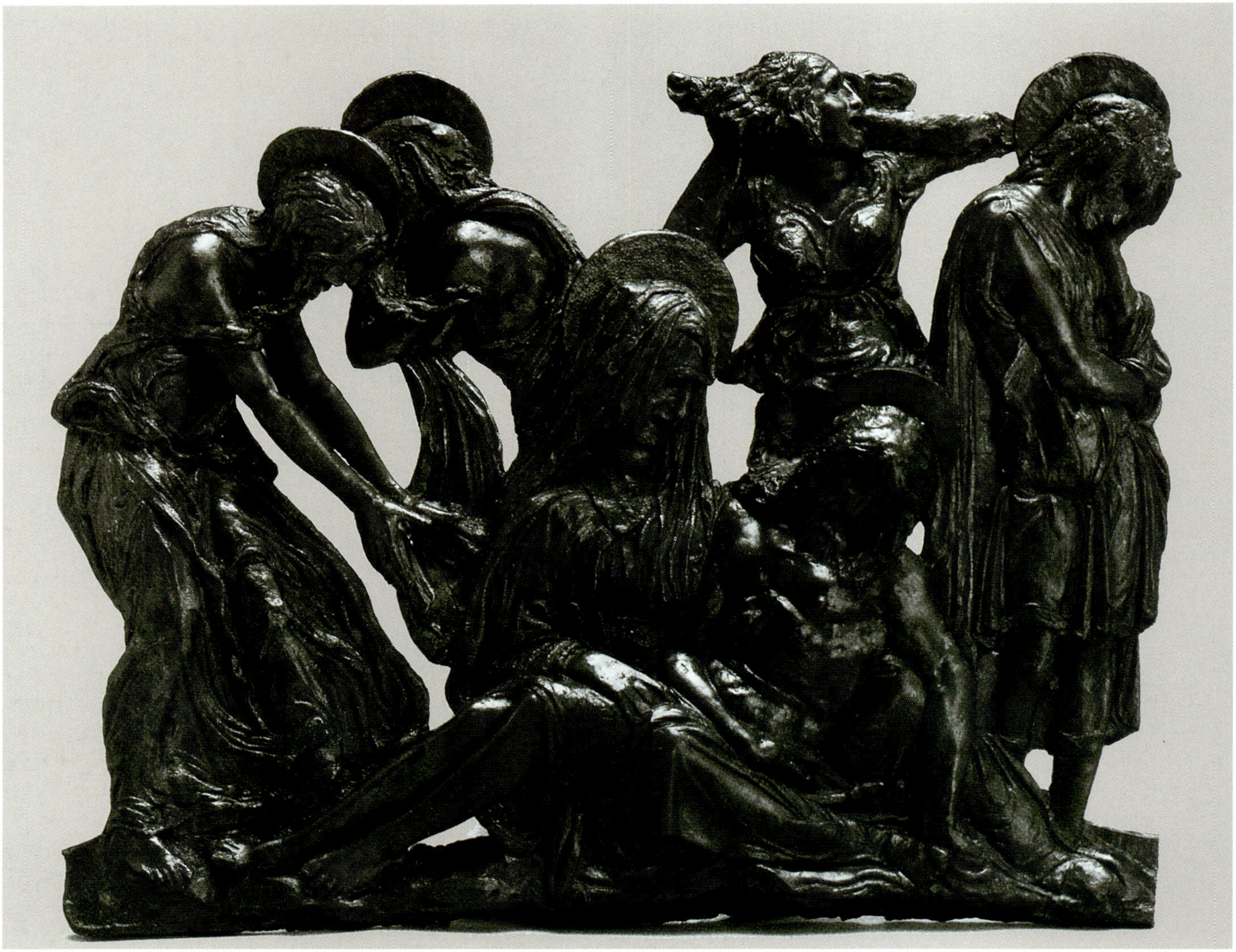

Lamentation, *by Donatello, in bronze. This relief was modelled in wax then cast in bronze. The piercing adds drama to the image. (V&A Museum, London)*

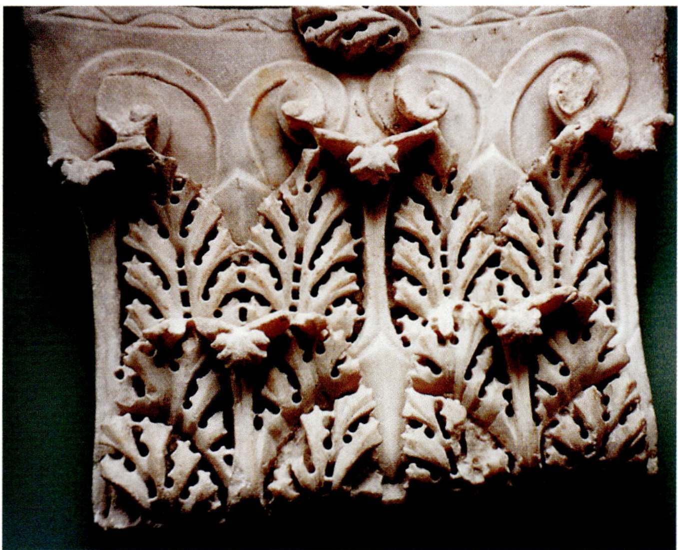

Marble relief carving, Italian. This is a clear example of a pierced relief paver that exploits the quality of the marble to great effect.

OPPOSITE: Panel from the doors of death, *by Giacomo Manzu, from St Peter's, Rome. Clearly visible are the lines drawn in the clay and the volume built up accordingly. The artist's hand prints are also visible.*

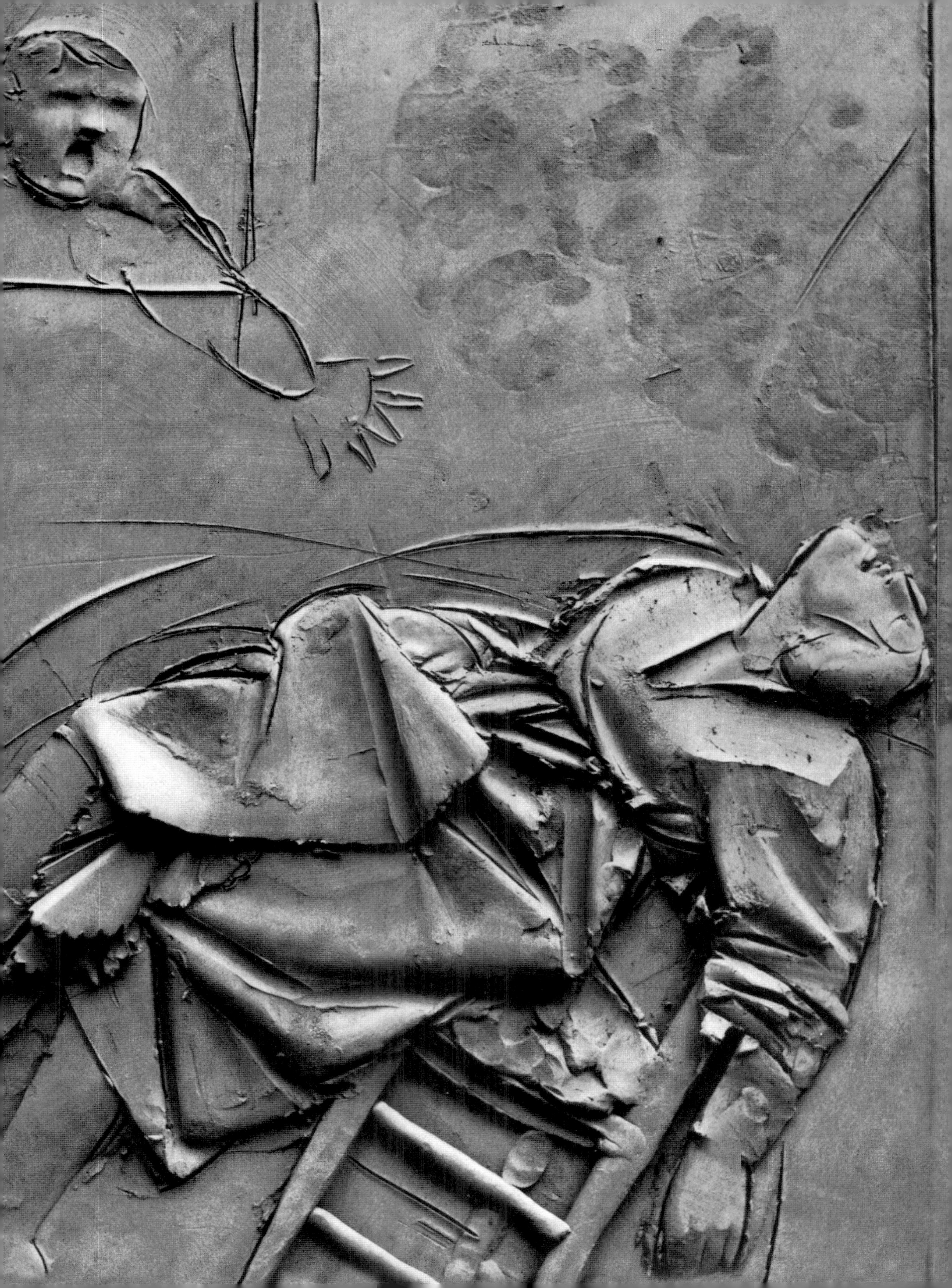

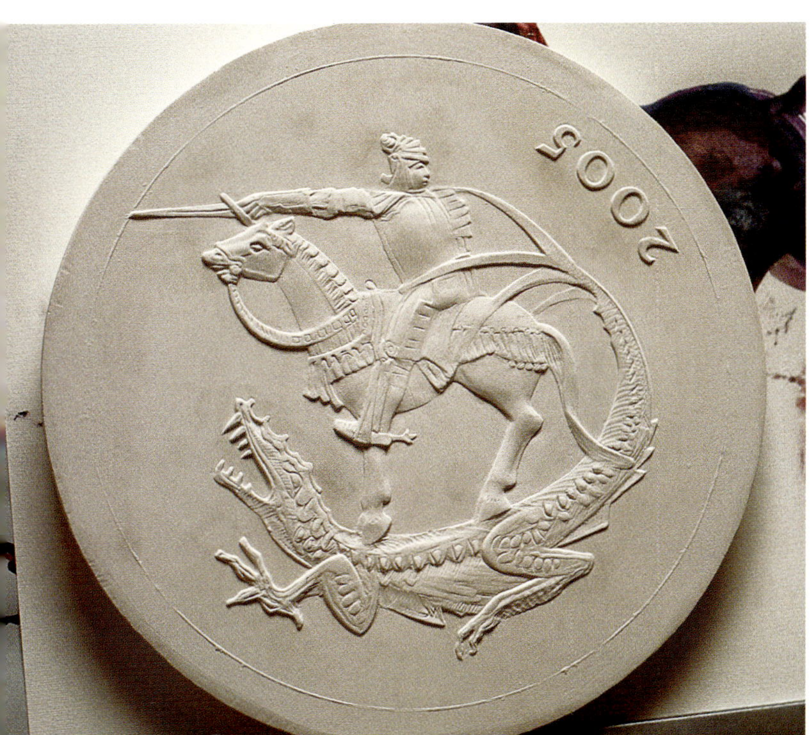

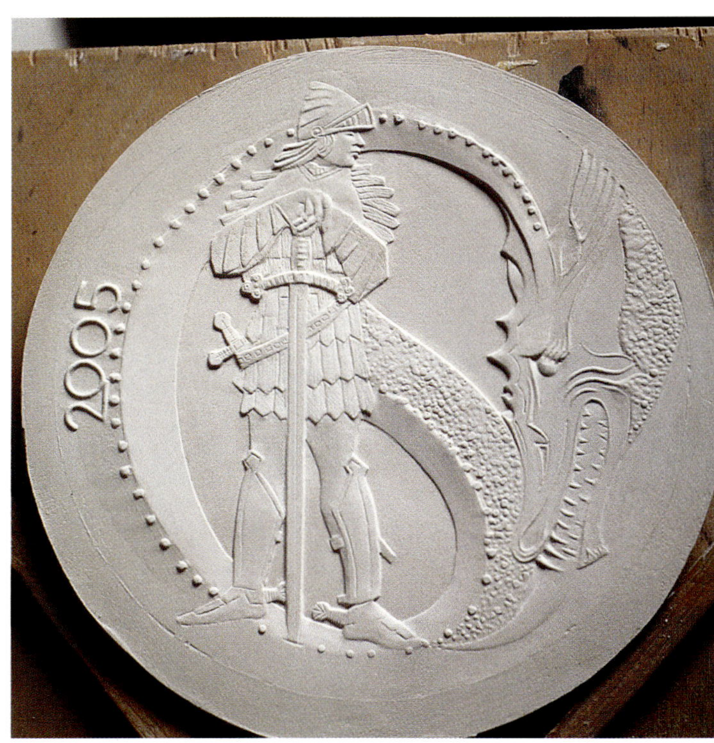

Plaster patterns for a coin, by John W. Mills.

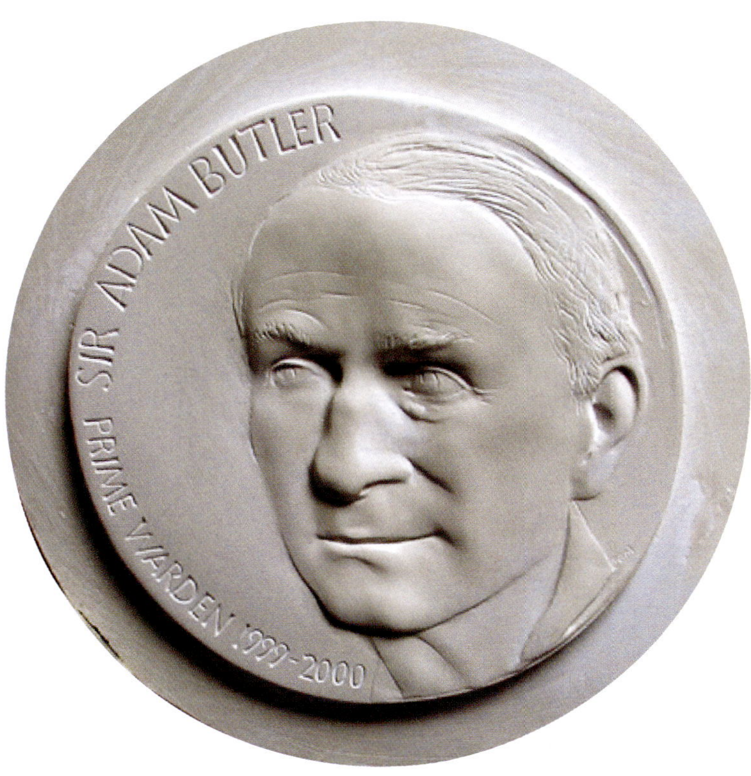

Plaster pattern for a medal, a portrait of Sir Adam Butler, Prime Warden, *by John W. Mills.*

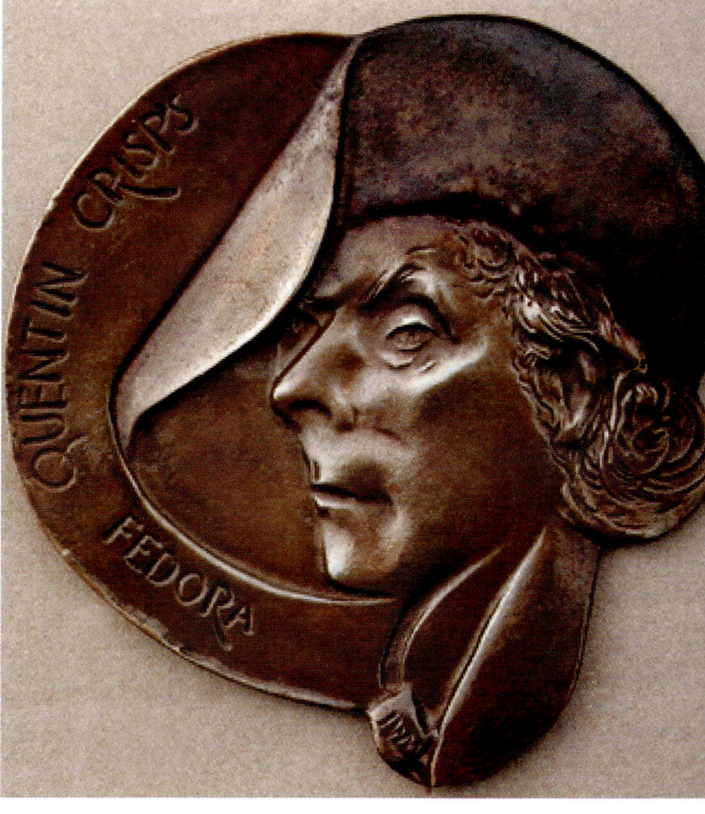

Quentin Crisp's Fedora, *by John W. Mills, in bronze. An eccentrically shaped cast medal.*

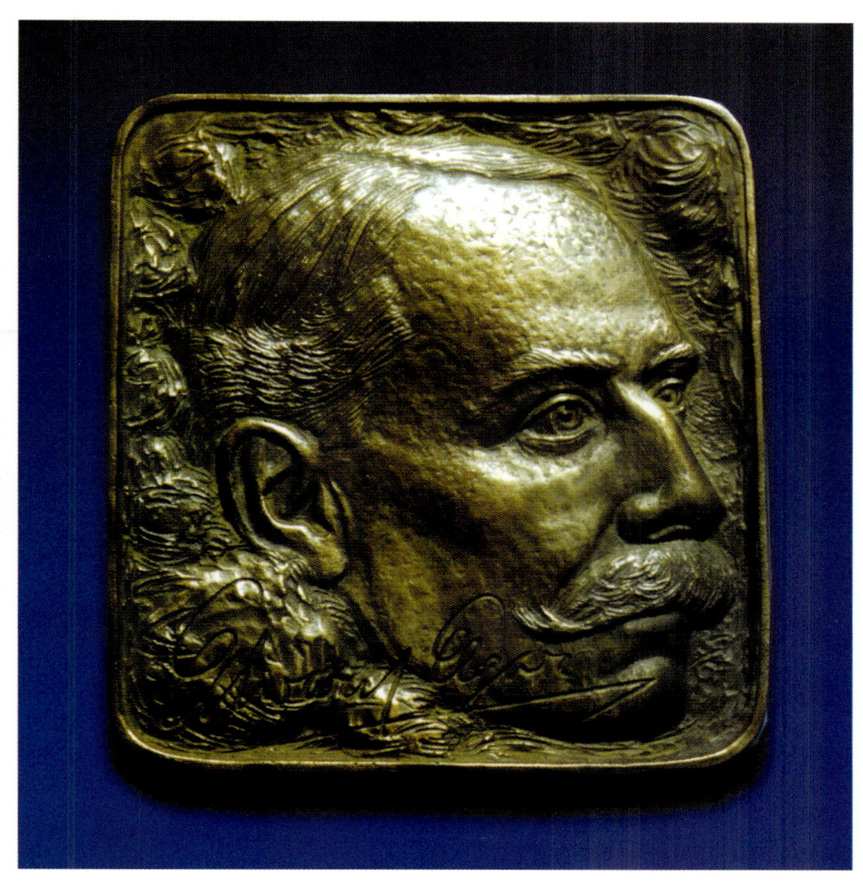

Medal relief portraits 'Elgar' (ABOVE) and 'Marion' (RIGHT) by Robert Elderton – good example of work by a master engraver.

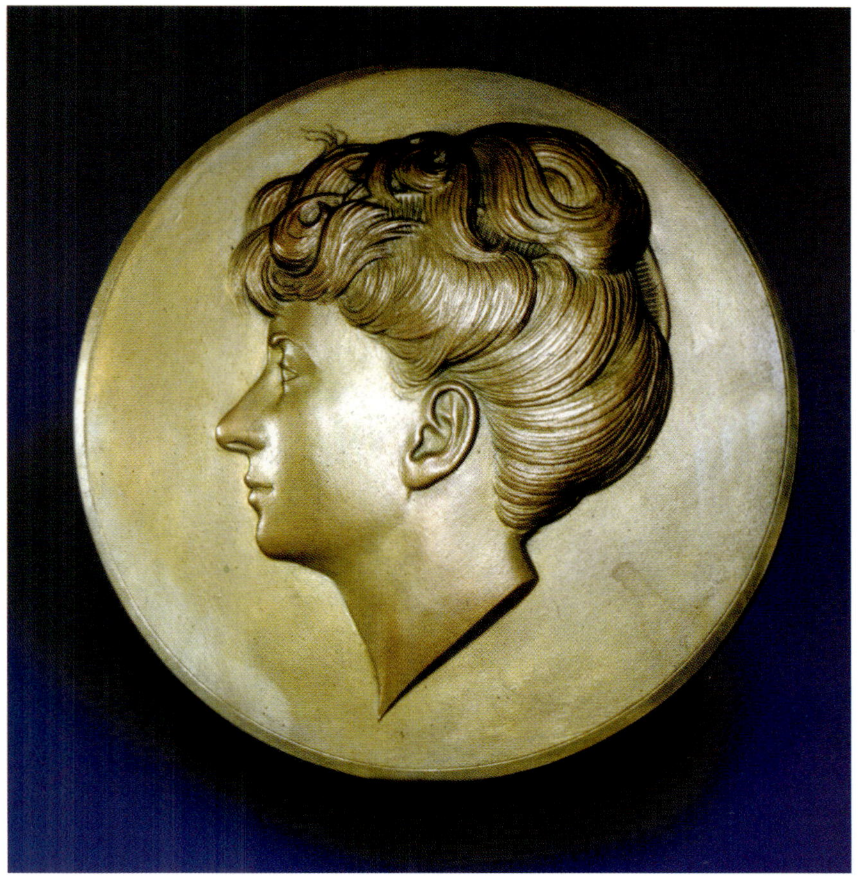

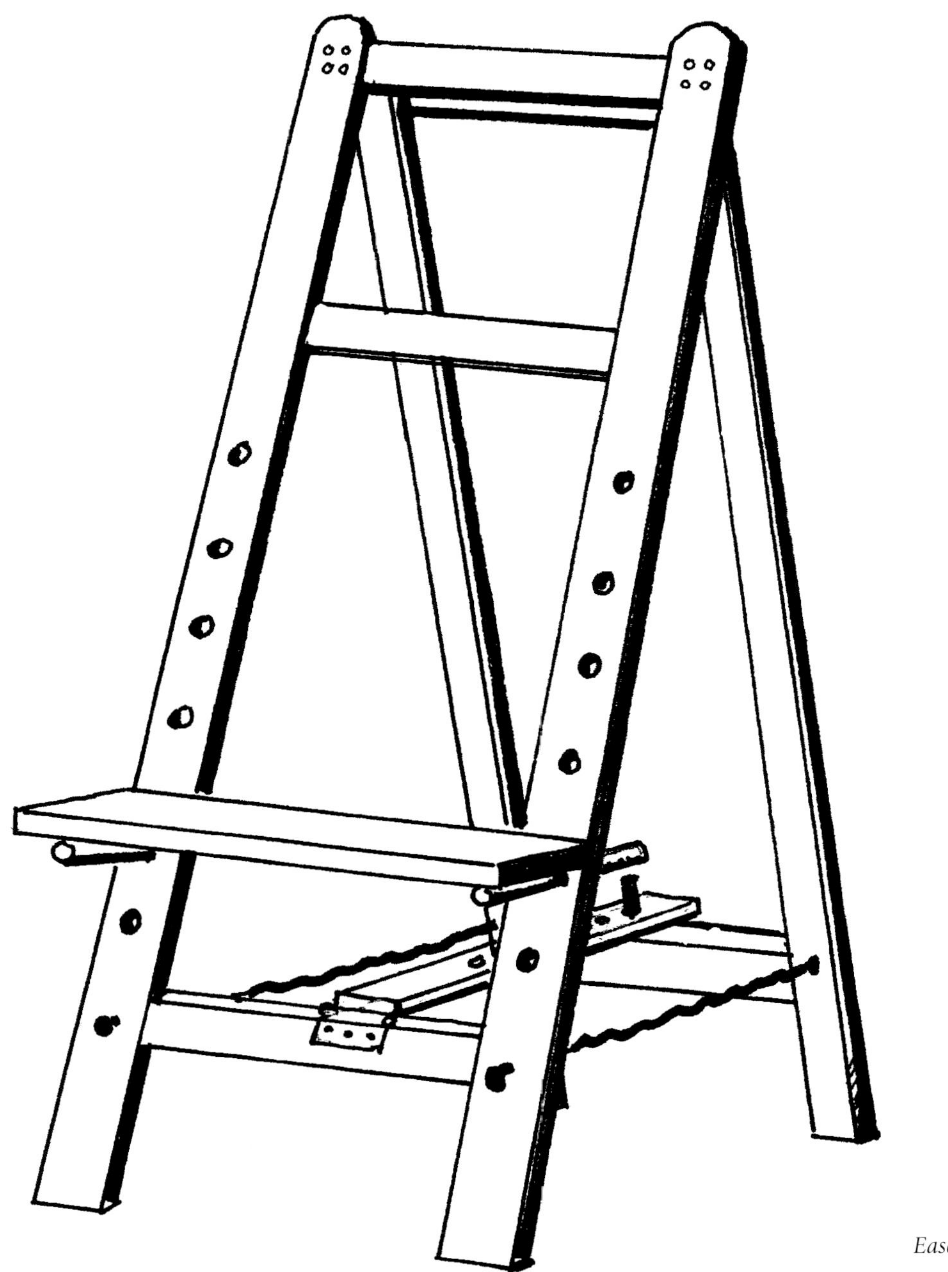

Easel.

images to be discovered will fascinate the mind and the eye, exposing the keen student to the richness of work that is so often taken for granted simply as decoration.

Relief sculpture is probably the most widely distributed art form. Decorative cast iron was shipped all over the world in the 1700s from Ironbridge in Shropshire as ships' ballast. These sections of relief sculpture were eventually assembled to make fine balconies to embellish many of the world's newer cities, such as Sydney and New Orleans. These refined examples of relief work often led to the formation of foundries in those countries to make their own versions. Charleston in South Carolina, USA, was one place that became an important centre for such cast iron and produced some remarkable relief decoration with a uniquely Southern style.

The Ancient Assyrian Palace reliefs are among the most accomplished early examples of descriptive relief sculpture and the British Museum in London houses a very fine collection. They are sophisticated in their narrative complexity finding the means of expressing movement, alluding to large terrain and water, depicting human and animal activity of all kinds, all expressed by the straightforward cutting

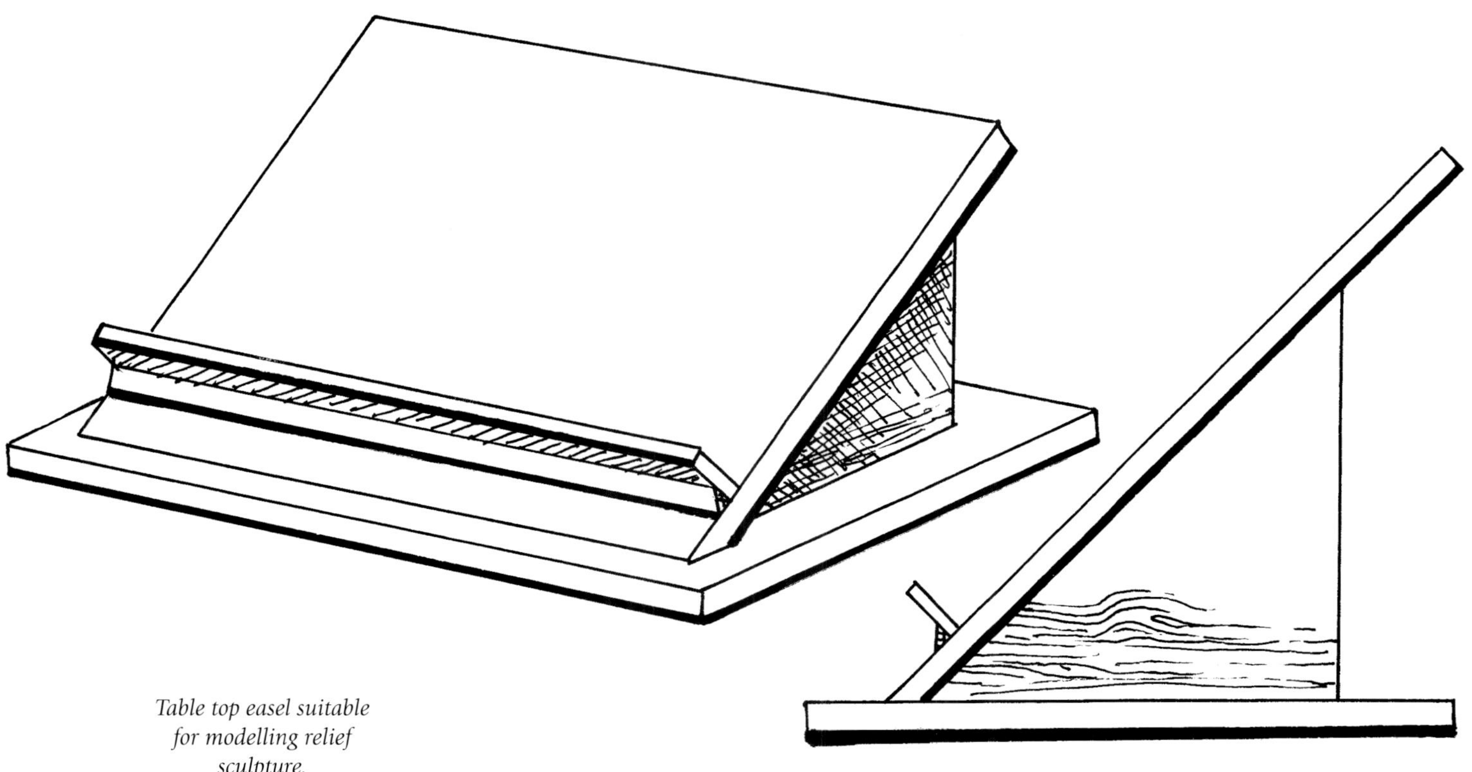

Table top easel suitable for modelling relief sculpture.

of soft limestone to create bas relief. There are also examples in this collection of similar Assyrian relief work made from metal, an early alloy based on copper. Many buildings of the Aztecs in Ancient Mexico feature this apparently simple method of relief decorations, which are also storytelling images, but of a larger, bolder design, carved from a much harder stone than that employed by the Assyrians. And such examples are repeated across the globe in all cultures. The Inuit carvers of the far north of Canada, where there is a distinct shortage of materials for sculpture, did not use the sophisticated system of depicting space using the science of single-point perspective illusion, which was invented in the Italian Renaissance. The narrative runs across the flat plane with very little suggestion of spatial depth, and the solidity and importance of the object or personality is expressed using an almost linear technique, with little depiction of actual form; the quality and clarity of the imagery is achieved by superb drawing. This kind of relief with vertical outlines to the imagery is made today in all sizes and using all materials.

Particularly skilful examples of this kind are practised on a much smaller scale in the production of struck coins and medals, known as numismatism. This art form demands a relief image drawn and modelled with a very shallow but vertical depth, to allow for the process of striking. The weight of a very heavy drop press is used to drive (strike) the image from the negative die (mould) into the surface of the object, to make the coin or medal. The poundage used to make this striking is many tons and the slightest undercut in the relief will lock the coin into its die. This vertical depth is known as the 'draft', which enables the 'draw'; as the terms imply, this allows for the two sections of the die to lift off the struck coin or medal. Coin relief sculpture is restricted to the size of current coinage in all its sizes, although the common practice is to model the master pattern at about 7in (175mm); this pattern is then reduced in size mechanically to whatever is required by the particular coin value.

A cast medal is not restricted in this way and this allows for a more free modelling approach to the relief. Today, there is a fairly active association of medallists all over the world, who are carrying on the tradition of medal-making. At the same time, many of them are experimenting with alternative shapes and materials to enhance the tradition, producing works that are really sculptures that are small enough to be held easily in the hand. Although the traditional medal shapes are circular and rectangular, modern medallists do not restrict themselves to these, and are creating some very interesting small objects. Portrait medals have been a popular source of promotion, both of the individual and of the state, since Roman times, and to a degree this is still one of the functions of relief sculpture.

Fine drawing is the key to all relief sculpture, no matter how large or small, and no matter how high or low the projected image stands out from or is cut into the flat surface. This is particularly subtle when perspective is employed to imply depth. In what has become a western tradition, a working knowledge and practice of the laws of perspective drawing are necessary. The advantage is that the full volume of a form can be implied; where necessary, the form can be turned at its drawn profile and may be undercut to provide a strong shadow that gives the illusion of depth and solidity. The temple carvings that are an integral part of the religious culture of India are fine examples of this technique. Carved from a very fine-grained lime-stone, they develop the relief to a very complex degree using the entire range of projected relief, from the very low to the very high. They include figures that are so fully expressed in the round that they hardly show any attachment to the fabric of the building. They were designed to exploit the very harsh bright light of the latitudes in which they were set, and cast shadows provided the drama that was very much part of the scheme, enabling the story and characters to be recognized from a distance.

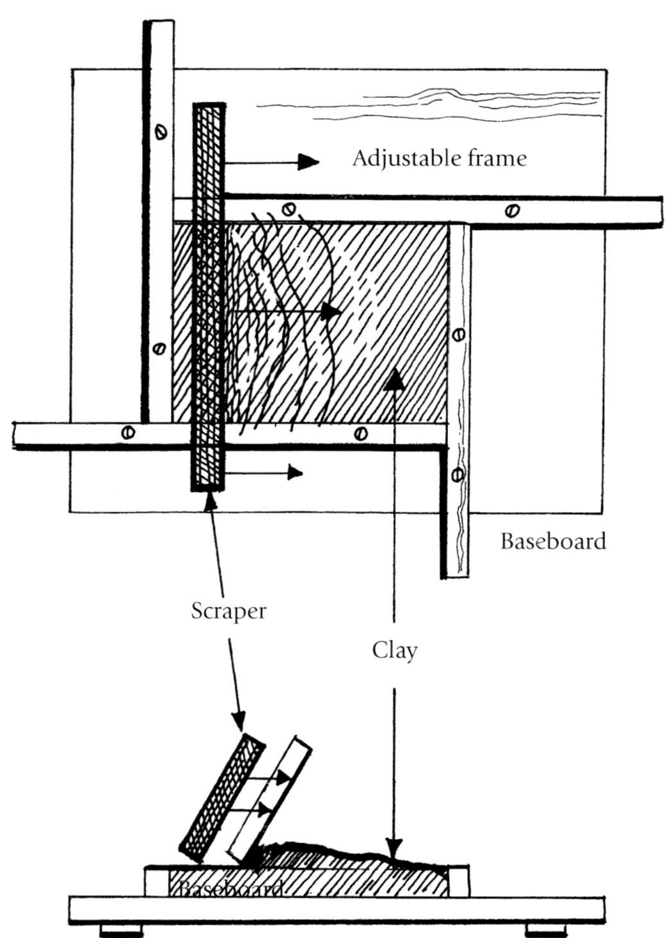

Making a simple flat clay shape to make relief. The frame is adjustable.

The same techniques were used by the Greeks in carving the friezes of the Parthenon (known in part as the Elgin Marbles and held in the British Museum), exploiting the deep cast shadows. The Romans also utilized the play of strong moving natural light across a relief in their designs, which they carved almost in the round, with deep undercuts to gain the greatest dramatic effect. A good example of this is Trajan's Column, a full-sized plaster cast of which dominates the plaster courts of the Victoria and Albert Museum in London. The picture stories of Emperor Trajan's war campaigns cover the column from its base to its top, cut in relief and clearly discernible as self-aggrandizing propaganda narratives. The V&A plaster courts are unique in the UK and are therefore an absolute must-see experience for sculptors at all stages of development.

In order to understand relief sculpture better, you can carry out a simple practical exercise. Flatten some clay, either by simply pressing it on to a flat, preferably smooth surface or by making a frame (see the illustration opposite). Then, with a pointed instrument, draw a simple object, preferably not a figure. Make the drawing as well as you can but in outline only; the outline is simply a device that helps identify the place where a solid form turns away from view. Although the line is universally accepted as a useful drawing tool, those concerned with three-dimensional expression should remember that it is a graphic invention necessary to plan an image on a two-dimensional surface. To continue the exercise, having drawn the outline on the clay, use softer clay to try to model the form that is alluded to within those outlines. Try this in a number of projections from the flat surface, from a very low relief, via any number of gradual projections, until the form is almost projecting in the round. Try to get a feel for expressing the form without undercuts and then, by gradually increasing the projection, cut under the form corresponding as much as possible to the original drawn line. This allows the play of light and shade to help create the 3D illusion. This will become clearer with practice and will be quite satisfying; remember that the relief sculpture only works from a single viewpoint.

This exercise is useful when introducing to sculpture a group of new students who are fairly confident and familiar with drawing on paper. It should help them gradually to comprehend the transition from two- to three-dimensional thinking. The exercise continues by modelling the human figure in relief with the same emphasis on drawing on the prepared clay and then making the appropriate projections of form from the flat surface according to the real volumes of the model. A particular challenge when making a figurative relief is to draw and model the image, especially the head in full face. Resolving the drawing and modelling of the nose, for instance, with a very restricted projection, pre-

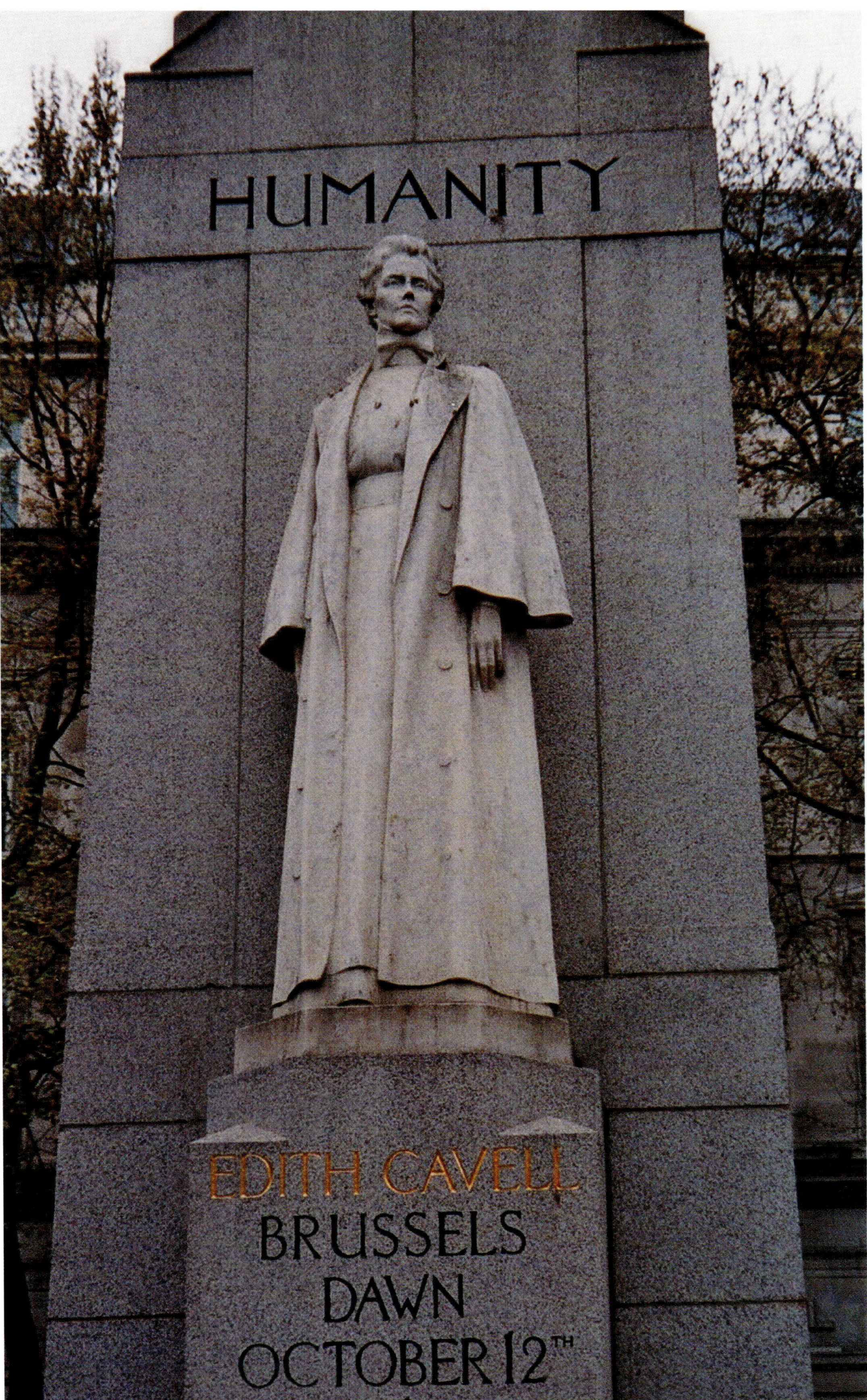

Edith Cavell Memorial, *by George Frampton, London – a very sensitive figure carved from a hard limestone.*

sents a very tricky task to master and is a good test of both drawing and modelling skills. It is fascinating to study the work of really good medallists to see how they manage this taxing problem and unravel the techniques they apply to full-frontal representation in relief.

Because the relief represents the transition from two- to three-dimensional thought, it also lends itself to a mixing of different materials, which can be used to make collage and assemblage pieces and will involve the artist in the various cutting and gluing technicalities. The point at this stage is to try as many variations as possible and enjoy the search. This practice may lead to a better understanding of a number of styles of art: in cubism, for instance, the representation of solid form in two dimensions was made by combining many views of a single item, in an attempt to state its complete physical identity. Collage was often employed to do this, and by the process of addition, the image was gradually projected from the flat surface to make relief sculpture, eventually venturing in the round to become assemblage. George Fullard was one of the most accomplished of British sculptors to use this process. He conjured up powerful images from disparate found objects and sometimes, like Picasso, had them cast in bronze. Without the quality of colour and accidental texture of the found objects, the image was much altered, but the power of Fullard's silhouettes and the gestures of the images he conjured were strong enough to stand and maintain their own presence. If a good sculpture emerges from such research and experimentation, the sculptor should grab the bonus with both hands and learn from the experience.

7

Modelling the Figure

A wide range of modelling skills are required to be able to model the figure satisfactorily, and they can be acquired only with practice. It is wise to experiment with a variety of modelling media, but the basic substance of clay offers the best range of possibilities and will help the sculptor to develop personal skills and artistic identity relatively quickly – and this must be the eventual aim of all artists. After making a small number of studies, in the form of sketch models or maquettes (see Chapter 2), the desire in most ambitious sculptors is to proceed to making larger versions. In doing this, he or she will find out how well the preliminary studies have prepared the way. Have they provided enough information to work freely at a larger scale or do they leave the sculptor wondering what to do next? Do they indicate whether or not a vital armature is needed and do they allow for the design and making of the armature, should it be necessary? (See Chapter 3.) Although it is possible to plough straight in to the making of a large figure without much preparation, but with a good sense of freedom and pleasure, such élan may be short-lived if there is no datum against which to measure the progress of the work.

I get a great degree of satisfaction from working on a large image as long as I have made thorough preparations for doing so. This means I always allow in my mind the thought that, should a fresh idea occur to me during the making process, despite the maquette searches already made, I should make that alternative too.

Making a sculpture based on the human figure is a serious challenge and such sculptures are seen and assessed in the light of unique standards – those set by human beings, not only in their creative output but also in their own physical presence. Work will be judged either by the other artists or by observers according to mankind's long tradition. Because of the thousands of years of cultural references of all kinds it is very easy to see faults in a figurative work. It is less easy to find fault with something that is entirely made up, in other words, sculptures that are truly abstract. There are many artists worldwide working in this way today, but the basic elements of the figure need to be kept uppermost in the mind at all times, to provide that firm basis against

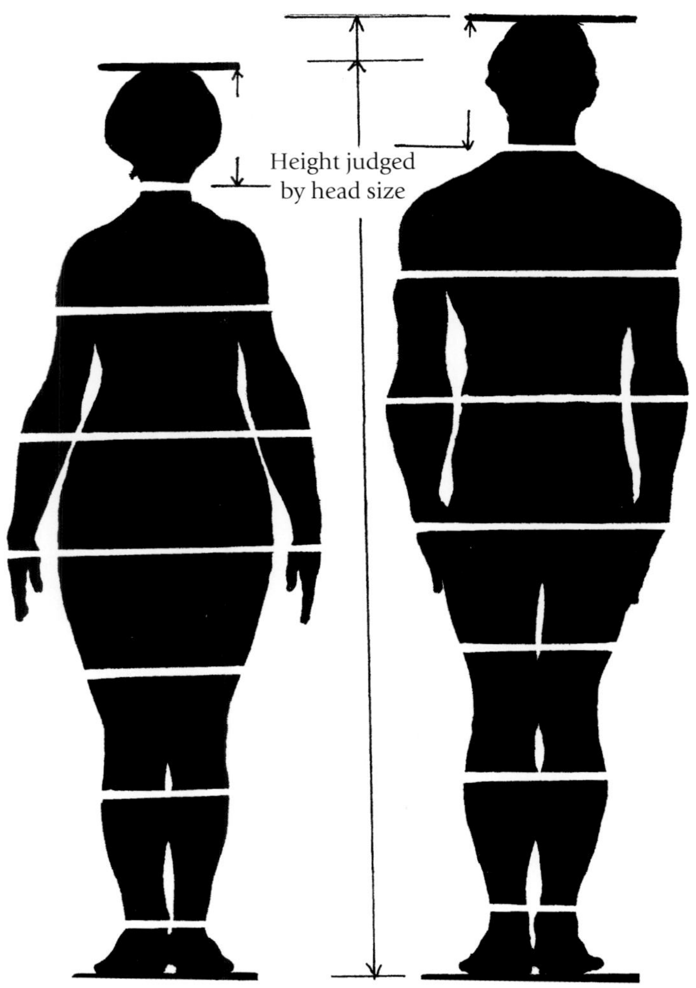

The basic characteristics of the male and female forms.

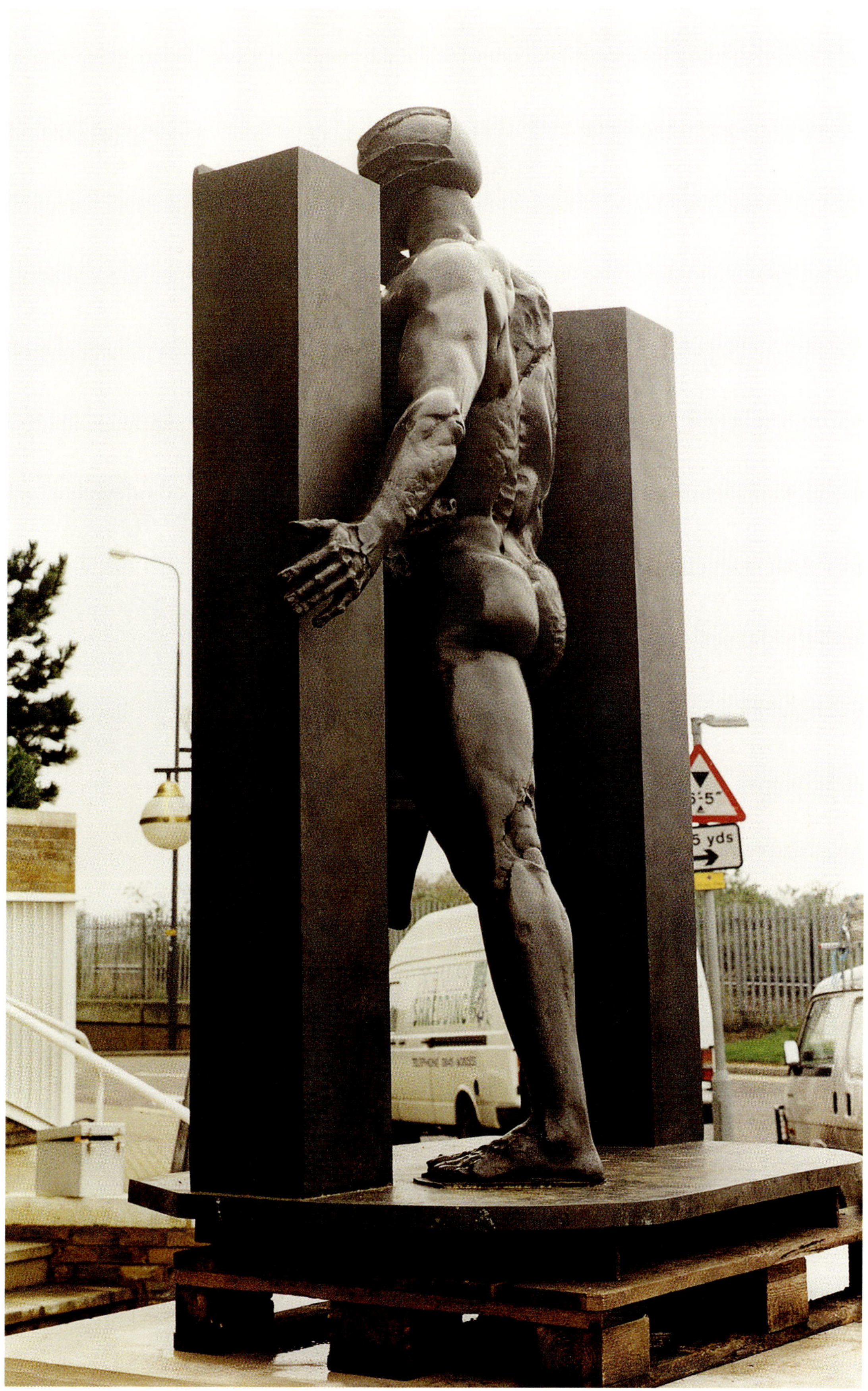

LEFT AND OPPOSITE:
L'homme passant la porte, *by Ipoustegy, in bronze. This powerful figure shows a fine understanding of human anatomy used to define the sculptor's idea.*

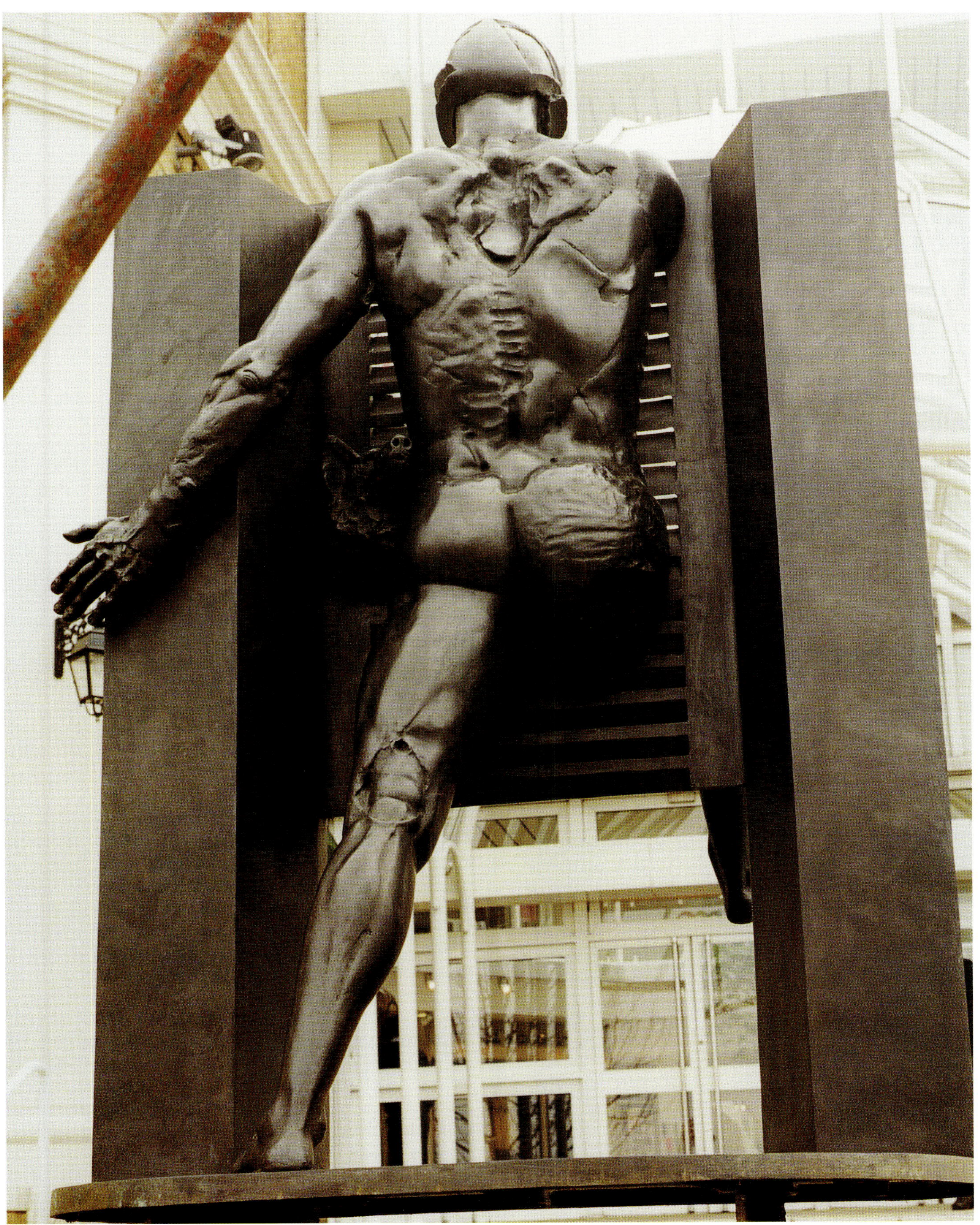

which the work can be assessed. Human proportions are easily identifiable and if the sculptor wishes to move away from that familiar human pattern, to make manifest a particular idea, it is that basic awareness that makes it possible; it becomes a matter of choice, which in turn leads to an interpretation of the human figure.

Regardless of the medium being used to make a figure, it is a useful mental game as the sculpture progresses to imagine the figure or figures confronting you in real life, in action, maybe walking towards you. Does the figure or group of figures look possible? Often the answer will be 'no'. There may be a deformity, deviating to a greater or lesser degree from the normal, emphasizing those elements of reality that are the datum base for sculpting the human figure. The artist then has to ask further questions: 'Shall I retain that deformity? Is it a possible enhancement of the idea?' Sometimes it might be, thus providing another stimulus. Imagining in this way can help the beginner and encourage a habit of self-appraisal relative to any personal perception of reality.

Fundamental proportions are an important factor. Broad shoulders and narrow hips usually signify a male, while narrow shoulders and broad hips are usually female. Because of this naturally broader hip width the arms of the female figure have a different configuration from the arms of a male. The real height of the average figure is seven and half times the size of the head, but this measurement is often changed to create an effective visual impact. By changing the size of the head the implied scale of the sculpture is affected. No matter how large or small the size the overall figure may be, a large head implies a smaller perceived scale; conversely, a small head implies a larger perceived scale. The length of the arms outstretched is equal to the height of the figure from head to foot. Arms including the hands reach to the middle of the thigh and in a well-built person the measurement from head to crotch is equal to that of the crotch to the feet. The corners of the mouth in repose are usually level with the centre of the eyes. The length of the foot is equal to that of the hand, which is equal to the length of the face, and so on. Artists through the ages have examined and played with the human proportions seeking an ideal, a kind of academic fundamentalism, but in those sculptures that are good enough to make the heart race, reality is inherently understood but then put to personal use by the sculptor.

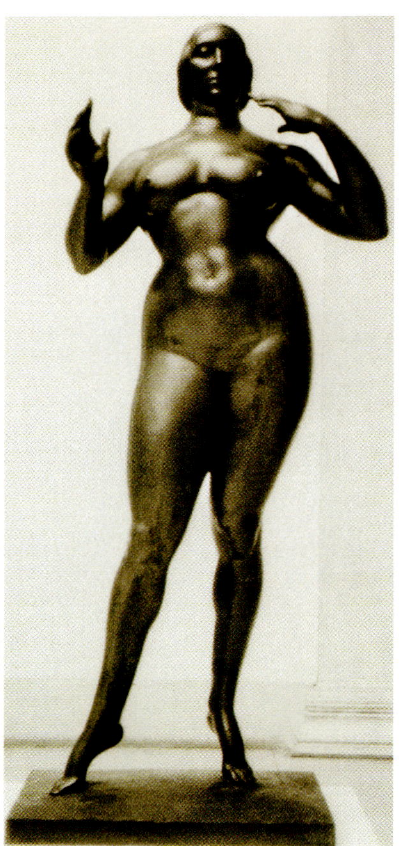

Standing Woman, *by Gaston Lachaise, in bronze. Although made in the USA, this image has a typically Northern European flavour in its interpretation. (Albrigh Knox Collection, Buffalo, USA)*

A non-medical working knowledge of the subject of human anatomy also aids the artist's expression. Paying too little attention to human anatomy may lead to ridicule (hence the importance of self-questioning), but it is also important to avoid paying too much attention to anatomical accuracy, as this can be a hindrance to expression. The balance to be struck is a very personal one and can make the difference between creating a naked figure and a nude figure. A naked figure is simply the image of a person stripped of clothing, apparently vulnerable in a hostile world, susceptible to man's vagaries and to those of the natural world. The nude figure by contrast is one that will appear to sit comfortably in all its connotations; it will be happy, often proud in the skin created for it by the artist, and this will have been arrived at by observing and interpreting reality, then making adjustments to be able to use it to best express the subject and the story.

Students often ask what anatomy they should study. 'Visual anatomy' is my usual reply; by this I mean the anatomy that confronts everyone on a daily basis, that which is understood from the external visual appearance of the figure. After all, most of the time the sculptor will be trying to make its sculptural equivalent to be perceived also only from the outside, but implying an understanding of the underlying complex organic physiology. In truth we all know more than we think about our body.

An understanding of the human skeleton and its basic elements is always useful, partly because the skeleton can often indicate the best solution for the design of an armature. In simple descriptive terms, the skeleton can be broken down into a set of simple formulas, the most important element of which is the spine, the articulated column of support. This column is supported above the legs by the load-bearing pelvis, a dish-shaped form with sockets at each side, which accommodate the leg joints with a rigid fixing to the spine at the rear. The legs are two

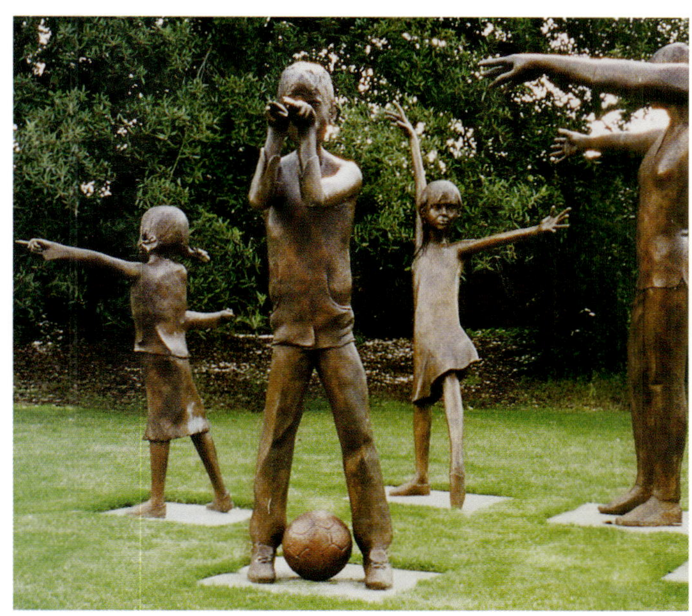

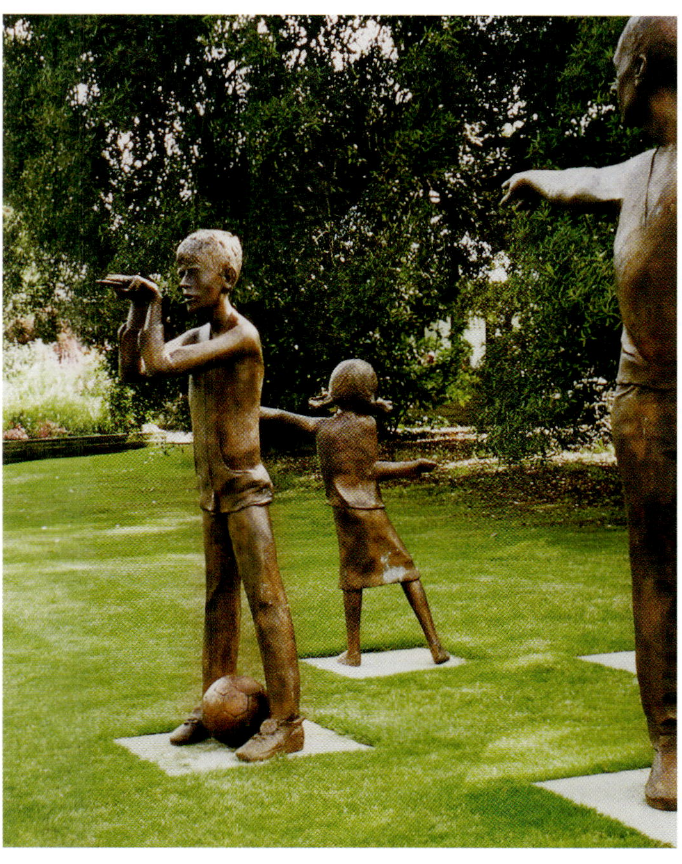

The Family, by John W. Mills, in bronze (2000). Made one and a quarter life size.

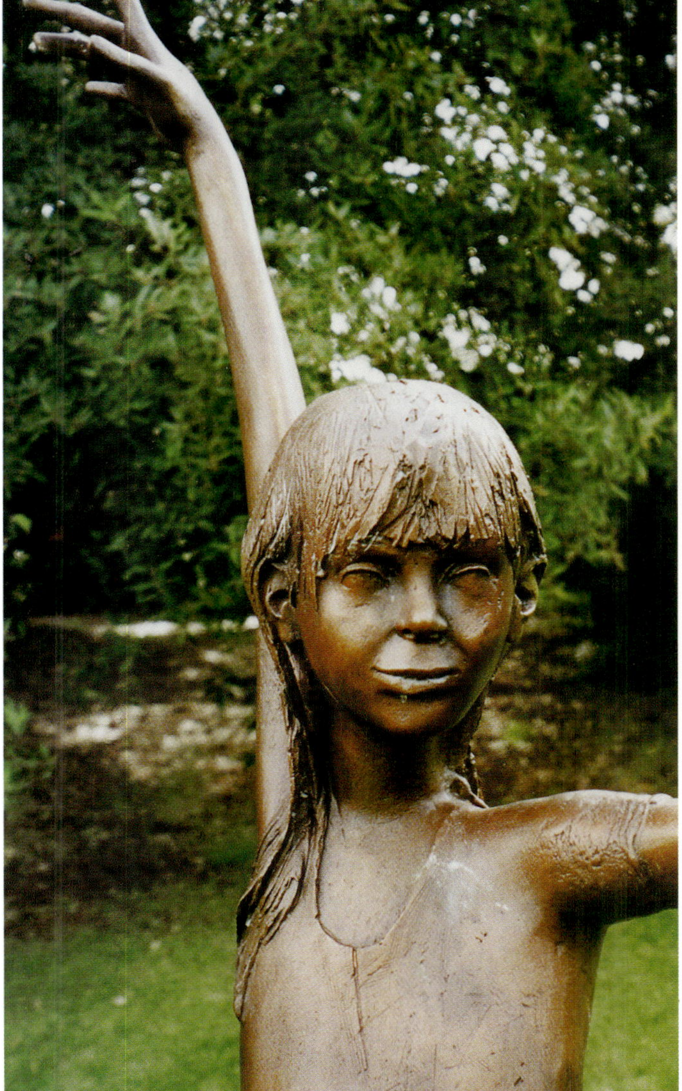

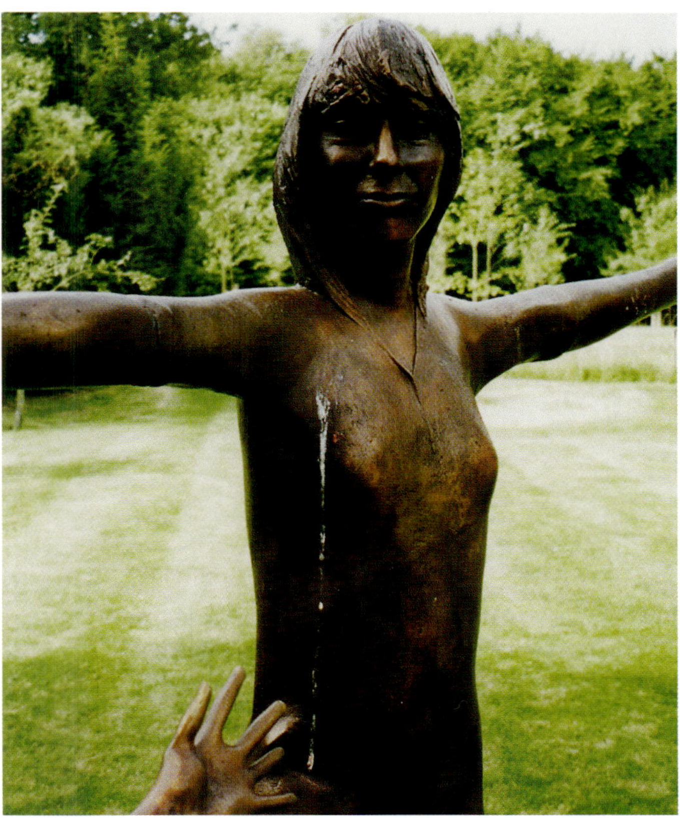

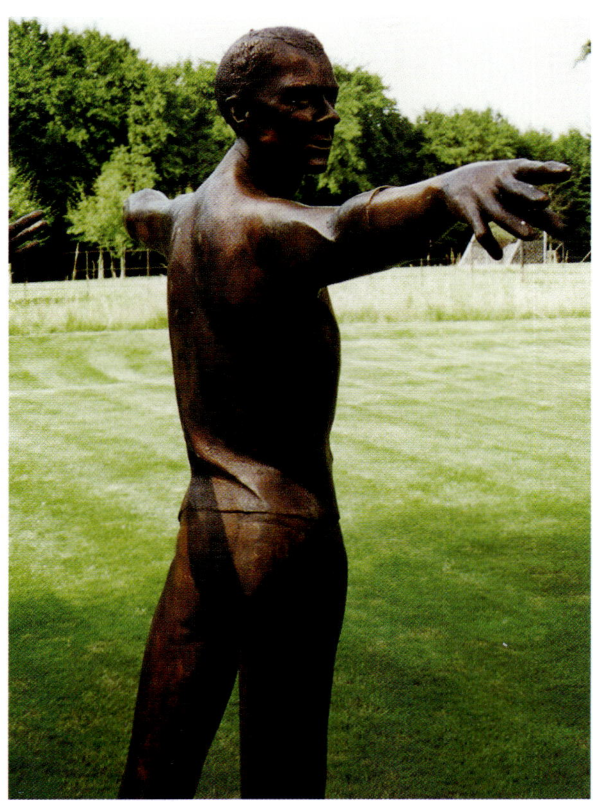

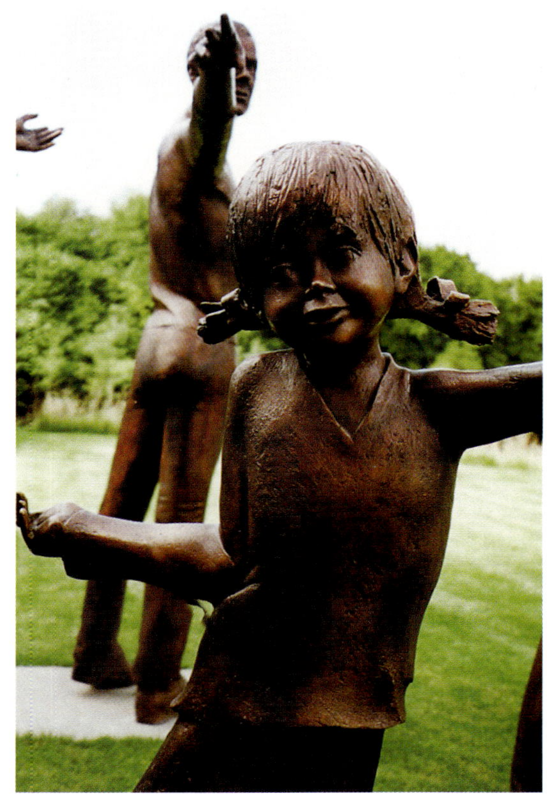

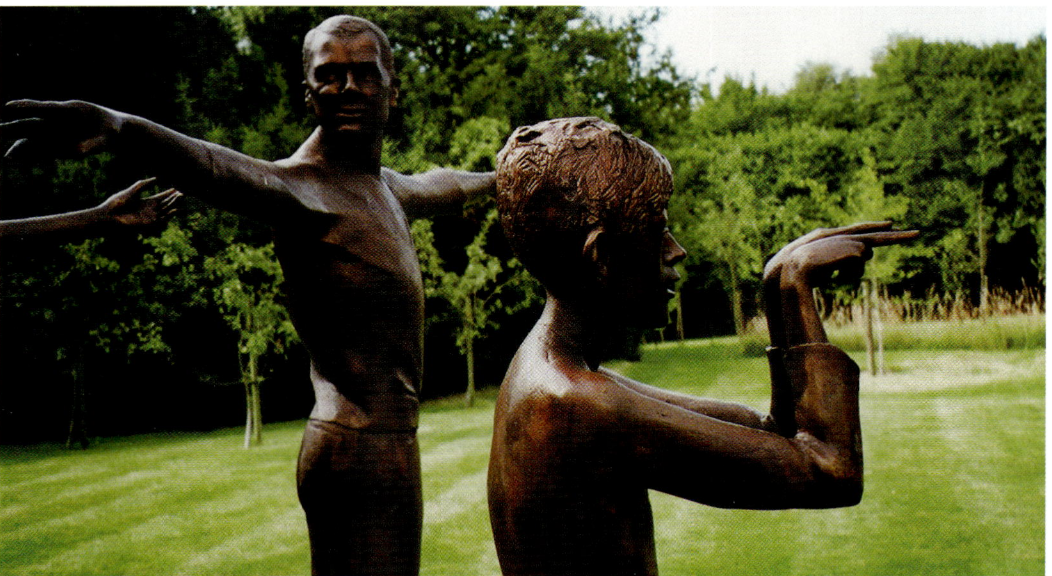

The Family, *by John W. Mills, in bronze (2000). Made one and a quarter life size.*

smaller columns jointed roughly half-way down at the knees. The rib cage is in effect a flexible basket of small bones attached at the back to the upper spine. From the top of the rib cage hangs a yoke of bones, including those of the arms. Surmounting the spine is the skull, a strong, roughly ovoid object. Hands and feet are a collection of articulating small bones that give strength and flexibility. This plain description may seem simplistic but, coupled to the inherent understanding of the human being that everyone has, it serves as a neat aid to thinking when starting to make a sculpture using the figure.

The function and articulation of the skeleton and its components as it affects daily life are also important, but only to the point of being aware of that fundamental awareness that enables a person to take care of him or herself. For example, everyone knows that their spine is not only a strong supporting structure but also made up of small linked elements that make it very flexible, capable of

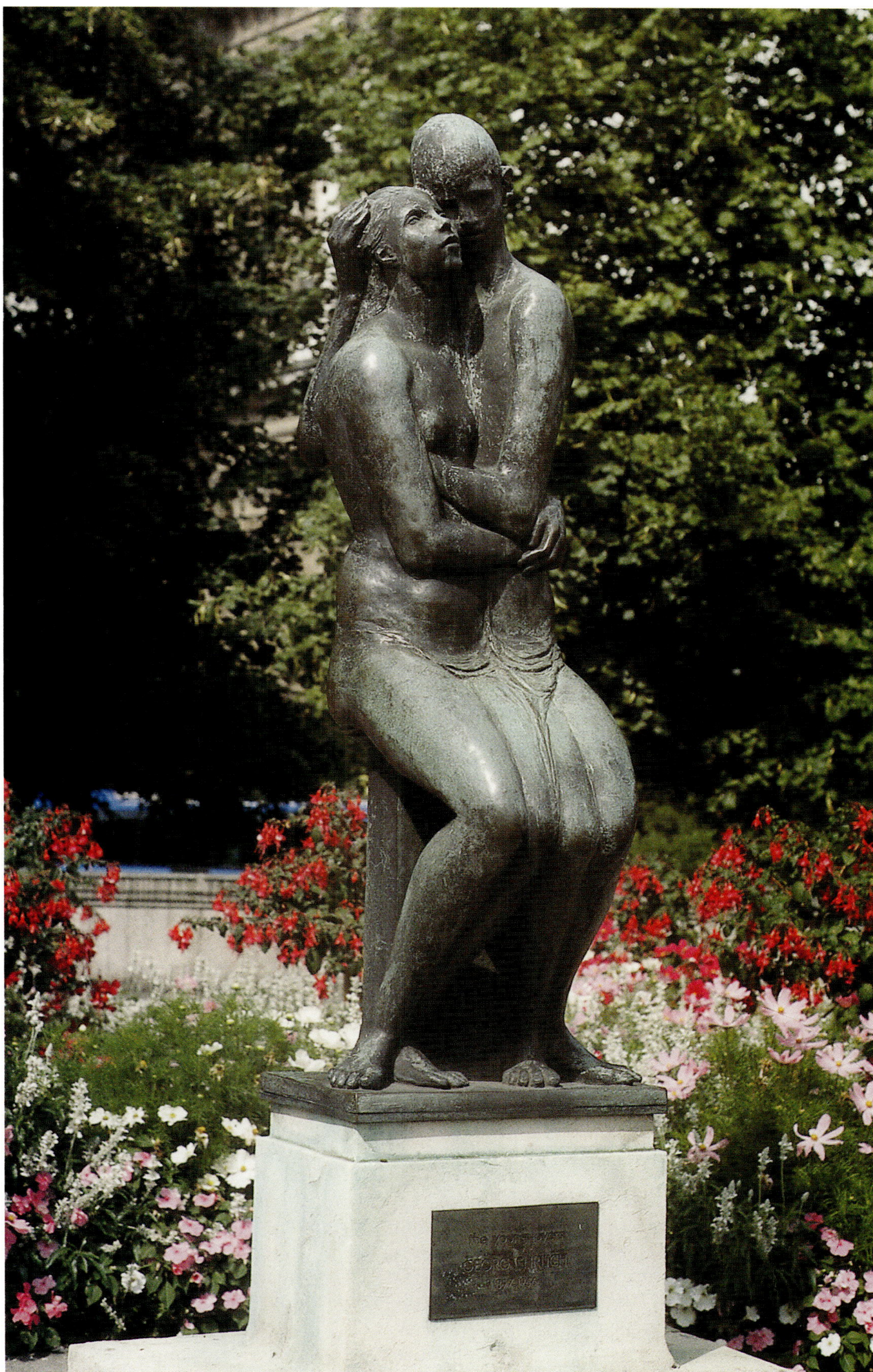

Lovers, *by George Eurlich. (St Paul's, London)*

extreme movement, especially in the young and healthy. This is a fundamental fact that is common to everyone, while the shape of the spine and the disposition of curves vary from person to person, establishing their particular individuality. Other fundamental facts are that the ribcage provides a flexible protection for vital organs, and the skull offers a hard protective cover to the delicate and vulnerable brain. What is important to the artist is the unique shapes they make and how they are disposed on top of and along the spine; this observable phenomenon differs from one individual to another. The pelvis too has a vital role to play in human anatomy; to the sculptor it is the rigid link that transfers the flexible strength and energy of the spine to the legs. It is different from the collarbone girdle, which can swing and move conveying in its extreme movement a kind of windmill-like action to the arms.

The articulation of all the joints of the body needs to be understood in all their basic functions as hinges and shock absorbers. Well-drawn, carved and modelled joints on a figurative sculpture will help to make that figure more believable. It is important that the difference between a knee and an elbow is clearly shown, even though they are both hinges, as are the joints of the fingers. Attention to the rotational function of the ball and socket joints at the shoulder and hips will help to give a feeling of true movement to the sculptured figure, and the particular action of the wrist when properly shown will add strength to the perception of the implied movement of the arm. The ankles are the joints that deal constantly with the greatest physical load, yet they remain flexible and springy under the body's weight, acting as very efficient shock absorbers. Feet have been described as being like a 'springy wattle of interwoven small forms'; they aid the balance and stability that are necessary if the person is to be able to walk. Good feet on a carved or modelled figure make for a better result; similarly, good ears make a better portrait sculpture.

Musculature must be treated with respect, but without awe. Remember that it is the individual's appearance that is paramount and as this can be observed it is the true reference. There are many books on anatomy, some medical and others aimed specifically at artists. Arthur Thomson's *A Handbook of Anatomy for Art Students*, after its first publication in about 1920, became required reading for many students, and was essential for most art-school examinations in the next twenty years or so. In the preface to his fifth edition of that book, Thomson recalls a first meeting with an artist of repute who told him that the first thing he did after passing his exams was 'to burn your bloody book'. Thomson went on to say that after his initial resentment to the remark he came to realize the truth, which is that a book is no substitute for observation. The absorbing fact of human anatomy is that, despite all people having all the same component parts, the shape and disposition of those components are infinitely variable, making up the amazing mix of men, women and children encountered in daily life. My own realization of this diversity came during my National Service when I was a Physical Training Instructor. Every two weeks, approximately two hundred new recruits arrived in the gymnasium providing the spectacle of that number of assorted male bodies, exercising and using various apparatus on a daily basis. This became for me the most stimulating anatomy lesson I could have dreamed of. Academic anatomy had been part of my art school life for seven years, but the real lesson was there before me – all those bodies, each complete and fit and working, but so different in shape and size, were for an aspiring sculptor quite fascinating. Unfortunately, the equivalent experience for studying female anatomy on that scale was not made available to me...

The body's outward appearance is dictated by muscle over bone covered by skin and, having become conscious of the importance of the skeleton, the sculptor needs to become visually familiar with musculature. Muscles are those observable forms, both large and small, that move, flex and relax as the figure moves. They have the peculiar characteristic of not travelling in a sraight line between points of skeletal contact. With the assistance of tendons and ligaments, their job is to combine with the structure of the skeleton to provide the power for movement of all the body's functions – large and small, powerful and subtle. They connect to the skeleton at strategic points that have evolved to maintain a perfect equilibrium as the muscles power actuates movement. The complexity of the fixtures to the bones dictates the shape of muscles that curve and twist, layer upon layer, to create the strongest possible sustainable connection. Twisting forms create a greater surface tension than those that follow a straight line between points of contact and therefore provide greater power for their function. This curving principle is an underlying design factor in the formation of muscles. In view of the modernist maxim, that 'form follows function', young sculptors need to pay heed to the appearance of shapes made up of curving forms; in particular, studying those with an upward living dynamic will help to enhance the quality of the forms that are produced.

One word of warning: in being aware of the vital subject of human anatomy, the sculptor must also give specific attention to his or her own back, joints and heart. The young are easily tempted to pick up a heavy weight and move it without thinking, but this is foolish and useful only in the very short term. Whenever possible, it is more sensible to use additional power, of both the human and mechanical kind; if the back, heart and joints are protected, you will certainly last longer and possibly produce more sculpture. Becoming more aware of your own anatomy – its musculature and functions, particularly in acts of strength and movement, and the consequent load-bearing capacity of the relative limbs and joints – will lead to a greater awareness and empathy between you and the figure or figures you are making.

8

Carving the Figure

Creating a sculpture of the whole figure or a combination of whole figures makes fascinating demands on all sculptors, putting to the test the artist's ability to conceive an idea, compose all the compositional elements, and tell the story in all its required detail. Figurative sculpture is a challenge in every medium; carving the figure, from whatever material is chosen, is an additional challenge.

Materials

Exploiting the Material

It is important to be familiar with the nature of the material to be carved and its consequent influence on the sculpture to be made. There is an essential difference between natural materials that have only compressive strength and those that have tensile tenacity; this is shown in the difference, for example, between hard, dense granite and soft, even-fibred lime wood. It is impossible to make a tall, slender, free-standing figure using granite while such a sculpture is easily carved in lime wood.

The degree of compressive and tensile strength varies from one material to another and these two factors can dictate the design of a sculpture. The slender, more naturalistic figures that distinguish the marble sculptures of the Hellenistic Greek period were only achievable by adding compositional elements that gave external support to the figure; these might take the form of a column, a weapon, a fragment of tree, an animal, or any similar item. In more sophisticated narratives, other figures would be involved in the design. Free-standing sculptures that explore comprehensively the compressive strength of the stone or marble are those that include more than one figure in the composition. Group compositions give the artist the opportunity to combine figures according to the block from which they were carved, each figure providing support for the other. One famous example of this is the group Triumph of Youth Over Old Age by Michelangelo, in which he created a basic spiral design, combining the two figures in a strong, twisting configuration. The nature of the design is such that the sculpture is imbued with strength and equilibrium; these qualities existed in the quarried marble block and the artist's knowledge and experience enabled him to exploit them with the utmost confidence.

This use of a spiralling pattern in figure composition, which seeks to utilize the quality inherent in the stone, was often copied by other sculptors of the Renaissance and in later periods of European art history. Danish sculptor Gustave Vigeland spent the greater part of his life on a single commission making enormous number of figures in many combinations, from single images to groups of many characters, to create what has become known as the Vigeland Sculpture Park in Oslo. He used granite for most of the carving and designed all of the work according to the demands of that stone. Many of the pieces are columnar in shape; fig-

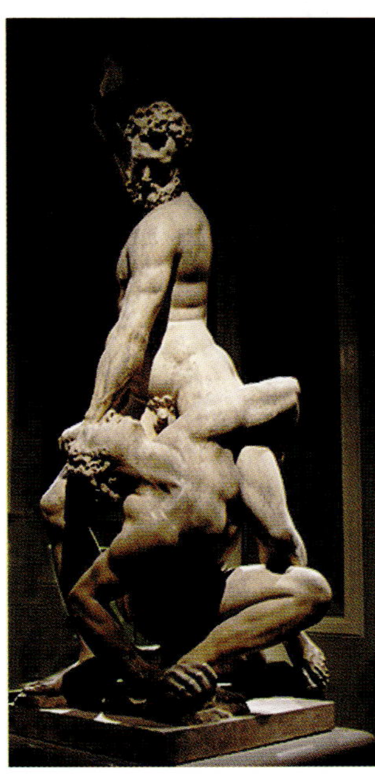

Samson and a Philistine, *by Giambologna, in marble. The spiral dynamic of Michelangelo is exploited to the full by Giambologna. (V&A Museum, Plaster Courts, London)*

ures are often piled one upon another to retain all of the compressive strength of the hard, dense material. Clearly, where the artist has a good understanding of the stone and its properties, he or she will find a way to resolve a particular creative problem.

Hardness and Colour

Stone is rich in variety in terms of both hardness and colour, ranging from tough, igneous rock such as granite through the diminishing hardnesses of various limestones to the softer sandstone The most favoured of the softer stones for carving are probably alabaster and soapstone, both of which are rich in colour, and polish quite easily. Soapstone is often given to beginners to carve because it is relatively easy to deal with and the good colour that appears as it is polished provides much encouragement. Alabaster is also soft, and is as colourful as soapstone, but it is tender and can be easily stunned when hit directly, leaving a white bruise mark that penetrates to a depth of an inch (25mm) or so, spoiling the translucency of the stone. It needs to be cut using sharp chisels rather than carved using the coarser carving tools that are more suitable for other types of stone (see the illustration opposite).

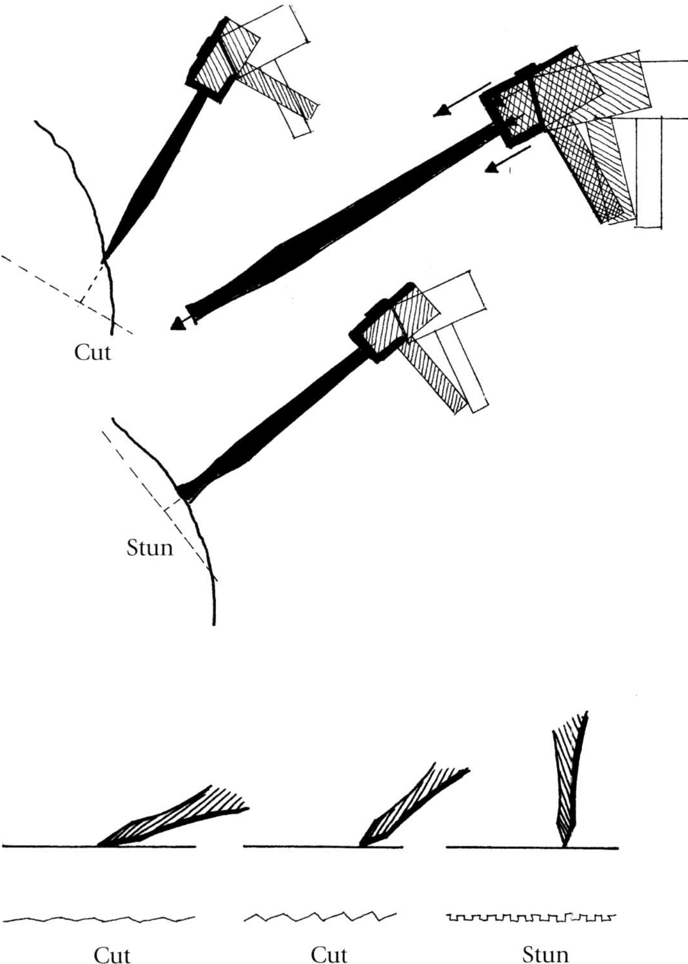

Diagrams of the angle and striking position of the chisel and hammer. Three examples of the angle of cut and stun.

The colour of natural materials is certainly one of their enchantments and this applies particularly to marble and the softer limestones, which are often used for inlaid work of a decorative architectural nature as well as for more exotic coloured sculptures.

Wood has a more restricted range of colour than stone, but it still ranges from the dense black of ebony to the paleness of blond lime wood. In the case of wood, it is the huge variety of grain structures that provide the great attraction and one of the skills of wood carving is to exploit whenever possible the combination of grain and colour of the wood chosen for the sculpture. Care must be taken in determining where the markings will occur; in the wrong place, they can spoil an image, or at least affect adversely the perception of the image. Sometimes the grain can seem to swirl around a shape, giving attention to a form or detail that does not need such emphasis. Such markings can also occur in stone, showing up only when it receives a final polish, and a flaw like this can spoil a carving, particularly a piece in pure white marble. A client may even reject a finished work that shows such a mark, and this is one of the hazards of carving wood and stone. Resolving such problems is always a test the ingenuity of the artist.

The sculptors of the Baroque period in Europe were particularly fond of using marbles of different colours in a single sculpture. The Romans had also used the practice of inlay, but it was the seventeenth and eighteenth centuries that saw a real explosion of this kind of decorative sculpture, which was influenced by an elaborate, almost over-exuberant, use of colour in stone, bronze, timber and ceramic. Highly skilled cabinetmakers exploited various colours and textures in furniture, making intricate patterns and picture marquetry using wood and wood veneers from around the world. Lorenzo Bernini in Rome during this period exploited almost all of the materials, sometimes in a single project. The exuberance with which he indulged his sculptures and their Baroque settings is sometimes almost overwhelming. He expressed himself with such flamboyant theatricality that, even when he was not using colour, the manner in which he carved the marble reflected the cornucopia of skills so typical of the Baroque show-off.

Making a Sculpture

Getting Started

The world of carved sculptural expression is a rich one, and there is no better way of finding out about it than getting out of the studio to encounter it in all its manifestations, in town- and cityscapes, as well as in museums, churches, palaces and castles. It seems that everything man has made has required decoration of some kind, sometimes simple and sometimes complicated and sophisticated, but always fascinating, particularly to the eyes of those who also aspire to make sculptural images.

There is no substitute for actually making a sculpture. The hands-on experience of dealing with a material and forming an image is unique, and will always be unique, no matter how experienced a sculptor becomes. The beginner can do no better than to find a small piece of carvable material – stone, soft concrete block, chalk, wood of whatever variety, or almost anything else you can get hold of (as a schoolboy, I used to carve small images from the stumps of candles) – take the simplest of tools required to get started, and have a go. Do not be too ambitious, but begin with simple things and try to work at a size that will enable you to complete the work in a reasonable time scale, so that you can enjoy the excitement of completing an image. The

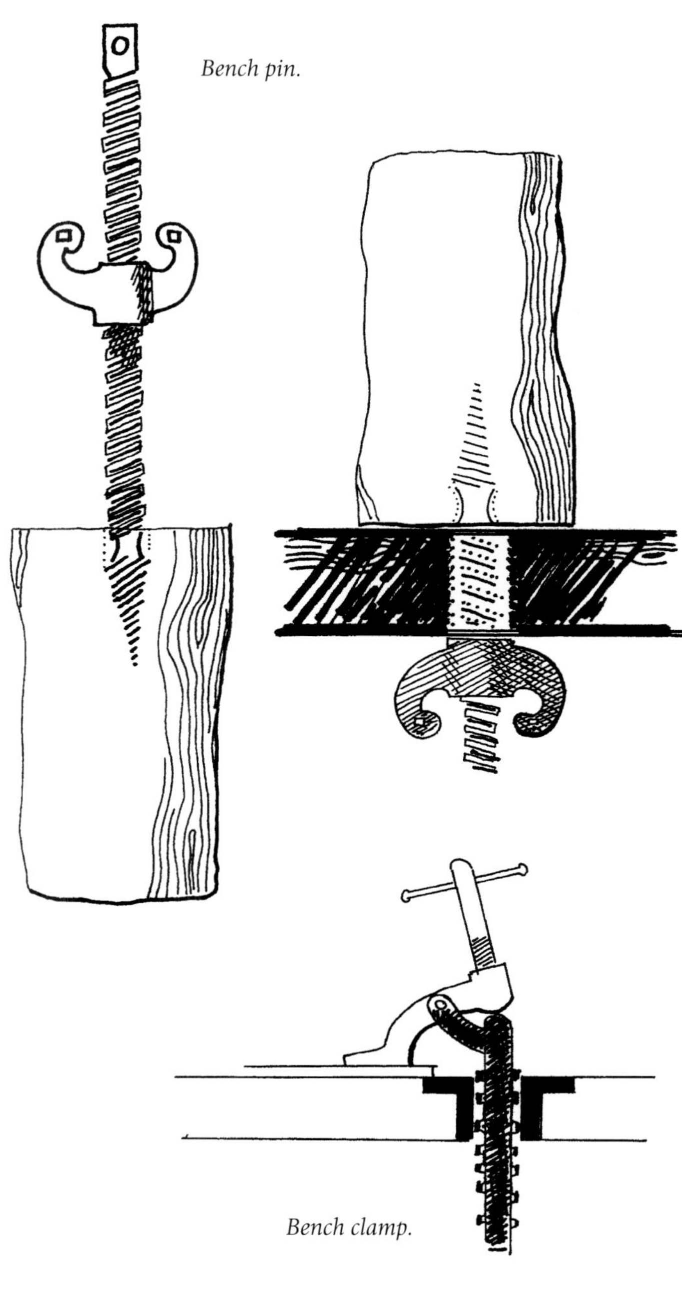

Bench pin.

Bench clamp.

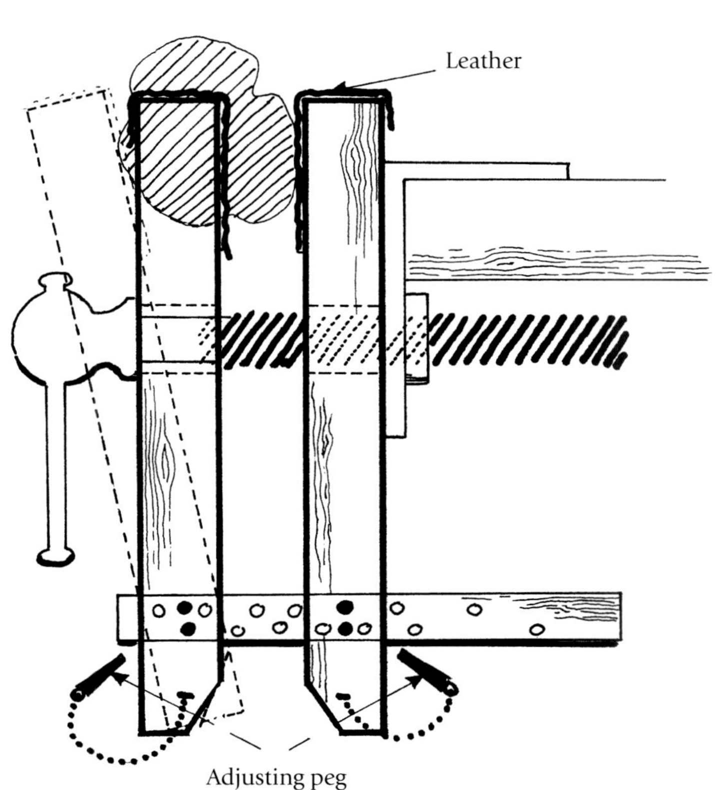

The Gillespie adjustable vice.

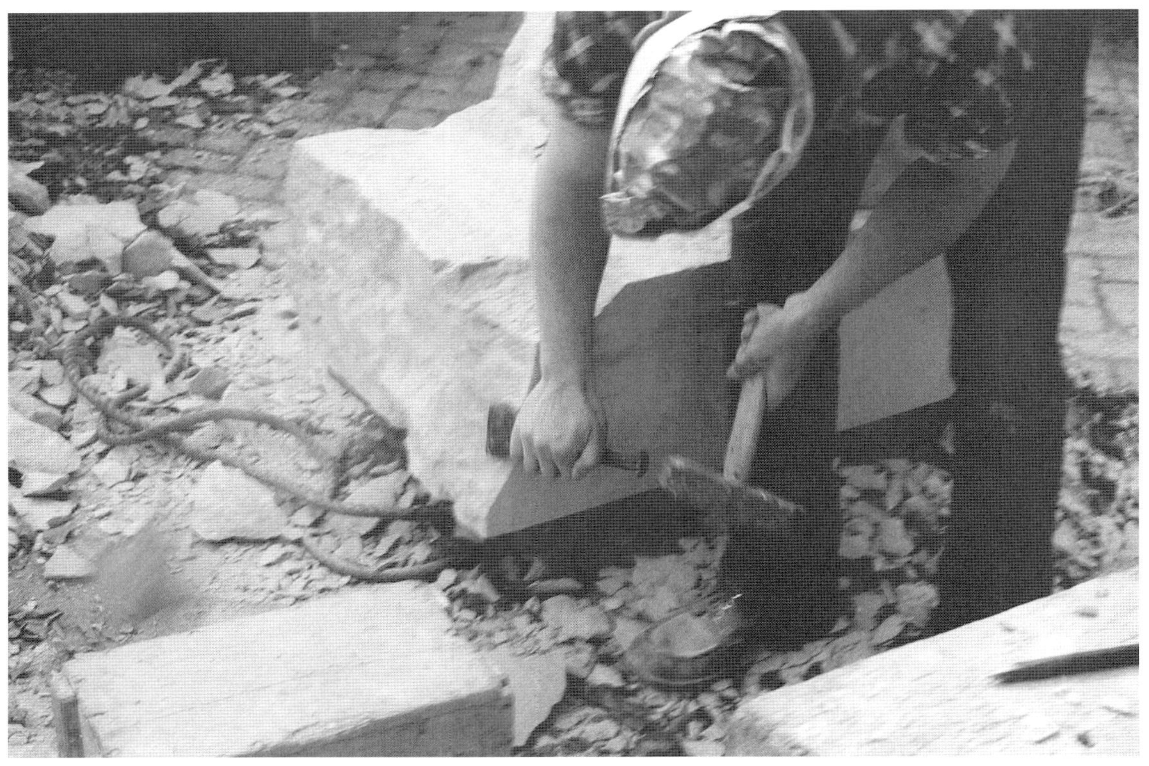

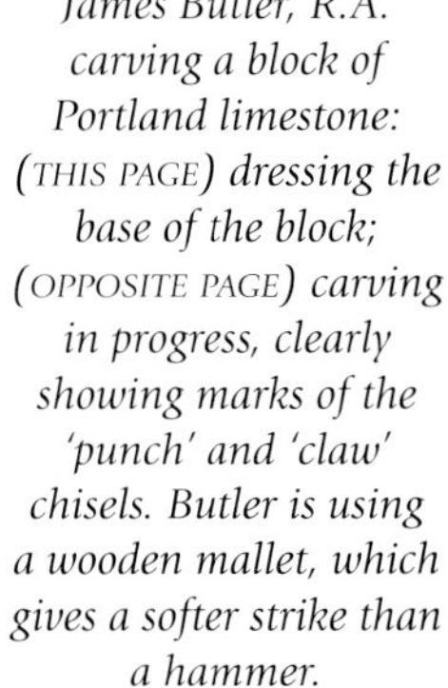

James Butler, R.A. carving a block of Portland limestone: (THIS PAGE) dressing the base of the block; (OPPOSITE PAGE) carving in progress, clearly showing marks of the 'punch' and 'claw' chisels. Butler is using a wooden mallet, which gives a softer strike than a hammer.

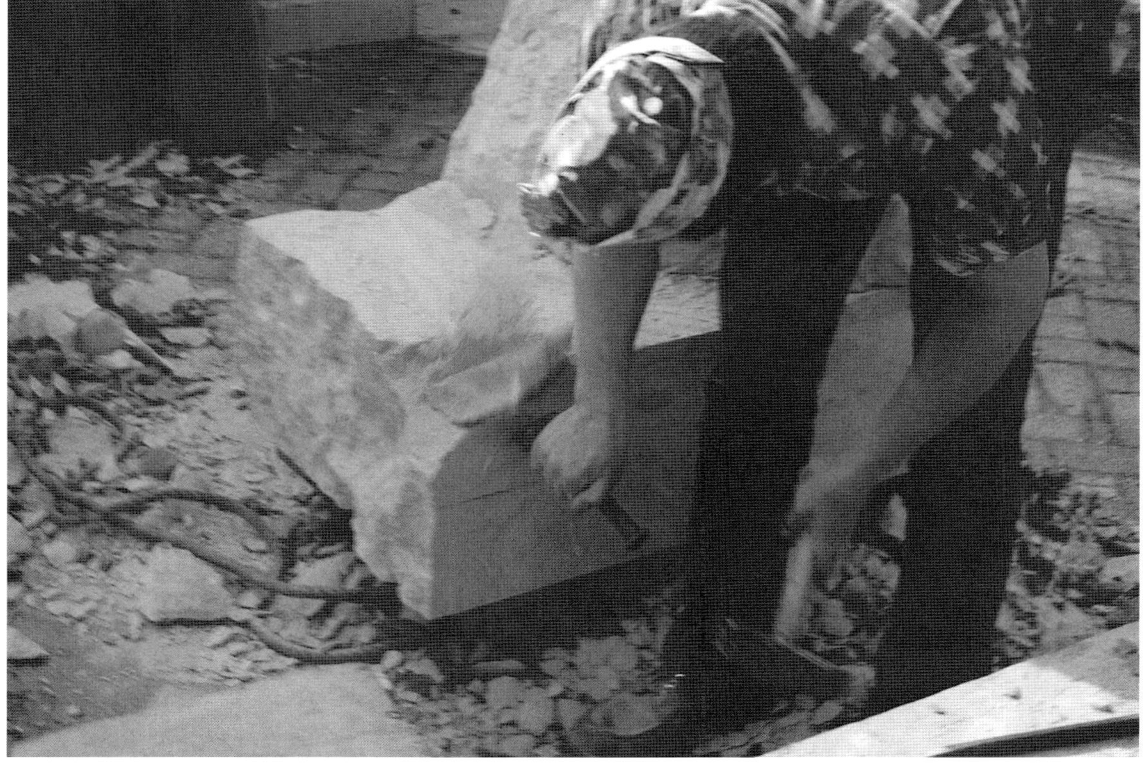

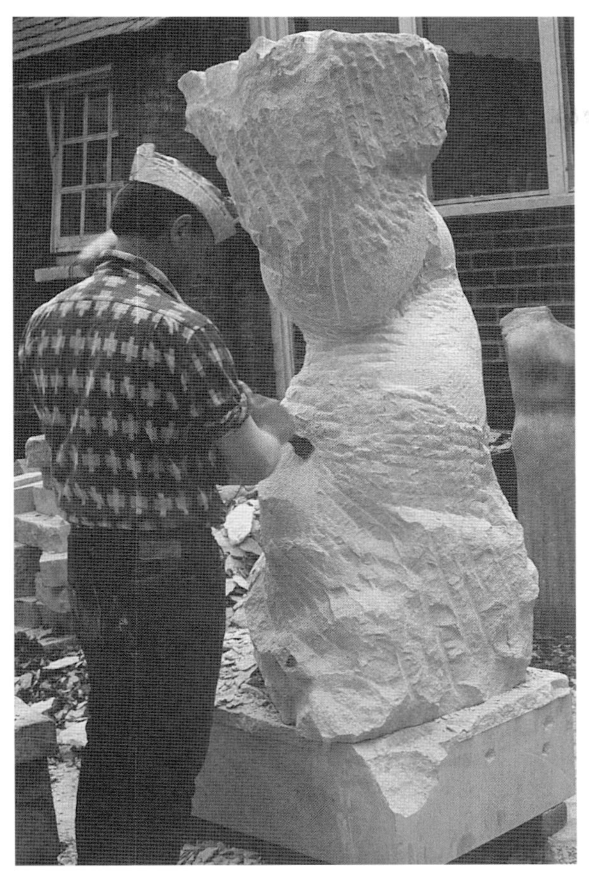

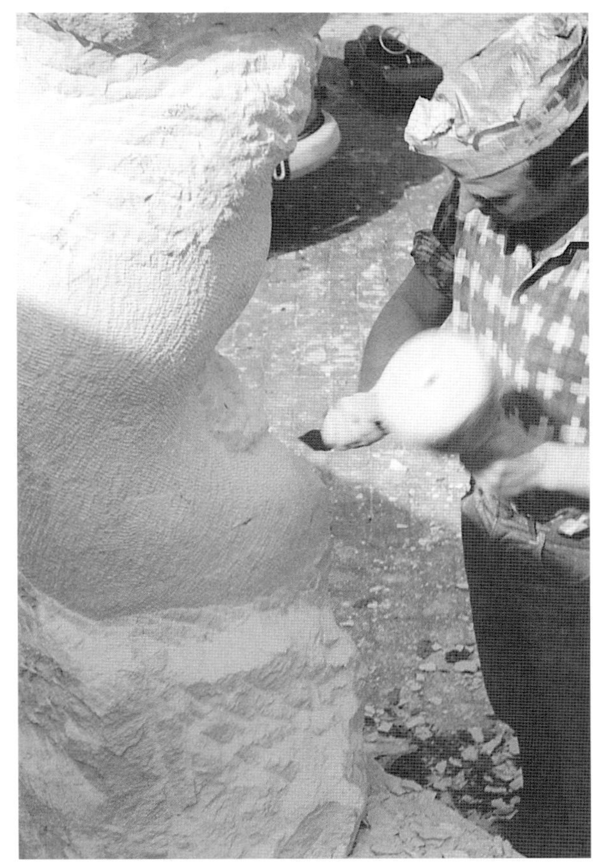

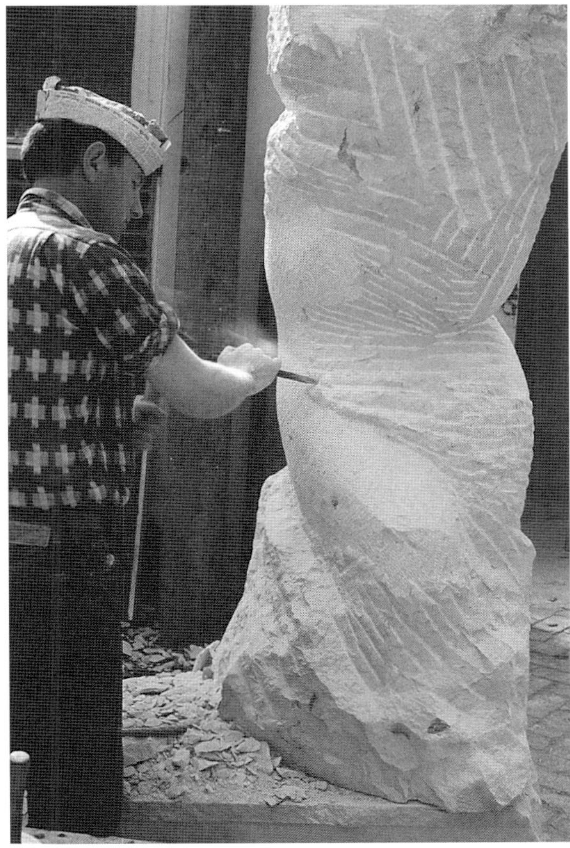

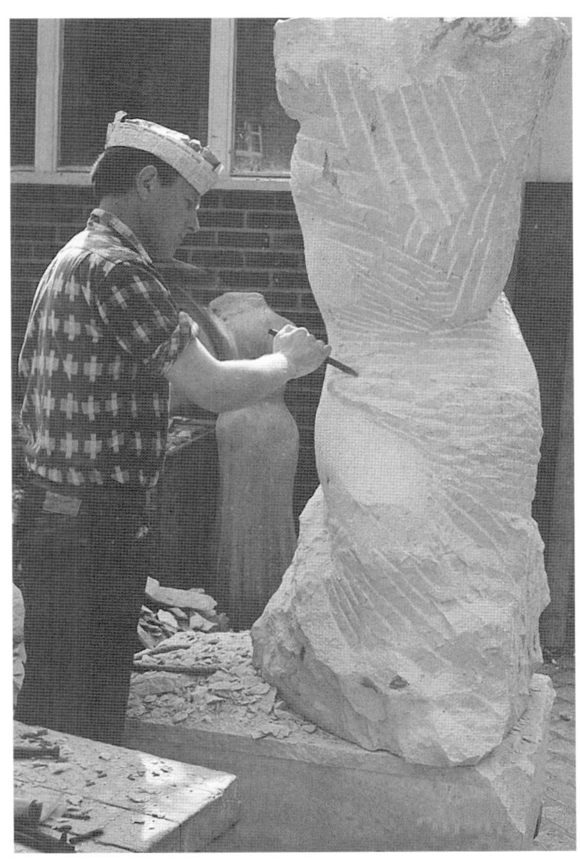

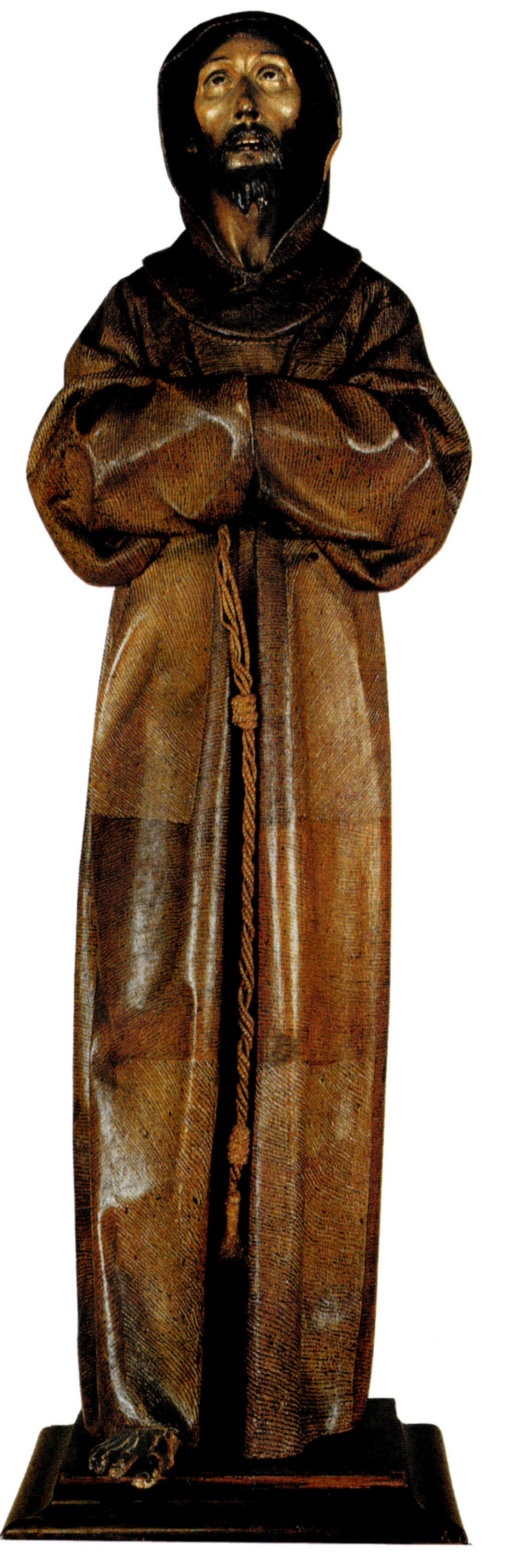

St Francis, *Spanish polychromatic woodcarving. This is a fine example of a gesso-covered and painted woodcarving, which also retains the character of the original log shape. (Louvre, Paris)*

objective at this stage should be to get the feel of working with the subtractive process of carving. If the object is larger than can be safely held in the hand, set up the material to be as comfortable to work with as possible. For stone or any other hard material, use a sand bag, a cushion or a sand box to hold the work safely and to absorb shock from the hammer. If you are carving wood, use a suitable vice with soft jaws (see the illustration on page 115). At this stage it is not wise to invest in sophisticated sets of tools, tempting as they may be in the shop; after all, you may turn out to be a modeller rather than a carver. Choose a range of simple tools such as chisels, rasps, rifflers, knives, and so on, that can be multi-purpose. Always try to make sure the tools you do use are suitable and sharp – more accidents happen with blunt tools than with sharp ones – and wear suitable gloves and protective glasses or goggles.

Try to design the image so that the whole thing is contained within the block you have chosen, or if it is wood, plan for it to allow the greatest freedom of design, but with a balanced composition. There are two reasons for doing this: first, you are more likely to have a good experience of working according to the block and therefore exploiting the characteristic strength of the chosen material; and second, the sculpture will stand with confidence, in balance, when it is completed. Even on the small scale the beginner should work hard at considering these design factors, so that their consideration gradually becomes instinctive.

My personal preference is for all movement to be contained within the base area of the sculpture, no matter how active or exuberant the image may be. Balance and equilibrium are significant factors in the perception of any three-dimensional object, large or small, and are especially relevant in large heavy sculptures, where any slight imbalance becomes obvious and upsetting. The slightest deviation from a state of equilibrium becomes magnified in the eye of the beholder and will intimidate the viewer, giving the impression that the sculpture is likely to topple over.

Making Larger Carvings

When the time comes to make a large carving there are several ways to proceed, according to what you wish to achieve. The experienced sculptor will either design for a stone or a bulk of timber already in the studio – all carvers collect lumps of stone and wood whenever it comes their way – or will find a piece of either material to fit an idea he or she wishes to resolve in a certain way. The sculptor working to commission will design according to the site and if the site is on a building, and the stone is already part of the fabric of the building, then the design will have to be worked with those relatively restricting factors in mind.

For a free-standing sculpture, a single standing figure, for example, the block of stone will need to be trued and made to stand correctly. This means dressing off the base of the block to make a flat surface on which the sculpture will stand in equilibrium (see the illustration on page 88). Time and care must be given to this stage, because it is almost impossible to do it later. Attention to a proper balance of the block also applies to bulky wood carving, although it is a little easier to sling and turn timber than stone and therefore more feasible to true a base after carving the image; however, this is not best practice.

Once the block is standing correctly, the actual carving can start. On the assumption that maquettes have been resolved, and any working model made if the work is very large, these should be placed in good relationship to the block to allow the sculptor to see their correlation easily at all times while working. Diagrams can be drawn on the block indicating the image within and the waste material that needs to be removed. If there are large areas of waste to be cut away, try to cut these out as large as possible; the lumps removed may be useful for carving smaller items later. Try not to whittle the block down by repeatedly carving the image over and over. Whatever material is being used, the task is to remove the waste efficiently so that the resolution of the image can be achieved by refining the forms and surfaces as you go. The initial work is done with large, hard-working tools – the punch on stone and the large gouge or axe on timbers. This stage is referred to as blocking out or roughing out.

The roughing-out tools will continue to be used until the image demands that the sculptor take up more refined tools, to cut and carve finer form and some detail. This refining procedure will be repeated, paying attention to detail according to the planned image, until the sculpture is done. The final surfaces of both stone and timber may require the use of abrasives, ranging from coarse-grit stone blocks to the finest sandpaper or sheets of emery. The artist needs to become as familiar with abrasive materials as possible, in order to make the right choices at this stage, to produce the best effect.

Safety

A good design concept provides another benefit that must be considered: safety for both the sculpture and for the public when it is placed on site in the public domain. No matter how well the site is supervized, any sculpture will receive attention, sometimes of a malicious kind. It is better to try to anticipate such attention and plan the sculpture accordingly. For example, extensions from the body mass of the sculpture are always vulnerable, especially those made of stone, and so should be avoided. Such extremities

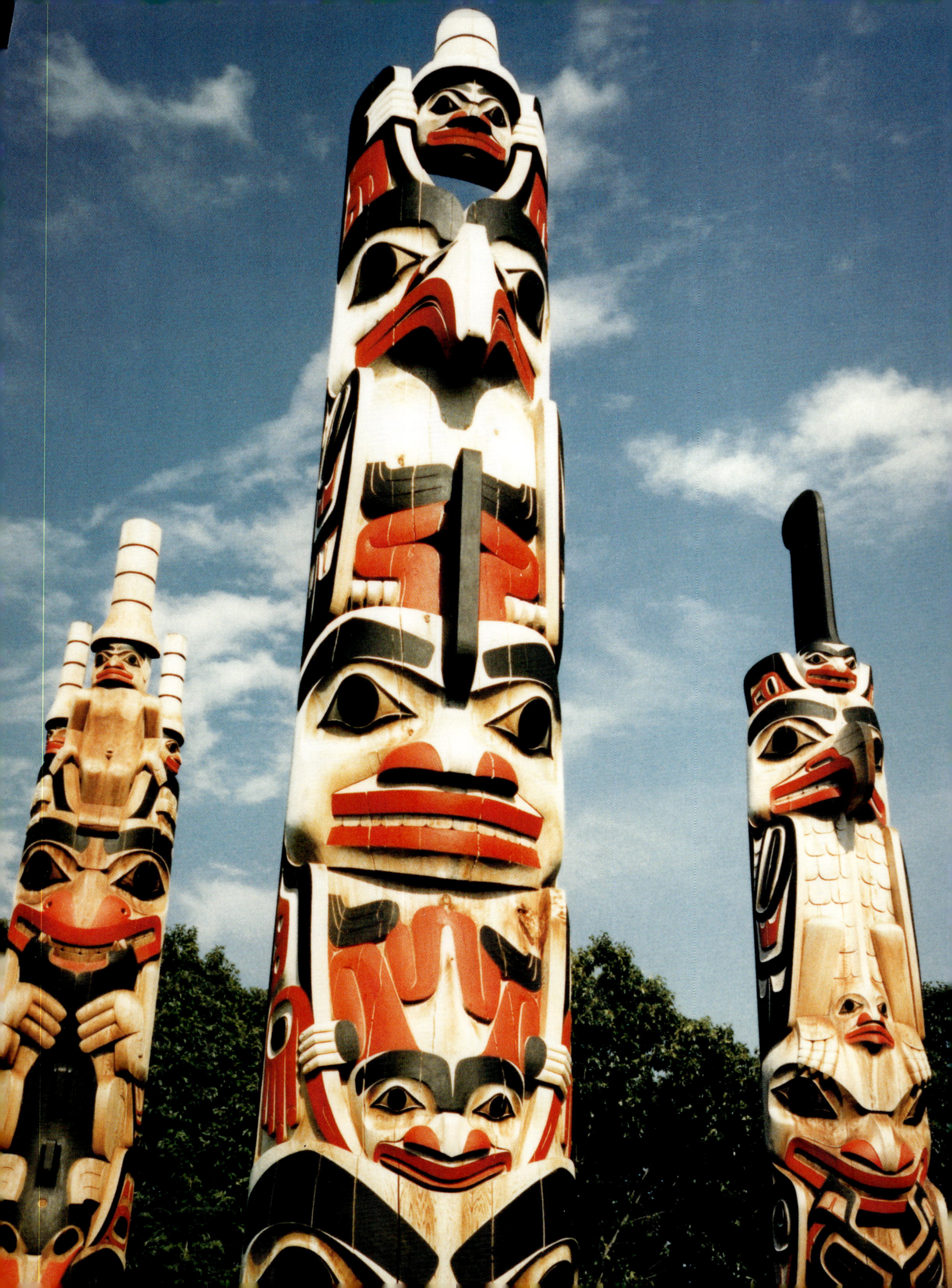

may be made in bronze or other metals with some degree of safety, but the temptation to climb up or swing on an outstretched form will always prove irresistible to some members of the public.

Although wood will permit a greater range of slender extension than stone, it has a limited strength and as a result is not necessarily suited to a public site. Large wooden totem-like sculptures are possible, and such pieces are found in many parts of the world, used in public ceremonial events as well as becoming sculptural elements to a landscape.

Getting to know the relative properties and qualities of the materials of sculpture will help the sculptor to exploit them with confidence. All materials for public works should be considered thoroughly in terms of safety, and this concern may restrict the artist's freedom of expression. However, public liability is an important factor when a sculpture is placed in a public site, and a matter for serious professional practice, which will include contracts, planning permission, ownership, copyright and intellectual rights, and insurance, as well as third-party responsibilities.

In the mean time, the most important thing for the younger sculptor is to enjoy the process of learning about making sculpture, and to gain the greatest pleasure from doing so, at the same time having some awareness of what is involved in the professional world of sculpture.

OPPOSITE: *Totem pole. (Pepisco collection, White Plains, New York, USA)*

9

Basic Casting

With the exception of modelling for terracotta, which involves baking (firing) clay to produce the final product, nearly all other modelling procedures need to be moulded and cast at various stages in the production of the final work. The casting process requires the manufacture of a negative mould (female), from which the original subject can be removed and replaced with a more durable material to make the positive cast (male). This casting procedure has been practised ever since mankind devised ways of making and reproducing vessels and implements for the household, weapons of war and for hunting, as well as for the making of icons for worship. It is found throughout modern industry, from heavy engineering making gargantuan castings to injection-moulding machines producing all kinds of plastic products. There have been many technical refinements according to the final material, the product and its complexity, but the basic principles remain the same: a mould (negative) is required from which a casting (positive) can be made.

The sculptor of the twenty-first century has available most of the industrial casting processes and materials; some are very old, while others are very new. Even the most cursory research of the world of sculpture will reveal pieces made in a wide range of resins reinforced with glass- and carbon-fibre, as well as all the cast metals. Even the most adventurous sculptor, exploring new materials and processes, will need an understanding of the basic principle of moulding and casting in order to make sense of new processes quickly enough to be able to put them to good use.

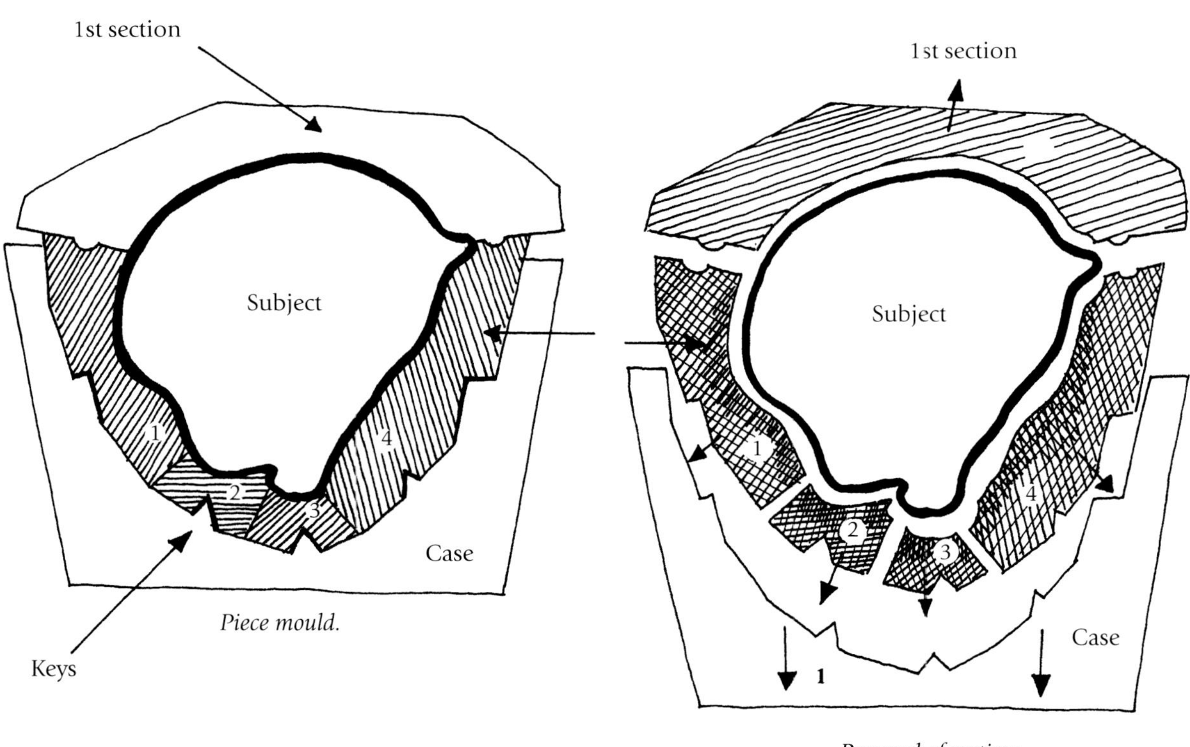

Piece mould.

Removal of sections.

Mould Types

Waste Mould and Piece Mould

The moulds made most frequently in the studio are the waste mould and the piece mould. Traditionally both types are made using plaster of Paris. The waste mould is made by placing a layer of plaster over a soft clay (natural or synthetic) original and, as its name suggests, it is designed to eventually become a waste product; removing the original clay after the plaster has hardened makes the hollow mould (negative). The hollow mould is then filled with plaster or some other hardening material, which is allowed to set hard to become the positive cast (male). When this is done, the mould is simply chipped away to become waste, revealing the cast.

The piece mould can be made over almost any original, hard or soft, and is designed to allow more than one casting to be made. This means that every undercut shape and form needs a separate section of mould that can be easily removed, both from the original subject and subsequently from the cast. Each separate section fits into a master mould (jacket), which holds them in the correct position for filling with the chosen casting medium (see the illustrations on page 122).

Flexible Moulds

Plaster of Paris is not the only moulding and casting medium. Almost any material that involves the mixing together of substances that become hard as a result can be used to make both moulds and casts. Choosing the most appropriate and effective substance for the job in hand takes some experience. Flexible moulds are probably the most common alternative to the waste and piece moulds. Most people will be familiar with the simple rubber moulds that can be bought to make castings of children's comic characters, which can then be painted. Such moulds are made from two types of compounds – hot-melting and cold-curing substances – none of which are materials for beginners to use, since they are both costly and complex. The hot-melting compounds are polyvinyl chlorides (vina-mould), which are reusable. Therefore, after a high initial cost for melting equipment and the compounds, the method can be relatively economical and was widely used in the 1960s and 70s. They serve a purpose, but they are smelly, difficult to use and the high melting temperature involved (108 degrees centigrade) makes them quite dangerous and means they can only be used on subjects that will not be damaged by the heat.

Cold-curing rubber compounds, referred to industrially as RTV (room-temperature vulcanizing) compounds, have succeeded the hot-melt substances in most cases, since they may be moulded over a much wider range of materials. Their application is less dangerous and they are relatively easy to use. Basically two-part compounds, when mixed together in the correct proportion they create a fine flexible material that is very suitable for mould-making and capable of reproducing the finest detail. They are silicone- or polyurethane-based and so require the respect that all resins demand at all times.

Techniques for Making Moulds

Basics

The techniques for using the new compounds are based on the basic principles of waste and piece moulding. Sculptors are advised to explore the newer materials and processes once they have mastered the basics of flexible moulding, which are described here (see the illustrations on page 124, a series of photographs showing a small figure being moulded using a cold-curing silicone rubber, and cast in a bronze-filled polyester resin, sometimes referred to as bonded bronze. Bronze-filled resins are sometimes referred to as 'cold-cast bronze', but this is a misnomer, as bronze cannot be cast cold. 'Bonded bronze' is a more accurate description.)

To mould an uncomplicated form, cover it with a shell of plaster of Paris about half an inch (25mm) thick (perhaps a little thicker for beginners). The shell is put on in two coats, the first of which is coloured, by dissolving a little yellow or blue powdered pigment in the clean water before adding the plaster. The second layer is added, using the plaster without colouring, and then built up to the required thickness. The coloured layer will act as a warning when chipping off the mould, to avoid any damage to the casting. Once the plaster shell has hardened, scoop out the clay to make the hollow negative (the mould).

Complex forms offer other kinds of problems, and different solutions with every new sculpture. The moulds need to be made up of a number of sections and pieces that can be lifted off the clay to allow for its removal, plus any armature used to support the clay while modelling. The planned removal of the pieces also facilitates the preparation of the mould surface and placing of the chosen filling to make the

FLEXIBLE CASTING

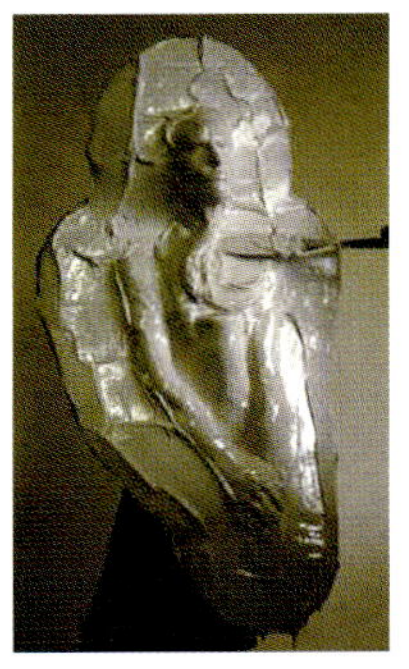

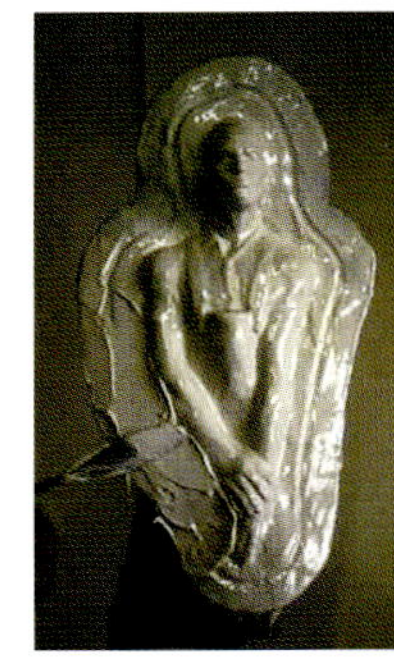

1. LEFT: *Applying the second layer.*

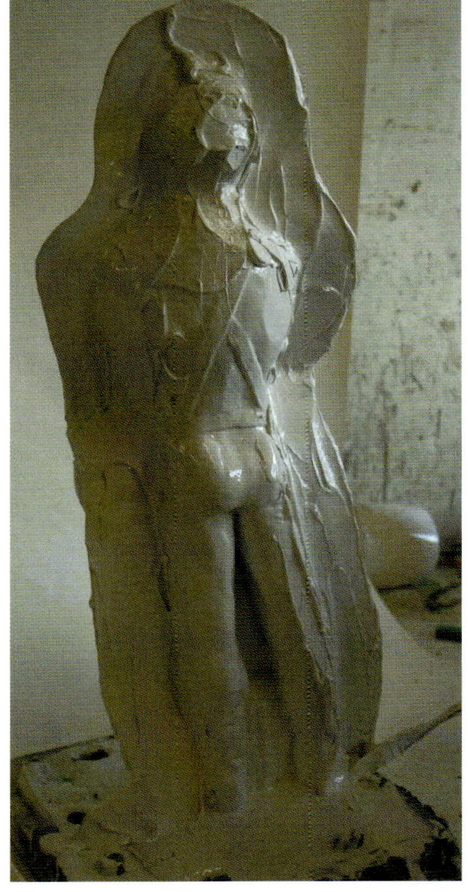

2. LEFT: *Applying the silicone to the back of the figure.*

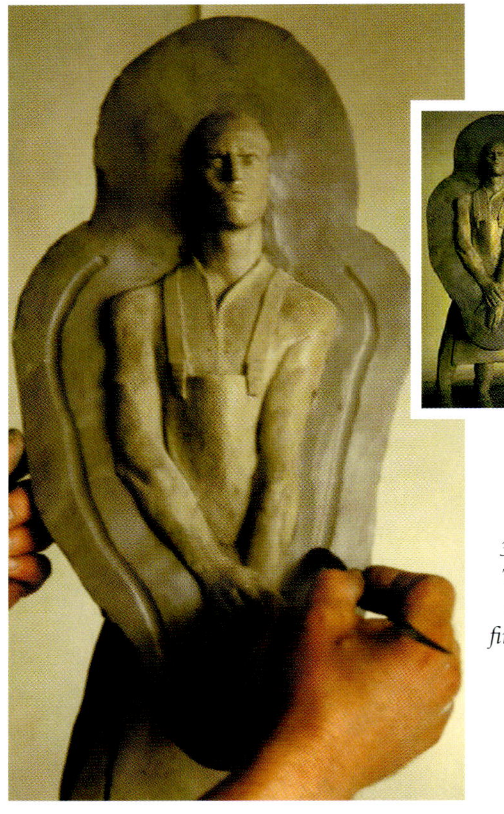

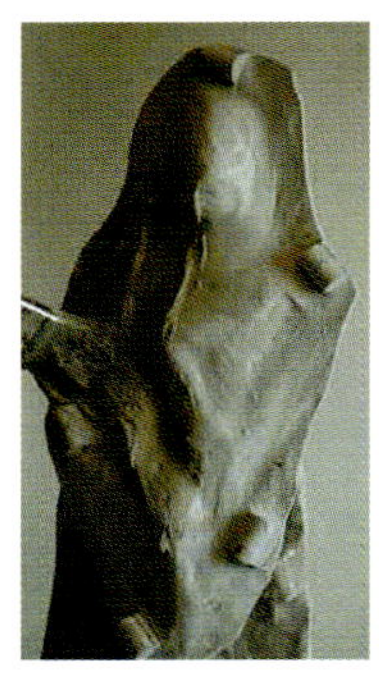

3. LEFT AND INSET: *The first clay wall and applying the first registration key.*

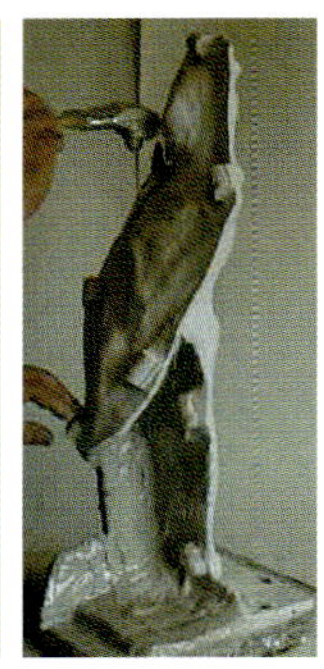

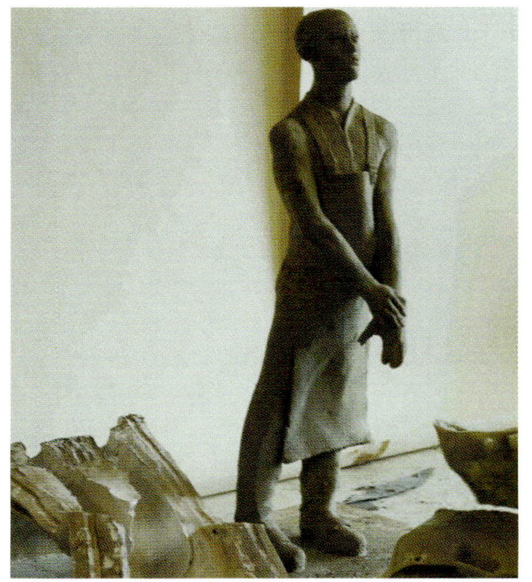

5. LEFT: *The original clay with part of the completed mould.*

4. FROM LEFT TO RIGHT: *Increaing the thickness of the rubber and making the fibre glass case.*

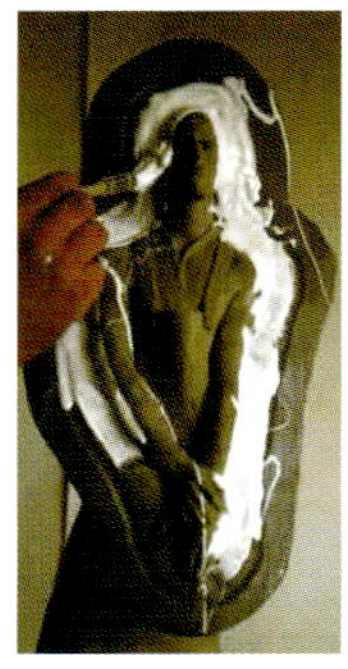

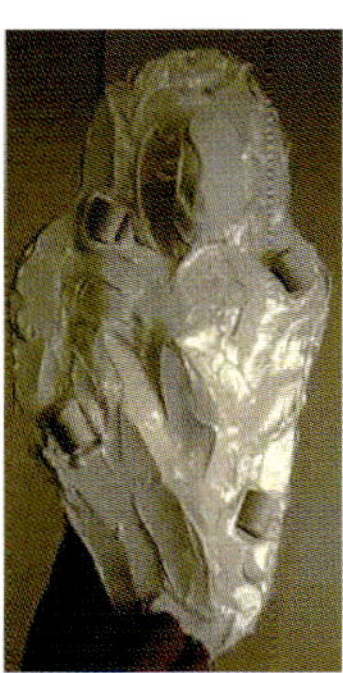

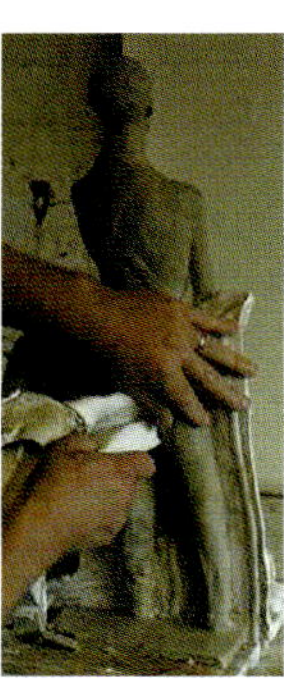

6. FROM LEFT TO RIGHT: *Painting on the first coat of silicone; registration keys in the rubber; and peeling the rubber from the clay.*

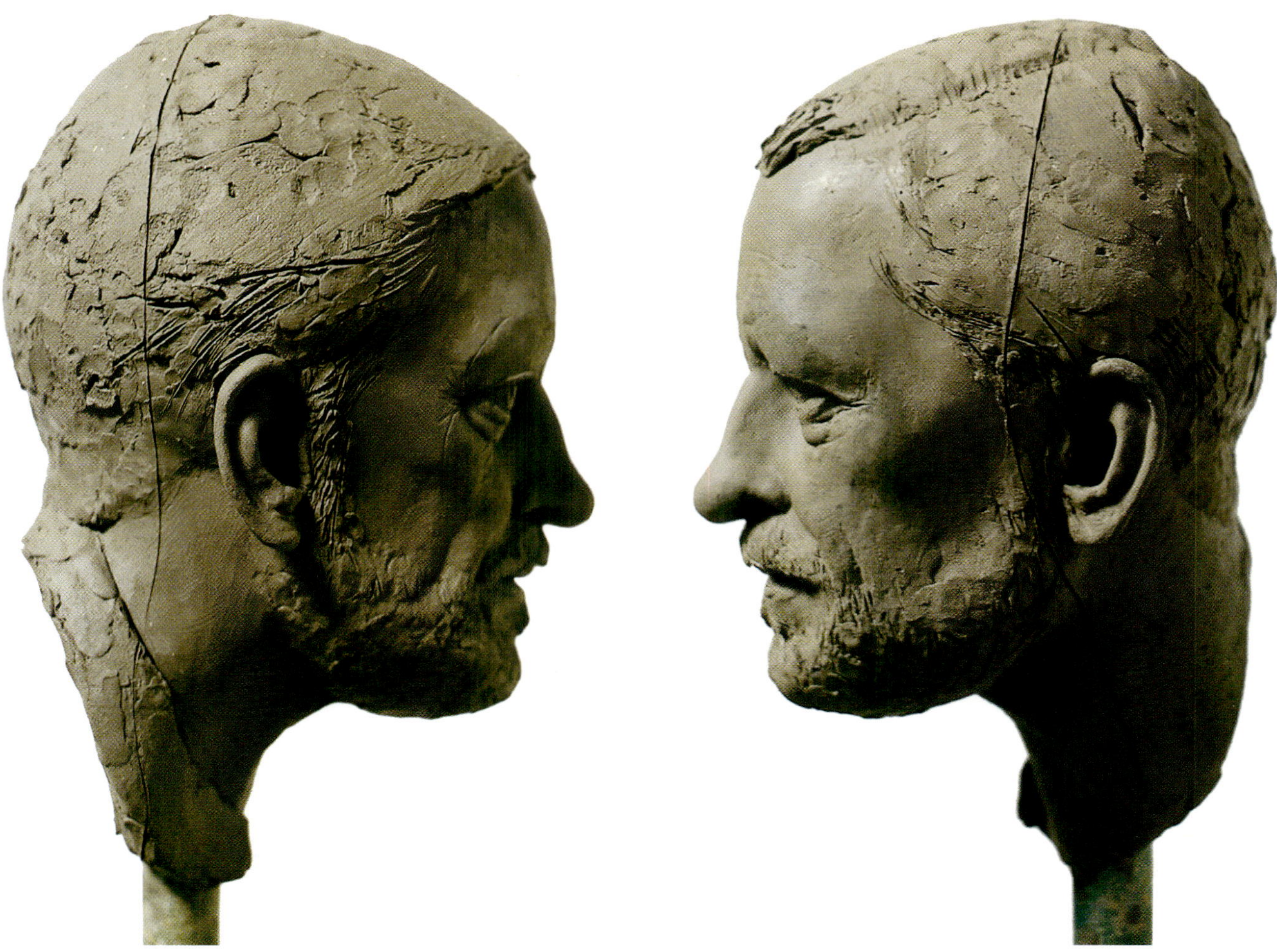

ABOVE: *Marking the seam on the clay. Note that the line is diagonal so there will be one ear in each of the two sections.*

casting. Clay or metal walls (the latter of 1/500in gauge non-ferrous shim) are composed around the subject to divide it into the appropriate number of sections that will allow the removal of the clay and any armature; these divisions are called the 'seams'.

The number of pieces will vary, from a simple two-piece mould to complex moulds with many pieces, but no matter how many sections are required the principle is the same. The mould is divided in such a way as to create a main section (the main mould), which contains the bulk of the sculpture to ensure the greatest volumetric accuracy of the final cast; the pieces, known as caps, fit on to this main mould and have a very specific role. The plan of the mould sections and caps must allow for access to the whole of the mould's inner surfaces in all cases. This is especially important with large castings that are to be made hollow. The sections and caps must cater for the preparation of the whole mould surface to be followed by layers of filler applied to those surfaces, together with any reinforcing required.

As much care as possible must be taken when designing and making a mould, regardless of its type and the technique to be used. Time taken at this stage is time saved later; particularly on large works, such planning can be critical, so it is important never to penny pinch on time or on materials.

Making Shim Walls

Brass is the best metal for the shim walls because it has a certain spring to it that allows the shims to be pushed hard into the clay without buckling. Other metals are usually too soft and more difficult to work with. If brass is not available, use a metal that has a fair degree of firmness, and is rigid enough to be pressed firmly into the clay. The shim is best handled by cutting it into strips approximately 2in (50mm) to 3in (75mm) long and ¼in (6mm) wider than the estimated planned thickness of the mould; this ¼in (6mm) is the allowance required to push the shim into the soft clay. The actual thickness of the mould will vary according to the size of the work being dealt with and may be anything from

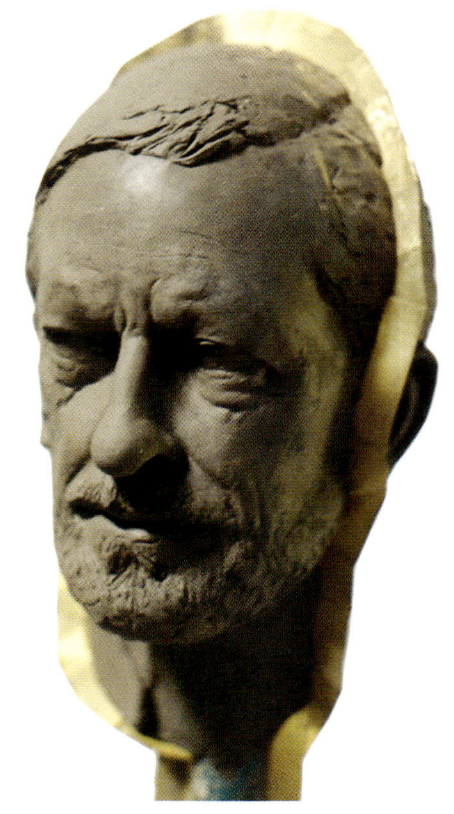

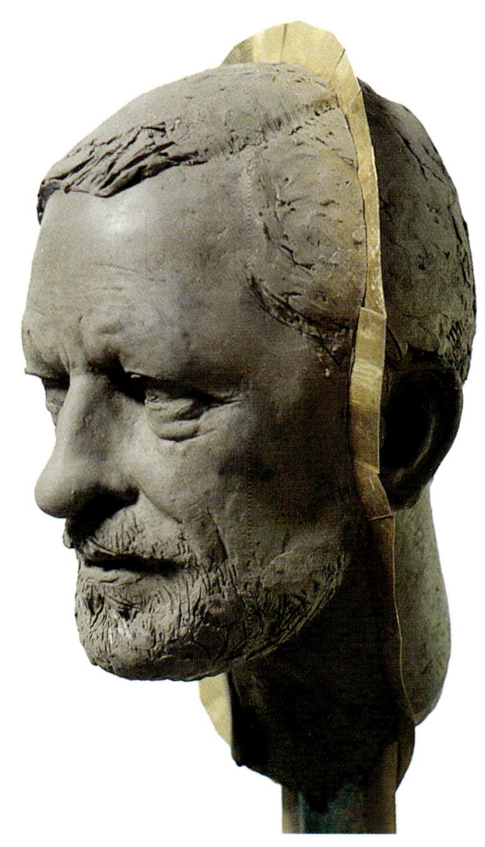

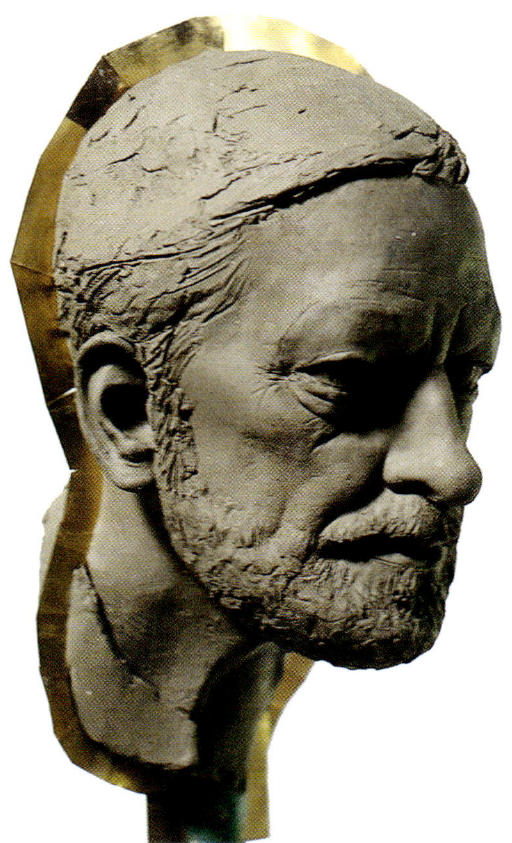

THIS PAGE: *The brass shims pushed into the clay.*

½in (12mm) to 1in (25mm) thick. These measurements are approximate, but no mould need be thicker than 1in (25mm) as long as it is properly reinforced. Remember that the waste mould has to be chipped away; keeping the mould thickness to a minimum will make it safer for the cast during the chipping-out procedure.

With a thin-bladed knife, carefully draw the planned dividing lines (the seams) in the clay, then cut and place the metal shims along the line, pressing each piece securely into the clay, trying to keep the shim wall as vertical as possible. If they are allowed to slope inwards, the cap will be locked in; sloping outwards is better. Try to visualize the release and subsequent removal of each cap as you are making it and judge the angle of the shim wall accordingly. Overlapping each shim a little as you proceed will help to make it firm, and you should continue cutting and trimming as you go. The objective is to make a precise shim wall of equal height around each section (cap), which will eventually be removed. The top edge of the wall needs to be as level as possible, so be sure to cut off any sharp projections. This edge will be scraped clean after each application of plaster and any sharp projections can hinder this necessary scraping and also cause serious cuts to the hands as you apply the plaster of Paris to make the mould; it is best to keep blood off the mould. The thickness of the shim (1/5000in) determines the thickness of the seam, which occurs as a proud thin line in the cast.

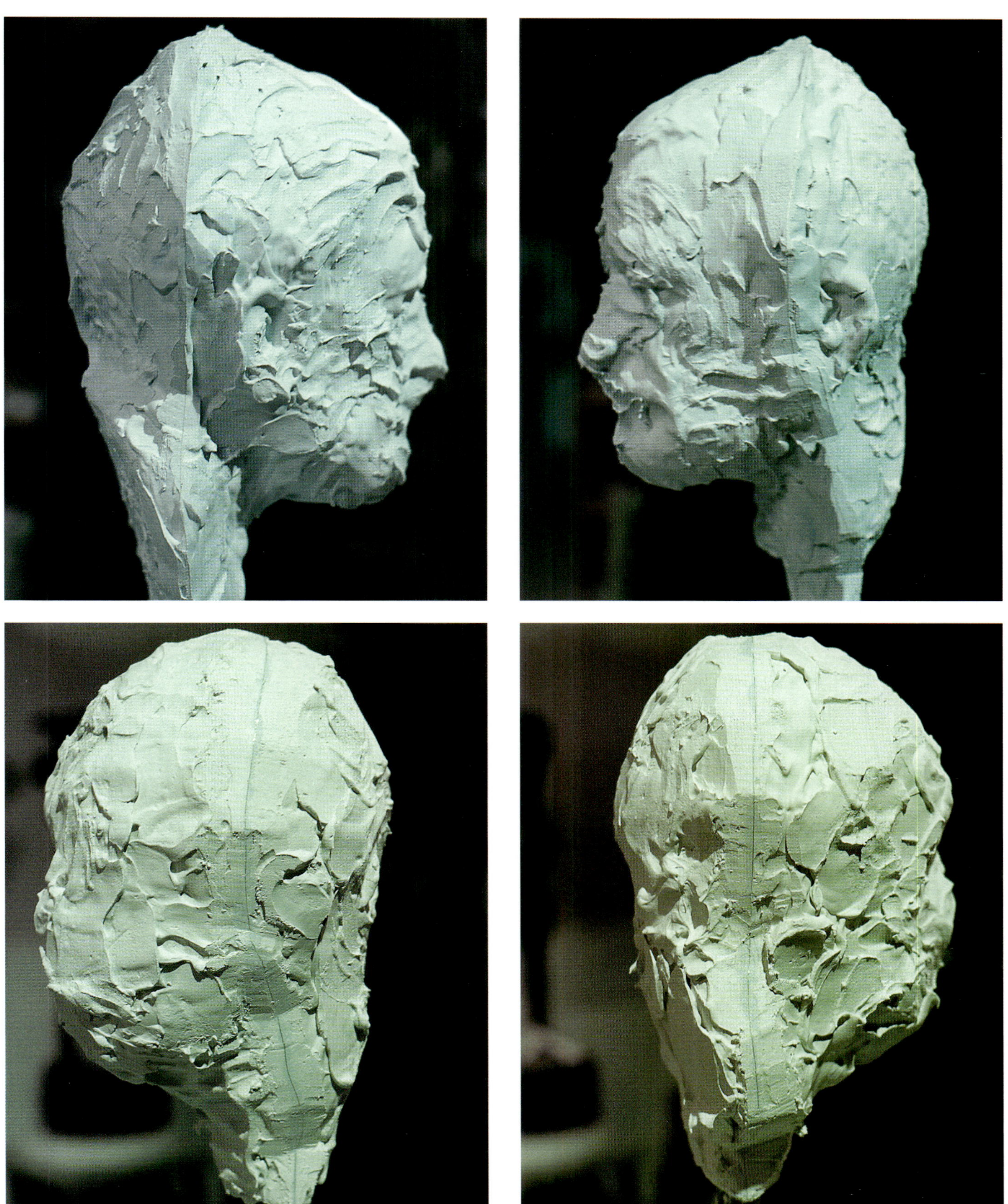

TOP LEFT AND RIGHT: *Making the coloured first coat of plaster.*
BOTTOM LEFT AND RIGHT: *The completed mould showing the seam after scraping.*

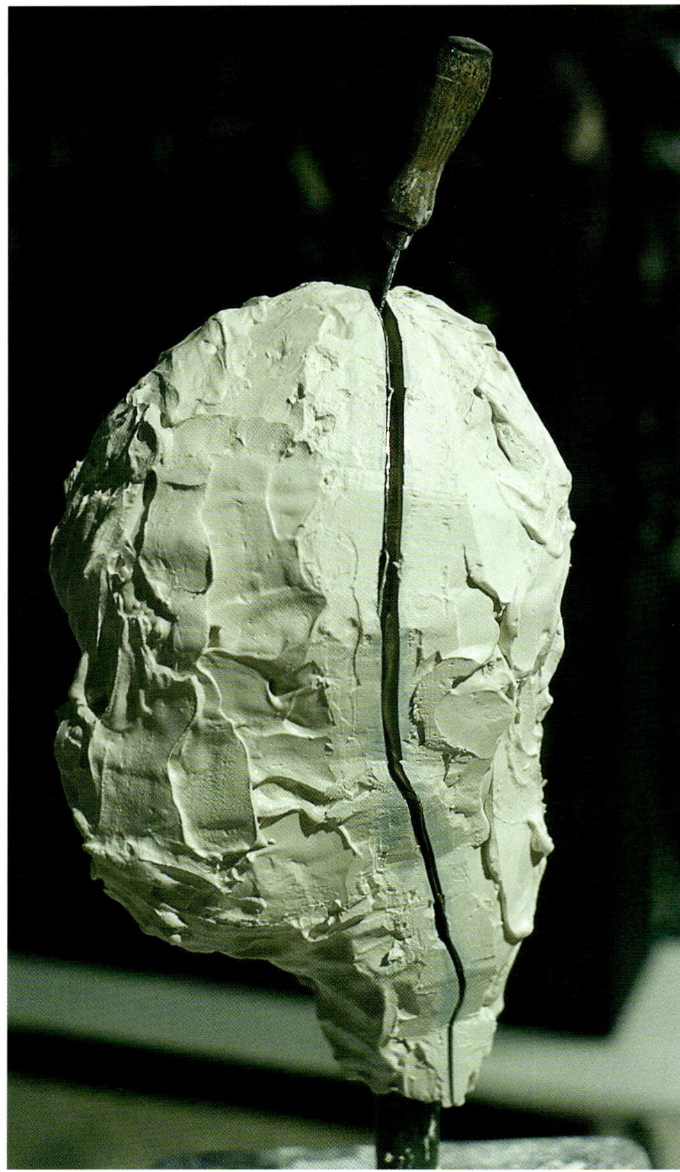

The mould being prised open.

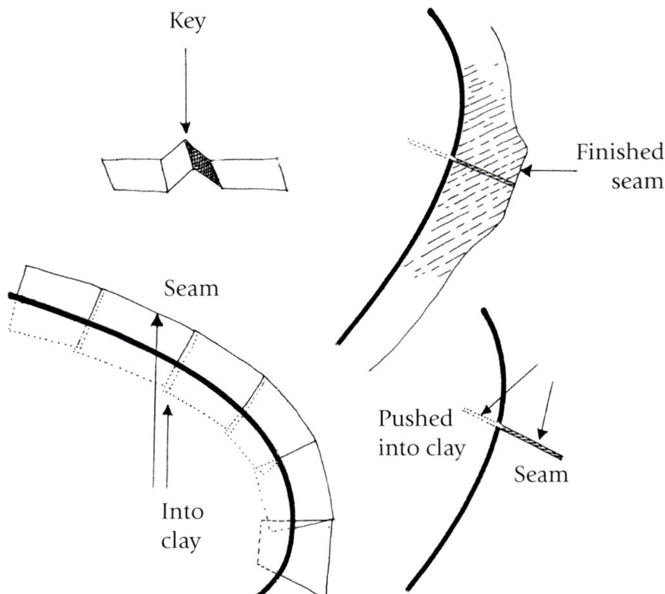

Shim placed to make the sections of waste mould.

Where the sections of the mould meet this is known as the 'flash'; the thinner the flash the more volumetrically accurate the cast will be.

It is often the case that a limb or other feature of a sculpture will extend in front of the bulk of the figure. If this extension were to be covered with plaster it would be impossible for the clay and armature to be removed. In such instances, it is necessary to make a window cap (see the illustration opposite) – a completely independent cap that is not connected with other shims of other seams in the mould design. Removing the separate cap will give access to the clay and armature pertaining to that limb or extension, plus all the subsequent processes described above.

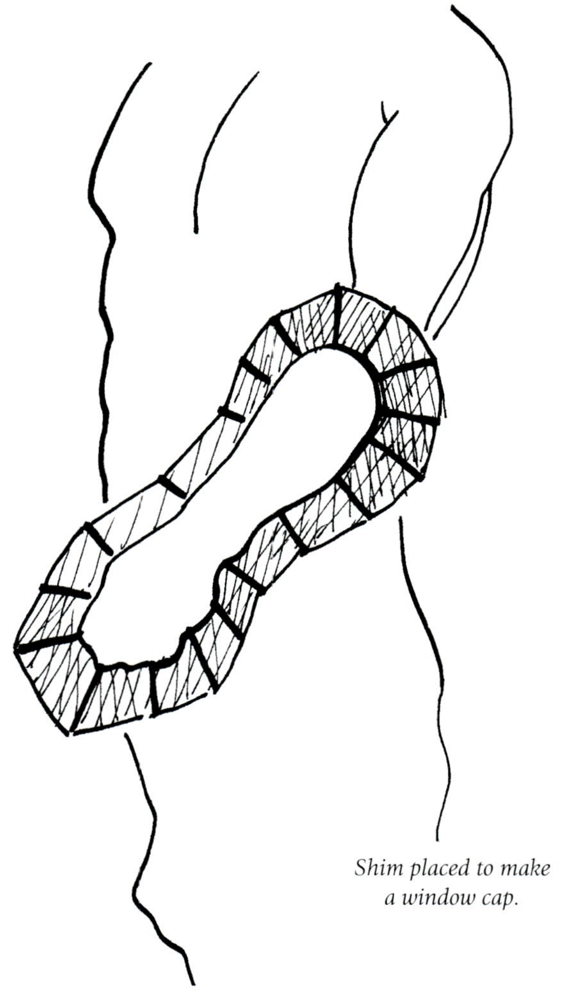

Shim placed to make a window cap.

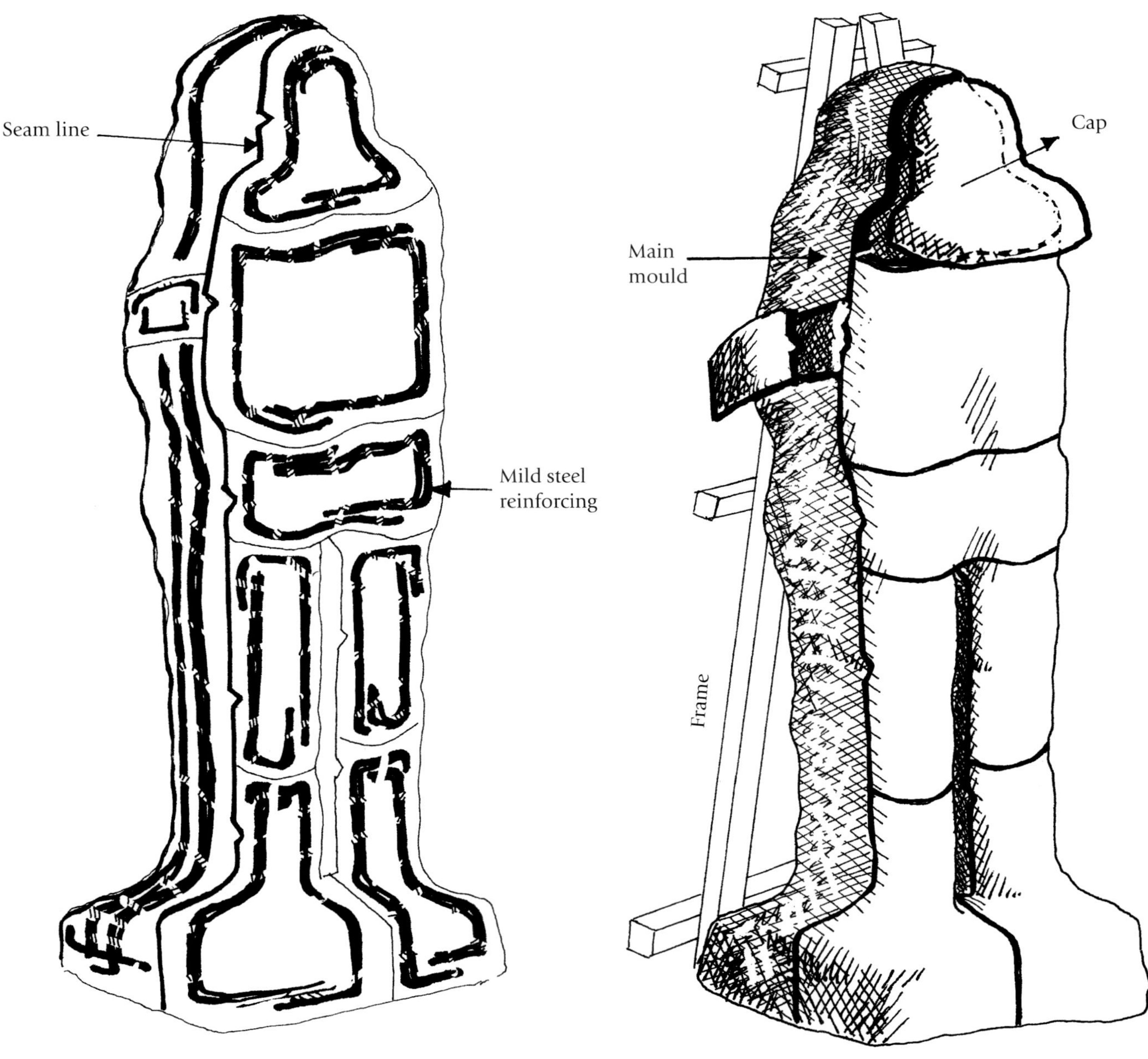

Basic principle: mild steel reinforcing.

Mould sections or 'caps'.

Coating and Reinforcing

When the shim wall has been completed, the whole assembly of clay and shim is covered with plaster of Paris. The first layer is coloured to create a warning coat that helps when chipping off the mould, indicating when the cast surface is near. The mould is built up evenly over the entire head or figure. The shim wall acts as a guide to building this even thickness. Any mild steel or other reinforcing that is needed to strengthen the mould should be placed over the coloured layer. Reinforcing is designed to provide tensile strength to the plaster, which is naturally very brittle and liable to break (see the illustration above for an indication of how to plan the reinforcing). The rule of thumb is to place the mild steel reinforcing around the perimeter of each section on both sides of the shim wall. Bending the metal takes time but it should hug the first layer as close as possible. Make sure the reinforcing is continuous, which means that each piece of mild steel should overlap its partner. The size of the mild steel used will vary according to the size of the mould. I use a complexity of ½in (12mm) steel on large moulds.

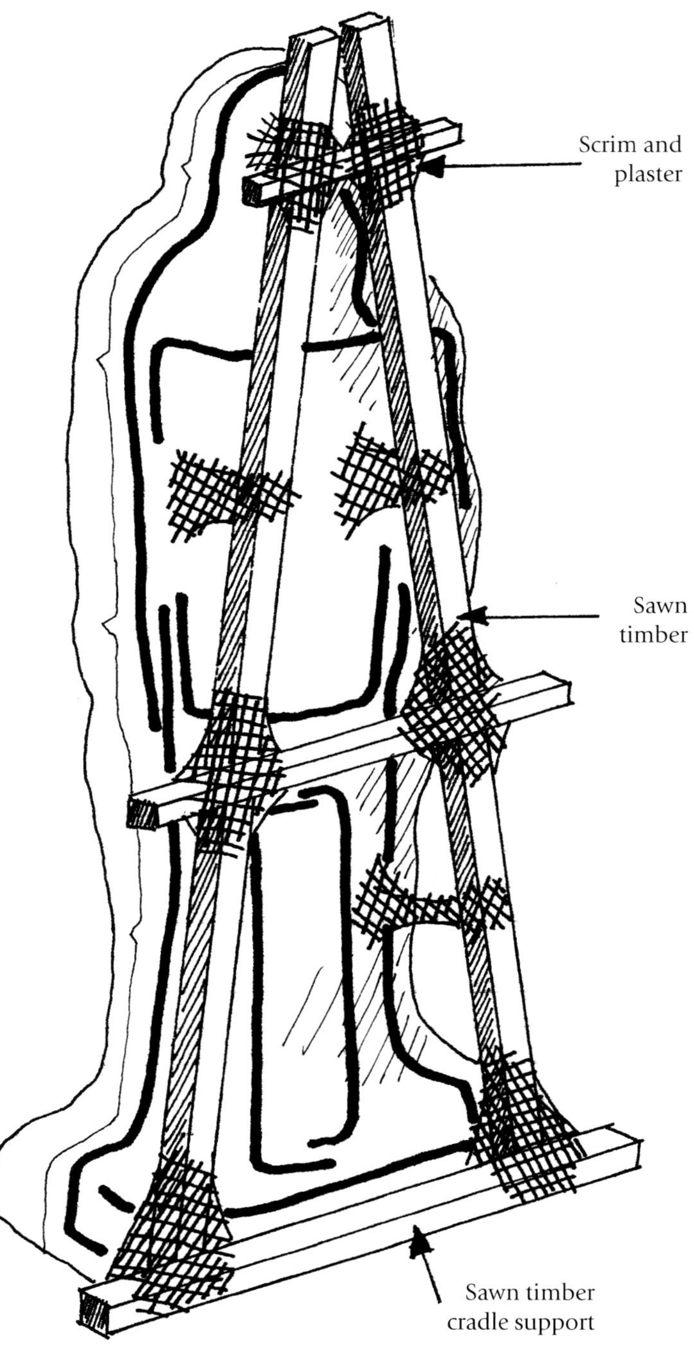

A cradle support.

The plaster is built up on both sides of the shim to make a firm base against which to lever when you come to open the mould and remove the sections. Scraping the top edge of the shim after each application of plaster should create a flat surface along the length of the seam, with the bright shim showing all the way round (see the illustration on pages 127 and 131). If the shim does not show along the seam's length, the cap is liable to break when leverage is applied to remove it.

Making a Cradle

For large moulds it will be necessary to make a sawn timber cradle (see the illustration opposite), which is fixed to the main mould using plaster and scrim. The cradle should be designed to be strong enough to support and protect the plaster mould during any lifting and manoeuvring, which is done by handling the cradle rather than the mould itself. This will allow the brittle plaster of the mould to be as thin as possible, which will prove to be an advantage when it comes to chipping off the waste mould when the cast is ready. Sawn timber is better than planed because the rough wood surface makes a better key for the plaster. This combination of materials is used not only for the strength it affords but also for the relative ease with which it can be cut away from the main mould to chip out the cast.

The plaster is left to harden for at least a couple of hours but preferably overnight.

Making Clay Walls

The mould sections (caps) can also be made by means of clay walls, with the thickness of the seam revealed by layers of clay thinned down with water. Plan carefully each section to be made, as each cap has to be completed separately; try to work this out logically, establishing an order of procedure. The plan should involve making a main mould first and then the caps, which helps to get the caps to register accurately with the main mould. Make each section (cap) separately, working to the plan, usually starting at the bottom of the sculpture. Numbering each cap as it is completed should ensure a successful reassembly of the mould sections.

Mark the seam division in the clay with a sharp knife, then roll out lengths of clay that can be flattened and cut into strips of about ½in (12mm) wide, and thick enough to stay in place on the clay original. The clay strip should be softer than the master subject, but if this is not possible dust a little French chalk (talcum powder) along the line to prevent the two clays sticking together. Place the clay strips along the marked line, with the smoothest side on the line; this will eventually become the seam. Little buttresses of clay placed on the opposite side will help the wall to stay in place. Be careful to make this wall as accurately as possible – remember that care taken at this stage saves time later.

When the wall has been completed, plaster of Paris is applied against the smooth surface, the first coat being coloured to create a warning layer. Complete the build of the main mould in this way, adding any reinforcing as required and when that is satisfactory remove the clay wall. The exposed plaster seam surface then needs to be treated by cutting any locating keys, if these are required (see the

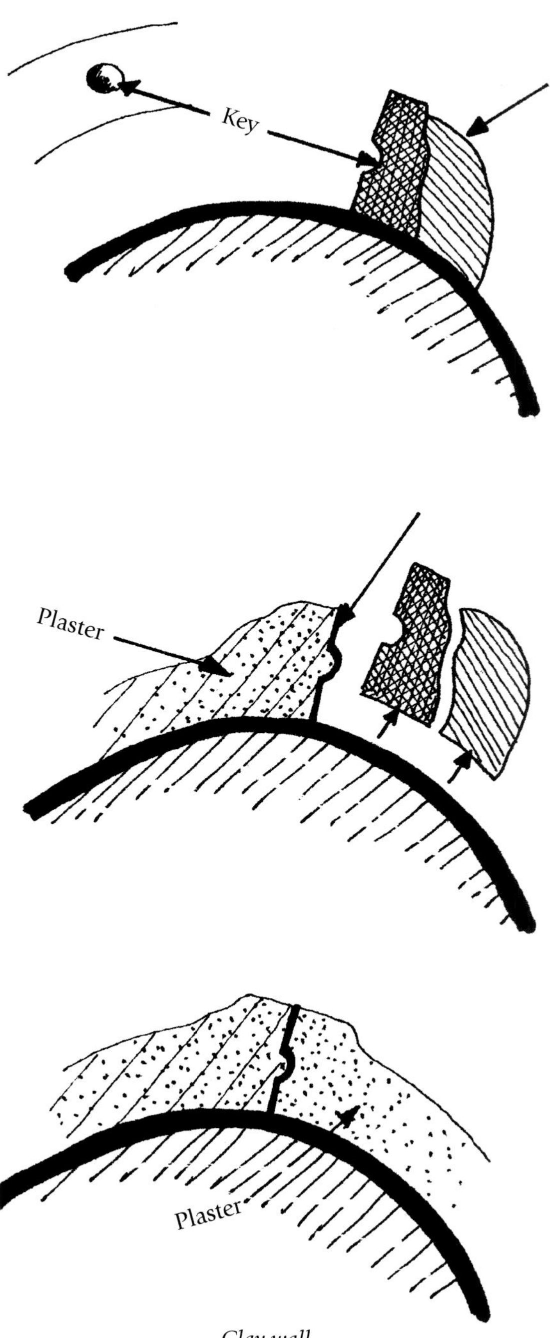

Clay wall.

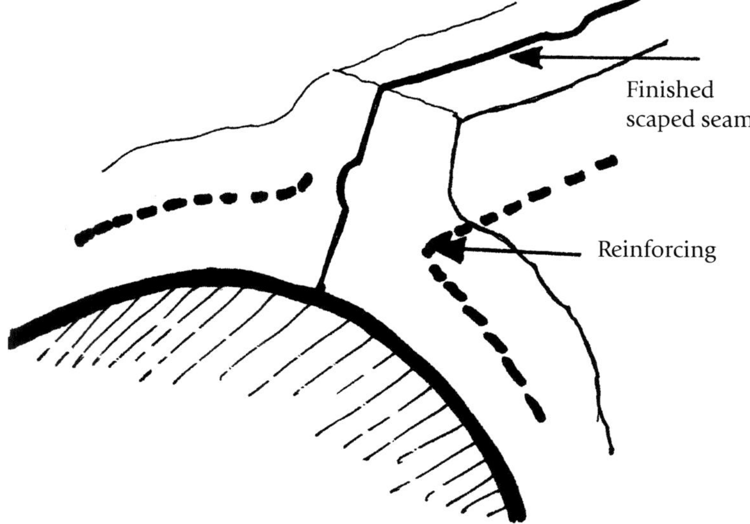

Steps in clay wall mould making.

illustration above). The keys need to be cut as cleanly as possible. Straight cuts can be done easily with a sharp knife or chisel, while circular button shapes are best made using the tip of round-ended steel spatula or knife. Do not be tempted to make the shapes too deep, as they will only break and be rendered useless. When enough points have been located and cut, the whole seam plaster surface needs to be coated with a thin wash of slip (a water and clay mix); this is the parting agent that will stop the next layer of plaster sticking to the it.

Having completed the preparation of the seam surface proceed to the making of the first cap; it will become obvious here that only one cap can be made at a time, because the clay wall has to be removed before continuing. When the plaster of the first section has set and hardened, remove the clay wall and its supports, and treat the seam surface ready for the next cap. For a simple two-piece mould, go ahead and make the second section by placing the plaster directly against the painted seam side, build the colour warning coat plus any reinforcing required, and make the plaster thickness equal to the first, making sure the seam edges are strong. If there are more than two caps to be made, each has to go through the same procedure until the mould is complete. Scraping after each application of plaster should flatten the top edge of each seam line (see the illustration above); the fine line of clay wash will be revealed to indicate where the seam is and should show along the whole length of all the seams. Leave the mould to harden for at least two hours, but preferably overnight.

Opening the Mould

Both kinds of mould are opened by pouring water over the seam edges, inserting a strong blade into the seam, and gently levering the cap at a number of points evenly distributed along its length. Do not try to rush this exercise or use too much force; slow, gentle pressure is what is required. For large moulds it is a useful ploy to include lugs of clay at the top edge of the seam, as these will eventually make little reservoirs for water to collect in to help in opening the mould. As plaster hardens, exothermic heat is created and this leads to suction between the plaster and the clay. Water seeping through the seam as it is prised open will break this suction with natural clay; with synthetic clay the exothermic heat itself will soften the clay enough to allow the caps to be easily removed by gentle but firm levering. Once the caps have been taken off the clay they should be stored, standing on an edge. Left flat, they will gradually warp and will not fit evenly together when the mould is reassembled for casting.

Once the caps have been removed and safely stored, the clay plus all armature material must be removed to complete the hollow mould. This must be done carefully to avoid scratching or breaking off protrusions on the mould surface. Natural clay will leave a fine deposit on the mould surface and this needs to be cleaned off by washing with clean water using a soft brush. Synthetic clay leaves no deposit and the softened clay will pull away from the surface quite easily, leaving it clean and ready for the next step. After removing all traces of clay, repair any air bubbles, cracks or breaks in the mould while the plaster mould is still fresh. When all repairs are complete, the caps should be tried in place to make sure they fit correctly, and any adjustments made to those that may have warped a little or been damaged as they were lifted from the clay. Such repairs are made using small mixes of plaster, making sure that the older plaster is wet and able to receive the new mixture without sucking out the water required to make it set and stick. Scrape off any protrusions that prevent a good fit, and make any necessary adjustments to get as good a fit as possible.

The surface of the mould must then be prepared with a release/parting agent, a medium that prevents the filling sticking to the mould. A soft soap solution is the most commonly used release agent for plaster to plaster. This solution is brushed on to the mould using a soft brush for five to ten minutes and made to lather, and then left to stand for a further 10–15 minutes. The oil from the soap seals the open pores of the plaster, preventing a bond between the mould and plaster cast. Surplus soap is removed with a clean brush

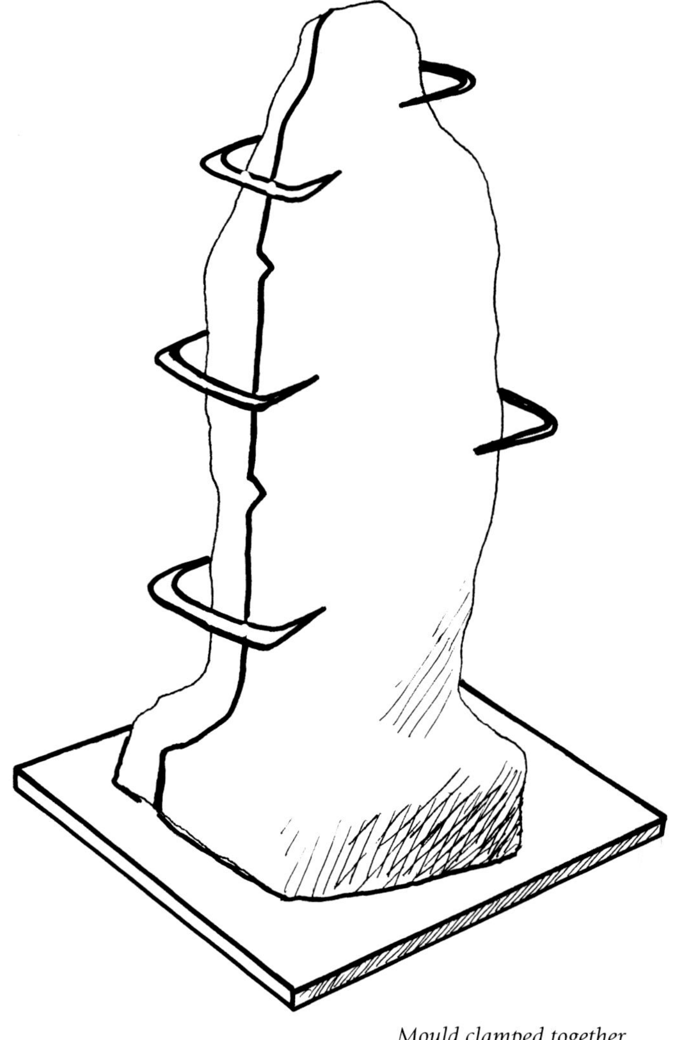

Mould clamped together.

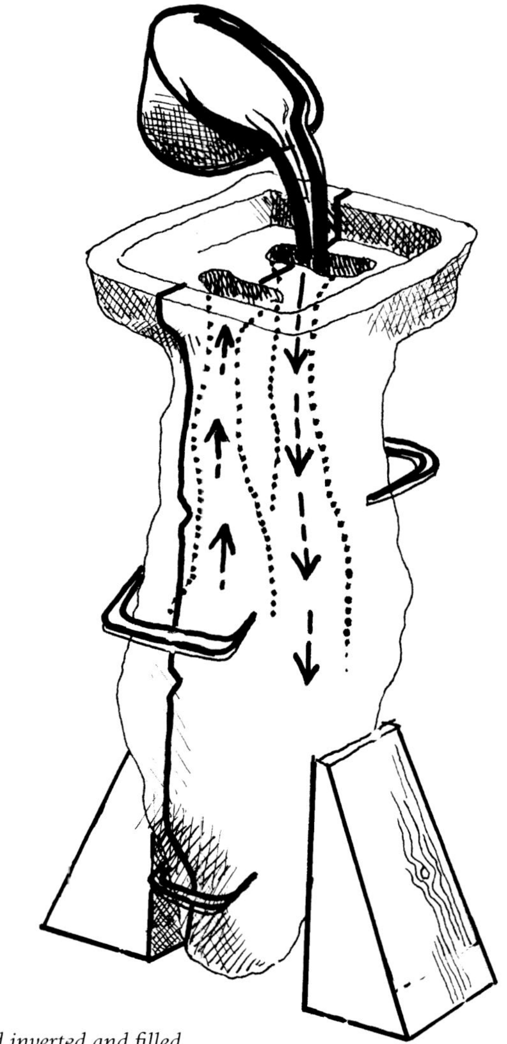

Mould inverted and filled.

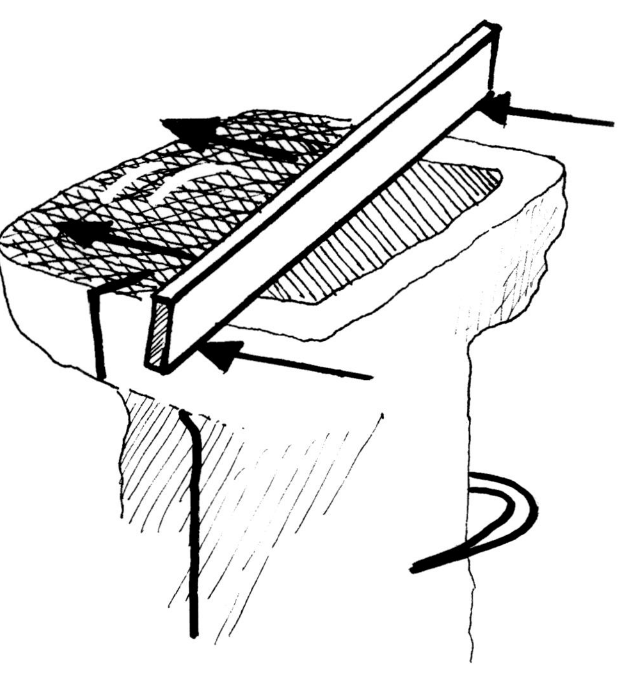

Levelling the fill at the base of the mould.

and the mould surface is brushed with the merest trace of thin oil – just enough to make a small spot in the palm of the hand; do not be tempted to apply a heavy coat of oil as this will cause a bad cast surface. The whole mould should now be left soaking in clean water to become saturated; this prevents any water being sucked from the fresh plaster as it is placed in the mould to make the casting.

When making a cast using a material other than plaster of Paris, the procedures are the basically the same, but be certain to research the appropriate release/parting agent for that substance.

Making a Casting

Filling the Mould

Once they have been cleaned, prepared and soaked, simple small moulds can be inverted, suitably supported and filled solid with fresh plaster of Paris. Gently vibrating the mould as it is filled will release any air that might be trapped in the mould; and in the poured plaster mix. The filling is then left to set and harden. It is a good idea to invert the mould and filling once it has set, so that it hardens with moisture gathering at the base. If reinforcing is required it can be fixed in position prior to completing the filling, using small blobs of plaster and making sure that the mould sections fit correctly after it has been placed. This reinforcing can become quite complex when the sculpture being cast is a figure or a composition of figures, and each limb requires support (see the illustration below).

Most large castings are made hollow because a hollow form is stronger than a solid one, and therefore more durable. The hollow cast is also lighter and consequently easier to transport and move around the studio. Careful planning of the mould is essential to making a good cast and in large works this means allowing for the process of applying the filler to each surface separately. On both the main mould and the caps, the seam surfaces need to kept clean at all times and tested frequently to ensure a good fit is maintained; the closer the fit, the better the seam thick-

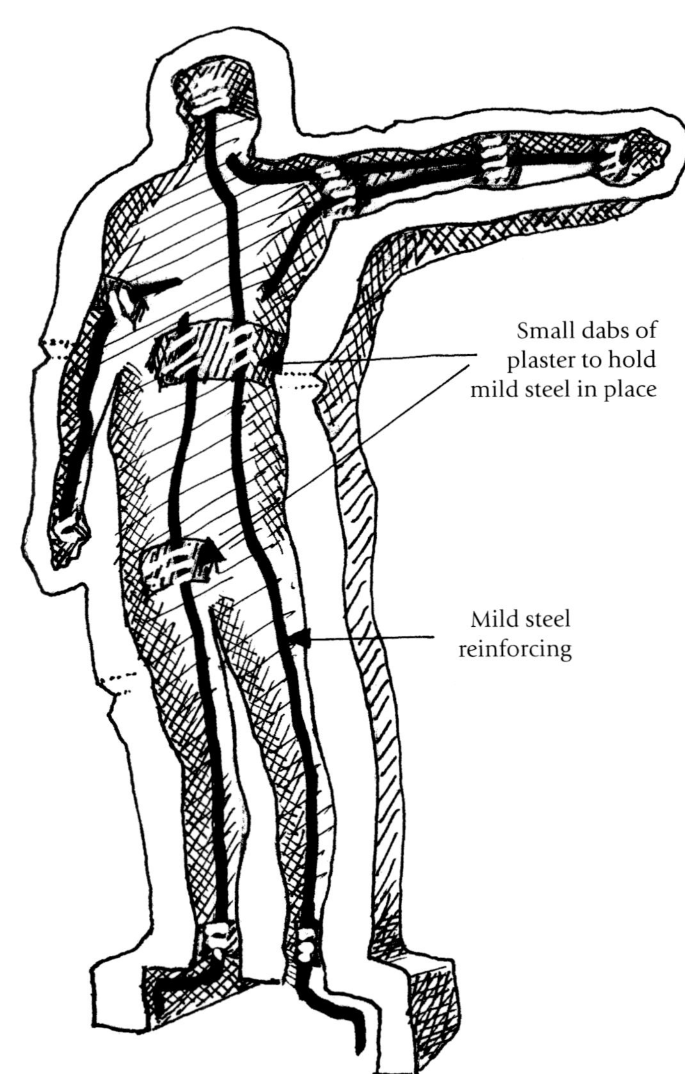

Reinforcing placed in the mould to strengthen the cast.

ness and volumetric accuracy. The sections of larger moulds are filled and assembled to a given plan, usually in the same order as they are removed from the clay. Often the caps are filled first and then fixed to the master mould as that is filled, but there are no rules – just apply common sense in the planning.

As the casting progresses the seams are filled and strengthened to make as strong a bond as possible. The hollow plaster cast requires some fibrous reinforcing and this is supplied by applying jute scrim in layers (laminations) after the initial layer of plaster is placed against the mould surface to guarantee the reproduction of surface detail.

Chipping Out

When the filling has been completed, the whole assembly is left to harden, preferably in its vertical position. Cleaning the area around the mould is a wise precaution (indeed, it is always good studio practice to clean as you go along, no matter what you are working on); at the chipping-out stage, the waste material will create a surprisingly large quantity of plaster debris. Trying to work on piled-up plaster chippings can make life quite uncomfortable, especially if it is layered on top of the mess that is inevitably created as the mould is made.

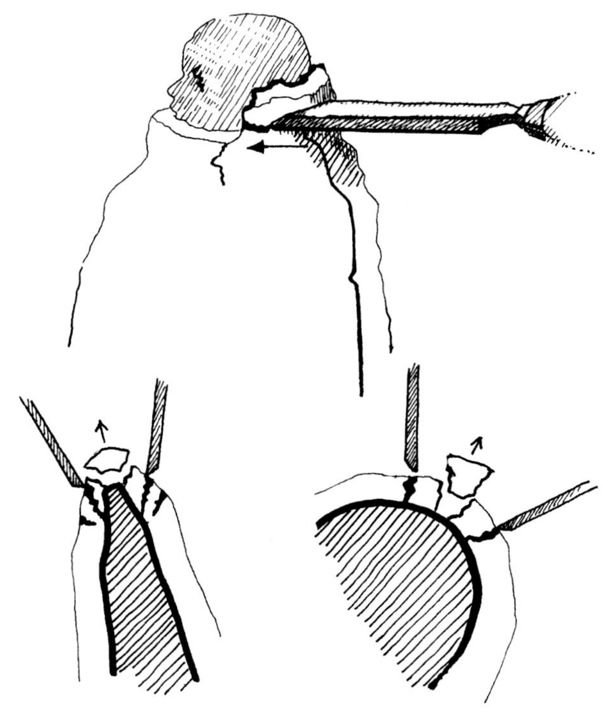

Suggested direction of the chisel when chipping out.

The next step is the actual chipping-out process. This is often exciting, especially for the first-timer, and it is always a pleasure gradually to reveal a good casting. A wooden mallet and blunt chisels of various sizes are used to chip away the mould. The objective is to cause the mould to break away from the cast surface and sharp tools will cut the plaster, preventing this. Starting from the top, usually the head of a figure, chip at the mould with the chisel aimed approximately at right-angles to the cast surface, taking small chips at a time. Do not be tempted to prise off large sections of mould because this will too often lead to details being snapped off in the process. Chipping carefully will expose the warning coat first, giving the signal that the cast surface is near by. Continue careful chipping and the mould will break away from that surface, leaving it clean. Continue to work in this manner, progressing down the mould, until the casting stands completely free.

The whole chipping-out exercise is best done slowly and carefully, erring on the side of caution and ending up with a complete casting, rather than rushing and finding yourself with a collection of broken pieces.

When the mould has been removed, clear away the detritus and inspect the casting for flaws. Using a pointed metal tool, pick out the little bits of coloured plaster that have lodged in the detail and then carefully scrape and remove the seam flash. This is the raised plaster line that is in place of the shim or clay wall division of the mould sections. Try to remove this without too much damage to the cast surface around it. When everything is cleaned off, check again for any repairs that need to be done – there may be small air bubbles or places where the plaster filling did not reach. Make the repairs by adding fresh plaster, ensuring that the area is wet, so that the new plaster will adhere. A small sable brush charged with cold clean water will help to blend the new plaster into the cast surface. This is another skill that can only be acquired by practice, so make as many moulds and castings as you can.

With skill and experience, it is possible to mould and cast almost anything, by one means or another, by choosing the appropriate casting material and knowing the techniques that go with it. A sculptor with limited casting skills may try to model to accommodate his or her poor technique, but this is a situation to be avoided. Acquiring the basic practical skills will allow the artist the greatest creative freedom, and it is certainly worth learning such skills early in your career.

10

Enlarging or Scaling Up

Once a suitable maquette or working model has been resolved, the art of enlarging or scaling up comes into play. Methods and their associated skills are many and varied – some techniques are common to most professional studios, while others are more idiosyncratic and personalized. All the methods may be used for enlarging, as well as for reducing or scaling down an image, most commonly used in the production of coins and medals. The task of the professional craftsman who specializes in the enlarging and reducing processes is to reproduce with the greatest accuracy, at a predetermined and appropriate size and scale, what the artist has presented in the maquette or working model. This is a highly skilled operation and, if it is not supervised sufficiently closely by the artist, to safeguard those qualities inherent in all good maquettes, it can become merely a mechanical copying exercise.

A good maquette shows a freshness of modelling or carving, and freedom of thought, and these are qualities that should be preserved. They are there because working on a small-scale sculpture allows for a relaxed, almost casual handling of the modelling or carving material, with a minimum attention to detail and a great concentration on gesture and action. These qualities should not be lost when scaling up, but they can easily be understated when using a laboured mechanical enlarging procedure. The sculptor also needs to be tuned in to any new aspect of an image that might present itself as the work moves from one stage in its development to another, and should be able to choose to take advantage of any unexpected quality that may be revealed. This design practice should be jealously guarded, even when using the skills of a trained operative, craftsman or artisan; the artist should control the work at all stages of its development.

Sophisticated machinery is gradually entering the world of sculpture, coming particularly from the world of industrial product design, and especially those businesses associated with vehicle and aircraft design that use complex computer systems. Computerized scanning and machine programming are dramatic examples of such technology, offering more than a hint of what might happen as the processes evolve and become more widely available. In

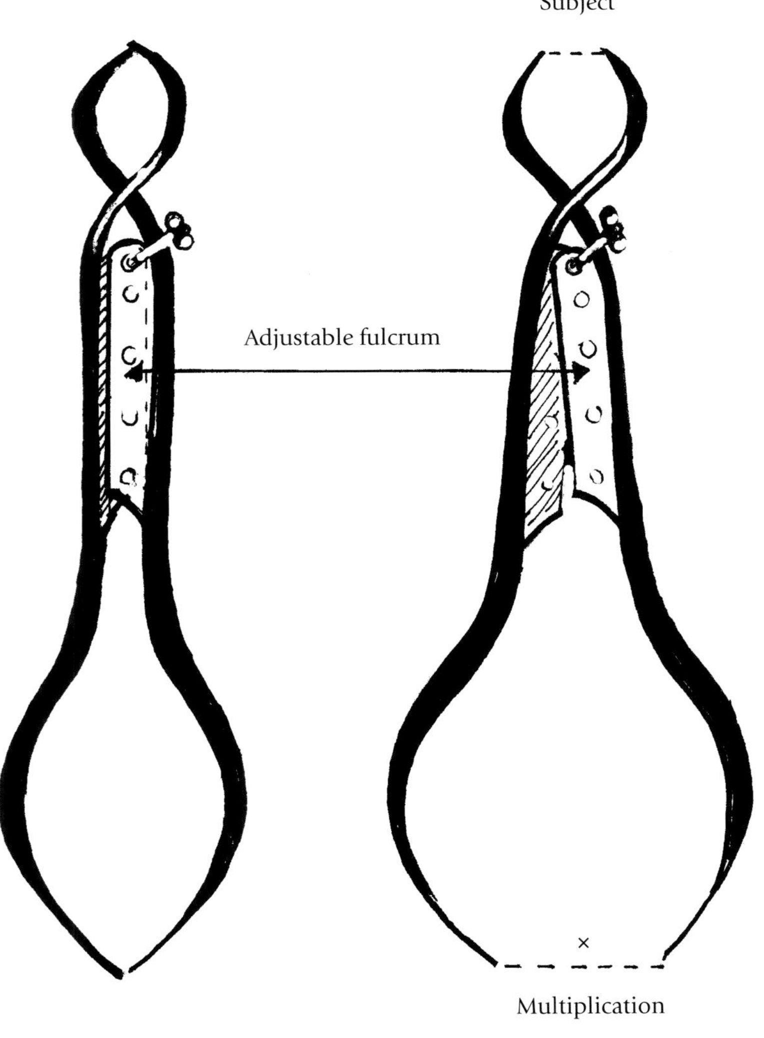

Proportional callipers.

these times of exciting technology, it is even more critical for the artist to be present as the work is scanned and machined. In that way, he or she will be able to take advantage of the certain surprises that will occur and will require some creative input. Sophisticated computer-based techniques are slowly becoming studio-friendly just as the computer itself has become a user-friendly tool. The latest computerized pantographic systems that guide laser-cutting equipment to work all kinds of materials are examples of this but as yet they are rare and expensive. They will surely become more popular as they become more affordable.

Exciting as the future may be for those who are fascinated by technology, in the mean time there are any number of simpler mechanical studio aids to enlarging. These range from the basic measuring stick, usually a specific length of wood made into a rule, two- or four-sided, with calibration marked on each face showing various multiplied dimensions, to the more sophisticated proportional double-ended callipers. These are specially constructed callipers with a sliding fulcrum that can be adjusted in such a manner as to allow a dimension measured at one end to be automatically shown at specific multiplication at the other end (see the illustration on page 135).

If it is to be successful, the enlarging process has certain basic but constant requirements that must be kept in mind at all times. It does not matter whether the work is based on a maquette or a working model, whether the sculptor is make the enlargement or placing it with a professional who would rather scale up from a working model. Of course, not all maquettes are to be enlarged – sometimes they are just for play, exploring the nuances of thinking in the round – but all working models are built to specific measurements relative in all proportions to the final sculpture. Most sculptors develop a preference for working to a comfortable size when exploring any idea, and even those small studies that are not to be enlarged often conform to this. Practice tends to direct the hands and thoughts to a working size that can be easily enlarged by simple multiplication. For instance, 4in times three makes 12in, or 10cm multiplied by three makes 30cm, and when such simple calculations are kept in mind, with time it will become almost automatic. Sculpture usually means the

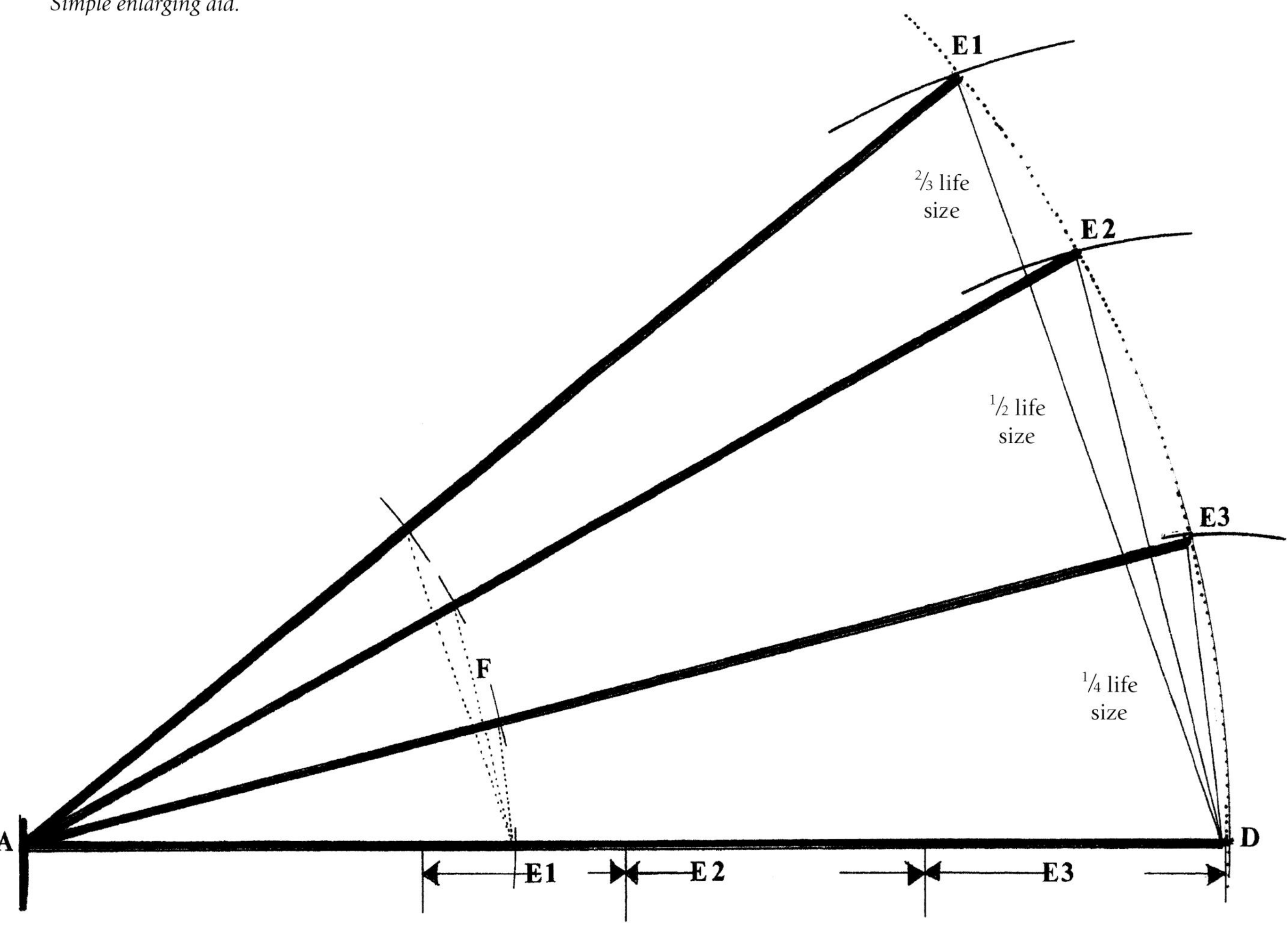

Simple enlarging aid.

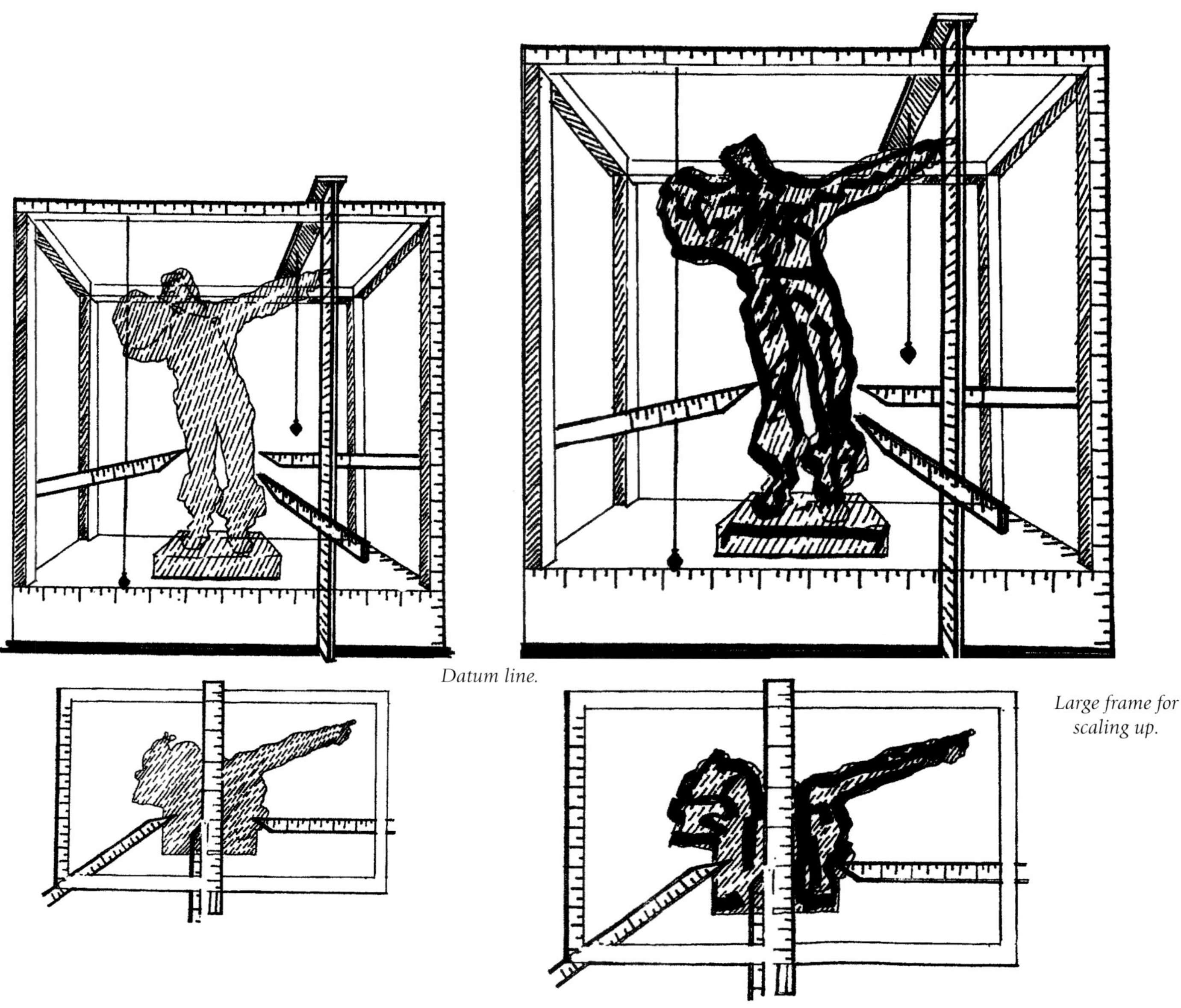

Datum line.

Large frame for scaling up.

making of a unique thing. Each work is a one-off object and not easily subjected to repeatable mathematical processes that aid mass production. Employing the simplest methods of calculation will help the sculptor to gain a good basic understanding of the requirements that enable enlarging to progress satisfactorily through all its stages.

The most important requirement for any enlarging procedure is a constant datum point. This can be a specific measurement of an item in the composition of the maquette or working model, a certain measurement along a fixed base line, or an external system of measuring if the subject does not present an obvious datum point. Whatever is chosen, it must remain unchanged during the enlarging process; changing the datum will affect all other calibrations. This demand for a fixed datum may seem to be a limiting factor in the production of sculpture, but the sculptor must train him or herself from the earliest start to consider the possibility of enlarging, and should adopt the simplest calculating system. If this advice is followed, it becomes an aid rather than a problem. A constant datum point is absolutely essential when a commission is undertaken, and the sculptor is designing for a specific site and material. In this case, he or she will probably have to communicate technical needs to other skilled craftsmen, who will always require as much accurate information as possible.

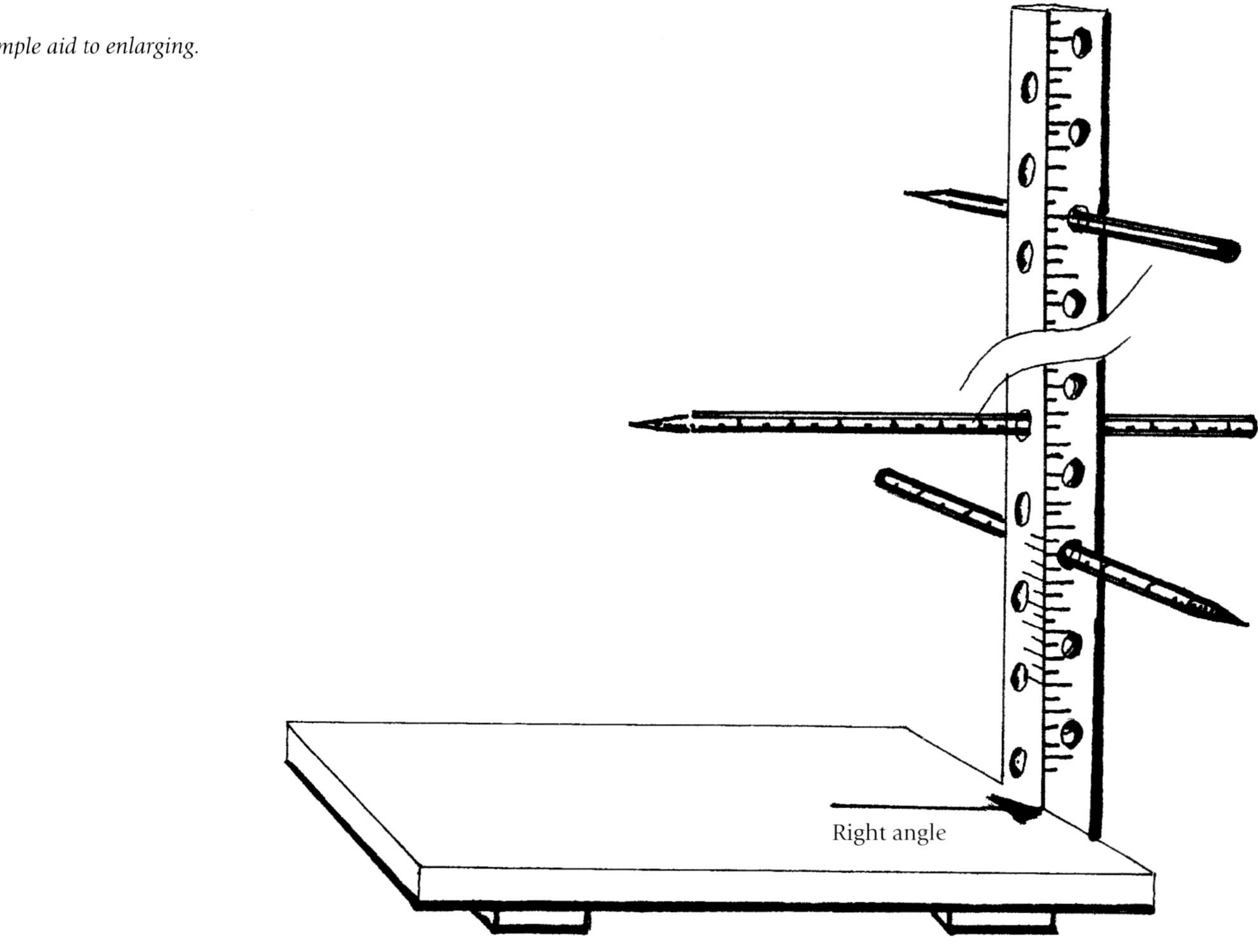

Simple aid to enlarging.

Methods

Grid System

The grid system, often referred to as squaring up, represents probably the most common technique for enlarging work of all kinds and is frequently used in all the visual arts. In sculpture, it is particularly useful when enlarging a flat surface such as relief sculpture, but it can also be adapted to help enlarge three-dimensional subjects that are the cut from a block that has at least one flat surface. The system involves first drawing a grid of squares on the work to be scaled up, choosing a suitable arithmetic size, then drawing a similar grid on the material for the enlargement, multiplied accordingly. Both grids must be calibrated and numbered for easy charting. The numbers selected must be suitable for the size of the original subject to be enlarged, and allow for a simple but logical multiplication of the first grid; as always, the simpler the calculations, the easier the enlarging work will be.

Now, on the small grid that has been drawn on the maquette or over a drawing, the artist has to identify and select the important features of the image or images to be enlarged. The selected features then need to be charted on the chosen material according to both squared grids, taking plenty of time and care. It is wise to choose large parts of the subject to start with, then gradually concentrate on the smaller parts as the work progresses. On large blocks of material, the squared-up image can be drawn on opposite sides of the block, one side reversed to the other, then the overall image can be fretted out using tools that are suitable for that material.

The drawn grid system can be used to enlarge a relief sculpture to be carved or modelled. If there is a need to calculate the projections on a high relief, the same grid system will need to be made from a side view of the maquette, then charted according to the two grids to establish the maximum projection of the relief. This technique is usually employed when the enlargement is very big and the height in relief from the flat surface is critical.

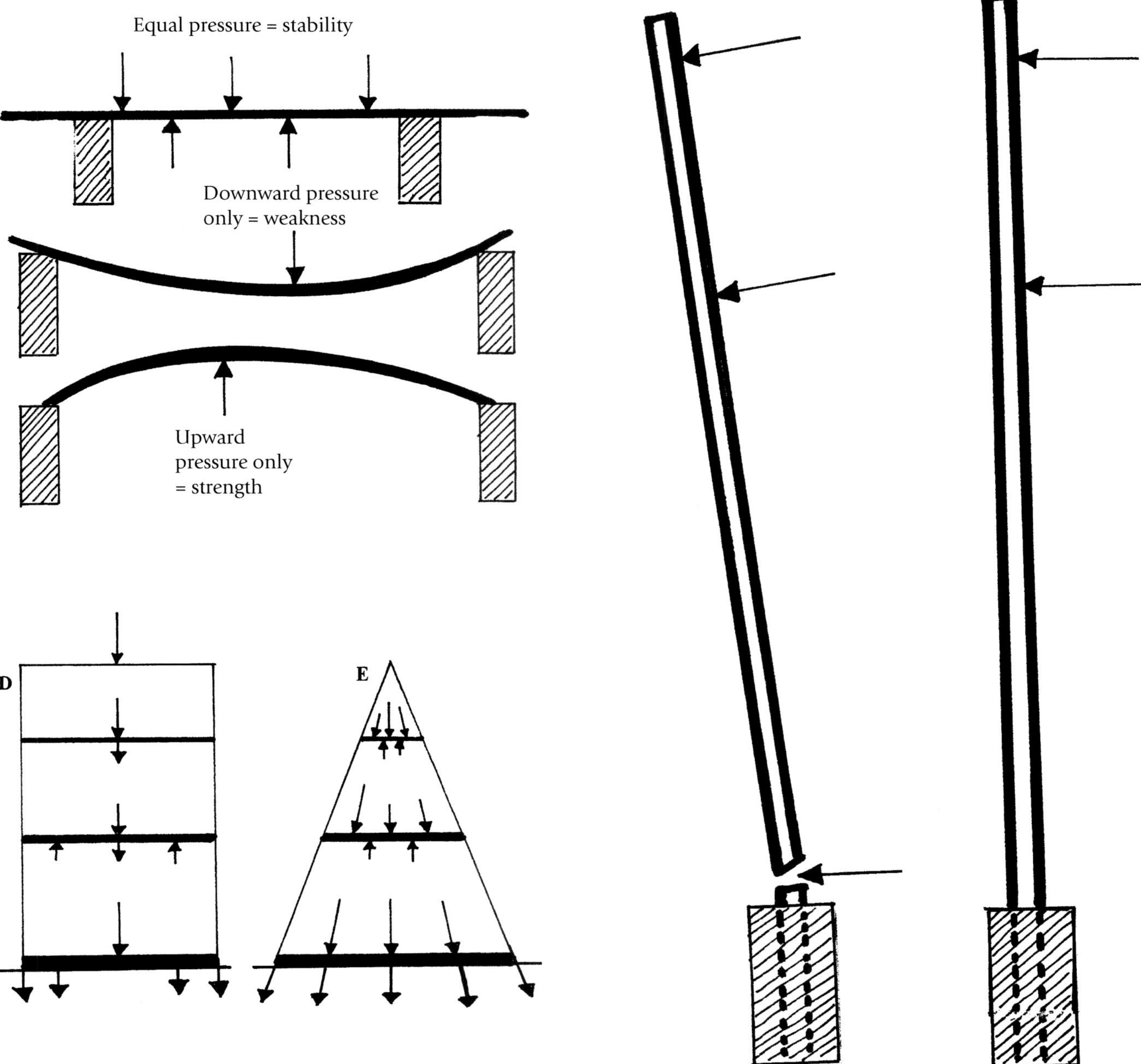

Block and pyramidal form under compression = stability.

Pressure on tall forms causes breakage.

Box-Frame Method

One of the most useful mechanical systems that can be easily made in the studio is that of the box-frame method. This is a three-dimensional version of the grid method, and is made up of two open box frameworks, one small and the other large, but made in exact proportional relation to each other (see the illustration on page 137). The small box frame will eventually house the maquette or working model and the larger frame will accommodate the material for the enlargement at the planned size. Each box must have a fixed horizontal base or platform, and time should be taken to ensure true levels, vertical and horizontal, using a good levelling aid such as a spirit level. Calibration marks are drawn on all horizontal and vertical surfaces, also proportionally, scaling up by multiplication from the smaller to the larger frame. To assure true verticality, a plumb line should be suspended at strategic points on or in both boxes. Pointers of varying length are devised to allow measuring inwards from and up and down the vertical members of the frames, each

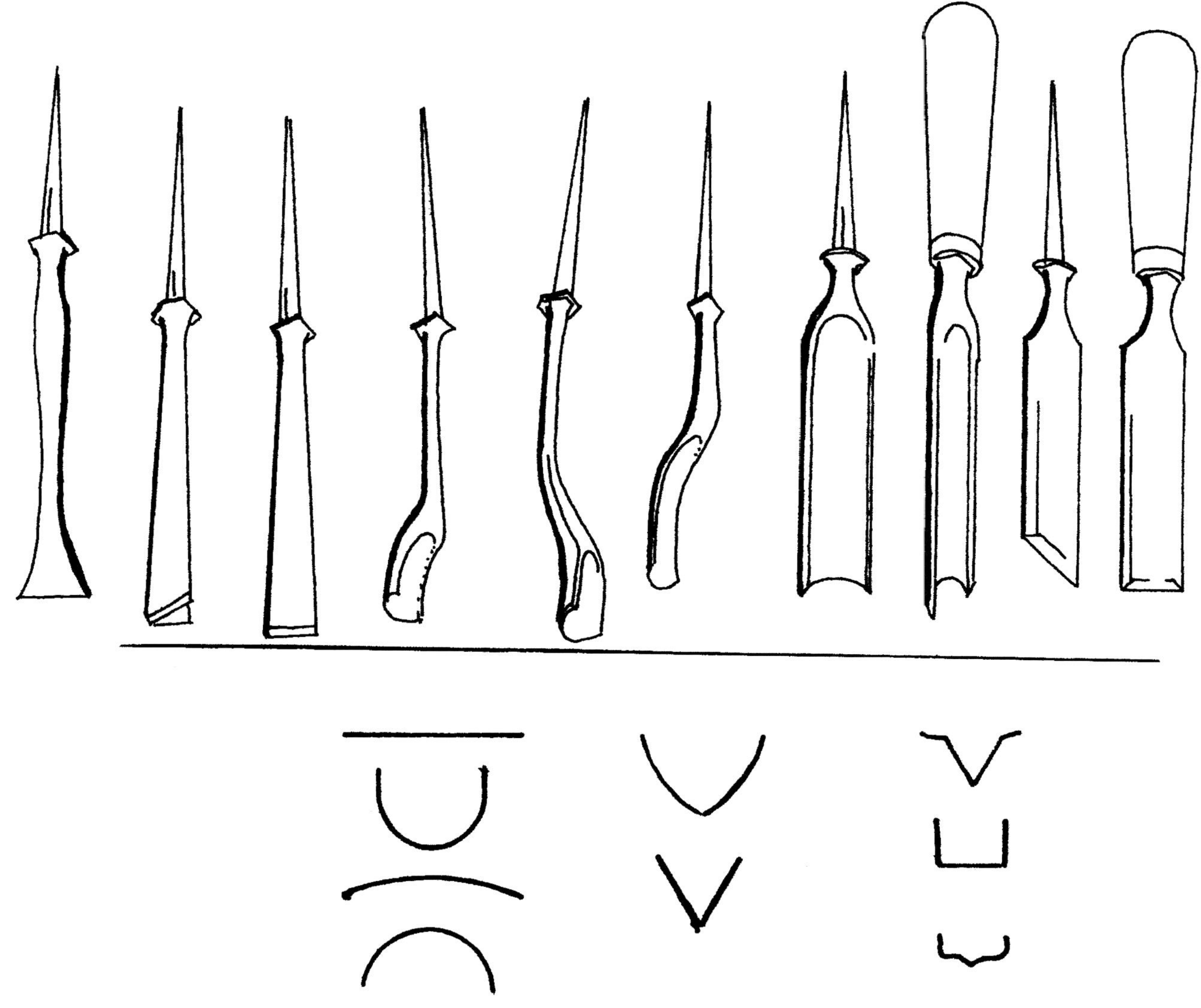

Shapes of woodcarving gouges.

pointer bearing the correct proportional calibrating marks to allow for measuring at any height or position. The larger framework is designed so that it can be easily assembled and demounted to enable carving or modelling, or any other sculpture technique, to be carried out.

When the two box frames have been made, it will become obvious that the maquette or working model should be placed centrally inside the smaller frame. Then, using the proportional calibrating pointers on the two frames, fixed points of reference can be identified and marked on the working model. The points can be marked with spots of paint or chalk, or, if the smaller work is clay or wax, by carefully pushing pointed pins or a stick into the surface. The larger frame echoes the smaller calibrations but at the correct proportional enlargement. The material to be worked on – stone or wood for carving or an armature if the sculpture is to be modelled – is placed centrally in the larger frame in the same orientation as the maquette or working model in the smaller box. The fixed reference points can then be detected on the larger work using the calibrated pointers, made to slide up and down the verticals and to be pushed horizontally in and out of the frame. Allowance in all calculations and measurements must be made for the carving (subtractive process) or for modelling (the additive procedure); this may be an obvious point but it is an important one.

As long as the horizontal and vertical features are good, constant and true, and the proportional calculations are correct, this method will enable the sculptor to work fairly freely and easily to scale on any chosen material. All such systems require attention to detail, however, and the discipline of enlarging is another that needs to be practised.

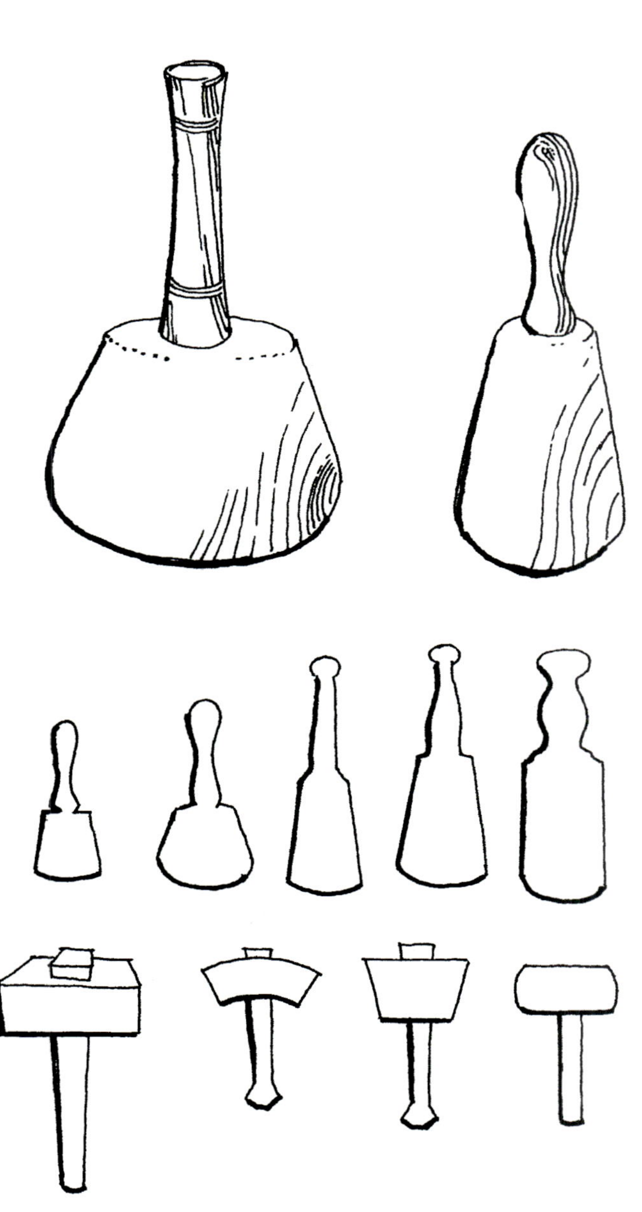

Profiles of carving mallets.

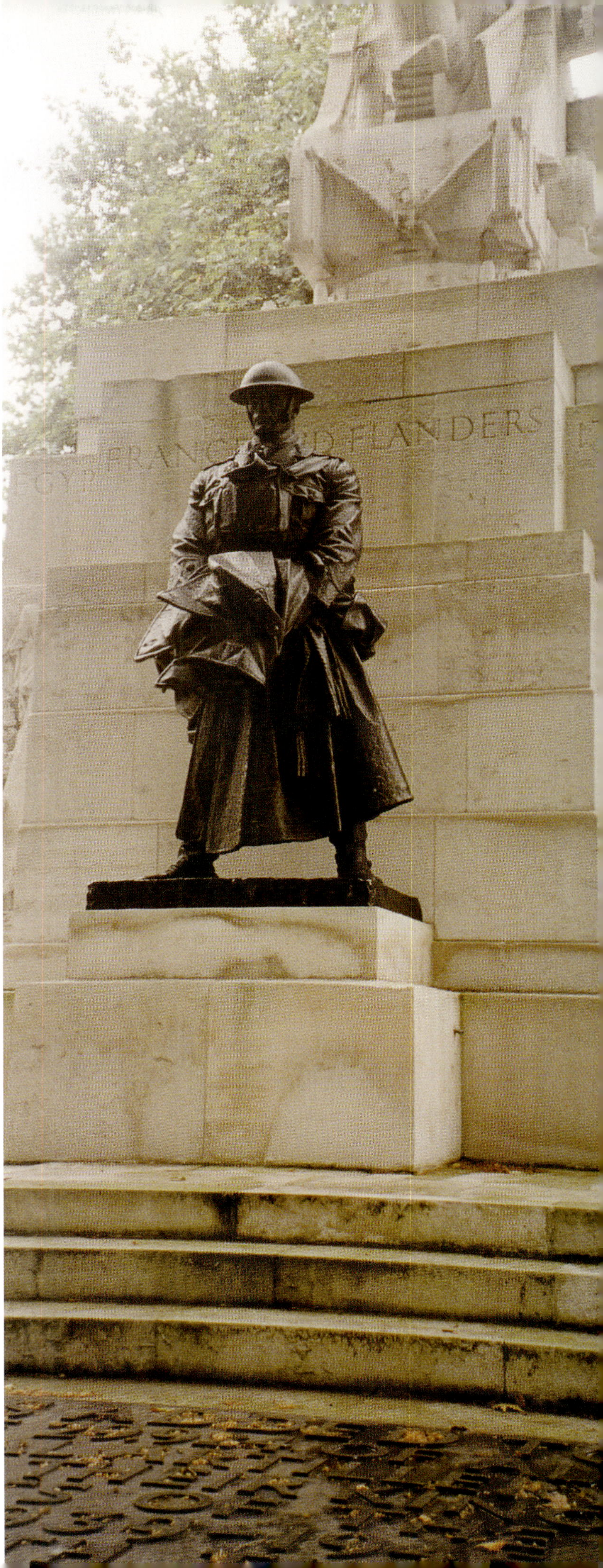

RIGHT: Royal Artillery Memorial, *by Sergeant Jagger, in bronze and Portland stone. A favourite sculpture among fellow sculptors who admire figurative narrative projects. (Hyde Park Corner, London)*

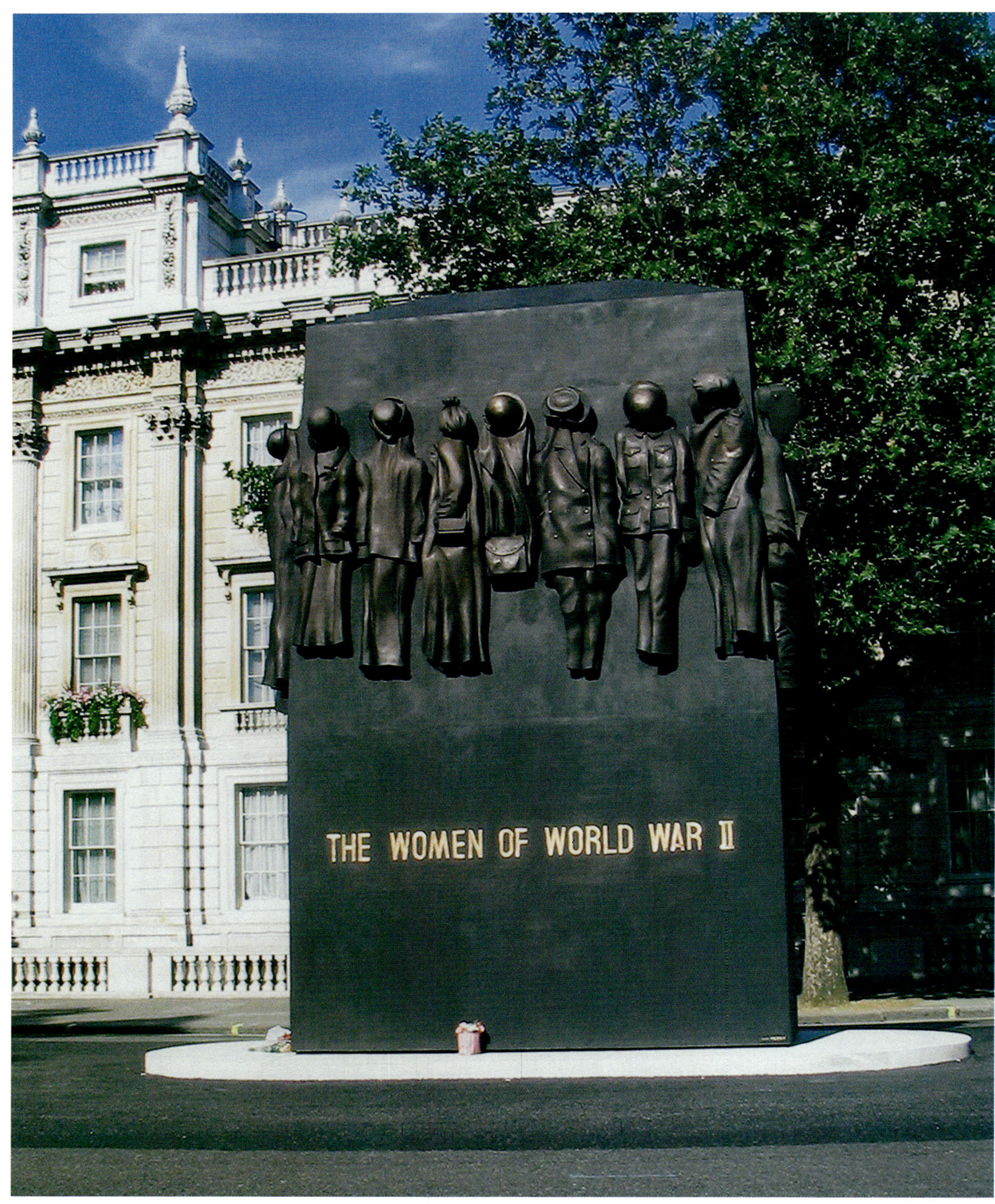

Monument to The Women of World War II, *by John W. Mills, in bronze (2005). (Whitehall, London)*

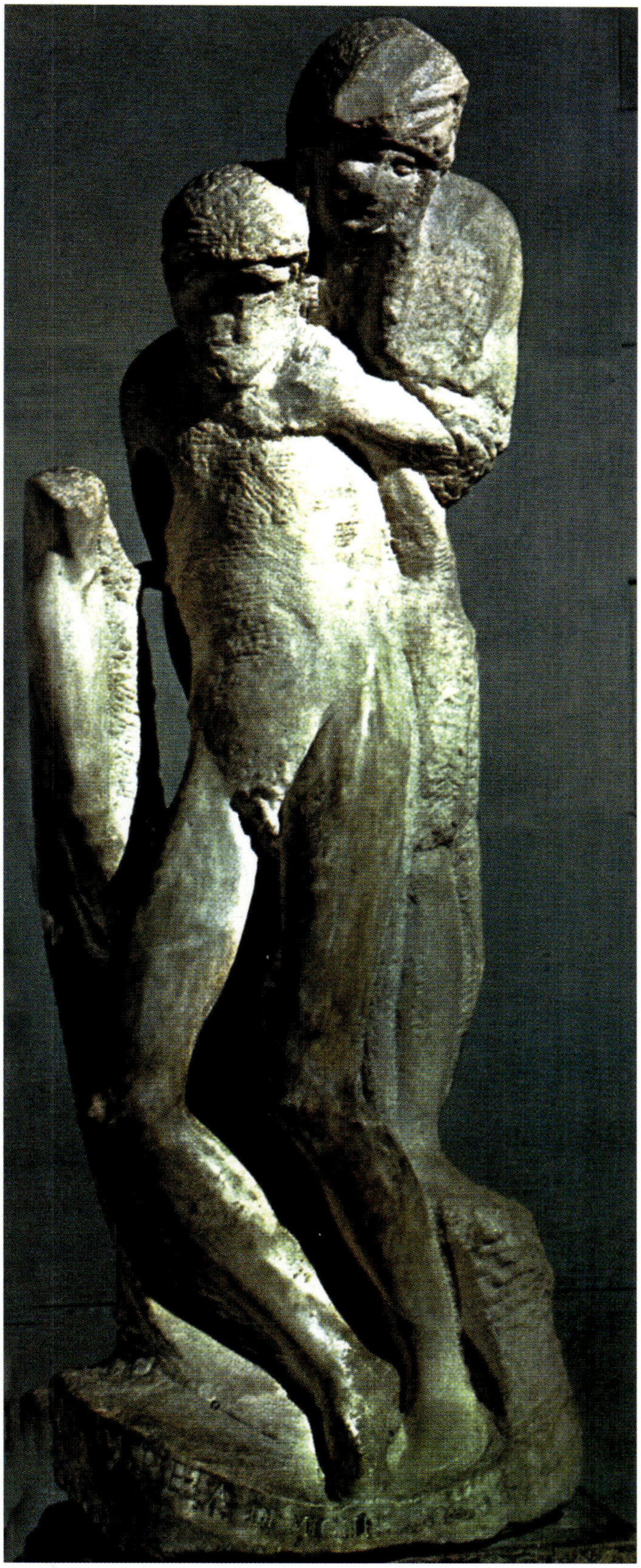

The Ronannini Pieta, *by Michelangelo, in marble – the sculpture that Michelangelo was modifying when he died, always searching for the image in the block. (Castello Sforza, Milan)*

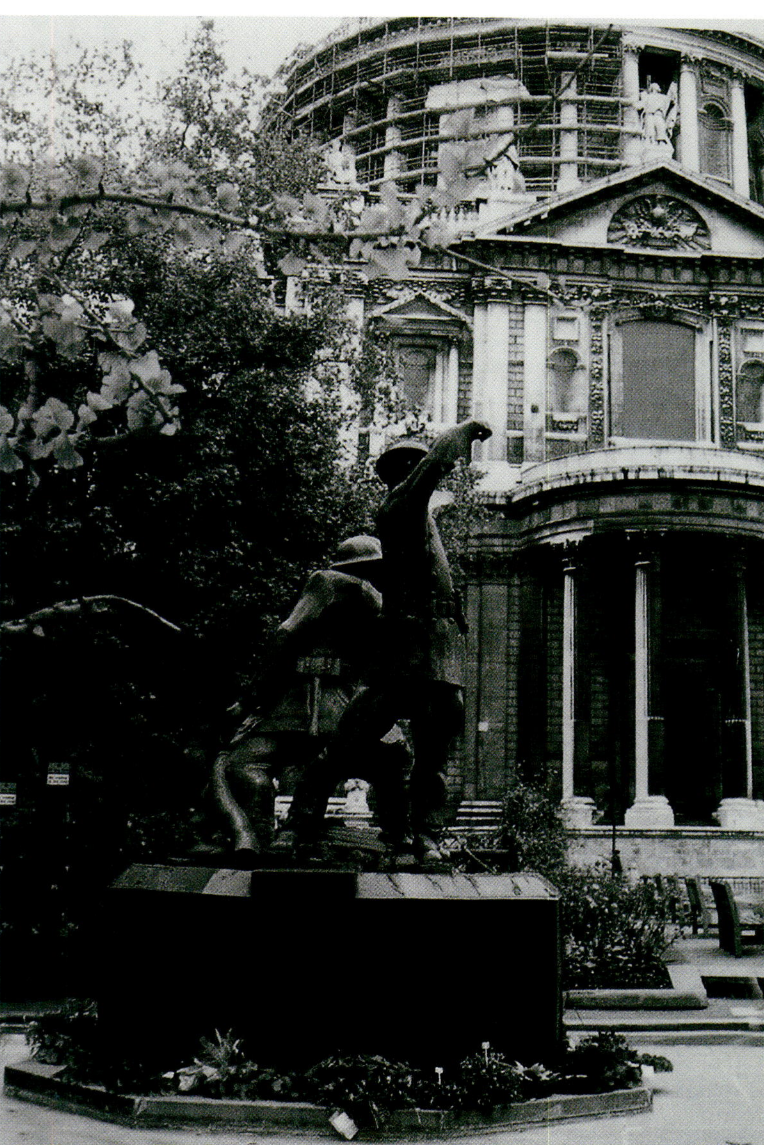

Blitz, *by John W. Mills, in bronze. (The National Firefighters Memorial, St Pauls, London)*

Index